HOOSIER
STATS
AND
FACTS
2008-09

HOCKEY STATS AND FACTS 2008-09

Darcy Norman

OVER TIME BOOKS

The Publisher: OverTime Books is an imprint of Éditions de la Montagne Verte

ISBN-13: 978-1-897277-34-8

Author: Darcy Norman
Project Director: J. Alexander Poulton
Editor: Carla MacKay
Book Design & Layout: Jodene Draven
Production: Jodene Draven, Alexander Luthor
Cover Design: Joy Dirto
Cover Image: Courtesy of Dreamstime; © Sparkia I Dreamstime.com

We acknowledge the financial support of the Government of Canada through the Book Publishing Industry Development Program for our publishing activities.

PC:P5

 Canadian   Patrimoine
Heritage   canadien

Contents

Introduction

With the 2008–09 NHL hockey season soon upon us, what more appropriate time than now to release a comprehensive yet compact book on the stats and facts that make up the nitty gritty of the 2007–08 hockey season? Beginning a book for an ongoing, yearly release was certainly a challenge—but not the usual sort of challenge writers and researchers often face. My problem wasn't finding enough information; it was how to decide which statistics out of many would be most appropriate for a book of this size. So, with hockey pool junkies, NHL fans and everyday hockey fans in general in mind, I whittled my choices down to just over 25 statistical categories, complemented by team pages, a comprehensive player registry and various other lists and stats that will be of interest to hockey fans everywhere. I really did want to pack as many tidbits into this book as I could, because all hockey fans understand the need to back up their arguments with hard facts and stats on why this player is better than that player, why this rookie was more of a star than another or why one team is so much better than a friend's favorite and always will be!

The arguments can go on and on, providing a glimpse into my problem of what to include in this book. What is important to a hockey fan? What do they want to know about a season that has just passed? Which stats pack the most punch, give the best representation of what I'm trying to do with this book?

A longtime hockey fan myself, as well a player in various leagues over the years, I have many memories of watching the game with friends, collecting and trading hockey cards and playing NHL videogames. All of these activities inevitably end up in some sort of heated discussion about either a player or team that particular season, or the history of that same player or team that, of course, makes them the best. Whether I was nine years old or the age I am now, the end goal was, and always will be, the same: how to prove my point. *Hockey Stats and Facts 2008–09* is exactly the quick reference guide for the job, and I hope other hockey fans will find it useful as well.

With this easy-to-use volume, trivia buffs can even get their fix with the team profiles topping each of the team pages. There really are just some instances when you might need to know exactly where the Detroit Red Wings' octopus-throwing tradition came from. Besides, it might just shut your belligerent hockey buddy up for a few seconds.

So grab that hockey buddy, settle in with a DVD of last season's highlights, a cold one, your newest guide to last year's hockey season and think ahead to this year's hockey pools and how to get ready to trump your friends' NHL knowledge over and over again.

Key to Abbreviations

#	Player number
%Tm	Percentage of team face-offs taken
+/-	Plus/Minus rating. Measures the team goal differential when a specific player is on the ice. Players' plus/minus stats get increased by one every time their team scores an even strength or short-handed goal while they are on the ice. Whenever the team is scored against while at even strength or on a power play when the player is on the ice, his plus/minus is decreased by one.
A	Assists
BkS	Blocked Shots*
Ctry	Country
DOB	Date of birth
FO%	Face-off winning percentage
FOL	Face-offs lost*
FOW	Face-offs won*
G	Goals
G/G	Goals per game
GA	Goals against
GA/G	Goals against per game
GAA	Goals against average
GF	Goals for
GF/G	Goals for per game
GP	Games played
GvA	Giveaways*
GW	Game-winning goals
Hits	Body checks*
Ht	Player height, in inches
L	Losses (goalie or team)
MsS	Missed shots. Shots taken for which the player is not granted a shot on goal.
Num	Overall draft number
OL	Overtime loss
OT	Overtime, Overtime goals (player) or Overtime losses (goalie or team)
P	Points
PIM	Penalties in minutes
PIM/G	Penalty minutes per game
PK%	Penalty killing percentage

Pos	Player's position
PP	Power-play goals
PP%	Power-play percentage
PPGA	Power-play goals against
PPO	Power-play opportunities
PPOA	Power-play opportunites against
PS	Penalty shots
PTS	Points
PTS%	Percentage of games in which at least one point is obtained
S	Shots or a player's shooting direction
S%	Shooting percentage
S/G	Shots per game
S/P	State or province
SA	Shots against
SA/G	Shots against per game
Sft/G	Shifts per game
SH or SHG	Short-handed goals
SHGA	Short-handed goals against
SO	Shutouts
SV	Saves
Sv%	Save percentage
T	Ties (goalie or team)
TkA	Takeaways*
TOI	Total time on ice
TOI/G	Time on ice per game
Tot	Total face-offs taken
W	Wins (goalie or team)
Wt	Player weight, in pounds
*	Represents a statistic measured subjectively by individual scorekeepers; it is important to keep comparisons in context, since no two scorekeepers will see the same play alike. Comparing teammates has more meaning than comparing players across teams.

Anaheim Ducks

Based in Anaheim, California, the Anaheim Ducks have one Stanley Cup win to their name (2007), have been in the NHL since 1993 and have always played their home games in the Honda Center. Members of the Pacific Division of the Western Conference, the Anaheim Ducks were once called the Mighty Ducks of Anaheim, a name based on the Disney movie *The Mighty Ducks*. Sold by Disney in 2005, the team name was changed prior to the start of the 2006–07 hockey season by its new owners to, of course, the current moniker of the Anaheim Ducks. The Ducks are one of only three teams in the NHL to have their team name scripted out on their current jerseys, rather than sport a team logo. The Anaheim mascot is a duck named Wild Wing; he has been with the team since its inception in 1993 and wears the number 93 on his jersey as a tribute.

Owners	General Manager	Coach
Henry & Susan Samueli	Bryan Burke	Randy Carlyle

2008 Record and Rankings

47-27-8, 2nd in Pacific Division

	Points	GF/G	GA/G	S/G	SA/G	PP %	PK %	PIM/G
	102	2.4	2.24	27.3	28	16.6	83.1	18.1
NHL Rank	4	28	2	25	10	20	12	30

Recent Top Draft Picks

Draft	Num.	Round	Player	Pos	Drafted From
2008 Entry	17	1	Jake Gardiner	D	Minnetonka H.S. (Minn.)
2008 Entry	35	2	Nicolas Deschamps	C	Chicoutimi Sagueneens (QMJHL)
2008 Entry	39	2	Eric O'Dell	C	Sudbury Wolves (OHL)
2007 Entry	19	1	Logan MacMillan	L	Halifax Mooseheads (QMJHL)
2007 Entry	42	2	Eric Tangradi	C	Belleville Bulls (OHL)
2007 Entry	63	3	Maxime Macenauer	C	Rouyn-Noranda Huskies (QMJHL)
2006 Entry	19	1	Mark Mitera	D	U. of Michigan (NCAA)
2006 Entry	38	2	Bryce Swan	R	Halifax Mooseheads (QMJHL)
2006 Entry	83	3	John de Gray	D	Brampton Battalion (OHL)

Shootout Record

GP	W	L	G	S	S%	GA	SA	Sv%
15	8	7	16	47	34	16	45	64

Team Leaders

	G			A			P
Corey Perry	29	Ryan Getzlaf	58	Ryan Getzlaf	82
Ryan Getzlaf	24	Chris Pronger	31	Corey Perry	54
Chris Kunitz	21	Chris Kunitz	29	Chris Kunitz	50
Todd Bertuzzi	14	Mathieu Schneider	27	Chris Pronger	43
Chris Pronger	12	Todd Bertuzzi	26	Todd Bertuzzi	40

	PIM		Hits		+/-
George Parros	183	Chris Kunitz	159	Ryan Getzlaf	32
Chris Pronger	128	Travis Moen	154	Kent Huskins	23
Corey Perry	108	Ryan Getzlaf	126	Mathieu Schneider	22
Todd Bertuzzi	97	Samuel Pahlsson	114	Corey Perry	12
Ryan Getzlaf	94	Francois Beauchemin	97	Sean O'Donnell	9

	PPG		SHG		Sht
Corey Perry	11	Samuel Pahlsson	3	Corey Perry	200
Chris Pronger	8	4 tied with	1	Chris Kunitz	196
Marc-Andre Bergeron	8			Ryan Getzlaf	185
3 tied with	7			Chris Pronger	182
				Francois Beauchemin	144

Goalies	GP	W	GAA	Sv%	SO
Jean-Sebastien Giguere	58	35	2.12	0.922	4
Jonas Hiller	23	10	2.06	0.927	0
J-Sebastien Aubin	19	5	3.19	0.886	0

Roster

Player	#	Pos	DOB	Hometown	S/P	Ctry	Ht	Wt	S
Carter, Ryan	20	C	Aug 03 '83	St. Paul	MN	USA	73	203	L
Ebbett, Andrew	48	C	Jan 02 '83	Vernon	BC	CAN	69	175	L
Getzlaf, Ryan	15	C	May 10 '85	Regina	SK	CAN	75	221	R
Marchant, Todd	22	C	Aug 12 '73	Buffalo	NY	USA	70	180	L
Niedermayer, Rob	44	C	Dec 28 '74	Cassiar	BC	CAN	74	200	L
Pahlsson, Samuel	26	C	Dec 17 '77	Ornskol		SWE	72	203	L
Platt, Geoff	20	C	Jul 10 '85	Mississauga	ON	CAN	69	175	L
Sutherby, Brian	17	C	Mar 01 '82	Edmonton	AB	CAN	75	210	L
Weight, Doug	39	C	Jan 21 '71	Detroit	MI	USA	71	196	L
Wirtanen, Petteri	56	C	May 28 '86	Hyvinkaa		FIN	73	207	L
Beauchemin, Francois	23	D	Jun 04 '80	Sorel	QC	CAN	72	213	L
Bergeron, Marc-Andre	7	D	Oct 13 '80	Trois-Rivières	QC	CAN	70	197	L
Dipenta, Joe	33	D	Feb 25 '79	Barrie	ON	CAN	74	199	R
Huskins, Kent	40	D	May 04 '79	Almont	ON	CAN	75	209	L
Kondratiev, Maxim	20	D	Jan 20 '83	Togliatti		RUS	73	197	L
Niedermayer, Scott	27	D	Aug 31 '73	Edmonton	AB	CAN	73	200	L
O'Donnell, Sean	21	D	Oct 13 '71	Ottawa	ON	CAN	75	234	L
Pronger, Chris	25	D	Oct 10 '74	Dryden	ON	CAN	78	213	L
Schneider, Mathieu	11	D	Jun 12 '69	New York	NY	USA	71	195	L
Kunitz, Chris	14	L	Sep 26 '79	Regina	SK	CAN	71	195	L
May, Brad	24	L	Nov 29 '71	Toronto	ON	CAN	73	218	L
Miller, Drew	18	L	Feb 17 '84	Dover	NJ	USA	74	165	L
Moen, Travis	32	L	Apr 06 '82	Swift Current	SK	CAN	74	215	L
Bertuzzi, Todd	4	R	Feb 02 '75	Sudbury	ON	CAN	75	231	L
King, Jason	42	R	Sep 14 '81	Corner Brook	NL	CAN	72	193	L
Mowers, Mark	28	R	Feb 16 '74	Decature	GA	USA	71	174	R
Parros, George	16	R	Dec 29 '79	Washington	PA	USA	77	229	R
Perry, Corey	10	R	May 16 '85	Peterborough	ON	CAN	75	209	R
Ryan, Bobby	54	R	Mar 17 '87	Cherry Hill	NJ	USA	73	218	R
Selanne, Teemu	8	R	Jul 03 '70	Helsinki		FIN	72	204	R

Goalies	#	Pos	DOB	Hometown	S/P	Ctry	Ht	Wt	C
Aubin, J-Sebastien	30	G	Jul 19 '77	Montreal	QC	CAN	71	180	R
Giguere, Jean-Sebastien	35	G	May 16 '77	Montreal	QC	CAN	73	201	L
Hiller, Jonas	1	G	Feb 12 '82	Felben Wellhausen		CZE	74	196	R

Regular Season Schedule

October 2008	Visitor	Home
Thu Oct 9, 2008	Ducks	Sharks
Sun Oct 12, 2008	Coyotes	Ducks
Tue Oct 14, 2008	Ducks	Kings
Wed Oct 15, 2008	Oilers	Ducks
Fri Oct 17, 2008	Sharks	Ducks
Sun Oct 19, 2008	Hurricanes	Ducks
Tue Oct 21, 2008	Ducks	Maple Leafs
Fri Oct 24, 2008	Ducks	Senators
Sat Oct 25, 2008	Ducks	Canadiens
Mon Oct 27, 2008	Ducks	Blue Jackets
Wed Oct 29, 2008	Red Wings	Ducks
Fri Oct 31, 2008	Canucks	Ducks

November 2008	Visitor	Home
Sun Nov 2, 2008	Flames	Ducks
Tue Nov 4, 2008	Ducks	Kings
Wed Nov 5, 2008	Blues	Ducks
Fri Nov 7, 2008	Stars	Ducks
Sun Nov 9, 2008	Panthers	Ducks
Fri Nov 14, 2008	Predators	Ducks
Sun Nov 16, 2008	Kings	Ducks
Wed Nov 19, 2008	Capitals	Ducks
Fri Nov 21, 2008	Ducks	Blues
Sat Nov 22, 2008	Ducks	Stars
Mon Nov 24, 2008	Avalanche	Ducks
Fri Nov 28, 2008	Blackhawks	Ducks
Sun Nov 30, 2008	Ducks	Hurricanes

December 2008	Visitor	Home
Mon Dec 1, 2008	Ducks	Red Wings
Wed Dec 3, 2008	Ducks	Blackhawks
Sun Dec 7, 2008	Blue Jackets	Ducks
Wed Dec 10, 2008	Blues	Ducks
Thu Dec 11, 2008	Ducks	Sharks
Sun Dec 14, 2008	Wild	Ducks
Tue Dec 16, 2008	Rangers	Ducks
Fri Dec 19, 2008	Ducks	Oilers
Mon Dec 22, 2008	Ducks	Canucks
Tue Dec 23, 2008	Ducks	Flames
Sat Dec 27, 2008	Ducks	Stars
Sun Dec 28, 2008	Ducks	Blues
Wed Dec 31, 2008	Blue Jackets	Ducks

January 2009	Visitor	Home
Fri Jan 2, 2009	Flyers	Ducks
Sun Jan 4, 2009	Coyotes	Ducks
Tue Jan 6, 2009	Kings	Ducks
Thu Jan 8, 2009	Ducks	Kings

January 2009, cont.	Visitor	Home
Fri Jan 9, 2009	Lightning	Ducks
Sun Jan 11, 2009	Devils	Ducks
Wed Jan 14, 2009	Red Wings	Ducks
Fri Jan 16, 2009	Ducks	Penguins
Sat Jan 17, 2009	Ducks	Wild
Tue Jan 20, 2009	Ducks	Rangers
Wed Jan 21, 2009	Ducks	Islanders
Tue Jan 27, 2009	Ducks	Coyotes
Wed Jan 28, 2009	Blackhawks	Ducks
Sat Jan 31, 2009	Ducks	Avalanche

February 2009	Visitor	Home
Mon Feb 2, 2009	Sabres	Ducks
Wed Feb 4, 2009	Ducks	Wild
Thu Feb 5, 2009	Ducks	Predators
Sat Feb 7, 2009	Ducks	Flames
Wed Feb 11, 2009	Flames	Ducks
Sun Feb 15, 2009	Thrashers	Ducks
Wed Feb 18, 2009	Kings	Ducks
Fri Feb 20, 2009	Ducks	Red Wings
Sat Feb 21, 2009	Ducks	Blue Jackets
Tue Feb 24, 2009	Ducks	Sabres
Thu Feb 26, 2009	Ducks	Bruins
Sat Feb 28, 2009	Ducks	Stars

March 2009	Visitor	Home
Tue Mar 3, 2009	Ducks	Blackhawks
Fri Mar 6, 2009	Stars	Ducks
Sun Mar 8, 2009	Wild	Ducks
Wed Mar 11, 2009	Canucks	Ducks
Sun Mar 15, 2009	Sharks	Ducks
Wed Mar 18, 2009	Predators	Ducks
Thu Mar 19, 2009	Ducks	Coyotes
Sun Mar 22, 2009	Coyotes	Ducks
Tue Mar 24, 2009	Ducks	Predators
Wed Mar 25, 2009	Ducks	Avalanche
Fri Mar 27, 2009	Oilers	Ducks
Sun Mar 29, 2009	Avalanche	Ducks
Tue Mar 31, 2009	Ducks	Oilers

April 2009	Visitor	Home
Thu Apr 2, 2009	Ducks	Canucks
Sat Apr 4, 2009	Ducks	Sharks
Sun Apr 5, 2009	Sharks	Ducks
Fri Apr 10, 2009	Stars	Ducks
Sat Apr 11, 2009	Ducks	Coyotes

13

Atlanta Thrashers

Atlanta, Georgia, home of the Thrashers, has seen its home team make the Stanley Cup playoffs once (in the 2006–07 season) since the team's founding in 1999. Currently housed in the Philips Arena, the Thrashers are not the first NHL team Atlanta has supported. The Atlanta Flames made their move to Calgary in 1980, leaving Atlanta without an NHL franchise for 17 years. The Thrashers' title comes from a fan poll that voted in favor of naming the team after Georgia's state bird, the brown thrasher—a name that pulled through after being runner-up to the Flames title awarded to the original Atlanta team. In January 2008, the NHL All-Star Game was played in the Philips Arena for the first time, with the Eastern Conference All-Stars winning 8–7 over the Western Conference All-Stars.

Owner	General Manager	Coach
Atlanta Spirit, LLC	Don Waddell	John Anderson

2008 Record and Rankings

34-40-8, 4th in Southeast Division

	Points	GF/G	GA/G	S/G	SA/G	PP %	PK %	PIM/G
	76	2.52	3.24	25.8	33.9	16.5	78.8	13.1
NHL Rank	28	22	29	30	30	23	27	13

Recent Top Draft Picks

Draft	Num.	Round	Player	Pos	Drafted From
2008 Entry	3	1	Zach Bogosian	D	Peterborough Petes (OHL)
2008 Entry	29	1	Daultan Leveille	C	St. Catharines Falcons (GHJHL)
2008 Entry	64	3	Danick Paquette	R	Lewiston MAINEiacs (QMJHL)
2007 Entry	67	3	Spencer Machacek	R	Vancouver Giants (WHL)
2007 Entry	115	4	Niclas Lucenius	C	Tappara Tampere (FNL)
2007 Entry	175	6	John Albert	C	US National Under 18 Team
2006 Entry	12	1	Bryan Little	C	Barrie Colts (OHL)
2006 Entry	43	2	Riley Holzapfel	C	Moose Jaw Warriors (WHL)
2006 Entry	80	3	Michael Forney	L	Thief River Falls (MN H.S.)

Shootout Record

GP	W	L	G	S	S%	GA	SA	Sv%
15	9	6	17	51	33	12	49	76

Team Leaders

G		A		P	
Ilya Kovalchuk	52	Ilya Kovalchuk	35	Ilya Kovalchuk	87
Vyacheslav Kozlov	17	Mark Recchi	34	Mark Recchi	48
Bobby Holik	15	Eric Perrin	33	Eric Perrin	45
Mark Recchi	14	Tobias Enstrom	33	Vyacheslav Kozlov	41
Todd White	14	Vyacheslav Kozlov	24	Tobias Enstrom	38

PIM		Hits		+/-	
Eric Bouton	127	Garnet Excelby	176	Darren Haydar	4
Chris Thorburn	92	Bobby Holik	147	Colby Armstrong	4
Bobby Holik	90	Steve McCarthy	101	Niclas Havelid	2
Garnet Excelby	85	Chris Thorburn	89	Colin Stuart	2
Ken Klee	60	Colby Armstrong	85	J. Lav. Smotherman	2

PP		SHG		S	
Ilya Kovalchuk	16	Jim Slater	2	Ilya Kovalchuk	283
Mark Recchi	7	Ilya Kovalchuk	2	Vyacheslav Kozlov	161
Todd White	6	Eric Perrin	2	Bobby Holik	140
Vyacheslav Kozlov	5	Colin Stuart	1	Erik Christensen	132
Tobias Enstrom	4	Todd White	1	2 tied with	121

Goalies	GP	W	GAA	Sv%	SO
Kari Lehtonen	48	17	2.90	0.916	4
Johan Hedberg	36	14	3.46	0.892	1
Ondrej Pavelec	7	3	3.11	0.905	0

Roster

Player	#	Pos	DOB	Hometown	S/P	Ctry	Ht	Wt	S
Christensen, Erik	9	C	Dec 17 '83	Edmonton	AB	CAN	73	210	L
Doell, Kevin	45	C	Jul 15 '79	Saskatoon	SK	CAN	71	190	R
Holik, Bobby	16	C	Jan 01 '71	Jihlava		CZE	76	230	R
Little, Bryan	10	C	Nov 12 '87	Edmonton	AB	CAN	71	190	R
Perrin, Eric	11	C	Nov 01 '75	Laval	QC	CAN	69	180	L
Slater, Jim	23	C	Dec 09 '82	Petosky	MI	USA	72	195	L
White, Todd	12	C	May 21 '75	Kanata	ON	CAN	70	195	L
Enstrom, Tobias	39	D	Nov 05 '84	Nordingra		SWE	70	175	L
Excelby, Garnet	2	D	Aug 16 '81	Ste. Anne	MB	CAN	73	210	L
Havelid, Niclas	28	D	Apr 12 '73	Stockholm		SWE	72	200	L
Klee, Ken	22	D	Apr 24 '71	Indianapolis	IN	USA	73	210	R
Kwiatkowski, Joel	3	D	Mar 22 '77	Kindersley	SK	CAN	72	205	L
McCarthy, Steve	5	D	Feb 03 '81	Trail	BC	CAN	73	210	L
Popovic, Mark	7	D	Oct 11 '82	Stoney Creek	ON	CAN	73	210	L
Valabik, Boris	48	D	Feb 14 '86	Nitra		SVK	79	240	L
Zhitnik, Alexei	77	D	Oct 10 '72	Kiev		UKR	71	225	L
Boulton, Eric	36	L	Aug 17 '76	Halifax	NS	CAN	73	225	L
Kovalchuk, Ilya	17	L	Apr 15 '83	Tver		RUS	73	220	R
Kozlov, Vyacheslav	13	L	May 03 '72	Voskresensk		RUS	70	190	L
Larsen, Brad	29	L	Jun 28 '77	Nakusp	BC	CAN	72	210	L
Lav.-Smotherman, Jordan	50	L	May 11 '86	Corvallis	OR	USA	75	225	L
Sterling, Brett	21	L	Apr 24 '84	Los Angeles	CA	USA	67	180	L
Stuart, Colin	49	L	Jul 08 '82	Rochester	MN	USA	74	205	L
Armstrong, Colby	19	R	Nov 23 '82	Lloydminster	SK	CAN	74	190	R
Haydar, Darren	38	R	Oct 22 '79	Toronto	ON	CAN	69	170	R
Recchi, Mark	8	R	Feb 01 '68	Kamloops	BC	CAN	70	195	L
Thorburn, Chris	27	R	Jun 03 '83	Sault Ste. Marie	ON	CAN	75	225	R

Goalies	#	Pos	DOB	Hometown	S/P	Ctry	Ht	Wt	C
Hedberg, Johan	1	G	May 05 '73	Leksand		SWE	72	185	
Lehtonen, Kari	32	G	Nov 16 '83	Helsinki		FIN	76	205	L
Pavelec, Ondrej	33	G	Aug 31 '87	Kladno		CZE	74	200	L

Regular Season Schedule

October 2008	Visitor	Home
Fri Oct 10, 2008	Capitals	Thrashers
Sat Oct 11, 2008	Thrashers	Panthers
Tue Oct 14, 2008	Wild	Thrashers
Thu Oct 16, 2008	Devils	Thrashers
Sat Oct 18, 2008	Sabres	Thrashers
Tue Oct 21, 2008	Thrashers	Lightning
Fri Oct 24, 2008	Thrashers	Red Wings
Sat Oct 25, 2008	Thrashers	Bruins
Tue Oct 28, 2008	Flyers	Thrashers
Thu Oct 30, 2008	Thrashers	Rangers

November 2008	Visitor	Home
Sat Nov 1, 2008	Thrashers	Devils
Sun Nov 2, 2008	Panthers	Thrashers
Thu Nov 6, 2008	Islanders	Thrashers
Fri Nov 7, 2008	Thrashers	Sabres
Sun Nov 9, 2008	Thrashers	Hurricanes
Fri Nov 14, 2008	Hurricanes	Thrashers
Sun Nov 16, 2008	Thrashers	Flyers
Thu Nov 20, 2008	Penguins	Thrashers
Sat Nov 22, 2008	Blue Jackets	Thrashers
Tue Nov 25, 2008	Thrashers	Maple Leafs
Wed Nov 26, 2008	Thrashers	Capitals
Fri Nov 28, 2008	Predators	Thrashers
Sun Nov 30, 2008	Blues	Thrashers

December 2008	Visitor	Home
Tue Dec 2, 2008	Thrashers	Canadiens
Wed Dec 3, 2008	Thrashers	Senators
Sat Dec 6, 2008	Thrashers	Islanders
Wed Dec 10, 2008	Rangers	Thrashers
Fri Dec 12, 2008	Bruins	Thrashers
Sat Dec 13, 2008	Thrashers	Bruins
Tue Dec 16, 2008	Thrashers	Senators
Thu Dec 18, 2008	Penguins	Thrashers
Sat Dec 20, 2008	Lightning	Thrashers
Mon Dec 22, 2008	Maple Leafs	Thrashers
Tue Dec 23, 2008	Thrashers	Islanders
Fri Dec 26, 2008	Hurricanes	Thrashers
Sun Dec 28, 2008	Bruins	Thrashers
Tue Dec 30, 2008	Thrashers	Maple Leafs
Wed Dec 31, 2008	Thrashers	Hurricanes

January 2009	Visitor	Home
Fri Jan 2, 2009	Canucks	Thrashers
Sun Jan 4, 2009	Lightning	Thrashers
Tue Jan 6, 2009	Thrashers	Penguins
Thu Jan 8, 2009	Thrashers	Devils

January 2009, cont.	Visitor	Home
Sat Jan 10, 2009	Thrashers	Panthers
Wed Jan 14, 2009	Senators	Thrashers
Fri Jan 16, 2009	Maple Leafs	Thrashers
Sat Jan 17, 2009	Thrashers	Predators
Tue Jan 20, 2009	Canadiens	Thrashers
Wed Jan 21, 2009	Thrashers	Flyers
Tue Jan 27, 2009	Thrashers	Stars
Thu Jan 29, 2009	Islanders	Thrashers
Sat Jan 31, 2009	Thrashers	Hurricanes

February 2009	Visitor	Home
Tue Feb 3, 2009	Thrashers	Rangers
Fri Feb 6, 2009	Devils	Thrashers
Sun Feb 8, 2009	Flyers	Thrashers
Tue Feb 10, 2009	Thrashers	Lightning
Wed Feb 11, 2009	Blackhawks	Thrashers
Sun Feb 15, 2009	Thrashers	Ducks
Mon Feb 16, 2009	Thrashers	Kings
Thu Feb 19, 2009	Thrashers	Coyotes
Sat Feb 21, 2009	Thrashers	Sharks
Tue Feb 24, 2009	Avalanche	Thrashers
Thu Feb 26, 2009	Thrashers	Capitals
Sat Feb 28, 2009	Hurricanes	Thrashers

March 2009	Visitor	Home
Tue Mar 3, 2009	Panthers	Thrashers
Fri Mar 6, 2009	Canadiens	Thrashers
Sun Mar 8, 2009	Flames	Thrashers
Tue Mar 10, 2009	Thrashers	Avalanche
Thu Mar 12, 2009	Thrashers	Oilers
Sat Mar 14, 2009	Thrashers	Sabres
Mon Mar 16, 2009	Capitals	Thrashers
Tue Mar 17, 2009	Thrashers	Penguins
Fri Mar 20, 2009	Red Wings	Thrashers
Sat Mar 21, 2009	Thrashers	Lightning
Tue Mar 24, 2009	Thrashers	Canadiens
Thu Mar 26, 2009	Rangers	Thrashers
Sat Mar 28, 2009	Senators	Thrashers

April 2009	Visitor	Home
Wed Apr 1, 2009	Sabres	Thrashers
Fri Apr 3, 2009	Thrashers	Panthers
Sun Apr 5, 2009	Thrashers	Capitals
Tue Apr 7, 2009	Capitals	Thrashers
Thu Apr 9, 2009	Panthers	Thrashers
Sat Apr 11, 2009	Lightning	Thrashers

17

Boston Bruins

One of the Original Six teams, the Boston Bruins, based in Boston, Massachusetts, have been skating and scoring since 1924. Their home arena is the TD Banknorth Garden, which the team has been playing in since 1995 after leaving Boston Gardens where they had played since 1928. The Bruins have won five Stanley Cups, the last of which was awarded in 1972. With such a rich NHL history, the Bruins made a change to their jerseys prior to the 2007–08 season, but unlike many other teams, did not stray far from its previous design. Fans now see a new logo, basically Boston's recognizable letter "B," and a brand new shoulder patch closely based on the main jersey logo until the 1931–32 season. Boston has also had 45 of its team's players inducted into the Hockey Hall of Fame. These players span the team's rosters from 1926 to 2000.

Owner	General Manager	Coach
Jeremy Jacobs	Peter Chiarelli	Claude Julien

2008 Record and Rankings

42-29-12, 3rd in Northeast Division

	Points	GF/G	GA/G	S/G	SA/G	PP %	PK %	PIM/G
	94	2.51	2.62	28.5	30.5	17.6	78.6	13
NHL Rank	14	24	11	20	22	16	28	11

Recent Top Draft Picks

Draft	Num.	Round	Player	Pos	Drafted From
2008 Entry	16	1	Joe Colborne	C	Camrose Kodiaks (AJHL)
2008 Entry	47	2	Maxime Sauve	C	Val-d'Or Foreurs (QMJHL)
2008 Entry	77	3	Michael Hutchinson	G	Barrie Colts (OHL)
2007 Entry	8	1	Zach Hamill	C	Everett Silvertips (WHL)
2007 Entry	35	2	Tommy Cross	D	Westminster H.S. (Conn.)
2007 Entry	130	5	Denis Reul	D	Heilbronn Falcons (GerObL)
2006 Entry	5	1	Phil Kessel	C	U. of Minnesota (NCAA)
2006 Entry	37	2	Yuri Alexandrov	D	Cherepovets Severstal (Russia)
2006 Entry	50	2	Milan Lucic	L	Vancouver Giants (WHL)

Shootout Record

GP	W	L	G	S	S%	GA	SA	Sv%
13	6	7	8	35	23	11	36	69

Team Leaders

	G		A		P
Marco Sturm	27	Marc Savard	63	Marc Savard	78
Chuck Kobasew	22	Zdeno Chara	34	Marco Sturm	56
Phil Kessel	19	Marco Sturm	29	Zdeno Chara	51
Zdeno Chara	17	Dennis Wideman	23	Chuck Kobasew	39
Glen Murray	17	Glen Metropolit	22	Phil Kessel	37

	PIM		Hits		+/-
Zdeno Chara	114	Zdeno Chara	223	Zdeno Chara	14
Milan Lucic	89	Milan Lucic	181	Dennis Wideman	11
Mark Stuart	81	Aaron Ward	143	Marco Sturm	11
Jeremy Reich	78	Mark Stuart	101	P.J. Axelsson	11
Shawn Thornton	74	Chuck Kobasew	86	Aaron Ward	9

	PPG		SHG		Sht
Marco Sturm	10	Chuck Kobasew	3	Marco Sturm	229
Dennis Wideman	9	P.J. Axelsson	2	Phil Kessel	213
Zdeno Chara	9	4 tied with	1	Zdeno Chara	207
Glen Murray	7			Marc Savard	196
Chuck Kobasew	6			Dennis Wideman	171

Goalies	GP	W	GAA	Sv%	SO
Tim Thomas	57	28	2.44	0.921	3
Alex Auld	32	12	2.68	0.907	3
Manny Fernandez	4	2	3.93	0.832	1
Tuukka Rask	4	2	3.26	0.886	0

Roster

Player	#	Pos	DOB	Hometown	S/P	Ctry	Ht	Wt	S
Bergeron, Patrice	37	C	Jul 24 '85	Ancienne-Lorette	QC	CAN	74	194	R
Kessel, Phil	81	C	Oct 02 '87	Madison	WI	USA	72	180	R
Krejci, David	46	C	Apr 28 '86	Sternberk		CZE	72	177	R
Metropolit, Glen	13	C	Jun 25 '74	Toronto	ON	CAN	70	193	R
Nokelainen, Petteri	56	C	Jan 16 '86	Imatra		FIN	73	191	R
Reich, Jeremy	53	C	Feb 11 '79	Craik	SK	CAN	73	203	L
Savard, Marc	91	C	Jul 17 '77	Ottawa	ON	CAN	70	191	L
Sobotka, Vladimir	60	C	Jul 02 '87	Trebic		CZE	70	183	L
Alberts, Andrew	41	D	Jun 30 '81	Minneapolis	MN	USA	77	218	L
Allen, Bobby	38	D	Nov 14 '78	Weymouth	MA	USA	72	201	L
Chara, Zdeno	33	D	Mar 18 '77	Trencin		SVK	81	255	L
Ference, Andrew	21	D	Mar 17 '79	Edmonton	AB	CAN	71	189	L
Hnidy, Shane	34	D	Nov 08 '75	Neepawa	MB	CAN	74	204	R
Hunwick, Matt	48	D	May 21 '85	Warren	MI	USA	71	190	L
Lashoff, Matt	49	D	Sep 29 '86	East Greenbush	NY	USA	74	204	L
Stuart, Mark	45	D	Apr 27 '84	Rochester	MN	USA	74	213	L
Ward, Aaron	44	D	Jan 17 '73	Windsor	ON	CAN	74	209	R
Wideman, Dennis	6	D	Mar 20 '83	Kitchener	ON	CAN	72	196	R
Axelsson, P.J.	11	L	Feb 26 '75	Kungalv		SWE	73	188	L
Lucic, Milan	17	L	Jun 07 '88	Vancouver	BC	CAN	76	220	L
Pelletier, Pascal	42	L	Jun 16 '83	Labrador City	NL	CAN	71	195	L
Schaefer, Peter	72	L	Jul 12 '77	Regina	SK	CAN	73	200	L
Sturm, Marco	16	L	Sep 08 '78	Dingolfing		DEU	72	194	L
Thornton, Shawn	22	L	Jul 23 '77	Oshawa	ON	CAN	74	217	R
Hoggan, Jeff	32	R	Feb 01 '78	Hope	BC	CAN	73	188	L
Kobasew, Chuck	12	R	Apr 17 '82	Vancouver	BC	CAN	72	192	R
Murray, Glen	27	R	Nov 01 '72	Halifax	NS	CAN	75	218	R

Goalies	#	Pos	DOB	Hometown	S/P	Ctry	Ht	Wt	C
Fernandez, Manny	35	G	Aug 27 '74	Etobicoke	ON	CAN	72	207	L
Rask, Tuukka	40	G	Mar 10 '87	Savonlinna		FIN	75	169	L
Thomas, Tim	30	G	Apr 15 '74	Flint	MI	USA	71	201	L

Regular Season Schedule

October 2008	Visitor	Home
Thu Oct 9, 2008	Bruins	Avalanche
Sat Oct 11, 2008	Bruins	Wild
Wed Oct 15, 2008	Bruins	Canadiens
Sat Oct 18, 2008	Bruins	Senators
Mon Oct 20, 2008	Penguins	Bruins
Tue Oct 21, 2008	Bruins	Sabres
Thu Oct 23, 2008	Maple Leafs	Bruins
Sat Oct 25, 2008	Thrashers	Bruins
Mon Oct 27, 2008	Bruins	Oilers
Tue Oct 28, 2008	Bruins	Canucks
Thu Oct 30, 2008	Bruins	Flames

November 2008	Visitor	Home
Sat Nov 1, 2008	Stars	Bruins
Thu Nov 6, 2008	Maple Leafs	Bruins
Sat Nov 8, 2008	Sabres	Bruins
Wed Nov 12, 2008	Bruins	Blackhawks
Thu Nov 13, 2008	Canadiens	Bruins
Sat Nov 15, 2008	Bruins	Rangers
Mon Nov 17, 2008	Bruins	Maple Leafs
Wed Nov 19, 2008	Sabres	Bruins
Fri Nov 21, 2008	Panthers	Bruins
Sat Nov 22, 2008	Bruins	Canadiens
Wed Nov 26, 2008	Bruins	Sabres
Fri Nov 28, 2008	Islanders	Bruins
Sat Nov 29, 2008	Red Wings	Bruins

December 2008	Visitor	Home
Thu Dec 4, 2008	Bruins	Lightning
Sat Dec 6, 2008	Bruins	Panthers
Mon Dec 8, 2008	Lightning	Bruins
Wed Dec 10, 2008	Bruins	Capitals
Fri Dec 12, 2008	Bruins	Thrashers
Sat Dec 13, 2008	Thrashers	Bruins
Thu Dec 18, 2008	Maple Leafs	Bruins
Sat Dec 20, 2008	Hurricanes	Bruins
Sun Dec 21, 2008	Bruins	Blues
Tue Dec 23, 2008	Bruins	Devils
Sat Dec 27, 2008	Bruins	Hurricanes
Sun Dec 28, 2008	Bruins	Thrashers
Tue Dec 30, 2008	Bruins	Penguins

January 2009	Visitor	Home
Thu Jan 1, 2009	Penguins	Bruins
Sat Jan 3, 2009	Sabres	Bruins
Tue Jan 6, 2009	Wild	Bruins
Thu Jan 8, 2009	Senators	Bruins
Sat Jan 10, 2009	Hurricanes	Bruins

January 2009, cont.	Visitor	Home
Tue Jan 13, 2009	Canadiens	Bruins
Thu Jan 15, 2009	Bruins	Islanders
Sat Jan 17, 2009	Bruins	Capitals
Mon Jan 19, 2009	Blues	Bruins
Wed Jan 21, 2009	Bruins	Maple Leafs
Tue Jan 27, 2009	Capitals	Bruins
Thu Jan 29, 2009	Devils	Bruins
Sat Jan 31, 2009	Rangers	Bruins

February 2009	Visitor	Home
Sun Feb 1, 2009	Bruins	Canadiens
Wed Feb 4, 2009	Bruins	Flyers
Thu Feb 5, 2009	Bruins	Senators
Sat Feb 7, 2009	Flyers	Bruins
Tue Feb 10, 2009	Sharks	Bruins
Fri Feb 13, 2009	Bruins	Devils
Sat Feb 14, 2009	Bruins	Predators
Tue Feb 17, 2009	Bruins	Hurricanes
Sat Feb 21, 2009	Bruins	Panthers
Sun Feb 22, 2009	Bruins	Lightning
Tue Feb 24, 2009	Panthers	Bruins
Thu Feb 26, 2009	Ducks	Bruins
Sat Feb 28, 2009	Capitals	Bruins

March 2009	Visitor	Home
Tue Mar 3, 2009	Flyers	Bruins
Thu Mar 5, 2009	Coyotes	Bruins
Sat Mar 7, 2009	Blackhawks	Bruins
Sun Mar 8, 2009	Bruins	Rangers
Tue Mar 10, 2009	Bruins	Blue Jackets
Thu Mar 12, 2009	Senators	Bruins
Sat Mar 14, 2009	Islanders	Bruins
Sun Mar 15, 2009	Bruins	Penguins
Thu Mar 19, 2009	Kings	Bruins
Sun Mar 22, 2009	Devils	Bruins
Sat Mar 28, 2009	Bruins	Maple Leafs
Sun Mar 29, 2009	Bruins	Flyers
Tue Mar 31, 2009	Lightning	Bruins

April 2009	Visitor	Home
Thu Apr 2, 2009	Senators	Bruins
Sat Apr 4, 2009	Rangers	Bruins
Tue Apr 7, 2009	Bruins	Senators
Thu Apr 9, 2009	Canadiens	Bruins
Sat Apr 11, 2009	Bruins	Sabres
Sun Apr 12, 2009	Bruins	Islanders

Buffalo Sabres

Founded in 1970, the Buffalo Sabres are the home team of Buffalo, New York. Wanting to be different from many other sports teams in Buffalo whose names were "bison" or a name of the same ilk, Buffalo's first owners immediately started up a name-the-team contest, resulting in the name that has stuck through to today: the Sabres. Chosen because one of the owners thought this weapon was one to be carried by a leader and was a weapon that is swift and strong on both offense and defense, the Sabres have yet to win a Stanley Cup, although they have been division champions for five of their seasons in the NHL. Losing 3–1 to the Montreal Canadiens in April 2008 put the Sabres out of Stanley Cup contention and they became only the third team in NHL history to go from finishing first overall in regular season standings to finishing out of the playoffs in the following year.

Owner	General Manager	Coach
Thomas Golisano	Darcy Regier	Lindy Ruff

2008 Record and Rankings

39-31-12, 4th in the Northeast Division

	Points	GF/G	GA/G	S/G	SA/G	PP %	PK %	PIM/G
	90	3.06	2.84	30.2	28.4	18	83.2	12.2
NHL Rank	18	4	22	8	12	14	11	6

Recent Top Draft Picks

Draft	Num.	Round	Player	Pos	Drafted From
2008 Entry	12	1	Tyler Myers	D	Kelowna Rockets (WHL)
2008 Entry	26	1	Tyler Ennis	C	Medicine Hat Tigers (WHL)
2008 Entry	44	2	Luke Adam	C	St. John's Fog Devils (QMJHL)
2007 Entry	31	2	T.J. Brennan	D	St. John's Fog Devils (QMJHL)
2007 Entry	59	2	Drew Schiestel	D	Mississauga IceDogs (OHL)
2007 Entry	89	3	Corey Tropp	R	Sioux Falls Stampede (USHL)
2006 Entry	24	1	Dennis Persson	D	Vasteras IK (Swe-1)
2006 Entry	46	2	Jhonas Enroth	G	Sodertalje SK (SEL)
2006 Entry	57	2	Mike Weber	D	Windsor Spitfires (OHL)

Shootout Record

GP	W	L	G	S	S%	GA	SA	Sv%
13	4	9	12	43	28	17	43	61

Team Leaders

	G		A		P
Thomas Vanek	36	Jason Pominville	53	Derek Roy	81
Derek Roy	32	Derek Roy	49	Jason Pominville	80
Jason Pominville	27	Tim Connolly	33	Thomas Vanek	64
Ales Kotalik	23	Thomas Vanek	28	Jochen Hecht	49
Jochen Hecht	22	Jochen Hecht	27	Ales Kotalik	43

	PIM		Hits		+/-
Andrew Peters	100	Paul Gaustad	199	Jason Pominville	16
Paul Gaustad	85	Toni Lydman	159	Derek Roy	13
Toni Lydman	74	Steve Bernier	157	Mike Weber	12
Adam Mair	66	Ales Kotalik	139	Daniel Paille	9
2 tied with	64	2 tied with	112	Jaroslav Spacek	7

	PPG		SHG		Sht
Thomas Vanek	19	Derek Roy	3	Thomas Vanek	240
Ales Kotalik	12	Daniel Paille	3	Jason Pominville	232
Jaroslav Spacek	7	Tim Connolly	1	Jochen Hecht	229
Derek Roy	6	Jochen Hecht	1	Derek Roy	218
Paul Gaustad	5	Jason Pominville	1	Ales Kotalik	207

Goalies	GP	W	GAA	Sv%	SO
Ryan Miller	76	36	2.64	0.906	3
Jocelyn Thibault	12	3	3.31	0.869	2

Roster

Player	#	Pos	DOB	Hometown	S/P	Ctry	Ht	Wt	S
Connolly, Tim	19	C	May 07 '81	Syracuse	NY	USA	73	190	R
Gaustad, Paul	28	C	Feb 03 '82	Fargo	ND	USA	77	225	L
Hecht, Jochen	55	C	Jun 21 '77	Mannheim		DEU	73	191	L
Mair, Adam	22	C	Feb 15 '79	Hamilton	ON	CAN	73	208	R
Roy, Derek	9	C	May 04 '83	Ottawa	ON	CAN	69	188	L
Ryan, Michael	37	C	May 16 '80	Boston	MA	USA	73	188	L
Funk, Michael	3	D	Aug 15 '86	Abbotsford	BC	CAN	76	199	L
Kalinin, Dmitri	45	D	Jul 22 '80	Chelyabinsk		RUS	75	206	L
Lydman, Toni	5	D	Sep 25 '77	Lahti		FIN	73	204	L
Numminen, Teppo	27	D	Jul 03 '68	Tampere		FIN	74	198	R
Paetsch, Nathan	38	D	Mar 30 '83	Leroy	SK	CAN	73	198	L
Pratt, Nolan	4	D	Aug 14 '75	Fort McMurray	AB	CAN	75	207	L
Sekera, Andrej	44	D	Jun 08 '86	Bojnice		SVK	72	191	L
Spacek, Jaroslav	6	D	Feb 11 '74	Rokycany		CZE	71	204	L
Tallinder, Henrik	10	D	Jan 10 '79	Stockholm		SWE	75	214	L
Weber, Mike	34	D	Dec 16 '87	Pittsburgh	PA	USA	74	199	L
Gragnani, Marc-Andre	17	L	Mar 11 '87	Montreal	QC	CAN	73	180	L
MacArthur, Clarke	41	L	Apr 06 '85	Lloydminster	AB	CAN	71	191	L
Paille, Daniel	20	L	Apr 15 '84	Welland	ON	CAN	72	197	L
Peters, Andrew	76	L	May 05 '80	St. Catharines	ON	CAN	76	247	L
Vanek, Thomas	26	L	Jan 19 '84	Vienna		AUT	74	208	R
Afinogenov, Maxim	61	R	Sep 04 '79	Moscow		RUS	72	191	L
Bernier, Steve	56	R	Mar 31 '85	Quebec City	QC	CAN	74	225	R
Kaleta, Patrick	36	R	Jun 08 '86	Buffalo	NY	USA	71	195	R
Kotalik, Ales	12	R	Dec 23 '78	Jindr Hradec		CZE	73	227	R
Pominville, Jason	29	R	Nov 30 '82	Repentigny	QC	CAN	72	186	R
Stafford, Drew	21	R	Oct 30 '85	Milwaukee	WI	USA	74	202	R

Goalies	#	Pos	DOB	Hometown	S/P	Ctry	Ht	Wt	C
Miller, Ryan	30	G	Jul 17 '80	East Lansing	MI	USA	74	166	L
Thibault, Jocelyn	35	G	Jan 12 '75	Montreal	QC	CAN	71	169	L

Regular Season Schedule

October 2008	Visitor	Home
Fri Oct 10, 2008	Canadiens	Sabres
Mon Oct 13, 2008	Sabres	Islanders
Wed Oct 15, 2008	Sabres	Rangers
Fri Oct 17, 2008	Canucks	Sabres
Sat Oct 18, 2008	Sabres	Thrashers
Tue Oct 21, 2008	Bruins	Sabres
Thu Oct 23, 2008	Sabres	Wild
Sat Oct 25, 2008	Sabres	Avalanche
Mon Oct 27, 2008	Senators	Sabres
Thu Oct 30, 2008	Lightning	Sabres

November 2008	Visitor	Home
Sat Nov 1, 2008	Capitals	Sabres
Mon Nov 3, 2008	Sabres	Devils
Fri Nov 7, 2008	Thrashers	Sabres
Sat Nov 8, 2008	Sabres	Bruins
Wed Nov 12, 2008	Blues	Sabres
Fri Nov 14, 2008	Blue Jackets	Sabres
Sat Nov 15, 2008	Sabres	Penguins
Wed Nov 19, 2008	Sabres	Bruins
Fri Nov 21, 2008	Flyers	Sabres
Sat Nov 22, 2008	Islanders	Sabres
Wed Nov 26, 2008	Bruins	Sabres
Fri Nov 28, 2008	Penguins	Sabres
Sat Nov 29, 2008	Sabres	Canadiens

December 2008	Visitor	Home
Mon Dec 1, 2008	Predators	Sabres
Thu Dec 4, 2008	Sabres	Panthers
Sat Dec 6, 2008	Sabres	Lightning
Mon Dec 8, 2008	Sabres	Penguins
Wed Dec 10, 2008	Lightning	Sabres
Fri Dec 12, 2008	Maple Leafs	Sabres
Sat Dec 13, 2008	Sabres	Devils
Wed Dec 17, 2008	Devils	Sabres
Fri Dec 19, 2008	Kings	Sabres
Sat Dec 20, 2008	Sabres	Canadiens
Mon Dec 22, 2008	Penguins	Sabres
Fri Dec 26, 2008	Sabres	Capitals
Sat Dec 27, 2008	Islanders	Sabres
Tue Dec 30, 2008	Capitals	Sabres

January 2009	Visitor	Home
Thu Jan 1, 2009	Sabres	Maple Leafs
Sat Jan 3, 2009	Sabres	Bruins
Tue Jan 6, 2009	Senators	Sabres
Fri Jan 9, 2009	Rangers	Sabres
Sat Jan 10, 2009	Sabres	Red Wings

January 2009, cont.	Visitor	Home
Wed Jan 14, 2009	Sabres	Blackhawks
Thu Jan 15, 2009	Sabres	Stars
Sat Jan 17, 2009	Hurricanes	Sabres
Mon Jan 19, 2009	Sabres	Panthers
Wed Jan 21, 2009	Sabres	Lightning
Tue Jan 27, 2009	Sabres	Oilers
Wed Jan 28, 2009	Sabres	Flames
Sat Jan 31, 2009	Sabres	Coyotes

February 2009	Visitor	Home
Mon Feb 2, 2009	Sabres	Ducks
Wed Feb 4, 2009	Maple Leafs	Sabres
Fri Feb 6, 2009	Canadiens	Sabres
Sat Feb 7, 2009	Sabres	Senators
Wed Feb 11, 2009	Senators	Sabres
Fri Feb 13, 2009	Sharks	Sabres
Sun Feb 15, 2009	Hurricanes	Sabres
Tue Feb 17, 2009	Sabres	Maple Leafs
Thu Feb 19, 2009	Sabres	Flyers
Sat Feb 21, 2009	Rangers	Sabres
Tue Feb 24, 2009	Ducks	Sabres
Thu Feb 26, 2009	Sabres	Hurricanes
Sat Feb 28, 2009	Sabres	Islanders

March 2009	Visitor	Home
Wed Mar 4, 2009	Canadiens	Sabres
Fri Mar 6, 2009	Coyotes	Sabres
Sat Mar 7, 2009	Sabres	Senators
Tue Mar 10, 2009	Sabres	Flyers
Thu Mar 12, 2009	Panthers	Sabres
Sat Mar 14, 2009	Thrashers	Sabres
Tue Mar 17, 2009	Sabres	Senators
Fri Mar 20, 2009	Flyers	Sabres
Sat Mar 21, 2009	Sabres	Rangers
Wed Mar 25, 2009	Panthers	Sabres
Fri Mar 27, 2009	Maple Leafs	Sabres
Sat Mar 28, 2009	Sabres	Canadiens

April 2009	Visitor	Home
Wed Apr 1, 2009	Sabres	Thrashers
Fri Apr 3, 2009	Sabres	Capitals
Sat Apr 4, 2009	Devils	Sabres
Mon Apr 6, 2009	Red Wings	Sabres
Wed Apr 8, 2009	Sabres	Maple Leafs
Thu Apr 9, 2009	Sabres	Hurricanes
Sat Apr 11, 2009	Bruins	Sabres

Calgary Flames

One of two Albertan teams, the Calgary Flames are based in Calgary, Alberta. They are the third professional hockey franchise the city has seen, following the Calgary Tigers (1921–26) and the Calgary Cowboys (1975–77), and were founded in 1980 after being bought from Atlanta. The Flames have one Stanley Cup win—the 1989 pitting against the Montreal Canadiens, which is also the last time two Canadian teams have gone head to head for this holy grail of hockey. Calgary currently plays in the Pengrowth Saddledome, home to many rival games between the Flames and the Edmonton Oilers—games otherwise known as Battles of Alberta. Things have become so heated between these two teams that the Flames' mascot, Harvey the Hound (the first NHL team mascot), once had his tongue ripped out by Oilers head coach Craig MacTavish as the mascot harassed the bench.

Owners	General Manager	Coach
Murray Edwards (chairman), Harley Hotchkiss (governor), Alvin G. Libin, Allan P. Markin, Jeff McCaig, Clayton H. Riddell, Byron J. Seaman, Daryl Seaman	Darryl Sutter	Mike Keenan

2008 Record and Rankings

42-30-10, 3rd in Northwest Division

	Points	GF/G	GA/G	S/G	SA/G	PP %	PK %	PIM/G
	94	2.76	2.73	28.2	28.5	16.8	81.5	16.4
NHL Rank	15	14	15	21	13	19	20	26

Recent Top Draft Picks

Draft	Num.	Round	Player	Pos	Drafted From
2008 Entry	25	1	Greg Nemisz	C	Windsor Spitfires (OHL)
2008 Entry	48	2	Mitch Wahl	C	Spokane Chiefs (WHL)
2008 Entry	78	3	Lance Bouma	C	Vancouver Giants (WHL)
2007 Entry	24	1	Mikael Backlund	C	Vasteras IK (Swe-1)
2007 Entry	70	3	John Negrin	D	Kootenay Ice (WHL)
2007 Entry	116	4	Keith Aulie	D	Brandon Wheat Kings (WHL)
2006 Entry	26	1	Leland Irving	G	Everett Silvertips (WHL)
2006 Entry	87	3	John Armstrong	C	Plymouth Whalers (OHL)
2006 Entry	89	3	Aaron Marvin	C	Warroad H.S. (Minn.)

Shootout Record

GP	W	L	G	S	S%	GA	SA	Sv%
6	3	3	7	18	39	6	17	65

Team Leaders

G		A		P	
Jarome Iginla	50	Jarome Iginla	48	Jarome Iginla	98
Daymond Langkow	30	Dion Phaneuf	43	Kristian Huselius	66
Kristian Huselius	25	Kristian Huselius	41	Daymond Langkow	65
Alex Tanguay	18	Alex Tanguay	40	Dion Phaneuf	60
Dion Phaneuf	17	Daymond Langkow	35	Alex Tanguay	58

PIM		Hits		+/-	
Dion Phaneuf	182	Dion Phaneuf	194	Jarome Iginla	27
Eric Godard	171	Cory Sarich	157	Daymond Langkow	16
Cory Sarich	135	Robyn Regehr	154	Adrian Aucoin	13
James Vandermeer	110	James Vandermeer	124	Dion Phaneuf	12
Jarome Iginla	83	2 tied with	98	2 tied with	11

PPG		SHG		Sht	
Jarome Iginla	15	Alex Tanguay	2	Jarome Iginla	338
Daymond Langkow	14	Matthew Lombardi	2	Dion Phaneuf	263
Dion Phaneuf	10	5 tied with	1	Kristian Huselius	202
Kristian Huselius	6			Daymond Langkow	201
Adrian Aucoin	5			Matthew Lombardi	181

Goalies	GP	W	GAA	Sv%	SO
Miikka Kiprusoff	76	39	2.69	0.906	2
Curtis Joseph	9	3	2.55	0.906	0
Curtis McElhinney	5	0	2.00	0.902	0
Matt Keetley	1	0	0.00	1.000	0

Roster

Player	#	Pos	DOB	Hometown	S/P	Ctry	Ht	Wt	S
Boyd, Dustin	41	C	Jul 16 '86	Winnipeg	MB	CAN	72	187	L
Conroy, Craig	24	C	Sep 04 '71	Potsdam	NY	USA	74	193	R
Langkow Daymond	22	C	Sep 27 '76	Edmonton	AB	CAN	70	183	L
Lombardi, Matthew	18	C	Mar 18 '82	Montreal	QC	CAN	72	198	L
Primeau, Wayne	19	C	Jun 04 '76	Scarborough	ON	CAN	76	225	L
Smith, Mark	16	C	Oct 24 '77	Edmonton	AB	CAN	70	200	L
Yelle, Stephane	7	C	May 09 '74	Ottawa	ON	CAN	74	182	L
Aucoin, Adrian	33	D	Jul 03 '73	Ottawa	ON	CAN	74	212	R
Eriksson, Anders	8	D	Jan 09 '75	Bollnas		SWE	75	224	L
Hale, David	21	D	Jun 18 '81	Colorado Springs	CO	USA	73	208	L
Phaneuf, Dion	3	D	Apr 10 '85	Edmonton	AB	CAN	75	214	L
Ramholt, Tim	47	D	Nov 02 '84	Zurich		CHE	73	194	L
Regehr, Robyn	28	D	Apr 19 '80	Recife		BRA	75	225	L
Sarich, Cory	6	D	Aug 16 '78	Saskatoon	SK	CAN	76	207	R
Vandermeer, James	4	D	Feb 21 '80	Caroline	AB	CAN	73	211	L
Warrener, Rhett	44	D	Jan 27 '76	Shaunavon	SK	CAN	73	203	R
Huselius, Kristian	20	L	Nov 10 '78	Osterhani		SWE	73	179	L
Moss, David	25	L	Dec 28 '81	Livonia	MI	USA	75	200	L
Nilson, Marcus	26	L	Mar 01 '78	Balsta		SWE	74	189	R
Nystrom, Eric	23	L	Feb 14 '83	Syosset	NY	USA	73	193	L
Tanguay, Alex	40	L	Nov 21 '79	Ste-Justine	QC	CAN	73	189	L
Godard, Eric	17	R	Mar 07 '80	Vernon	BC	CAN	76	214	R
Iginla, Jarome	12	R	Jul 01 '77	Edmonton	AB	CAN	73	207	R
Nolan, Owen	11	R	Feb 12 '72	Belfast		IRL	73	214	R

Goalies	#	Pos	DOB	Hometown	S/P	Ctry	Ht	Wt	C
Joseph, Curtis	31	G	Apr 29 '67	Keswick	ON	CAN	71	193	L
Keetley, Matt	36	G	Apr 27 '86	Medicine Hat	AB	CAN	73	187	R
Kiprusoff, Miikka	34	G	Oct 26 '76	Turku		FIN	73	184	L
McElhinney, Curtis	32	G	May 23 '83	London	ON	CAN	74	193	L

Regular Season Schedule

October 2008	Visitor	Home
Thu Oct 9, 2008	Flames	Canucks
Sat Oct 11, 2008	Canucks	Flames
Tue Oct 14, 2008	Avalanche	Flames
Fri Oct 17, 2008	Oilers	Flames
Sat Oct 18, 2008	Flames	Oilers
Tue Oct 21, 2008	Capitals	Flames
Thu Oct 23, 2008	Flames	Predators
Sat Oct 25, 2008	Flames	Coyotes
Tue Oct 28, 2008	Avalanche	Flames
Thu Oct 30, 2008	Bruins	Flames

November 2008	Visitor	Home
Sat Nov 1, 2008	Flames	Kings
Sun Nov 2, 2008	Flames	Ducks
Tue Nov 4, 2008	Coyotes	Flames
Thu Nov 6, 2008	Predators	Flames
Sat Nov 8, 2008	Flames	Blue Jackets
Sun Nov 9, 2008	Flames	Blackhawks
Tue Nov 11, 2008	Maple Leafs	Flames
Thu Nov 13, 2008	Flames	Sharks
Tue Nov 18, 2008	Avalanche	Flames
Thu Nov 20, 2008	Flames	Avalanche
Sat Nov 22, 2008	Red Wings	Flames
Tue Nov 25, 2008	Kings	Flames
Thu Nov 27, 2008	Flames	Canucks
Sat Nov 29, 2008	Canucks	Flames

December 2008	Visitor	Home
Tue Dec 2, 2008	Stars	Flames
Fri Dec 5, 2008	Flames	Blues
Sun Dec 7, 2008	Flames	Rangers
Tue Dec 9, 2008	Flames	Canadiens
Wed Dec 10, 2008	Flames	Red Wings
Fri Dec 12, 2008	Panthers	Flames
Tue Dec 16, 2008	Flames	Blues
Wed Dec 17, 2008	Flames	Wild
Fri Dec 19, 2008	Blackhawks	Flames
Tue Dec 23, 2008	Ducks	Flames
Sat Dec 27, 2008	Senators	Flames
Mon Dec 29, 2008	Wild	Flames
Wed Dec 31, 2008	Oilers	Flames

January 2009	Visitor	Home
Sat Jan 3, 2009	Flames	Predators
Sun Jan 4, 2009	Flames	Blackhawks
Tue Jan 6, 2009	Sharks	Flames
Thu Jan 8, 2009	Islanders	Flames
Tue Jan 13, 2009	Blues	Flames

January 2009, cont.	Visitor	Home
Thu Jan 15, 2009	Flames	Sharks
Sat Jan 17, 2009	Coyotes	Flames
Sun Jan 18, 2009	Flames	Avalanche
Wed Jan 21, 2009	Blue Jackets	Flames
Wed Jan 28, 2009	Sabres	Flames
Fri Jan 30, 2009	Predators	Flames

February 2009	Visitor	Home
Mon Feb 2, 2009	Flames	Avalanche
Tue Feb 3, 2009	Flames	Stars
Thu Feb 5, 2009	Blackhawks	Flames
Sat Feb 7, 2009	Ducks	Flames
Mon Feb 9, 2009	Canadiens	Flames
Wed Feb 11, 2009	Flames	Ducks
Thu Feb 12, 2009	Flames	Kings
Sat Feb 14, 2009	Flames	Coyotes
Tue Feb 17, 2009	Canucks	Flames
Thu Feb 19, 2009	Flames	Wild
Sat Feb 21, 2009	Flames	Oilers
Tue Feb 24, 2009	Blue Jackets	Flames
Fri Feb 27, 2009	Wild	Flames

March 2009	Visitor	Home
Sun Mar 1, 2009	Lightning	Flames
Tue Mar 3, 2009	Flames	Senators
Thu Mar 5, 2009	Flames	Flyers
Fri Mar 6, 2009	Flames	Hurricanes
Sun Mar 8, 2009	Flames	Thrashers
Tue Mar 10, 2009	Flames	Devils
Thu Mar 12, 2009	Flames	Red Wings
Sat Mar 14, 2009	Flames	Maple Leafs
Wed Mar 18, 2009	Stars	Flames
Fri Mar 20, 2009	Blues	Flames
Mon Mar 23, 2009	Red Wings	Flames
Wed Mar 25, 2009	Flames	Penguins
Thu Mar 26, 2009	Flames	Blue Jackets
Sat Mar 28, 2009	Wild	Flames
Mon Mar 30, 2009	Sharks	Flames

April 2009	Visitor	Home
Thu Apr 2, 2009	Flames	Stars
Fri Apr 3, 2009	Flames	Wild
Mon Apr 6, 2009	Kings	Flames
Tue Apr 7, 2009	Flames	Canucks
Fri Apr 10, 2009	Flames	Oilers
Sat Apr 11, 2009	Oilers	Flames

Carolina Hurricanes

The Carolina Hurricanes are the home team of Raleigh, North Carolina, and some who were fans prior to 1997 might also know them as the Hartford Whalers. Fans might also remember Glen Wesley, who announced his retirement in 2008 and was the last remaining Carolina player from the Whalers days. The Hurricanes had their best season to date in 2005–06, finishing with a 52–22–8 record, 112 points and breaking the previous franchise record set by the 1986–87 Whalers. This was also the year Carolina won their only Stanley Cup. Remarkably, however, this was also the year the team set the record as the only NHL team in history to lose nine or more games in a year's playoffs, but still win the Cup. The Carolina Hurricanes call the RBC Center home ice.

Owner	General Manager	Coach
Peter Karmanos	Jim Rutherford	Peter Laviolette

2008 Record and Rankings

43-33-6, 2nd in Southeast Division

	Points	GF/G	GA/G	S/G	SA/G	PP %	PK %	PIM/G
	92	3.05	3	32.5	28.9	18.8	78.9	14.4
NHL Rank	16	5	25	2	16	8	26	23

Recent Top Draft Picks

Draft	Num.	Round	Player	Pos	Drafted From
2008 Entry	14	1	Zach Boychuk	C	Lethbridge Hurricanes (WHL)
2008 Entry	45	2	Zac Dalpe	C	Penticton Vees (BCHL)
2008 Entry	105	4	Michal Jordan	D	Plymouth Whalers (OHL)
2007 Entry	11	1	Brandon Sutter	C	Red Deer Rebels (WHL)
2007 Entry	72	3	Drayson Bowman	L	Spokane Chiefs (WHL)
2007 Entry	102	4	Justin McCrae	C	Saskatoon Blades (WHL)
2006 Entry	63	2	Jamie McBain	D	US National Under 18 Team
2006 Entry	93	3	Harrison Reed	C	Sarnia Sting (OHL)
2006 Entry	123	4	Bobby Hughes	C	Kingston Frontenacs (OHL)

Shootout Record

GP	W	L	G	S	S%	GA	SA	Sv%
5	2	3	7	14	50	8	14	43

Team Leaders

	G		A		P
Eric Staal	38	Eric Staal	44	Eric Staal	82
Ray Whitney	25	Ray Whitney	36	Ray Whitney	61
Erik Cole	22	Matt Cullen	36	Erik Cole	51
Rod Brind'Amour	19	Joseph Corvo	35	Rod Brind'Amour	51
2 tied with	14	Rod Brind'Amour	32	Matt Cullen	49

	PIM		Hits		+/-
Scott Walker	115	Erik Cole	186	Bret Hedican	17
Tuomo Ruutu	91	Tuomo Ruutu	171	Joseph Corvo	17
Tim Gleason	84	Tim Gleason	151	Dennis Seidenberg	6
Erik Cole	76	Niclas Wallin	134	Chad Larose	6
Wade Brookbank	76	Dennis Seidenberg	110	2 tied with	5

	PPG		SHG		Sht
Eric Staal	14	Scott Walker	2	Eric Staal	310
Erik Cole	10	Trevor Letowski	1	Erik Cole	216
Matt Cullen	8	Chad Larose	1	Ray Whitney	204
Jeffrey Hamilton	7			Joseph Corvo	167
3 tied with	6			Rod Brind'Amour	151

Goalies	GP	W	GAA	Sv%	SO
Cam Ward	69	37	2.75	0.904	4
John Grahame	17	5	3.75	0.875	0
Michael Leighton	3	1	2.66	0.897	0

Roster

Player	#	Pos	DOB	Hometown	S/P	Ctry	Ht	Wt	S
Brind'Amour, Rod	17	C	Aug 09 '70	Ottawa	ON	CAN	73	205	L
Cullen, Matt	8	C	Nov 02 '76	Virginia	MN	USA	73	200	L
Hamilton, Jeffrey	51	C	Sep 04 '77	Dayton	OH	USA	70	185	R
Jensen, Joe	34	C	Feb 06 '83	Plymouth	MN	USA	71	180	L
Larose, Chad	59	C	Mar 27 '82	Fraser	MI	USA	70	181	R
Nolan, Brandon	36	C	Jul 18 '83	St. Catharines	ON	CAN	73	192	L
Ruutu, Tuomo	15	C	Feb 16 '83	Vantaa		FIN	72	200	L
Staal, Eric	12	C	Oct 29 '84	Thunder Bay	ON	CAN	76	205	L
Borer, Casey	53	D	Jul 28 '85	Minneapolis	MN	USA	74	205	L
Conboy, Tim	38	D	Mar 22 '82	Farmington	MN	USA	74	210	R
Corvo, Joseph	77	D	Jun 20 '77	Oak Park	IL	USA	72	204	R
Gleason, Tim	42	D	Jan 29 '83	Clawson	MI	USA	72	217	L
Hedican, Bret	6	D	Aug 10 '70	St. Paul	MN	USA	74	210	L
Kaberle, Frantisek	5	D	Nov 08 '73	Kladno		CZE	72	190	L
Mormina, Joey	29	D	Jun 29 '82	Montreal	QC	CAN	78	220	L
Seidenberg, Dennis	4	D	Jul 18 '81	Schwenningen		DEU	73	210	L
Tanabe, David	45	D	Jul 19 '80	White Bear Lake	MN	USA	73	212	R
Wallin, Niclas	7	D	Feb 20 '75	Boden		SWE	75	220	L
Wesley, Glen	2	D	Oct 02 '68	Red Deer	AB	CAN	73	207	L
Bayda, Ryan	18	L	Dec 09 '80	Saskatoon	SK	CAN	71	185	L
Brookbank, Wade	28	L	Sep 29 '77	Lanigan	SK	CAN	76	225	L
Cole, Erik	26	L	Nov 06 '78	Oswego	NY	USA	74	205	L
Samsonov, Sergei	14	L	Oct 27 '78	Moscow		RUS	68	188	R
Whitney, Ray	13	L	May 08 '72	Fort Saskatchewan	AB	CAN	70	180	R
Aucoin, Keith	37	R	Nov 06 '78	Waltham	MA	USA	69	187	L
Eaves, Patrick	44	R	May 01 '84	Calgary	AB	CAN	71	190	R
Letowski, Trevor	19	R	Apr 05 '77	Thunder Bay	ON	CAN	70	180	R
Walker, Scott	24	R	Jul 19 '73	Cambridge	ON	CAN	70	196	R
Williams, Justin	11	R	Oct 04 '81	Cobourg	ON	CAN	73	195	R

Goalies	#	Pos	DOB	Hometown	S/P	Ctry	Ht	Wt	C
Grahame, John	47	G	Aug 31 '75	Denver	CO	USA	75	220	L
Leighton, Michael	49	G	May 19 '81	Petrolia	ON	CAN	75	186	L
Ward, Cam	30	G	Feb 29 '84	Saskatoon	SK	CAN	73	200	L

Regular Season Schedule

October 2008	Visitor	Home
Fri Oct 10, 2008	Panthers	Hurricanes
Sat Oct 11, 2008	Hurricanes	Lightning
Mon Oct 13, 2008	Red Wings	Hurricanes
Fri Oct 17, 2008	Hurricanes	Kings
Sun Oct 19, 2008	Hurricanes	Ducks
Thu Oct 23, 2008	Hurricanes	Penguins
Sat Oct 25, 2008	Hurricanes	Islanders
Tue Oct 28, 2008	Hurricanes	Canadiens
Thu Oct 30, 2008	Hurricanes	Blues

November 2008	Visitor	Home
Sat Nov 1, 2008	Oilers	Hurricanes
Sun Nov 2, 2008	Maple Leafs	Hurricanes
Tue Nov 4, 2008	Hurricanes	Maple Leafs
Thu Nov 6, 2008	Hurricanes	Capitals
Fri Nov 7, 2008	Senators	Hurricanes
Sun Nov 9, 2008	Thrashers	Hurricanes
Wed Nov 12, 2008	Capitals	Hurricanes
Fri Nov 14, 2008	Hurricanes	Thrashers
Sun Nov 16, 2008	Lightning	Hurricanes
Tue Nov 18, 2008	Canadiens	Hurricanes
Fri Nov 21, 2008	Coyotes	Hurricanes
Sun Nov 23, 2008	Predators	Hurricanes
Mon Nov 24, 2008	Hurricanes	Panthers
Wed Nov 26, 2008	Flyers	Hurricanes
Fri Nov 28, 2008	Hurricanes	Flyers
Sun Nov 30, 2008	Ducks	Hurricanes

December 2008	Visitor	Home
Thu Dec 4, 2008	Penguins	Hurricanes
Sat Dec 6, 2008	Flyers	Hurricanes
Sun Dec 7, 2008	Capitals	Hurricanes
Thu Dec 11, 2008	Hurricanes	Flyers
Sat Dec 13, 2008	Hurricanes	Rangers
Tue Dec 16, 2008	Canadiens	Hurricanes
Thu Dec 18, 2008	Panthers	Hurricanes
Sat Dec 20, 2008	Hurricanes	Bruins
Sun Dec 21, 2008	Hurricanes	Canadiens
Tue Dec 23, 2008	Hurricanes	Wild
Fri Dec 26, 2008	Hurricanes	Thrashers
Sat Dec 27, 2008	Bruins	Hurricanes
Wed Dec 31, 2008	Thrashers	Hurricanes

January 2009	Visitor	Home
Fri Jan 2, 2009	Blues	Hurricanes
Sat Jan 3, 2009	Hurricanes	Lightning
Tue Jan 6, 2009	Devils	Hurricanes
Thu Jan 8, 2009	Hurricanes	Panthers

January 2009, cont.	Visitor	Home
Sat Jan 10, 2009	Hurricanes	Bruins
Tue Jan 13, 2009	Hurricanes	Senators
Thu Jan 15, 2009	Maple Leafs	Hurricanes
Sat Jan 17, 2009	Hurricanes	Sabres
Mon Jan 19, 2009	Hurricanes	Maple Leafs
Tue Jan 20, 2009	Hurricanes	Penguins
Tue Jan 27, 2009	Hurricanes	Rangers
Thu Jan 29, 2009	Lightning	Hurricanes
Sat Jan 31, 2009	Thrashers	Hurricanes

February 2009	Visitor	Home
Tue Feb 3, 2009	Hurricanes	Canucks
Thu Feb 5, 2009	Hurricanes	Sharks
Sat Feb 7, 2009	Hurricanes	Coyotes
Thu Feb 12, 2009	Panthers	Hurricanes
Sat Feb 14, 2009	Blue Jackets	Hurricanes
Sun Feb 15, 2009	Hurricanes	Sabres
Tue Feb 17, 2009	Bruins	Hurricanes
Thu Feb 19, 2009	Hurricanes	Islanders
Fri Feb 20, 2009	Lightning	Hurricanes
Sun Feb 22, 2009	Avalanche	Hurricanes
Tue Feb 24, 2009	Hurricanes	Senators
Thu Feb 26, 2009	Sabres	Hurricanes
Sat Feb 28, 2009	Hurricanes	Thrashers

March 2009	Visitor	Home
Tue Mar 3, 2009	Hurricanes	Capitals
Fri Mar 6, 2009	Flames	Hurricanes
Sat Mar 7, 2009	Hurricanes	Lightning
Mon Mar 9, 2009	Rangers	Hurricanes
Wed Mar 11, 2009	Hurricanes	Blackhawks
Thu Mar 12, 2009	Hurricanes	Stars
Sat Mar 14, 2009	Hurricanes	Capitals
Wed Mar 18, 2009	Devils	Hurricanes
Fri Mar 20, 2009	Islanders	Hurricanes
Sat Mar 21, 2009	Capitals	Hurricanes
Mon Mar 23, 2009	Hurricanes	Panthers
Wed Mar 25, 2009	Senators	Hurricanes
Sat Mar 28, 2009	Hurricanes	Devils

April 2009	Visitor	Home
Thu Apr 2, 2009	Rangers	Hurricanes
Sat Apr 4, 2009	Penguins	Hurricanes
Tue Apr 7, 2009	Islanders	Hurricanes
Thu Apr 9, 2009	Sabres	Hurricanes
Sat Apr 11, 2009	Hurricanes	Devils

33

Chicago Blackhawks

With three Stanley Cups and 13 division titles to their name since their founding in 1926 (then the Chicago Black Hawks), this team can also take pride in being one of the Original Six. However, despite having won three Cups, the Blackhawks are stuck in the longest drought of any current NHL team. The Blackhawks' team name origins go back to World War I, as the team's founder, Frederic McLaughlin, was a commander with the 333rd Machine Gun Battalion of the 86th Infantry Division, nicknamed the Blackhawk Division, and thus, the inspiration for McLaughlin's team name. And the Blackhawk history lives on, as in May 2008, it was reported that the Blackhawks are set to host the 2009 Winter Classic on a temporary ice rink at Wrigley Field on New Year's Day against fellow Original Six team, the Detroit Red Wings.

Owner	General Manager	Coach
Rocky Wirtz	Dale Tallon	Denis Savard

2008 Record and Rankings

40-34-8, 3rd in Central Division

	Points	GF/G	GA/G	S/G	SA/G	PP %	PK %	PIM/G
	88	2.85	2.82	28	28.6	15.9	82.1	16.9
NHL Rank	21	10	20	22	14	24	17	27

Recent Top Draft Picks

Draft	Num.	Round	Player	Pos	Drafted From
2008 Entry	11	1	Kyle Beach	C	Everett Silvertips (WHL)
2008 Entry	68	3	Shawn Lalonde	D	Belleville Bulls (OHL)
2008 Entry	132	5	Teigan Zahn	D	Saskatoon Blades (WHL)
2007 Entry	1	1	Patrick Kane	R	London Knights (OHL)
2007 Entry	38	2	Billy Sweatt	L	Colorado College (NCAA)
2007 Entry	56	2	Akim Aliu	R	Sudbury Wolves (OHL)
2006 Entry	3	1	Jonathan Toews	C	U. of North Dakota (NCAA)
2006 Entry	33	2	Igor Makarov	R	Krylja-2 (Russia)
2006 Entry	61	2	Simon Danis-Pepin	D	U. of Maine (NCAA)

Shootout Record

GP	W	L	G	S	S%	GA	SA	Sv%
9	5	4	10	26	38	9	28	68

Team Leaders

	G		A		P	
Patrick Sharp	36	Patrick Kane	51	Patrick Kane	72
Jonathan Toews	24	Robert Lang	33	Patrick Sharp	62
Patrick Kane	21	Jonathan Toews	30	Jonathan Toews	54
Robert Lang	21	Patrick Sharp	26	Robert Lang	54
Dustin Byfuglien	19	2 tied with	23	2 tied with	36

	PIM		Hits		+/-	
Adam Burish	214	Brent Seabrook	167	Duncan Keith	30
James Wisniewski	103	Andrew Ladd	138	Patrick Sharp	23
Brent Seabrook	90	Dustin Byfuglien	137	Andrew Ladd	13
Ben Eager	89	Craig Adams	117	Brent Seabrook	13
David Koci	68	James Wisniewski	113	James Wisniewski	12

	PPG		SHG		Sht	
Patrick Sharp	9	Patrick Sharp	7	Patrick Sharp	209
Robert Lang	7	Rene Bourque	5	Patrick Kane	191
Jonathan Toews	7	5 tied with	1	Robert Lang	172
Dustin Byfuglien	7			Dustin Byfuglien	163
Patrick Kane	7			Brent Seabrook	152

Goalies	GP	W	GAA	Sv%	SO
Nikolai Khabibulin	50	23	2.63	0.909	2
Patrick Lalime	32	16	2.82	0.897	1
Corey Crawford	5	1	2.14	0.929	1

Roster

Player	#	Pos	DOB	Hometown	S/P	Ctry	Ht	Wt	S
Adams, Kevyn	17	C	Oct 08 '74	Washington	DC	USA	73	200	R
Bolland, Dave	36	C	Jun 05 '86	Mimico	ON	CAN	72	176	R
Dowell, Jacob	49	C	Mar 04 '85	Eau Claire	WI	USA	72	202	L
Fraser, Colin	46	C	Jan 28 '85	Sicamous	BC	CAN	73	190	L
Kontiola, Petri	34	C	Oct 04 '84	Seinajoki		FIN	72	198	R
Lang, Robert	20	C	Dec 19 '70	Teplicev		CZE	75	216	R
Perreault, Yanic	94	C	Apr 04 '71	Sherbrooke	QC	CAN	71	185	L
St. Pierre, Martin	16	C	Aug 11 '83	Ottawa	ON	CAN	69	185	L
Toews, Jonathan	19	C	Apr 29 '88	Winnipeg	MB	CAN	74	203	L
Williams, Jason	29	C	Aug 11 '80	London	ON	CAN	71	194	R
Barker, Cameron	25	D	Apr 04 '86	Winnipeg	MB	CAN	75	222	L
Hendry, Jordan	42	D	Feb 23 '84	Nokomis	SK	CAN	72	196	L
Hjalmarsson, Niklas	41	D	Jun 06 '87	Eksjo		SWE	75	196	L
Keith, Duncan	2	D	Jul 16 '83	Winnipeg	MB	CAN	72	195	L
Richmond, Danny	44	D	Aug 01 '84	Chicago	IL	USA	72	192	L
Seabrook, Brent	7	D	Apr 20 '85	Richmond	BC	CAN	75	220	R
Sopel, Brent	5	D	Jan 07 '77	Calgary	AB	CAN	74	205	R
Wisniewski, James	43	D	Feb 21 '84	Canton	MI	USA	72	207	R
Zyuzin, Andrei	27	D	Jan 21 '78	Ufa		RUS	73	208	L
Berti, Adam	45	L	Jul 01 '86	Scarborough	ON	CAN	75	207	L
Bickell, Bryan	38	L	Mar 09 '86	Bowmanville	ON	CAN	76	226	L
Bourque, Rene	12	L	Dec 10 '81	Lac La Biche	AB	CAN	74	213	L
Eager, Ben	55	L	Jan 22 '84	Ottawa	ON	CAN	75	225	L
Koci, David	48	L	May 12 '81	Prague		CZE	78	238	L
Ladd, Andrew	16	L	Dec 12 '85	Maple Ridge	BC	CAN	74	201	L
Adams, Craig	28	R	Apr 26 '77	Seria		BRN	72	200	R
Blunden, Michael	28	R	Dec 15 '86	Toronto	ON	CAN	75	207	R
Brouwer, Troy	26	R	Aug 17 '85	Vancouver	BC	CAN	75	220	R
Burish, Adam	37	R	Jan 06 '83	Madison	WI	USA	73	189	R
Byfuglien, Dustin	52	R	Mar 27 '85	Minneapolis	MN	USA	75	246	R
Havlat, Martin	24	R	Apr 19 '81	Mlada Boleslav		CZE	73	204	L
Kane, Patrick	88	R	Nov 19 '88	Buffalo	NY	USA	70	163	L
Sharp, Patrick	10	R	Dec 27 '81	Thunder Bay	ON	CAN	73	197	R
Skille, Jack	11	R	May 19 '87	Madison	WI	USA	73	198	R
Versteeg, Kris	32	R	May 13 '86	Lethbridge	AB	CAN	70	179	R

Goalies	#	Pos	DOB	Hometown	S/P	Ctry	Ht	Wt	C
Khabibulin, Nikolai	39	G	Jan 13 '73	Sverdlovsk		RUS	73	208	
Lalime, Patrick	40	G	Jul 07 '74	St. Bonaventur	QC	CAN	75	189	L

Regular Season Schedule

October 2008	Visitor	Home
Fri Oct 10, 2008	Blackhawks	Rangers
Sat Oct 11, 2008	Blackhawks	Capitals
Mon Oct 13, 2008	Predators	Blackhawks
Wed Oct 15, 2008	Coyotes	Blackhawks
Sat Oct 18, 2008	Blackhawks	Blues
Sun Oct 19, 2008	Canucks	Blackhawks
Wed Oct 22, 2008	Oilers	Blackhawks
Sat Oct 25, 2008	Red Wings	Blackhawks
Mon Oct 27, 2008	Blackhawks	Wild
Fri Oct 31, 2008	Stars	Blackhawks

November 2008	Visitor	Home
Sat Nov 1, 2008	Blackhawks	Blue Jackets
Mon Nov 3, 2008	Avalanche	Blackhawks
Sun Nov 9, 2008	Flames	Blackhawks
Wed Nov 12, 2008	Bruins	Blackhawks
Fri Nov 14, 2008	Blues	Blackhawks
Sun Nov 16, 2008	Sharks	Blackhawks
Tue Nov 18, 2008	Blackhawks	Coyotes
Thu Nov 20, 2008	Blackhawks	Stars
Sat Nov 22, 2008	Blackhawks	Maple Leafs
Wed Nov 26, 2008	Blackhawks	Sharks
Fri Nov 28, 2008	Blackhawks	Ducks
Sat Nov 29, 2008	Blackhawks	Kings

December 2008	Visitor	Home
Wed Dec 3, 2008	Ducks	Blackhawks
Sat Dec 6, 2008	Blackhawks	Red Wings
Sun Dec 7, 2008	Coyotes	Blackhawks
Wed Dec 10, 2008	Senators	Blackhawks
Fri Dec 12, 2008	Blackhawks	Avalanche
Sun Dec 14, 2008	Blue Jackets	Blackhawks
Tue Dec 16, 2008	Blackhawks	Oilers
Fri Dec 19, 2008	Blackhawks	Flames
Sat Dec 20, 2008	Blackhawks	Canucks
Fri Dec 26, 2008	Flyers	Blackhawks
Sun Dec 28, 2008	Blackhawks	Wild
Tue Dec 30, 2008	Blackhawks	Red Wings

January 2009	Visitor	Home
Thu Jan 1, 2009	Red Wings	Blackhawks (Wrigley Field)
Sun Jan 4, 2009	Flames	Blackhawks
Tue Jan 6, 2009	Blackhawks	Coyotes
Thu Jan 8, 2009	Blackhawks	Avalanche
Sat Jan 10, 2009	Blackhawks	Predators
Sun Jan 11, 2009	Predators	Blackhawks
Wed Jan 14, 2009	Sabres	Blackhawks

January 2009, cont.	Visitor	Home
Fri Jan 16, 2009	Rangers	Blackhawks
Sat Jan 17, 2009	Blackhawks	Blues
Mon Jan 19, 2009	Wild	Blackhawks
Wed Jan 21, 2009	Blues	Blackhawks
Wed Jan 28, 2009	Blackhawks	Ducks
Thu Jan 29, 2009	Blackhawks	Kings
Sat Jan 31, 2009	Blackhawks	Sharks

February 2009	Visitor	Home
Tue Feb 3, 2009	Blackhawks	Oilers
Thu Feb 5, 2009	Blackhawks	Flames
Sat Feb 7, 2009	Blackhawks	Canucks
Wed Feb 11, 2009	Blackhawks	Thrashers
Fri Feb 13, 2009	Blackhawks	Blues
Sat Feb 14, 2009	Stars	Blackhawks
Tue Feb 17, 2009	Blackhawks	Lightning
Thu Feb 19, 2009	Blackhawks	Panthers
Sat Feb 21, 2009	Blackhawks	Stars
Sun Feb 22, 2009	Wild	Blackhawks
Tue Feb 24, 2009	Blackhawks	Predators
Fri Feb 27, 2009	Penguins	Blackhawks

March 2009	Visitor	Home
Sun Mar 1, 2009	Kings	Blackhawks
Tue Mar 3, 2009	Ducks	Blackhawks
Sat Mar 7, 2009	Blackhawks	Bruins
Sun Mar 8, 2009	Avalanche	Blackhawks
Wed Mar 11, 2009	Hurricanes	Blackhawks
Fri Mar 13, 2009	Blue Jackets	Blackhawks
Sun Mar 15, 2009	Islanders	Blackhawks
Tue Mar 17, 2009	Blackhawks	Devils
Wed Mar 18, 2009	Blackhawks	Blue Jackets
Fri Mar 20, 2009	Oilers	Blackhawks
Sun Mar 22, 2009	Kings	Blackhawks
Wed Mar 25, 2009	Sharks	Blackhawks
Fri Mar 27, 2009	Devils	Blackhawks
Sun Mar 29, 2009	Canucks	Blackhawks
Tue Mar 31, 2009	Blackhawks	Canadiens

April 2009	Visitor	Home
Wed Apr 1, 2009	Blues	Blackhawks
Fri Apr 3, 2009	Predators	Blackhawks
Sun Apr 5, 2009	Blackhawks	Blue Jackets
Tue Apr 7, 2009	Blackhawks	Predators
Wed Apr 8, 2009	Blue Jackets	Blackhawks
Sat Apr 11, 2009	Blackhawks	Red Wings
Sun Apr 12, 2009	Red Wings	Blackhawks

Colorado Avalanche

Based in Denver, Colorado, the Colorado Avalanche are the winners of two Stanley Cups (1996 and 2001), and can also call themselves the only NHL team in history to win a Cup in their first season after a re-location to a new city. Originally the Quebec Nordiques from 1979–95, the franchise made the move to Denver and have since won eight division titles and gone to the playoffs in each of their first 10 seasons, with the streak ending in 2007. Fans of the Avalanche are some of the most loyal in hockey, proven by the fact that Colorado also holds the NHL record for longest consecutive attendance sellouts with 487. Fans also love to come out when the Detroit Red Wings are in town; a rivalry first developed in 1996, it has lasted through to today, partly because of the two teams having met five times in seven years in the Western Conference playoffs between 1996 and 2002. The Avalanche currently play in the Pepsi Center.

Owner	General Manager	Coach
Stan Kroenke	Francois Giguere	Tony Granato

2008 Record and Rankings

44-31-7, 2nd in Northwest Division

	Points	GF/G	GA/G	S/G	SA/G	PP %	PK %	PIM/G
	95	2.73	2.63	28.6	27.3	14.6	81.4	12.1
NHL Rank	11	15	12	19	5	28	21	5

Recent Top Draft Picks

Draft	Num.	Round	Player	Pos	Drafted From
2008 Entry	50	2	Cameron Gaunce	D	Mississauga St. Michael's Majors (OHL)
2008 Entry	61	2	Peter Delmas	G	Lewiston MAINEiacs (QMJHL)
2008 Entry	110	4	Kelsey Tessier	C	Quebec Remparts (QMJHL)
2007 Entry	14	1	Kevin Shattenkirk	D	US National Under 18 Team
2007 Entry	45	2	Colby Cohen	D	Lincoln Stars (USHL)
2007 Entry	49	2	Trevor Cann	G	Peterborough Petes (OHL)
2006 Entry	18	1	Chris Stewart	R	Kingston Frontenacs (OHL)
2006 Entry	51	2	Nigel Williams	D	US National Under 18 Team
2006 Entry	59	2	Codey Burki	C	Brandon Wheat Kings (WHL)

Shootout Record

GP	W	L	G	S	S%	GA	SA	Sv%
10	7	3	16	39	41	10	37	73

Team Leaders

	G		A		P
Milan Hejduk	29	Paul Stastny	47	Paul Stastny	71
Marek Stavos	26	Andrew Brunette	40	Andrew Brunette	59
Paul Stastny	24	Wojtek Wolski	30	Milan Hejduk	54
Andrew Brunette	19	Joe Sakic	27	Wojtek Wolski	48
Wojtek Wolski	18	John-Michael Liles	26	Joe Sakic	40

	PIM		Hits		+/-
Ian Laperriere	140	Ruslan Salei	162	Paul Stastny	22
Cody McLeod	120	Jeff Finger	121	Kurt Sauer	17
Adam Foote	107	Ben Guite	115	Marek Svatos	13
Ruslan Salei	98	Ian Laperriere	101	Jeff Finger	12
Scott Parker	70	Cody McLeod	98	Wojtek Wolski	10

	PPG		SHG		Sht
Milan Hejduk	8	Jeff Finger	1	Milan Hejduk	205
Andrew Brunette	7	Adam Foote	1	Tyler Arnason	179
Joe Sakic	5	Milan Hejduk	1	Ryan Smyth	168
John-Michael Liles	5			John-Michael Liles	163
2 tied with	4			Wojtek Wolski	158

Goalies	GP	W	GAA	Sv%	SO
Jose Theodore	53	28	2.44	0.910	3
Peter Budaj	35	16	2.57	0.903	0
Tyler Weiman	1	0	0.00	1.000	0

Roster

Player	#	Pos	DOB	Hometown	S/P	Ctry	Ht	Wt	S
Arnason, Tyler	39	C	Mar 16 '79	Oklahoma City	OK	USA	71	204	L
Forsberg, Peter	21	C	Jul 20 '73	Ornskoldsvik		SWE	72	205	L
Guite, Ben	28	C	Jul 17 '78	Montreal	QC	CAN	73	211	R
Hensick, T.J.	37	C	Dec 10 '85	Lansing	MI	USA	70	185	R
Hlinka, Jaroslav	17	C	Nov 10 '76	Prague		CZE	70	185	L
Richardson, Brad	12	C	Feb 04 '85	Belleville	ON	CAN	71	185	L
Sakic, Joe	19	C	Jul 07 '69	Burnaby	BC	CAN	71	195	L
Smith, Wyatt	10	C	Feb 13 '77	Thief River Falls	MN	USA	71	205	L
Stastny, Paul	26	C	Dec 27 '85	Quebec City	QC	CAN	72	205	L
Boychuk, Johnny	7	D	Jan 19 '84	Edmonton	AB	CAN	74	225	R
Clark, Brett	5	D	Dec 23 '76	Wapella	SK	CAN	72	195	L
Cumiskey, Kyle	48	D	Dec 02 '86	Abbotsford	BC	CAN	70	185	L
Finger, Jeff	6	D	Dec 18 '79	Houghton	MI	USA	73	205	R
Foote, Adam	52	D	Jul 10 '71	Toronto	ON	CAN	74	226	R
Hannan, Scott	22	D	Jan 23 '79	Richmond	BC	CAN	73	225	L
Leopold, Jordan	44	D	Aug 03 '80	Golden Valley	MN	USA	73	200	L
Liles, John-Michael	4	D	Nov 25 '80	Indianapolis	IN	USA	70	185	L
Salei, Ruslan	24	D	Nov 02 '74	Minsk		BLR	73	212	L
Sauer, Kurt	34	D	Jan 16 '81	St. Cloud	MN	USA	76	220	L
Brunette, Andrew	15	L	Aug 24 '73	Sudbury	ON	CAN	73	212	L
McLeod, Cody	55	L	Jun 26 '84	Binscarth	MB	CAN	74	210	L
Smyth, Ryan	94	L	Feb 21 '76	Banff	AB	CAN	73	190	L
Wolski, Wojtek	8	L	Feb 24 '86	Zabrze		POL	75	200	L
Hejduk, Milan	23	R	Feb 14 '76	Usti		CZE	72	190	R
Jones, David	54	R	Aug 10 '84	Guelph	ON	CAN	74	220	R
Laperriere, Ian	14	R	Jan 19 '74	Montreal	QC	CAN	73	200	R
McCormick, Cody	11	R	Apr 18 '83	London	ON	CAN	75	215	R
Parker, Scott	27	R	Jan 29 '78	Hanford	CA	USA	77	240	R
Svatos, Marek	40	R	Jun 17 '82	Kosice		SVK	70	185	R

Goalies	#	Pos	DOB	Hometown	S/P	Ctry	Ht	Wt	C
Budaj, Peter	31	G	Sep 18 '82	Banska Bystrica		SVK	73	200	L
Theodore, Jose	60	G	Sep 13 '76	Laval	QC	CAN	71	182	R
Weiman, Tyler	35	G	Jun 05 '84	Saskatoon	SK	CAN	71	180	L

Regular Season Schedule

October 2008	Visitor	Home
Thu Oct 9, 2008	Bruins	Avalanche
Sun Oct 12, 2008	Avalanche	Oilers
Tue Oct 14, 2008	Avalanche	Flames
Thu Oct 16, 2008	Flyers	Avalanche
Sat Oct 18, 2008	Avalanche	Stars
Mon Oct 20, 2008	Avalanche	Kings
Thu Oct 23, 2008	Oilers	Avalanche
Sat Oct 25, 2008	Sabres	Avalanche
Tue Oct 28, 2008	Avalanche	Flames
Thu Oct 30, 2008	Blue Jackets	Avalanche

November 2008	Visitor	Home
Sun Nov 2, 2008	Sharks	Avalanche
Mon Nov 3, 2008	Avalanche	Blackhawks
Thu Nov 6, 2008	Wild	Avalanche
Sat Nov 8, 2008	Predators	Avalanche
Wed Nov 12, 2008	Avalanche	Canucks
Sat Nov 15, 2008	Avalanche	Oilers
Tue Nov 18, 2008	Avalanche	Flames
Thu Nov 20, 2008	Flames	Avalanche
Sat Nov 22, 2008	Avalanche	Kings
Mon Nov 24, 2008	Avalanche	Ducks
Wed Nov 26, 2008	Blues	Avalanche
Fri Nov 28, 2008	Avalanche	Coyotes
Sat Nov 29, 2008	Lightning	Avalanche

December 2008	Visitor	Home
Mon Dec 1, 2008	Avalanche	Wild
Thu Dec 4, 2008	Avalanche	Predators
Fri Dec 5, 2008	Avalanche	Stars
Sun Dec 7, 2008	Canucks	Avalanche
Tue Dec 9, 2008	Kings	Avalanche
Fri Dec 12, 2008	Blackhawks	Avalanche
Mon Dec 15, 2008	Avalanche	Red Wings
Tue Dec 16, 2008	Avalanche	Flyers
Thu Dec 18, 2008	Avalanche	Lightning
Sun Dec 21, 2008	Avalanche	Panthers
Tue Dec 23, 2008	Coyotes	Avalanche
Sat Dec 27, 2008	Red Wings	Avalanche
Mon Dec 29, 2008	Predators	Avalanche
Wed Dec 31, 2008	Avalanche	Coyotes

January 2009	Visitor	Home
Fri Jan 2, 2009	Blue Jackets	Avalanche
Sun Jan 4, 2009	Wild	Avalanche
Tue Jan 6, 2009	Avalanche	Predators
Thu Jan 8, 2009	Blackhawks	Avalanche
Sat Jan 10, 2009	Penguins	Avalanche

January 2009, cont.	Visitor	Home
Tue Jan 13, 2009	Avalanche	Blue Jackets
Thu Jan 15, 2009	Avalanche	Blues
Fri Jan 16, 2009	Oilers	Avalanche
Sun Jan 18, 2009	Flames	Avalanche
Wed Jan 21, 2009	Kings	Avalanche
Tue Jan 27, 2009	Sharks	Avalanche
Thu Jan 29, 2009	Maple Leafs	Avalanche
Sat Jan 31, 2009	Ducks	Avalanche

February 2009	Visitor	Home
Mon Feb 2, 2009	Flames	Avalanche
Thu Feb 5, 2009	Stars	Avalanche
Sat Feb 7, 2009	Avalanche	Blues
Tue Feb 10, 2009	Avalanche	Blue Jackets
Wed Feb 11, 2009	Avalanche	Wild
Fri Feb 13, 2009	Canadiens	Avalanche
Sun Feb 15, 2009	Avalanche	Red Wings
Tue Feb 17, 2009	Senators	Avalanche
Fri Feb 20, 2009	Avalanche	Capitals
Sun Feb 22, 2009	Avalanche	Hurricanes
Tue Feb 24, 2009	Avalanche	Thrashers
Thu Feb 26, 2009	Avalanche	Devils
Sat Feb 28, 2009	Avalanche	Rangers

March 2009	Visitor	Home
Mon Mar 2, 2009	Avalanche	Islanders
Wed Mar 4, 2009	Red Wings	Avalanche
Sun Mar 8, 2009	Avalanche	Blackhawks
Tue Mar 10, 2009	Thrashers	Avalanche
Thu Mar 12, 2009	Wild	Avalanche
Sat Mar 14, 2009	Avalanche	Oilers
Sun Mar 15, 2009	Avalanche	Canucks
Tue Mar 17, 2009	Avalanche	Wild
Thu Mar 19, 2009	Oilers	Avalanche
Sun Mar 22, 2009	Avalanche	Sharks
Wed Mar 25, 2009	Ducks	Avalanche
Fri Mar 27, 2009	Canucks	Avalanche
Sun Mar 29, 2009	Avalanche	Ducks

April 2009	Visitor	Home
Wed Apr 1, 2009	Coyotes	Avalanche
Sun Apr 5, 2009	Avalanche	Canucks
Tue Apr 7, 2009	Avalanche	Sharks
Thu Apr 9, 2009	Stars	Avalanche
Sat Apr 11, 2009	Canucks	Avalanche
Sun Apr 12, 2009	Blues	Avalanche

Columbus Blue Jackets

Columbus, Ohio product, the Columbus Blue Jackets, are a fairly new team to the NHL, founded only eight years ago in 2000. The Blue Jackets are an expansion team of Columbus' ECHL team, the Columbus Chill. A tribute to Ohio's extensive Civil War history, the Blue Jackets' jerseys are red, white and blue and feature the flag of Ohio, with an alternate logo on the shoulder depicting a Civil War cap with two crossed hockey sticks. Home ice for the Columbus Blue Jackets is the Nationwide Arena, but as of yet, the team has never finished higher than third place in their division and are the only active NHL team to have never qualified for the Stanley Cup playoffs.

Owner	General Manager	Coach
John P. McConnell	Scott Howsom	Ken Hitchcock

2008 Record and Rankings

34-36-12, 4th in Central Division

	Points	GF/G	GA/G	S/G	SA/G	PP %	PK %	PIM/G
	80	2.32	2.56	29	27.4	14.9	83.3	16.2
NHL Rank	25	29	8	14	6	26	9	25

Recent Top Draft Picks

Draft	Num.	Round	Player	Pos	Drafted From
2008 Entry	6	1	Nikita Filatov	L	CSKA Jr. (Russia)
2008 Entry	37	2	Cody Goloubef	D	U. of Wisconsin (NCAA)
2008 Entry	107	4	Steven Delisle	D	Gatineau Olympiques (QMJHL)
2007 Entry	7	1	Jakub Voracek	R	Halifax Mooseheads (QMJHL)
2007 Entry	37	2	Stefan Legein	R	Mississauga IceDogs (OHL)
2007 Entry	53	2	Will Weber	D	Gaylord H.S. (Mich.)
2006 Entry	6	1	Derick Brassard	C	Drummondville Voltigeurs (QMJHL)
2006 Entry	69	3	Steve Mason	G	London Knights (OHL)
2006 Entry	85	3	Tom Sestito	L	Plymouth Whalers (OHL)

Shootout Record

GP	W	L	G	S	S%	GA	SA	Sv%
11	3	8	11	37	30	14	33	58

Team Leaders

G		A		P	
Rick Nash	38	Nikolai Zherdev	35	Rick Nash	69
Nikolai Zherdev	26	Rick Nash	31	Nikolai Zherdev	61
Jason Chimera	14	Michael Peca	26	Michael Peca	34
Manny Malhotra	11	Ron Hainsey	24	Ron Hainsey	32
Dan Fritsche	10	David Vyborny	19	Jason Chimera	31

PIM		Hits		+/-	
Jared Boll	226	Jan Hejda	148	Jan Hejda	20
Ole-Kristian Tollefsen	111	Jared Boll	135	Rostislav Klesla	7
Jason Chimera	98	Rostislav Klesla	107	Clay Wilson	3
Rick Nash	95	Jiri Novotny	103	Rick Nash	2
Michael Peca	64	Ole-Kristian Tollefsen	91	Dan Fritsche	2

PPG		SHG		Sht	
Rick Nash	10	Rick Nash	4	Rick Nash	329
Ron Hainsey	8	Jason Chimera	1	Nikolai Zherdev	254
Nikolai Zherdev	7	Ole-Kristian Tollefsen	1	Jason Chimera	198
Michael Peca	3	Dan Fritsche	1	Ron Hainsey	161
Rostislav Klesla	3			Rostislav Klesla	130

Goalies	GP	W	GAA	Sv%	SO
Pascal Leclaire	54	24	2.25	0.919	9
Fredrik Norrena	37	10	2.72	0.896	2
Daniel Lacosta	1	0	0.00	1.000	0

Roster

Player	#	Pos	DOB	Hometown	S/P	Ctry	Ht	Wt	S
Brassard, Derick	16	C	Sep 22 '87	Hull	QC	CAN	72	180	L
Brule, Gilbert	17	C	Jan 01 '87	Edmonton	AB	CAN	70	189	R
Fritsche, Dan	49	C	Jul 13 '85	Parma	OH	USA	73	206	R
Konopka, Zenon	28	C	Jan 02 '81	Niagara On The Lake	ON	CAN	73	213	L
Lindstrom, Joakim	38	C	Dec 05 '83	Skelleftea		SWE	72	187	L
MacKenzie, Derek	26	C	Jun 11 '81	Sudbury	ON	CAN	71	185	L
Malhotra, Manny	27	C	May 18 '80	Mississauga	ON	CAN	74	217	L
Murray, Andrew	51	C	Nov 06 '81	Selkirk	MB	CAN	74	210	L
Novotny, Jiri	12	C	Aug 12 '83	Pelhrimov		CZE	75	209	R
Peca, Michael	19	C	Mar 26 '74	Toronto	ON	CAN	71	181	R
Hainsey, Ron	6	D	Mar 24 '81	Bolton	CT	USA	75	209	L
Hejda, Jan	8	D	Jun 18 '78	Prague		CZE	75	229	L
Klesla, Rostislav	97	D	Mar 21 '82	Novy Jicin		CZE	75	220	L
Methot, Marc	29	D	Jun 21 '85	Ottawa	ON	CAN	74	196	L
Rome, Aaron	44	D	Sep 27 '83	Brandon	MB	CAN	73	204	L
Russell, Kris	2	D	May 02 '87	Red Deer	AB	CAN	70	168	L
Tarnstrom, Dick	23	D	Jan 20 '75	Sundbyberg		SWE	73	205	L
Tollefsen, Ole-Kristian	55	D	Mar 29 '84	Oslo		NOR	74	211	L
Westcott, Duvie	10	D	Oct 30 '77	Winnipeg	MB	CAN	71	196	R
Wilson, Clay	4	D	Apr 05 '83	Sturgeon Lake	MN	USA	72	195	L
Chimera, Jason	25	L	May 02 '79	Edmonton	AB	CAN	74	216	L
Modin, Fredrik	33	L	Oct 08 '74	Sundsvall		SWE	76	217	L
Nash, Rick	61	L	Jun 16 '84	Brampton	ON	CAN	76	218	L
Picard, Alexandre	21	L	Oct 09 '85	Les Saules	QC	CAN	74	208	L
Sestito, Tommy	43	L	Sep 28 '87	Utica	NY	USA	76	209	L
Boll, Jared	40	R	May 13 '86	Charlotte	NC	USA	74	206	R
Pineault, Adam	41	R	May 23 '86	Holyoke	MA	USA	73	201	R
Vyborny, David	9	R	Jan 22 '75	Jihlava		CZE	70	181	L
Zherdev, Nikolai	13	R	Nov 05 '84	Kiev		UKR	74	200	R

Goalies	#	Pos	DOB	Hometown	S/P	Ctry	Ht	Wt	C
Lacosta, Daniel	34	G	Mar 28 '86	Labrador City	NL	CAN	73	186	L
Leclaire, Pascal	31	G	Nov 07 '82	Repentigny	QC	CAN	74	197	L
Norrena, Fredrik	30	G	Nov 29 '73	Pietarsaari		FIN	72	189	L

Regular Season Schedule

October 2008	Visitor	Home
Fri Oct 10, 2008	Blue Jackets	Stars
Sat Oct 11, 2008	Blue Jackets	Coyotes
Tue Oct 14, 2008	Blue Jackets	Sharks
Fri Oct 17, 2008	Predators	Blue Jackets
Sat Oct 18, 2008	Blue Jackets	Predators
Tue Oct 21, 2008	Canucks	Blue Jackets
Fri Oct 24, 2008	Rangers	Blue Jackets
Sat Oct 25, 2008	Blue Jackets	Wild
Mon Oct 27, 2008	Ducks	Blue Jackets
Thu Oct 30, 2008	Blue Jackets	Avalanche

November 2008	Visitor	Home
Sat Nov 1, 2008	Blackhawks	Blue Jackets
Mon Nov 3, 2008	Blue Jackets	Islanders
Wed Nov 5, 2008	Oilers	Blue Jackets
Fri Nov 7, 2008	Canadiens	Blue Jackets
Sat Nov 8, 2008	Flames	Blue Jackets
Wed Nov 12, 2008	Coyotes	Blue Jackets
Fri Nov 14, 2008	Blue Jackets	Sabres
Sat Nov 15, 2008	Blue Jackets	Wild
Tue Nov 18, 2008	Oilers	Blue Jackets
Sat Nov 22, 2008	Blue Jackets	Thrashers
Wed Nov 26, 2008	Coyotes	Blue Jackets
Fri Nov 28, 2008	Blue Jackets	Red Wings
Sat Nov 29, 2008	Capitals	Blue Jackets

December 2008	Visitor	Home
Mon Dec 1, 2008	Canucks	Blue Jackets
Thu Dec 4, 2008	Blue Jackets	Sharks
Sat Dec 6, 2008	Blue Jackets	Kings
Sun Dec 7, 2008	Blue Jackets	Ducks
Thu Dec 11, 2008	Predators	Blue Jackets
Sat Dec 13, 2008	Islanders	Blue Jackets
Sun Dec 14, 2008	Blue Jackets	Blackhawks
Wed Dec 17, 2008	Sharks	Blue Jackets
Thu Dec 18, 2008	Blue Jackets	Stars
Sat Dec 20, 2008	Blue Jackets	Coyotes
Tue Dec 23, 2008	Kings	Blue Jackets
Sat Dec 27, 2008	Flyers	Blue Jackets
Mon Dec 29, 2008	Blue Jackets	Kings
Wed Dec 31, 2008	Blue Jackets	Ducks

January 2009	Visitor	Home
Fri Jan 2, 2009	Blue Jackets	Avalanche
Sat Jan 3, 2009	Blue Jackets	Blues
Tue Jan 6, 2009	Blue Jackets	Red Wings
Fri Jan 9, 2009	Blue Jackets	Capitals
Sat Jan 10, 2009	Wild	Blue Jackets

January 2009, cont.	Visitor	Home
Tue Jan 13, 2009	Avalanche	Blue Jackets
Fri Jan 16, 2009	Devils	Blue Jackets
Sun Jan 18, 2009	Blue Jackets	Canucks
Tue Jan 20, 2009	Blue Jackets	Oilers
Wed Jan 21, 2009	Blue Jackets	Flames
Tue Jan 27, 2009	Red Wings	Blue Jackets
Fri Jan 30, 2009	Senators	Blue Jackets
Sat Jan 31, 2009	Stars	Blue Jackets

February 2009	Visitor	Home
Tue Feb 3, 2009	Blues	Blue Jackets
Fri Feb 6, 2009	Blue Jackets	Penguins
Sat Feb 7, 2009	Sharks	Blue Jackets
Tue Feb 10, 2009	Avalanche	Blue Jackets
Fri Feb 13, 2009	Red Wings	Blue Jackets
Sat Feb 14, 2009	Blue Jackets	Hurricanes
Mon Feb 16, 2009	Stars	Blue Jackets
Wed Feb 18, 2009	Blues	Blue Jackets
Thu Feb 19, 2009	Blue Jackets	Maple Leafs
Sat Feb 21, 2009	Ducks	Blue Jackets
Tue Feb 24, 2009	Blue Jackets	Flames
Thu Feb 26, 2009	Blue Jackets	Oilers

March 2009	Visitor	Home
Sun Mar 1, 2009	Blue Jackets	Canucks
Tue Mar 3, 2009	Kings	Blue Jackets
Thu Mar 5, 2009	Blue Jackets	Predators
Sat Mar 7, 2009	Blue Jackets	Red Wings
Tue Mar 10, 2009	Bruins	Blue Jackets
Thu Mar 12, 2009	Penguins	Blue Jackets
Fri Mar 13, 2009	Blue Jackets	Blackhawks
Sun Mar 15, 2009	Red Wings	Blue Jackets
Wed Mar 18, 2009	Blackhawks	Blue Jackets
Sat Mar 21, 2009	Blue Jackets	Panthers
Tue Mar 24, 2009	Blue Jackets	Lightning
Thu Mar 26, 2009	Flames	Blue Jackets
Sat Mar 28, 2009	Blue Jackets	Blues
Sun Mar 29, 2009	Blues	Blue Jackets
Tue Mar 31, 2009	Predators	Blue Jackets

April 2009	Visitor	Home
Sat Apr 4, 2009	Blue Jackets	Predators
Sun Apr 5, 2009	Blackhawks	Blue Jackets
Wed Apr 8, 2009	Blue Jackets	Blackhawks
Fri Apr 10, 2009	Blue Jackets	Blues
Sat Apr 11, 2009	Wild	Blue Jackets

Dallas Stars

Stanley Cup champions in 1999, the Dallas Stars have their home in Dallas, Texas, and have been division champions seven times since the team's name and location change-over in 1993. Prior to this, the Stars were known as the Minnesota North Stars, based in Bloomington, Minnesota. Calling the American Airlines Center home ice during home games, Dallas fans have made it tradition to shout out "stars" when the word is sung during the U.S. national anthem. Pantera's song, *The Dallas Stars Fight Song*, is played every time the team comes back on the ice after each intermission.

Owner	General Manager	Coach
Tom Hicks	Brett Hull, Les Jackson	Dave Tippett

2008 Record and Rankings

45-30-7, 3rd in Pacific Division

	Points	GF/G	GA/G	S/G	SA/G	PP %	PK %	PIM/G
	97	2.89	2.49	26.7	26.1	18.1	85.6	14.3
NHL Rank	8	9	6	27	4	13	2	21

Recent Top Draft Picks

Draft	Num.	Round	Player	Pos	Drafted From
2008 Entry	59	2	Tyler Beskorowany	G	Owen Sound Attack (OHL)
2008 Entry	89	3	Scott Winkler	C	Russell Stover (Kansas City Midgets)
2008 Entry	149	5	Philip Larsen	D	Vastra Frolunda HC Goteborg (SEL)
2007 Entry	50	2	Nico Sacchetti	C	Virginia H.S. (Minn.)
2007 Entry	64	3	Sergei Korostin	R	Moscow Dynamo (Russia)
2007 Entry	112	4	Colton Sceviour	R	Portland Winter Hawks (WHL)
2006 Entry	27	1	Ivan Vishnevskiy	D	Rouyn-Noranda Huskies (QMJHL)
2006 Entry	90	3	Aaron Snow	L	Brampton Battalion (OHL)
2006 Entry	120	4	Richard Bachman	G	Cushing Academy (Mass H.S.)

Shootout Record

GP	W	L	G	S	S%	GA	SA	Sv%
8	5	3	10	28	36	9	29	69

Team Leaders

G		A		P	
Brenden Morrow	32	Mike Ribeiro	56	Mike Ribeiro	83
Mike Ribeiro	27	Brenden Morrow	42	Brenden Morrow	74
Niklas Hagman	27	Brad Richards	42	Brad Richards	62
Mike Modano	21	Mike Modano	36	Mike Modano	57
Brad Richards	20	Sergei Zubov	31	Niklas Hagman	41

PIM		Hits		+/-	
Steve Ott	147	Brenden Morrow	260	Brenden Morrow	23
Brenden Morrow	105	Stephane Robidas	220	Matt Niskanen	22
Krystofer Barch	105	Steve Ott	182	Mike Ribeiro	21
Stephane Robidas	85	Joel Lundqvist	88	Nicklas Grossman	10
Trevor Daley	85	Nicklas Grossman	87	Jere Lehtinen	9

PPG		SHG		Sht	
Brenden Morrow	12	Niklas Hagman	4	Brad Richards	249
Jere Lehtinen	9	Stu Barnes	2	Brenden Morrow	207
Brad Richards	9	Brenden Morrow	2	Mike Modano	200
Stephane Robidas	7	Brad Richards	2	Niklas Hagman	178
Mike Ribeiro	7	3 tied with	1	Stephane Robidas	153

Goalies	GP	W	GAA	Sv%	SO
Marty Turco	62	32	2.31	0.909	3
Johan Holmqvist	47	21	3.04	0.889	2
Tobias Stephan	1	0	1.97	0.950	0

Roster

Player	#	Pos	DOB	Hometown	S/P	Ctry	Ht	Wt	S
Barnes, Stu	14	C	Dec 25 '70	Spruce Grove	AB	CAN	71	182	R
Lundqvist, Joel	39	C	Mar 02 '82	Are		SWE	73	194	L
Modano, Mike	9	C	Jun 07 '70	Livonia	MI	USA	75	210	L
Ott, Steve	29	C	Aug 19 '82	Summerside	PE	CAN	72	193	L
Petersen, Toby	17	C	Oct 27 '78	Minneapolis	MN	USA	70	197	L
Ribeiro, Mike	63	C	Feb 10 '80	Montreal	QC	CAN	72	178	L
Richards, Brad	91	C	May 02 '80	Murray Harbour	PE	CAN	72	192	L
Boucher, Philippe	43	D	Mar 24 '73	St. Apollinaire	QC	CAN	75	218	R
Daley, Trevor	6	D	Oct 09 '83	Toronto	ON	CAN	71	207	L
Fistric, Mark	28	D	Jun 01 '86	Edmonton	AB	CAN	74	232	L
Grossman, Nicklas	2	D	Jan 22 '85	Stockholm		SWE	75	206	L
Jancevski, Dan	42	D	Jun 15 '81	Windsor	ON	CAN	75	218	L
Niskanen, Matt	5	D	Dec 06 '86	Virginia	MN	USA	72	194	R
Norstrom, Mattias	4	D	Jan 02 '72	Stockholm		SWE	74	210	L
Robidas, Stephane	3	D	Mar 03 '77	Sherbrooke	QC	CAN	71	190	R
Zubov, Sergei	56	D	Jul 22 '70	Moscow		RUS	73	198	R
Eriksson, Loui	21	L	Jul 17 '85	Goteborg		SWE	73	183	L
Hagman, Niklas	15	L	Dec 05 '79	Espoo		FIN	72	205	L
Morrow, Brenden	10	L	Jan 16 '79	Carlyle	SK	CAN	71	205	L
Winchester, Brad	16	L	Mar 01 '81	Madison	WI	USA	77	228	L
Barch, Krystofer	13	R	Mar 26 '80	Hamilton	ON	CAN	74	220	L
Conner, Chris	25	R	Dec 23 '83	Westland	MI	USA	68	180	L
Crombeen, Brandon	44	R	Jul 10 '85	Denver	CO	USA	74	212	R
Lehtinen, Jere	26	R	Jun 24 '73	Espoo		FIN	72	192	R
Miettinen, Antti	20	R	Jul 03 '80	Hameenl		FIN	72	190	L

Goalies	#	Pos	DOB	Hometown	S/P	Ctry	Ht	Wt	C
Holmqvist, Johan	40	G	May 24 '78	Tolfta		SWE	75	198	L
Stephan, Tobias	31	G	Jan 21 '84	Zürich		CHE	74	180	L
Turco, Marty	35	G	Aug 13 '75	Sault Ste. Marie	ON	CAN	71	185	L

Regular Season Schedule

October 2008	Visitor	Home
Fri Oct 10, 2008	Blue Jackets	Stars
Sat Oct 11, 2008	Stars	Predators
Wed Oct 15, 2008	Predators	Stars
Thu Oct 16, 2008	Stars	Blues
Sat Oct 18, 2008	Avalanche	Stars
Mon Oct 20, 2008	Stars	Rangers
Wed Oct 22, 2008	Stars	Devils
Thu Oct 23, 2008	Stars	Islanders
Sat Oct 25, 2008	Capitals	Stars
Wed Oct 29, 2008	Wild	Stars
Fri Oct 31, 2008	Stars	Blackhawks

November 2008	Visitor	Home
Sat Nov 1, 2008	Stars	Bruins
Fri Nov 7, 2008	Stars	Ducks
Sat Nov 8, 2008	Stars	Sharks
Tue Nov 11, 2008	Stars	Kings
Thu Nov 13, 2008	Kings	Stars
Sat Nov 15, 2008	Stars	Coyotes
Thu Nov 20, 2008	Blackhawks	Stars
Sat Nov 22, 2008	Ducks	Stars
Mon Nov 24, 2008	Stars	Flyers
Wed Nov 26, 2008	Stars	Wild
Fri Nov 28, 2008	Sharks	Stars
Sun Nov 30, 2008	Oilers	Stars

December 2008	Visitor	Home
Tue Dec 2, 2008	Stars	Flames
Wed Dec 3, 2008	Stars	Oilers
Fri Dec 5, 2008	Avalanche	Stars
Wed Dec 10, 2008	Coyotes	Stars
Fri Dec 12, 2008	Red Wings	Stars
Sat Dec 13, 2008	Stars	Predators
Tue Dec 16, 2008	Coyotes	Stars
Thu Dec 18, 2008	Blue Jackets	Stars
Sat Dec 20, 2008	Stars	Senators
Tue Dec 23, 2008	Stars	Maple Leafs
Sat Dec 27, 2008	Ducks	Stars
Mon Dec 29, 2008	Sharks	Stars
Wed Dec 31, 2008	Devils	Stars

January 2009	Visitor	Home
Sat Jan 3, 2009	Stars	Oilers
Sun Jan 4, 2009	Stars	Canucks
Thu Jan 8, 2009	Stars	Red Wings
Sat Jan 10, 2009	Stars	Coyotes
Mon Jan 12, 2009	Red Wings	Stars
Thu Jan 15, 2009	Sabres	Stars

January 2009, cont.	Visitor	Home
Sat Jan 17, 2009	Kings	Stars
Mon Jan 19, 2009	Stars	Lightning
Wed Jan 21, 2009	Stars	Panthers
Tue Jan 27, 2009	Thrashers	Stars
Thu Jan 29, 2009	Stars	Red Wings
Sat Jan 31, 2009	Stars	Blue Jackets

February 2009	Visitor	Home
Tue Feb 3, 2009	Flames	Stars
Thu Feb 5, 2009	Stars	Avalanche
Fri Feb 6, 2009	Rangers	Stars
Sun Feb 8, 2009	Predators	Stars
Wed Feb 11, 2009	Coyotes	Stars
Fri Feb 13, 2009	Canucks	Stars
Sat Feb 14, 2009	Stars	Blackhawks
Mon Feb 16, 2009	Stars	Blue Jackets
Thu Feb 19, 2009	Oilers	Stars
Sat Feb 21, 2009	Blackhawks	Stars
Mon Feb 23, 2009	Sharks	Stars
Thu Feb 26, 2009	Blues	Stars
Sat Feb 28, 2009	Ducks	Stars

March 2009	Visitor	Home
Sun Mar 1, 2009	Penguins	Stars
Tue Mar 3, 2009	Stars	Sharks
Thu Mar 5, 2009	Stars	Kings
Fri Mar 6, 2009	Stars	Ducks
Sun Mar 8, 2009	Canadiens	Stars
Tue Mar 10, 2009	Stars	Blues
Thu Mar 12, 2009	Hurricanes	Stars
Sat Mar 14, 2009	Wild	Stars
Tue Mar 17, 2009	Stars	Canucks
Wed Mar 18, 2009	Stars	Flames
Sat Mar 21, 2009	Stars	Sharks
Tue Mar 24, 2009	Canucks	Stars
Thu Mar 26, 2009	Kings	Stars
Sat Mar 28, 2009	Panthers	Stars
Mon Mar 30, 2009	Stars	Coyotes
Tue Mar 31, 2009	Stars	Kings

April 2009	Visitor	Home
Thu Apr 2, 2009	Flames	Stars
Sat Apr 4, 2009	Blues	Stars
Tue Apr 7, 2009	Stars	Wild
Thu Apr 9, 2009	Stars	Avalanche
Fri Apr 10, 2009	Stars	Ducks

Detroit Red Wings

Eleven-time Stanley Cup winners (most recently in 2008), the Detroit Red Wings have been entertaining fans in Detroit, Michigan, since 1926. The Red Wings are one of the Original Six teams and are so popular in the NHL that Detroit has been dubbed "Hockeytown." The team has made the playoffs the last 17 seasons in a row, which is the longest streak of post-season appearances in all of professional American sports. Playing in the 20,066-capacity Joe Louis Arena, Detroit has been home to Gordie Howe and Steve Yzerman, both of whom have their numbers retired and hold the top scoring spots in the Detroit franchise record books. They have also both been witness to the Legend of the Octopus tradition that persists at Detroit playoff home games, despite the NHL trying to ban this practice several times. The throwing of the eight-legged octopus is seen as good luck after the start of the tradition in 1952 saw the owner of a local fish market throw an octopus onto the ice, apparently symbolic of the eight wins it took for Detroit to win the Stanley Cup at the time. The Red Wings went on to win the Stanley Cup that year, as well as many years after that.

Owner	General Manager	Coach
Mike Ilitch	Ken Holland	Mike Babcock

2008 Record and Rankings

54-21-7, 1st in Central Division

	Points	GF/G	GA/G	S/G	SA/G	PP %	PK %	PIM/G
	115	3.07	2.18	34.4	23.5	20.7	84.0	11.4
NHL Rank	1	3	1	1	1	3	8	1

Recent Top Draft Picks

Draft	Num.	Round	Player	Pos	Drafted From
2008 Entry	30	1	Thomas McCollum	G	Guelph Storm (OHL)
2008 Entry	91	3	Max Nicastro	D	Chicago Steel (USHL)
2008 Entry	121	4	Gustav Nyquist	C	Malmo Jrs (Sweden)
2007 Entry	27	1	Brendan Smith	D	St. Michael's Buzzers (OPJHL)
2007 Entry	88	3	Joakim Andersson	C	Frolunda Jrs (Sweden)
2007 Entry	148	5	Randy Cameron	C	Moncton Wildcats (QMJHL)
2006 Entry	41	2	Cory Emmerton	L	Kingston Frontenacs (OHL)
2006 Entry	47	2	Shawn Matthias	C	Belleville Bulls (OHL)
2006 Entry	62	2	Dick Axelsson	L	Huddinge (Sweden)

Shootout Record

GP	W	L	G	S	S%	GA	SA	Sv%
10	5	5	12	30	40	11	28	61

Team Leaders

	G		A		P
Henrik Zetterberg	43	Pavel Datsyuk	66	Pavel Datsyuk	97
Pavel Datsyuk	31	Nicklas Lidstrom	60	Henrik Zetterberg	92
Johan Franzen	27	Henrik Zetterberg	49	Nicklas Lidstrom	70
Daniel Cleary	20	Brian Rafalski	42	Brian Rafalski	55
Tomas Holmstrom	20	2 tied with	29	2 tied with	42

	PIM		Hits		+/-
Aaron Downey	116	Andreas Lilja	133	Pavel Datsyuk	41
Andreas Lilja	93	Brad Stuart	118	Nicklas Lidstrom	40
Brad Stuart	69	Tomas Kopecky	111	Henrik Zetterberg	30
Kris Draper	68	Niklas Kronwall	93	Brian Rafalski	27
Tomas Holmstrom	58	2 tied with	92	Niklas Kronwall	25

	PPG		SHG		Sht
Henrik Zetterberg	16	Kris Draper	2	Henrik Zetterberg	358
Johan Franzen	14	Dallas Drake	1	Pavel Datsyuk	264
Tomas Holmstrom	11	Henrik Zetterberg	1	Mikael Samuelsson	249
Brian Rafalski	10	Pavel Datsyuk	1	Johan Franzen	199
Pavel Datsyuk	10			Nicklas Lidstrom	188

Goalies	GP	W	GAA	Sv%	SO
Chris Osgood	43	27	2.09	0.914	4
Dominik Hasek	41	27	2.14	0.902	5
James Howard	4	0	2.13	0.926	0

Roster

Player	#	Pos	DOB	Hometown	S/P	Ctry	Ht	Wt	S
Datsyuk, Pavel	13	C	Jul 20 '78	Sverdlovsk		RUS	71	194	L
Draper, Kris	33	C	May 24 '71	Toronto	ON	CAN	70	188	L
Filppula, Valtteri	51	C	Mar 20 '84	Vantaa		FIN	72	193	L
Hartigan, Mark	44	C	Oct 15 '77	Fort St. John	BC	CAN	72	200	L
Helm, Darren	43	C	Jan 21 '87	Winnipeg	MB	CAN	71	172	L
Hudler, Jiri	26	C	Jan 04 '84	Olomouc		CZE	70	182	L
Kopecky, Tomas	82	C	Feb 05 '82	Ilava		SVK	75	200	L
Ritola, Mattias	42	C	Mar 14 '87	Borlange		SWE	72	192	L
Zetterberg, Henrik	40	C	Oct 09 '80	Njurunda		SWE	71	195	L
Chelios, Chris	24	D	Jan 25 '62	Chicago	IL	USA	72	191	R
Ericsson, Jonathan	52	D	Mar 02 '84	Karlskrona		SWE	76	206	L
Kronwall, Niklas	55	D	Jan 12 '81	Stockholm		SWE	72	189	L
Lebda, Brett	22	D	Jan 15 '82	Buffalo Grove	IL	USA	69	195	L
Lidstrom, Nicklas	5	D	Apr 28 '70	Vasteras		SWE	73	189	L
Lilja, Andreas	3	D	Jul 13 '75	Helsin		SWE	75	220	L
Meech, Derek	14	D	Apr 21 '84	Winnipeg	MB	CAN	71	197	L
Quincey, Kyle	4	D	Aug 12 '85	Kitchener	ON	CAN	74	207	L
Rafalski, Brian	28	D	Sep 28 '73	Dearborn	MI	USA	70	191	R
Stafford, Garrett	36	D	Jan 28 '80	Los Angeles	CA	USA	72	195	R
Stuart, Brad	23	D	Nov 06 '79	Rocky Mountain House	AB	CAN	74	213	L
Abdelkader, Justin	8	L	Feb 25 '87	Muskegon	MI	USA	73	215	L
Holmstrom, Tomas	96	L	Jan 23 '73	Pieta		SWE	72	203	L
Maltby, Kirk	18	L	Dec 22 '72	Guelph	ON	CAN	72	193	R
Cleary, Daniel	11	R	Dec 18 '78	Carbonear	NL	CAN	72	210	L
Downey, Aaron	20	R	Aug 27 '74	Shelburne	ON	CAN	73	215	R
Drake, Dallas	17	R	Feb 04 '69	Trail	BC	CAN	72	186	L
Franzen, Johan	93	R	Dec 23 '79	Vetlanda		SWE	75	220	L
McCarty, Darren	25	R	Apr 01 '72	Burnaby	BC	CAN	73	210	R
Samuelsson, Mikael	37	R	Dec 23 '76	Mariefred		SWE	74	213	R

Goalies	#	Pos	DOB	Hometown	S/P	Ctry	Ht	Wt	C
Hasek, Dominik	39	G	Jan 29 '65	Pardubice		CZE	73	166	L
Howard, James	35	G	Mar 26 '84	Syracuse	NY	USA	72	205	L
Osgood, Chris	30	G	Nov 26 '72	Peace River	AB	CAN	70	178	L

Regular Season Schedule

October 2008	Visitor	Home
Thu Oct 9, 2008	Maple Leafs	Red Wings
Sat Oct 11, 2008	Red Wings	Senators
Mon Oct 13, 2008	Red Wings	Hurricanes
Thu Oct 16, 2008	Canucks	Red Wings
Sat Oct 18, 2008	Rangers	Red Wings
Wed Oct 22, 2008	Red Wings	Blues
Fri Oct 24, 2008	Thrashers	Red Wings
Sat Oct 25, 2008	Red Wings	Blackhawks
Mon Oct 27, 2008	Red Wings	Kings
Wed Oct 29, 2008	Red Wings	Ducks
Thu Oct 30, 2008	Red Wings	Sharks

November 2008	Visitor	Home
Sun Nov 2, 2008	Red Wings	Canucks
Sat Nov 8, 2008	Devils	Red Wings
Tue Nov 11, 2008	Penguins	Red Wings
Thu Nov 13, 2008	Red Wings	Lightning
Fri Nov 14, 2008	Red Wings	Panthers
Mon Nov 17, 2008	Oilers	Red Wings
Thu Nov 20, 2008	Red Wings	Oilers
Sat Nov 22, 2008	Red Wings	Flames
Mon Nov 24, 2008	Red Wings	Canucks
Wed Nov 26, 2008	Canadiens	Red Wings
Fri Nov 28, 2008	Blue Jackets	Red Wings
Sat Nov 29, 2008	Red Wings	Bruins

December 2008	Visitor	Home
Mon Dec 1, 2008	Ducks	Red Wings
Thu Dec 4, 2008	Canucks	Red Wings
Sat Dec 6, 2008	Blackhawks	Red Wings
Wed Dec 10, 2008	Flames	Red Wings
Fri Dec 12, 2008	Red Wings	Stars
Sat Dec 13, 2008	Red Wings	Coyotes
Mon Dec 15, 2008	Avalanche	Red Wings
Thu Dec 18, 2008	Sharks	Red Wings
Sat Dec 20, 2008	Kings	Red Wings
Tue Dec 23, 2008	Blues	Red Wings
Fri Dec 26, 2008	Red Wings	Predators
Sat Dec 27, 2008	Red Wings	Avalanche
Tue Dec 30, 2008	Blackhawks	Red Wings

January 2009	Visitor	Home
Thu Jan 1, 2009	Red Wings	Blackhawks (Wrigley Field)
Sat Jan 3, 2009	Red Wings	Wild
Tue Jan 6, 2009	Blue Jackets	Red Wings
Thu Jan 8, 2009	Stars	Red Wings
Sat Jan 10, 2009	Sabres	Red Wings

January 2009, cont.	Visitor	Home
Mon Jan 12, 2009	Red Wings	Stars
Wed Jan 14, 2009	Red Wings	Ducks
Thu Jan 15, 2009	Red Wings	Kings
Sat Jan 17, 2009	Red Wings	Sharks
Tue Jan 20, 2009	Red Wings	Coyotes
Tue Jan 27, 2009	Red Wings	Blue Jackets
Thu Jan 29, 2009	Stars	Red Wings
Sat Jan 31, 2009	Red Wings	Capitals

February 2009	Visitor	Home
Mon Feb 2, 2009	Blues	Red Wings
Wed Feb 4, 2009	Coyotes	Red Wings
Sat Feb 7, 2009	Oilers	Red Wings
Sun Feb 8, 2009	Red Wings	Penguins
Tue Feb 10, 2009	Red Wings	Predators
Thu Feb 12, 2009	Wild	Red Wings
Fri Feb 13, 2009	Red Wings	Blue Jackets
Sun Feb 15, 2009	Avalanche	Red Wings
Wed Feb 18, 2009	Predators	Red Wings
Fri Feb 20, 2009	Ducks	Red Wings
Sat Feb 21, 2009	Red Wings	Wild
Wed Feb 25, 2009	Sharks	Red Wings
Fri Feb 27, 2009	Kings	Red Wings
Sat Feb 28, 2009	Red Wings	Predators

March 2009	Visitor	Home
Tue Mar 3, 2009	Red Wings	Blues
Wed Mar 4, 2009	Red Wings	Avalanche
Sat Mar 7, 2009	Blue Jackets	Red Wings
Tue Mar 10, 2009	Coyotes	Red Wings
Thu Mar 12, 2009	Flames	Red Wings
Sat Mar 14, 2009	Red Wings	Blues
Sun Mar 15, 2009	Red Wings	Blue Jackets
Tue Mar 17, 2009	Flyers	Red Wings
Fri Mar 20, 2009	Red Wings	Thrashers
Mon Mar 23, 2009	Red Wings	Flames
Tue Mar 24, 2009	Red Wings	Oilers
Fri Mar 27, 2009	Islanders	Red Wings
Sun Mar 29, 2009	Predators	Red Wings

April 2009	Visitor	Home
Thu Apr 2, 2009	Blues	Red Wings
Sun Apr 5, 2009	Wild	Red Wings
Mon Apr 6, 2009	Red Wings	Sabres
Thu Apr 9, 2009	Predators	Red Wings
Sat Apr 11, 2009	Blackhawks	Red Wings
Sun Apr 12, 2009	Red Wings	Blackhawks

53

Edmonton Oilers

One-time home team to record-breaker Number 99 Wayne Gretzky, the Edmonton Oilers, based in Edmonton, Alberta, have won the Stanley Cup five times, the most recent of which was in 1990. This marked the end to the literal dynasty years (as honored by the NHL) during the 1980s when the Oilers were the dominant team in the NHL, collecting all of their Cup wins in this period, as well as obtaining six conference titles in a 21-team league over seven years. The Oilers made their most recent Stanley Cup run in 2006, but lost 3–1 in Game 7 to the Carolina Hurricanes. In the 2007–08 season, Edmonton was three points back of a playoff spot, but with Daryl Katz as the new owner and the impressive showing in 2008 by the Oilers' young players such as Sam Gagner and Andrew Cogliano, fans hope 2008–09 to be a season reminiscent of the Oiler-mania of the 1980s.

Owner	General Manager	Coach
Daryl Katz	Kevin Lowe	Craig MacTavish

2008 Record and Rankings

41-35-6, 4th in Northwest Division

	Points	GF/G	GA/G	S/G	SA/G	PP %	PK %	PIM/G
	88	2.68	3.01	26.3	31.4	16.6	84.7	14.3
NHL Rank	20	17	26	28	25	21	5	19

Recent Top Draft Picks

Draft	Num.	Round	Player	Pos	Drafted From
2008 Entry	22	1	Jordan Eberle	C	Regina Pats (WHL)
2008 Entry	103	4	Johan Motin	D	Bofors IK (Swe-1)
2008 Entry	133	5	Philippe Cornet	L	Rimouski Oceanic (QMJHL)
2007 Entry	6	1	Sam Gagner	C	London Knights (OHL)
2007 Entry	15	1	Alexandre Plante	D	Calgary Hitmen (WHL)
2007 Entry	21	1	Riley Nash	C	Salmon Arm Silverbacks (BCHL)
2006 Entry	45	2	Jeff Petry	D	Des Moines Buccaneers (USHL)
2006 Entry	75	3	Theo Peckham	D	Owen Sound Attack (OHL)
2006 Entry	133	5	Bryan Pitton	G	Brampton Battalion (OHL)

Shootout Record

GP	W	L	G	S	S%	GA	SA	Sv%
19	15	4	24	65	37	12	69	83

Team Leaders

	G		A		P
Dustin Penner	23	Ales Hemsky	51	Ales Hemsky	71
Shawn Horcoff	21	Sam Gagner	36	Shawn Horcoff	50
Ales Hemsky	20	Robert Nilsson	31	Sam Gagner	49
Andrew Cogliano	18	Shawn Horcoff	29	Dustin Penner	47
Curtis Glencross	15	Andrew Cogliano	27	Andrew Cogliano	45

	PIM		Hits		+/-
Zachery Stortini	201	Jarret Stoll	122	Robert Nilsson	8
Steve Staios	121	Dustin Penner	99	Curtis Glencross	8
Jarret Stoll	74	Zachery Stortini	99	Zachery Stortini	3
Ladislav Smid	58	Curtis Glencross	94	Denis Grebeshkov	2
Joni Pitkanen	56	Ladislav Smid	92	2 tied with	1

	PPG		SHG		Sht
Dustin Penner	13	Jarret Stoll	3	Dustin Penner	201
Jarret Stoll	8	Andrew Cogliano	2	Jarret Stoll	187
Ales Hemsky	8	Joni Pitkanen	1	Ales Hemsky	184
Shawn Horcoff	6	Kyle Brodziak	1	Sam Gagner	135
2 tied with	4			Kyle Brodziak	125

Goalies	GP	W	GAA	Sv%	SO
Mathieu Garon	47	26	2.66	0.913	4
Dwayne Roloson	43	15	3.05	0.901	0

Roster

Player	#	Pos	DOB	Hometown	S/P	Ctry	Ht	Wt	S
Brodziak, Kyle	51	C	May 25 '84	St. Paul	AB	CAN	74	209	R
Cogliano, Andrew	13	C	Jun 14 '87	Toronto	ON	CAN	70	184	L
Gagner, Sam	89	C	Aug 10 '89	London	ON	CAN	71	191	R
Horcoff, Shawn	10	C	Sep 17 '78	Trail	BC	CAN	73	208	L
Nilsson, Robert	12	C	Jan 10 '85	Calgary	AB	CAN	71	185	L
Pouliot, Marc-Antoine	78	C	May 22 '85	Quebec City	QC	CAN	74	200	R
Reasoner, Marty	19	C	Feb 26 '77	Honeoye Falls	NY	USA	73	202	L
Schremp, Rob	88	C	Jul 01 '86	Syracuse	NY	USA	71	200	L
Stoll, Jarret	16	C	Jun 24 '82	Melville	SK	CAN	73	210	R
Gilbert, Tom	77	D	Jan 10 '83	Minneapolis	MN	USA	75	206	R
Grebeshkov, Denis	37	D	Oct 11 '83	Yaroslavl		RUS	72	209	L
Greene, Matt	2	D	May 13 '83	Grand Ledge	MI	USA	75	233	R
Peckham, Theo	49	D	Nov 10 '87	Richmond Hill	ON	CAN	74	223	L
Pitkanen, Joni	25	D	Sep 19 '83	Oulu		FIN	75	214	L
Rourke, Allan	52	D	Mar 06 '80	Mississauga	ON	CAN	74	215	L
Roy, Mathieu	36	D	Aug 10 '83	St-Martins	QC	CAN	74	210	R
Smid, Ladislav	5	D	Feb 01 '86	Frydlant		CZE	75	226	L
Souray, Sheldon	44	D	Jul 13 '76	Elk Point	AB	CAN	76	233	L
Staios, Steve	24	D	Jul 28 '73	Hamilton	ON	CAN	73	200	R
Young, Bryan	76	D	Aug 06 '86	Ennismore	ON	CAN	73	191	L
Glencross, Curtis	20	L	Dec 28 '82	Kindersley	SK	CAN	73	195	L
Jacques, J-F	22	L	Apr 29 '85	Montreal	QC	CAN	76	225	L
Moreau, Ethan	18	L	Sep 22 '75	Huntsville	ON	CAN	74	220	L
Penner, Dustin	27	L	Sep 28 '82	Winkler	MB	CAN	76	245	L
Reddox, Liam	85	L	Jan 27 '86	Whitby	ON	CAN	70	180	L
Sanderson, Geoff	8	L	Feb 01 '72	Hay River	NT	CAN	72	190	L
Torres, Raffi	14	L	Oct 08 '81	Toronto	ON	CAN	72	215	L
Hemsky, Ales	83	R	Aug 13 '83	Pardubice		CZE	72	192	R
Pisani, Fernando	34	R	Dec 27 '76	Edmonton	AB	CAN	73	205	L
Stortini, Zachery	46	R	Sep 11 '85	Elliot Lake	ON	CAN	76	220	R

Goalies	#	Pos	DOB	Hometown	S/P	Ctry	Ht	Wt	C
Garon, Mathieu	32	G	Jan 09 '78	Chandler	QC	CAN	74	207	R
Roloson, Dwayne	35	G	Oct 12 '69	Simcoe	ON	CAN	73	180	L

Regular Season Schedule

October 2008	Visitor	Home
Sun Oct 12, 2008	Avalanche	Oilers
Wed Oct 15, 2008	Oilers	Ducks
Fri Oct 17, 2008	Oilers	Flames
Sat Oct 18, 2008	Flames	Oilers
Wed Oct 22, 2008	Oilers	Blackhawks
Thu Oct 23, 2008	Oilers	Avalanche
Sat Oct 25, 2008	Oilers	Canucks
Mon Oct 27, 2008	Bruins	Oilers
Thu Oct 30, 2008	Oilers	Predators

November 2008	Visitor	Home
Sat Nov 1, 2008	Oilers	Hurricanes
Sun Nov 2, 2008	Oilers	Flyers
Wed Nov 5, 2008	Oilers	Blue Jackets
Thu Nov 6, 2008	Oilers	Penguins
Sun Nov 9, 2008	Oilers	Devils
Mon Nov 10, 2008	Oilers	Rangers
Thu Nov 13, 2008	Maple Leafs	Oilers
Sat Nov 15, 2008	Avalanche	Oilers
Mon Nov 17, 2008	Oilers	Red Wings
Tue Nov 18, 2008	Oilers	Blue Jackets
Thu Nov 20, 2008	Red Wings	Oilers
Wed Nov 26, 2008	Kings	Oilers
Sat Nov 29, 2008	Oilers	Blues
Sun Nov 30, 2008	Oilers	Stars

December 2008	Visitor	Home
Wed Dec 3, 2008	Stars	Oilers
Fri Dec 5, 2008	Oilers	Kings
Sat Dec 6, 2008	Oilers	Sharks
Thu Dec 11, 2008	Panthers	Oilers
Sat Dec 13, 2008	Canucks	Oilers
Tue Dec 16, 2008	Blackhawks	Oilers
Wed Dec 17, 2008	Oilers	Canucks
Fri Dec 19, 2008	Ducks	Oilers
Mon Dec 22, 2008	Coyotes	Oilers
Fri Dec 26, 2008	Oilers	Canucks
Sun Dec 28, 2008	Predators	Oilers
Tue Dec 30, 2008	Senators	Oilers
Wed Dec 31, 2008	Oilers	Flames

January 2009	Visitor	Home
Sat Jan 3, 2009	Stars	Oilers
Mon Jan 5, 2009	Islanders	Oilers
Wed Jan 7, 2009	Canucks	Oilers
Fri Jan 9, 2009	Sharks	Oilers
Sun Jan 11, 2009	Blues	Oilers
Tue Jan 13, 2009	Oilers	Capitals

January 2009, cont.	Visitor	Home
Thu Jan 15, 2009	Oilers	Wild
Fri Jan 16, 2009	Oilers	Avalanche
Sun Jan 18, 2009	Coyotes	Oilers
Tue Jan 20, 2009	Blue Jackets	Oilers
Tue Jan 27, 2009	Sabres	Oilers
Fri Jan 30, 2009	Wild	Oilers

February 2009	Visitor	Home
Sun Feb 1, 2009	Predators	Oilers
Tue Feb 3, 2009	Blackhawks	Oilers
Thu Feb 5, 2009	Oilers	Blues
Sat Feb 7, 2009	Oilers	Red Wings
Sun Feb 8, 2009	Oilers	Wild
Wed Feb 11, 2009	Canadiens	Oilers
Sat Feb 14, 2009	Oilers	Kings
Mon Feb 16, 2009	Oilers	Coyotes
Tue Feb 17, 2009	Oilers	Sharks
Thu Feb 19, 2009	Oilers	Stars
Sat Feb 21, 2009	Flames	Oilers
Tue Feb 24, 2009	Lightning	Oilers
Thu Feb 26, 2009	Blue Jackets	Oilers
Sat Feb 28, 2009	Wild	Oilers

March 2009	Visitor	Home
Tue Mar 3, 2009	Oilers	Predators
Thu Mar 5, 2009	Oilers	Senators
Sat Mar 7, 2009	Oilers	Maple Leafs
Tue Mar 10, 2009	Oilers	Canadiens
Thu Mar 12, 2009	Thrashers	Oilers
Sat Mar 14, 2009	Avalanche	Oilers
Tue Mar 17, 2009	Blues	Oilers
Thu Mar 19, 2009	Oilers	Avalanche
Fri Mar 20, 2009	Oilers	Blackhawks
Sun Mar 22, 2009	Oilers	Wild
Tue Mar 24, 2009	Red Wings	Oilers
Thu Mar 26, 2009	Oilers	Coyotes
Fri Mar 27, 2009	Oilers	Ducks
Sun Mar 29, 2009	Wild	Oilers
Tue Mar 31, 2009	Ducks	Oilers

April 2009	Visitor	Home
Thu Apr 2, 2009	Sharks	Oilers
Sat Apr 4, 2009	Canucks	Oilers
Tue Apr 7, 2009	Kings	Oilers
Fri Apr 10, 2009	Flames	Oilers
Sat Apr 11, 2009	Oilers	Flames

Florida Panthers

The Florida Panthers play in the BankAtlantic Center in Sunrise, Florida, and have been Sunrise's team since 1993. Yet to win a Stanley Cup, the Panthers were Conference champions once, in 1996, but 2008 marked the seventh straight season the team has failed to make the playoffs. However, as of 2008, the Panthers are the only team in the NHL to have a lifetime winning percentage of .500 or better over the Montreal Canadiens, the winningest team in NHL history. Also in 2008, five-year captain (2003–08) and top points leader in the Panthers' franchise history, Olli Jokinen, was traded to the Phoenix Coyotes.

Owners	General Manager	Coach
Alan Cohen Bernie Kosar	Jacques Martin	Peter DeBoer

2008 Record and Rankings

38-35-9, 3rd in Southeast Division

	Points	GF/G	GA/G	S/G	SA/G	PP %	PK %	PIM/G
	85	2.57	2.68	31.1	33.6	19.2	82.4	12.5
NHL Rank	22	20	14	4	29	6	16	7

Recent Top Draft Picks

Draft	Num.	Round	Player	Pos	Drafted From
2008 Entry	31	2	Jacob Markstrom	G	Brynas Jrs. (Sweden)
2008 Entry	46	2	Colby Robak	D	Brandon Wheat Kings (WHL)
2008 Entry	80	3	Adam Comrie	D	Saginaw Spirit (OHL)
2007 Entry	10	1	Keaton Ellerby	D	Kamloops Blazers (WHL)
2007 Entry	40	2	Michal Repik	R	Vancouver Giants (WHL)
2007 Entry	71	3	Evgeny Dadonov	R	Chelyabinsk Traktor (Russia)
2006 Entry	10	1	Michael Frolik	L	Kladno (Czech)
2006 Entry	73	3	Brady Calla	R	Everett Silvertips (WHL)
2006 Entry	103	4	Michael Caruso	D	Guelph Storm (OHL)

Shootout Record

GP	W	L	G	S	S%	GA	SA	Sv%
11	5	6	9	41	22	11	41	73

Team Leaders

	G		A		P
Olli Jokinen	34	Olli Jokinen	37	Olli Jokinen	71
Nathan Horton	27	Nathan Horton	35	Nathan Horton	62
David Booth	22	Stephen Weiss	29	Stephen Weiss	42
Jay Bouwmeester	15	Brett McLean	23	David Booth	40
Richard Zednik	15	Jay Bouwmeester	22	2 tied with	37

	PIM		Hits		+/-
Nathan Horton	85	Gregory Campbell	156	Jassen Cullimore	21
Wade Belak	78	Branislav Mezei	115	Nathan Horton	15
Steve Montador	73	David Booth	113	Stephen Weiss	14
Jay Bouwmeester	72	Bryan Allen	112	David Booth	13
Gregory Campbell	72	Jay Bouwmeester	105	Kamil Kreps	10

	PPG		SHG		Sht
Olli Jokinen	18	Gregory Campbell	2	Olli Jokinen	341
Nathan Horton	9	Radek Dvorak	1	David Booth	228
Richard Zednik	6	Brett McLean	1	Nathan Horton	212
Rostislav Olesz	5			Jay Bouwmeester	182
2 tied with	4			Radek Dvorak	146

Goalies	GP	W	GAA	Sv%	SO
Tomas Vokoun	69	30	2.68	0.919	4
Craig Anderson	17	8	2.25	0.935	2

Roster

Player	#	Pos	DOB	Hometown	S/P	Ctry	Ht	Wt	S
Brine, David	45	C	Jan 06 '85	Truro	NS	CAN	73	201	L
Campbell, Gregory	11	C	Dec 17 '83	London	ON	CAN	72	194	L
Jokinen, Olli	12	C	Dec 05 '78	Kuopio		FIN	75	214	L
Kreps, Kamil	54	C	Nov 18 '84	Litomerice		CZE	74	194	R
Larman, Drew	50	C	May 15 '85	Buffalo	NY	USA	75	195	R
Matthias, Shawn	41	C	Feb 19 '88	Mississauga	ON	CAN	74	213	L
McLean, Brett	53	C	Aug 14 '78	Comox	BC	CAN	71	185	L
Murray, Garth	17	C	Sep 17 '82	Regina	SK	CAN	74	209	L
Stewart, Anthony	57	C	Jan 05 '85	La Salle	QC	CAN	74	239	R
Weiss, Stephen	9	C	Apr 03 '83	Toronto	ON	CAN	71	185	L
Allen, Bryan	5	D	Aug 21 '80	Kingston	ON	CAN	76	220	L
Bouwmeester, Jay	4	D	Sep 27 '83	Edmonton	AB	CAN	76	212	L
Cullimore, Jassen	22	D	Dec 04 '72	Simcoe	ON	CAN	77	235	L
Johansson, Magnus	6	D	Sep 04 '73	Linkoping		SWE	71	180	L
Lojek, Martin	47	D	Aug 19 '85	Brno		CZE	76	220	R
Mezei, Branislav	2	D	Oct 08 '80	Nitra		SVK	76	235	L
Montador, Steve	7	D	Dec 21 '79	Vancouver	BC	CAN	72	205	R
Murphy, Cory	21	D	Feb 13 '78	Kanata	ON	CAN	70	185	L
Skrastins, Karlis	3	D	Jul 09 '74	Riga		LVA	73	210	L
Van Ryn, Mike	26	D	May 14 '79	London	ON	CAN	73	198	R
Welch, Noah	27	D	Aug 26 '82	Brighton	MA	USA	76	218	L
Booth, David	10	L	Nov 24 '84	Detroit	MI	USA	72	212	L
Glass, Tanner	37	L	Nov 29 '83	Regina	SK	CAN	72	200	L
Meyer, Stefan	64	L	Jul 20 '85	Medicine Hat	SK	CAN	74	194	L
Olesz, Rostislav	85	L	Oct 10 '85	Bilovec		CZE	73	214	L
Peltonen, Ville	18	L	May 24 '73	Vantaa		FIN	71	182	L
Stumpel, Jozef	15	L	Jul 20 '72	Nitra		SVK	75	222	R
Belak, Wade	33	R	Jul 03 '76	Saskatoon	SK	CAN	77	221	R
Dvorak, Radek	14	R	Mar 09 '77	Tabor		CZE	74	200	R
Globke, Rob	51	R	Oct 24 '82	Farmington	MI	USA	74	208	R
Horton, Nathan	16	R	May 29 '85	Welland	ON	CAN	74	229	R
Zednik, Richard	20	R	Jan 06 '76	Bystrica		SVK	72	200	L

Goalies	#	Pos	DOB	Hometown	S/P	Ctry	Ht	Wt	C
Anderson, Craig	31	G	May 21 '81	Park Ridge	IL	USA	74	180	L
Vokoun, Tomas	29	G	Jul 02 '76	Karlovy Vary		CZE	72	195	R

Regular Season Schedule

October 2008	Visitor	Home
Fri Oct 10, 2008	Panthers	Hurricanes
Sat Oct 11, 2008	Thrashers	Panthers
Thu Oct 16, 2008	Wild	Panthers
Sat Oct 18, 2008	Islanders	Panthers
Mon Oct 20, 2008	Panthers	Canadiens
Wed Oct 22, 2008	Panthers	Senators
Fri Oct 24, 2008	Sharks	Panthers
Sat Oct 25, 2008	Panthers	Blues
Thu Oct 30, 2008	Senators	Panthers

November 2008	Visitor	Home
Sat Nov 1, 2008	Panthers	Predators
Sun Nov 2, 2008	Panthers	Thrashers
Thu Nov 6, 2008	Panthers	Kings
Sat Nov 8, 2008	Panthers	Coyotes
Sun Nov 9, 2008	Panthers	Ducks
Wed Nov 12, 2008	Lightning	Panthers
Fri Nov 14, 2008	Red Wings	Panthers
Tue Nov 18, 2008	Panthers	Lightning
Thu Nov 20, 2008	Panthers	Devils
Fri Nov 21, 2008	Panthers	Bruins
Mon Nov 24, 2008	Hurricanes	Panthers
Wed Nov 26, 2008	Devils	Panthers
Fri Nov 28, 2008	Rangers	Panthers
Sun Nov 30, 2008	Panthers	Rangers

December 2008	Visitor	Home
Tue Dec 2, 2008	Panthers	Capitals
Thu Dec 4, 2008	Sabres	Panthers
Sat Dec 6, 2008	Bruins	Panthers
Mon Dec 8, 2008	Panthers	Senators
Thu Dec 11, 2008	Panthers	Oilers
Fri Dec 12, 2008	Panthers	Flames
Sun Dec 14, 2008	Panthers	Canucks
Thu Dec 18, 2008	Panthers	Hurricanes
Sun Dec 21, 2008	Avalanche	Panthers
Tue Dec 23, 2008	Predators	Panthers
Fri Dec 26, 2008	Lightning	Panthers
Sat Dec 27, 2008	Panthers	Lightning
Mon Dec 29, 2008	Canadiens	Panthers
Wed Dec 31, 2008	Panthers	Islanders

January 2009	Visitor	Home
Sat Jan 3, 2009	Panthers	Penguins
Sun Jan 4, 2009	Panthers	Canadiens
Tue Jan 6, 2009	Panthers	Maple Leafs
Thu Jan 8, 2009	Hurricanes	Panthers
Sat Jan 10, 2009	Thrashers	Panthers

January 2009, cont.	Visitor	Home
Fri Jan 16, 2009	Flyers	Panthers
Sat Jan 17, 2009	Panthers	Lightning
Mon Jan 19, 2009	Sabres	Panthers
Wed Jan 21, 2009	Stars	Panthers
Tue Jan 27, 2009	Flyers	Panthers
Thu Jan 29, 2009	Canadiens	Panthers
Sat Jan 31, 2009	Panthers	Islanders

February 2009	Visitor	Home
Tue Feb 3, 2009	Panthers	Maple Leafs
Thu Feb 5, 2009	Islanders	Panthers
Sat Feb 7, 2009	Panthers	Capitals
Tue Feb 10, 2009	Maple Leafs	Panthers
Thu Feb 12, 2009	Panthers	Hurricanes
Fri Feb 13, 2009	Rangers	Panthers
Sun Feb 15, 2009	Capitals	Panthers
Tue Feb 17, 2009	Devils	Panthers
Thu Feb 19, 2009	Blackhawks	Panthers
Sat Feb 21, 2009	Bruins	Panthers
Tue Feb 24, 2009	Panthers	Bruins
Thu Feb 26, 2009	Panthers	Rangers
Sat Feb 28, 2009	Panthers	Devils

March 2009	Visitor	Home
Sun Mar 1, 2009	Panthers	Capitals
Tue Mar 3, 2009	Panthers	Thrashers
Thu Mar 5, 2009	Penguins	Panthers
Sat Mar 7, 2009	Blues	Panthers
Tue Mar 10, 2009	Panthers	Penguins
Thu Mar 12, 2009	Panthers	Sabres
Sat Mar 14, 2009	Lightning	Panthers
Tue Mar 17, 2009	Capitals	Panthers
Thu Mar 19, 2009	Maple Leafs	Panthers
Sat Mar 21, 2009	Blue Jackets	Panthers
Mon Mar 23, 2009	Hurricanes	Panthers
Wed Mar 25, 2009	Panthers	Sabres
Thu Mar 26, 2009	Panthers	Flyers
Sat Mar 28, 2009	Panthers	Stars
Tue Mar 31, 2009	Senators	Panthers

April 2009	Visitor	Home
Fri Apr 3, 2009	Thrashers	Panthers
Sun Apr 5, 2009	Penguins	Panthers
Tue Apr 7, 2009	Panthers	Flyers
Thu Apr 9, 2009	Panthers	Thrashers
Sat Apr 11, 2009	Capitals	Panthers

Los Angeles Kings

Based in Los Angeles, California, the Los Angeles Kings have yet to win a Stanley Cup, despite the hope fans felt in the 1992–93 season when the team won in their conference for the first and only time, advancing to the Cup finals, but losing to the Montreal Canadiens in five games. Wayne Gretkzy played with the Kings from 1988 to 1996, and in his first season with the franchise, won his ninth Hart Memorial Trophy as the league's Most Valuable Player. And, with 13 of the team's former players in the Hockey Hall of Fame, in 2008, the Kings failed to impress fans at the Staples Center, finishing the season with the second worst record in the NHL.

Owners	General Manager	Coach
Philip Anshutz	Dean Lombardi	Marc Crawford
Edward Roski, Jr.		

2008 Record and Rankings

32-43-7, 5th in Pacific Division

	Points	GF/G	GA/G	S/G	SA/G	PP %	PK %	PIM/G
	71	2.76	3.21	28.6	32	17.4	78.0	11.6
NHL Rank	30	13	28	18	28	17	30	2

Recent Top Draft Picks

Draft	Num.	Round	Player	Pos	Drafted From
2008 Entry	2	1	Drew Doughty	D	Guelph Storm (OHL)
2008 Entry	13	1	Colten Teubert	D	Regina Pats (WHL)
2008 Entry	32	2	Vyacheslav Vojnov	D	Chelyabinsk Traktor (Russia)
2007 Entry	4	1	Thomas Hickey	D	Seattle Thunderbirds (WHL)
2007 Entry	52	2	Oscar Moller	R	Chilliwack Bruins (WHL)
2007 Entry	61	2	Wayne Simmonds	R	Owen Sound Attack (OHL)
2006 Entry	11	1	Jonathan Bernier	G	Lewiston MAINEiacs (QMJHL)
2006 Entry	17	1	Trevor Lewis	C	Des Moines Buccaneers (USHL)
2006 Entry	48	2	Joey Ryan	D	Quebec Remparts (QMJHL)

Shootout Record

GP	W	L	G	S	S%	GA	SA	Sv%
8	5	3	12	29	41	10	27	63

Team Leaders

G		A		P	
Dustin Brown	33	Anze Kopitar	45	Anze Kopitar	77
Anze Kopitar	32	Alexander Frolov	44	Alexander Frolov	67
Alexander Frolov	23	Lubomir Visnovsky	33	Dustin Brown	60
Patrick O'Sullivan	22	Patrick O'Sullivan	31	Patrick O'Sullivan	53
Mike Cammalleri	19	Mike Cammalleri	28	Mike Cammalleri	47

PIM		Hits		+/-	
Raitis Ivanans	134	Dustin Brown	311	Derek Armstrong	4
Rob Blake	98	Raitis Ivanans	139	Brian Boyle	4
Jack Johnson	76	Derek Armstrong	106	Kevin Dallman	4
Derek Armstrong	63	John Zeiler	102	Peter Harrold	3
Dustin Brown	55	Patrick O'Sullivan	95	Matt Ellis	3

PPG		SHG		Sht	
Anze Kopitar	12	Michal Handzus	3	Patrick O'Sullivan	220
Dustin Brown	12	Patrick O'Sullivan	3	Dustin Brown	219
Mike Cammalleri	10	Anze Kopitar	2	Mike Cammalleri	210
Tom Preissing	6	Dustin Brown	2	Anze Kopitar	201
2 tied with	5	Matt Ellis	1	Alexander Frolov	160

Goalies	GP	W	GAA	Sv%	SO
Erik Ersberg	14	6	2.48	0.927	2
Dan Cloutier	9	2	3.44	0.887	0
Jonathan Bernier	4	1	4.03	0.864	0
Jonathan Quick	3	1	3.83	0.855	0
Daniel Taylor	1	0	6.00	0.800	0

Roster

Player	#	Pos	DOB	Hometown	S/P	Ctry	Ht	Wt	S
Armstrong, Derek	7	C	Apr 23 '73	Ottawa	ON	CAN	72	190	R
Boyle, Brian	22	C	Dec 18 '84	Hingham	MA	USA	78	222	L
Cammalleri, Mike	13	C	Jun 08 '82	Richmond Hill	ON	CAN	69	185	L
Handzus, Michal	26	C	Mar 11 '77	Banska Bystrica		SVK	77	217	L
Kopitar, Anze	11	C	Aug 24 '87	Jesenice		SVN	76	220	L
O'Sullivan, Patrick	12	C	Feb 01 '85	Winston	NC	USA	71	190	L
Purcell, Edward	54	C	Sep 08 '85	St. John's	NL	CAN	75	177	R
Blake, Rob	4	D	Dec 10 '69	Simcoe	ON	CAN	76	225	R
Dallman, Kevin	38	D	Feb 26 '81	Niagara Falls	ON	CAN	71	195	R
Harrold, Peter	5	D	Jun 08 '83	Kirtland Hills	OH	USA	71	195	R
Johnson, Jack	3	D	Jan 13 '87	Indianapolis	IN	USA	73	201	L
Klemm, Jon	25	D	Jan 08 '70	Cranbrook	BC	CAN	74	205	R
Preissing, Tom	42	D	Dec 03 '78	Arlington Heights	IL	USA	72	198	R
Visnovsky, Lubomir	17	D	Aug 11 '76	Topolcany		SVK	70	188	L
Brown, Dustin	23	L	Nov 04 '84	Ithaca	NY	USA	72	200	R
Calder, Kyle	19	L	Jan 05 '79	Mannville	AB	CAN	71	180	L
Ellis, Matt	8	L	Aug 31 '81	Welland	ON	CAN	72	207	L
Frolov, Alexander	24	L	Jun 19 '82	Moscow		RUS	74	210	R
Gauthier, Gabe	52	L	Jan 20 '84	Torrance	CA	USA	69	205	L
Giuliano, Jeff	29	L	Jun 20 '79	Nashua	NH	USA	69	205	R
Ivanans, Raitis	41	L	Jan 03 '79	Riga		LVA	75	263	L
Moulson, Matt	28	L	Nov 01 '83	North York	ON	CAN	73	210	L
Murray, Brady	15	L	Aug 17 '84	Brandon	MB	CAN	70	185	L
Nagy, Ladislav	47	L	Jun 01 '79	Saca		SVK	71	192	L
Thornton, Scott	27	L	Jan 09 '71	London	ON	CAN	75	220	L
Tukonen, Lauri	34	R	Sep 01 '86	Hyvinkaa		FIN	74	198	R
Willsie, Brian	21	R	Mar 16 '78	London	ON	CAN	73	202	R
Zeiler, John	73	R	Nov 21 '82	Jefferson Hills	PA	USA	72	193	R

Goalies	#	Pos	DOB	Hometown	S/P	Ctry	Ht	Wt	C
Bernier, Jonathan	45	G	Aug 07 '88	Laval	QC	CAN	72	177	L
Cloutier, Dan	39	G	Apr 22 '76	Mont-Laurier	QC	CAN	73	195	L
Ersberg, Erik	31	G	Mar 08 '82	Sala		SWE	71	182	L
LaBarbera, Jason	35	G	Jan 18 '80	Burnaby	BC	CAN	75	230	L
Quick, Jonathan	32	G	Jan 21 '86	Milford	CT	USA	72	180	L
Taylor, Daniel	46	G	Apr 28 '86	Plymouth		GBR	72	179	L

Regular Season Schedule

October 2008	Visitor	Home
Sat Oct 11, 2008	Kings	Sharks
Sun Oct 12, 2008	Sharks	Kings
Tue Oct 14, 2008	Ducks	Kings
Fri Oct 17, 2008	Hurricanes	Kings
Mon Oct 20, 2008	Avalanche	Kings
Fri Oct 24, 2008	Kings	Blues
Sat Oct 25, 2008	Kings	Predators
Mon Oct 27, 2008	Red Wings	Kings
Thu Oct 30, 2008	Canucks	Kings

November 2008	Visitor	Home
Sat Nov 1, 2008	Flames	Kings
Tue Nov 4, 2008	Ducks	Kings
Thu Nov 6, 2008	Panthers	Kings
Sat Nov 8, 2008	Blues	Kings
Tue Nov 11, 2008	Stars	Kings
Thu Nov 13, 2008	Kings	Stars
Sat Nov 15, 2008	Predators	Kings
Sun Nov 16, 2008	Kings	Ducks
Thu Nov 20, 2008	Capitals	Kings
Sat Nov 22, 2008	Avalanche	Kings
Tue Nov 25, 2008	Kings	Flames
Wed Nov 26, 2008	Kings	Oilers
Sat Nov 29, 2008	Blackhawks	Kings

December 2008	Visitor	Home
Mon Dec 1, 2008	Maple Leafs	Kings
Tue Dec 2, 2008	Kings	Coyotes
Fri Dec 5, 2008	Oilers	Kings
Sat Dec 6, 2008	Blue Jackets	Kings
Tue Dec 9, 2008	Kings	Avalanche
Thu Dec 11, 2008	Blues	Kings
Sat Dec 13, 2008	Wild	Kings
Mon Dec 15, 2008	Sharks	Kings
Wed Dec 17, 2008	Rangers	Kings
Fri Dec 19, 2008	Kings	Sabres
Sat Dec 20, 2008	Kings	Red Wings
Tue Dec 23, 2008	Kings	Blue Jackets
Fri Dec 26, 2008	Coyotes	Kings
Sat Dec 27, 2008	Kings	Coyotes
Mon Dec 29, 2008	Blue Jackets	Kings

January 2009	Visitor	Home
Sat Jan 3, 2009	Flyers	Kings
Tue Jan 6, 2009	Kings	Ducks
Thu Jan 8, 2009	Ducks	Kings
Sat Jan 10, 2009	Devils	Kings
Mon Jan 12, 2009	Lightning	Kings

January 2009, cont.	Visitor	Home
Thu Jan 15, 2009	Red Wings	Kings
Sat Jan 17, 2009	Kings	Stars
Tue Jan 20, 2009	Kings	Wild
Wed Jan 21, 2009	Kings	Avalanche
Thu Jan 29, 2009	Blackhawks	Kings
Sat Jan 31, 2009	Kings	Canadiens

February 2009	Visitor	Home
Tue Feb 3, 2009	Kings	Senators
Thu Feb 5, 2009	Kings	Capitals
Sat Feb 7, 2009	Kings	Devils
Tue Feb 10, 2009	Kings	Islanders
Thu Feb 12, 2009	Flames	Kings
Sat Feb 14, 2009	Oilers	Kings
Mon Feb 16, 2009	Thrashers	Kings
Wed Feb 18, 2009	Kings	Ducks
Thu Feb 19, 2009	Kings	Sharks
Sat Feb 21, 2009	Coyotes	Kings
Tue Feb 24, 2009	Kings	Wild
Wed Feb 25, 2009	Kings	Flyers
Fri Feb 27, 2009	Kings	Red Wings

March 2009	Visitor	Home
Sun Mar 1, 2009	Kings	Blackhawks
Tue Mar 3, 2009	Kings	Blue Jackets
Thu Mar 5, 2009	Stars	Kings
Sat Mar 7, 2009	Wild	Kings
Mon Mar 9, 2009	Canucks	Kings
Fri Mar 13, 2009	Kings	Canucks
Sat Mar 14, 2009	Kings	Sharks
Mon Mar 16, 2009	Predators	Kings
Thu Mar 19, 2009	Kings	Bruins
Fri Mar 20, 2009	Kings	Penguins
Sun Mar 22, 2009	Kings	Blackhawks
Tue Mar 24, 2009	Kings	Blues
Thu Mar 26, 2009	Kings	Stars
Sat Mar 28, 2009	Kings	Predators
Tue Mar 31, 2009	Stars	Kings

April 2009	Visitor	Home
Thu Apr 2, 2009	Kings	Coyotes
Sat Apr 4, 2009	Coyotes	Kings
Mon Apr 6, 2009	Kings	Flames
Tue Apr 7, 2009	Kings	Oilers
Thu Apr 9, 2009	Kings	Canucks
Sat Apr 11, 2009	Sharks	Kings

Minnesota Wild

Founded in 2000, the Minnesota Wild, home team to St. Paul, Minnesota, might be a young team in NHL history, but fans have quickly become loyal, as the team has sold out every game the Wild has played in their home arena, the Xcel Energy Center. Division champions in the 2007–08 season, the Wild also broke numerous franchise records this year, including most goals in a season (Marian Gaborik, with 42 goals and 83 points), and won their first-ever Northwest Division title, in a 3–1 win over the Calgary Flames. Since the Wild's introduction into the NHL eight years ago, they have never assigned the team a permanent captain, adopting the system of rotating the title monthly amongst its players, with some players taking the role more than once per season (the 2007–08 season saw Pavol Demitra, Brian Rolston, Mark Parrish, Nick Schultz and Gaborik as team captains).

Owner	General Manager	Coach
Craig Leipold	Doug Risebrough	Jacques Lemaire

2008 Record and Rankings

44-28-10, 1st in Northwest Division

	Points	GF/G	GA/G	S/G	SA/G	PP %	PK %	PIM/G
	98	2.68	2.56	27	30.1	18.9	85.2	13.4
NHL Rank	7	18	9	26	20	7	4	16

Recent Top Draft Picks

Draft	Num.	Round	Player	Pos	Drafted From
2008 Entry	23	1	Tyler Cuma	D	Ottawa 67's (OHL)
2008 Entry	55	2	Marco Scandella	D	Val d'Or Foreurs (QMJHL)
2008 Entry	115	4	Sean Lorenz	D	US National Under 18 Team
2007 Entry	16	1	Colton Gillies	C	Saskatoon Blades (WHL)
2007 Entry	110	4	Justin Falk	D	Spokane Chiefs (WHL)
2007 Entry	140	5	Cody Almond	C	Kelowna Rockets (WHL)
2006 Entry	9	1	James Sheppard	C	Cape Breton Screaming Eagles (QMJHL)
2006 Entry	40	2	Ondrej Fiala	L	Everett Silvertips (WHL)
2006 Entry	72	3	Cal Clutterbuck	R	Oshawa Generals (OHL)

Shootout Record

GP	W	L	G	S	S%	GA	SA	Sv%
15	8	7	16	47	34	16	45	64

Team Leaders

G		A		P	
Marian Gaborik	42	Pierre-Marc Bouchard	50	Marian Gaborik	83
Brian Rolston	31	Marian Gaborik	41	Pierre-Marc Bouchard	63
Mark Parrish	16	Pavol Demitra	39	Brian Rolston	59
Pavol Demitra	15	Mikko Koivu	31	Pavol Demitra	54
Brent Burns	15	2 tied with	28	Brent Burns	43

PIM		Hits		+/-	
Aaron Voros	141	Stephane Veilleux	113	Marian Gaborik	17
Todd Fedoruk	139	Nick Schultz	101	Mikko Koivu	13
Brent Burns	80	Brent Burns	99	Brent Burns	12
Derek Boogaard	74	Branko Radivojevic	98	Pierre-Marc Bouchard	11
Marian Gaborik	63	Aaron Voros	96	2 tied with	9

PPG		SHG		Sht	
Marian Gaborik	11	Brian Rolston	1	Brian Rolston	289
Brian Rolston	11	Marian Gaborik	1	Marian Gaborik	278
Brent Burns	8	Eric Belanger	1	Brent Burns	158
Mark Parrish	7			Mikko Koivu	144
Eric Belanger	7			Stephane Veilleux	136

Goalies	GP	W	GAA	Sv%	SO
Niklas Backstrom	58	33	2.31	0.920	4
Josh Harding	29	11	2.94	0.908	1

Roster

Player	#	Pos	DOB	Hometown	S/P	Ctry	Ht	Wt	S
Belanger, Eric	25	C	Dec 16 '77	Sherbrooke	QC	CAN	72	185	L
Bouchard, Pierre-Marc	96	C	Apr 27 '84	Sherbrooke	QC	CAN	70	171	L
Kelly, Steve	16	C	Oct 26 '76	Vancouver	BC	CAN	74	210	L
Koivu, Mikko	9	C	Mar 12 '83	Turku		FIN	74	200	L
Sheppard, James	15	C	Apr 25 '88	Halifax	NS	CAN	74	210	L
Walz, Wes	37	C	May 15 '70	Calgary	AB	CAN	71	190	R
Burns, Brent	8	D	Mar 09 '85	Ajax	ON	CAN	77	219	R
Carney, Keith	3	D	Feb 03 '70	Providence	RI	USA	73	207	L
Foster, Kurtis	26	D	Nov 24 '81	Carp	ON	CAN	77	220	R
Hill, Sean	6	D	Feb 14 '70	Duluth	MN	USA	72	204	R
Johnsson, Kim	5	D	Mar 16 '76	Malmo		SWE	73	193	L
Nummelin, Petteri	33	D	Nov 25 '72	Turku		FIN	70	188	L
Schultz, Nick	55	D	Aug 25 '82	Strasbourg	SK	CAN	73	200	L
Skoula, Martin	41	D	Oct 28 '79	Litomerice		CZE	75	226	L
Boogaard, Derek	24	L	Jun 23 '82	Saskatoon	SK	CAN	79	258	L
Fedoruk, Todd	17	L	Feb 13 '79	Redwater	AB	CAN	74	240	L
Pouliot, Benoit	67	L	Sep 29 '86	Alfred	ON	CAN	75	199	L
Simon, Chris	11	L	Jan 30 '72	Wawa	ON	CAN	75	232	L
Veilleux, Stephane	19	L	Nov 16 '81	St.-Georges de Beauce	QC	CAN	72	190	L
Voros, Aaron	34	L	Jul 02 '81	Vancouver	BC	CAN	75	205	L
Clutterbuck, Cal	22	R	Nov 18 '87	Welland	ON	CAN	71	213	R
Demitra, Pavol	38	R	Nov 29 '74	Dubnica		SVK	72	200	L
Foy, Matt	83	R	May 18 '83	Oakville	ON	CAN	74	228	R
Gaborik, Marian	10	R	Feb 14 '82	Trencin		SVK	73	199	L
Parrish, Mark	21	R	Feb 02 '77	Bloomington	MN	USA	71	199	R
Radivojevic, Branko	92	R	Nov 24 '80	Piestany		SVK	72	208	R
Rolston, Brian	12	R	Feb 21 '73	Flint	MI	USA	74	214	L

Goalies	#	Pos	DOB	Hometown	S/P	Ctry	Ht	Wt	C
Backstrom, Niklas	32	G	Feb 13 '78	Helsinki		FIN	73	196	L
Harding, Josh	29	G	Jun 18 '84	Regina	SK	CAN	73	197	R

Regular Season Schedule

October 2008	Visitor	Home
Sat Oct 11, 2008	Bruins	Wild
Tue Oct 14, 2008	Wild	Thrashers
Thu Oct 16, 2008	Wild	Panthers
Sat Oct 18, 2008	Wild	Lightning
Thu Oct 23, 2008	Sabres	Wild
Sat Oct 25, 2008	Blue Jackets	Wild
Mon Oct 27, 2008	Blackhawks	Wild
Wed Oct 29, 2008	Wild	Stars
Thu Oct 30, 2008	Canadiens	Wild

November 2008	Visitor	Home
Sat Nov 1, 2008	Wild	Coyotes
Tue Nov 4, 2008	Wild	Sharks
Thu Nov 6, 2008	Wild	Avalanche
Sat Nov 8, 2008	Wild	Canucks
Thu Nov 13, 2008	Coyotes	Wild
Sat Nov 15, 2008	Blue Jackets	Wild
Tue Nov 18, 2008	Wild	Penguins
Thu Nov 20, 2008	Canucks	Wild
Sat Nov 22, 2008	Blues	Wild
Mon Nov 24, 2008	Capitals	Wild
Wed Nov 26, 2008	Stars	Wild
Fri Nov 28, 2008	Lightning	Wild
Sat Nov 29, 2008	Wild	Predators

December 2008	Visitor	Home
Mon Dec 1, 2008	Avalanche	Wild
Wed Dec 3, 2008	Blues	Wild
Fri Dec 5, 2008	Canucks	Wild
Sat Dec 6, 2008	Wild	Predators
Thu Dec 11, 2008	Wild	Coyotes
Sat Dec 13, 2008	Wild	Kings
Sun Dec 14, 2008	Wild	Ducks
Wed Dec 17, 2008	Flames	Wild
Fri Dec 19, 2008	Islanders	Wild
Sat Dec 20, 2008	Wild	Blues
Tue Dec 23, 2008	Hurricanes	Wild
Sun Dec 28, 2008	Blackhawks	Wild
Mon Dec 29, 2008	Wild	Flames
Wed Dec 31, 2008	Sharks	Wild

January 2009	Visitor	Home
Sat Jan 3, 2009	Red Wings	Wild
Sun Jan 4, 2009	Wild	Avalanche
Tue Jan 6, 2009	Wild	Bruins
Thu Jan 8, 2009	Wild	Flyers
Sat Jan 10, 2009	Wild	Blue Jackets
Tue Jan 13, 2009	Coyotes	Wild

January 2009, cont.	Visitor	Home
Thu Jan 15, 2009	Oilers	Wild
Sat Jan 17, 2009	Ducks	Wild
Mon Jan 19, 2009	Wild	Blackhawks
Tue Jan 20, 2009	Kings	Wild
Tue Jan 27, 2009	Maple Leafs	Wild
Fri Jan 30, 2009	Wild	Oilers
Sat Jan 31, 2009	Wild	Canucks

February 2009	Visitor	Home
Wed Feb 4, 2009	Ducks	Wild
Fri Feb 6, 2009	Predators	Wild
Sun Feb 8, 2009	Oilers	Wild
Wed Feb 11, 2009	Avalanche	Wild
Thu Feb 12, 2009	Wild	Red Wings
Sat Feb 14, 2009	Senators	Wild
Thu Feb 19, 2009	Flames	Wild
Sat Feb 21, 2009	Red Wings	Wild
Sun Feb 22, 2009	Wild	Blackhawks
Tue Feb 24, 2009	Kings	Wild
Fri Feb 27, 2009	Wild	Flames
Sat Feb 28, 2009	Wild	Oilers

March 2009	Visitor	Home
Tue Mar 3, 2009	Wild	Canucks
Thu Mar 5, 2009	Wild	Sharks
Sat Mar 7, 2009	Wild	Kings
Sun Mar 8, 2009	Wild	Ducks
Tue Mar 10, 2009	Sharks	Wild
Thu Mar 12, 2009	Wild	Avalanche
Sat Mar 14, 2009	Wild	Stars
Sun Mar 15, 2009	Wild	Blues
Tue Mar 17, 2009	Avalanche	Wild
Fri Mar 20, 2009	Wild	Devils
Sun Mar 22, 2009	Oilers	Wild
Tue Mar 24, 2009	Wild	Rangers
Wed Mar 25, 2009	Wild	Islanders
Sat Mar 28, 2009	Wild	Flames
Sun Mar 29, 2009	Wild	Oilers
Tue Mar 31, 2009	Canucks	Wild

April 2009	Visitor	Home
Fri Apr 3, 2009	Flames	Wild
Sun Apr 5, 2009	Wild	Red Wings
Tue Apr 7, 2009	Stars	Wild
Fri Apr 10, 2009	Predators	Wild
Sat Apr 11, 2009	Wild	Blue Jackets

Montreal Canadiens

The oldest continuously operating professional hockey team, the only continuously operating team to predate the NHL and the most successful of all NHL teams, the Montreal Canadiens are cloaked in hockey history. Founded in 1909, eight years before the founding of the NHL, the Canadiens are one of the Original Six teams and have 24 Stanley Cup wins to their name. Their last Cup win in 1993 marks the last time a Canadian team won the Stanley Cup. Often called the Habs (short for the French nickname of Les Habitants), the Canadiens play in the Bell Centre in Montreal, Quebec, and are celebrating their 100th anniversary in 2009, when they will host the 2009 NHL All-Star Game. Division champions in the 2007–08 season, the Canadiens have been home team to such hockey greats as Maurice Richard, Guy Lafleur and Patrick Roy.

Owner	General Manager	Coach
George Gillett Jr.	Bob Gainey	Guy Carbonneau

2008 Record and Rankings

47-25-10, 1st in Northeast Division

	Points	GF/G	GA/G	S/G	SA/G	PP %	PK %	PIM/G
	104	3.13	2.63	29.1	31.6	24.1	82.5	13.3
NHL Rank	3	2	13	13	26	1	15	15

Recent Top Draft Picks

Draft	Num.	Round	Player	Pos	Drafted From
2008 Entry	56	2	Danny Kristo	R	US National Under 18 Team
2008 Entry	86	3	Steve Quailer	R	Sioux City Musketeers (USHL)
2008 Entry	116	4	Jason Missiaen	G	Peterborough Petes (OHL)
2007 Entry	12	1	Ryan McDonagh	D	Cretin Derham Hall H.S. (Minn.)
2007 Entry	22	1	Max Pacioretty	L	Sioux City Musketeers (USHL)
2007 Entry	43	2	P.K. Subban	D	Belleville Bulls (OHL)
2006 Entry	20	1	David Fischer	D	Apple Valley H.S. (Minn)
2006 Entry	49	2	Ben Maxwell	C	Kootenay Ice (WHL)
2006 Entry	53	2	Mathieu Carle	D	Acadie-Bathurst Titan (QMJHL)

Shootout Record

GP	W	L	G	S	S%	GA	SA	Sv%
11	5	6	9	37	24	10	38	74

Team Leaders

	G		A		P
Alex Kovalev	35	Alex Kovalev	49	Alex Kovalev	84
Tomas Plekanec	29	Mark Streit	49	Tomas Plekanec	69
Christopher Higgins	27	Andrei Markov	42	Mark Streit	62
Andrei Kostitsyn	26	Tomas Plekanec	40	Andrei Markov	58
3 tied with	16	Saku Koivu	40	Saku Koivu	56

	PIM		Hits		+/-
Tom Kostopoulos	113	Michael Komisarek	266	Alex Kovalev	18
Michael Komisarek	101	Francis Bouillon	168	Tomas Plekanec	15
Saku Koivu	93	Roman Hamrlik	138	Andrei Kostitsyn	15
Alex Kovalev	70	Guillaume Latendresse	134	3 tied with	9
Andrei Markov	63	Tom Kostopoulos	128		

	PPG		SHG		Sht
Alex Kovalev	17	Tom Kostopoulos	3	Christopher Higgins	241
Tomas Plekanec	12	Tomas Plekanec	2	Alex Kovalev	230
Andrei Kostitsyn	12	Sergei Kostitsyn	1	Tomas Plekanec	186
Christopher Higgins	12	Andrei Markov	1	Mark Streit	165
Andrei Markov	10	Mathieu Dandenault	1	Andrei Kostitsyn	150

Goalies	GP	W	GAA	Sv%	SO
Carey Price	41	24	2.56	0.920	3
Jaroslav Halak	6	2	2.11	0.934	1

Roster

Player	#	Pos	DOB	Hometown	S/P	Ctry	Ht	Wt	S
Chipchura, Kyle	28	C	Feb 19 '86	Westlock	AB	CAN	74	204	L
Grabovski, Mikhail	54	C	Jan 31 '84	Potsdam		DEU	71	179	L
Koivu, Saku	11	C	Nov 23 '74	Turku		FIN	70	187	L
Lapierre, Maxim	40	C	Mar 29 '85	Saint-Léonard	QC	CAN	74	200	R
Locke, Corey	45	C	May 08 '84	Toronto	ON	CAN	69	169	L
Plekanec, Tomas	14	C	Oct 31 '82	Kladno		CZE	70	194	L
Smolinski, Bryan	20	C	Dec 27 '71	Toledo	OH	USA	73	203	R
Bouillon, Francis	51	D	Oct 17 '75	New York	NY	USA	68	196	L
Brisebois, Patrice	71	D	Jan 27 '71	Montréal	QC	CAN	74	196	R
Gorges, Josh	26	D	Aug 14 '84	Kelowna	BC	CAN	73	195	L
Hamrlik, Roman	44	D	Apr 12 '74	Zlin		CZE	74	215	L
Komisarek, Michael	8	D	Jan 19 '82	West Islip	NY	USA	76	240	R
Markov, Andrei	79	D	Dec 20 '78	Voskresensk		RUS	72	204	L
O'Byrne, Ryan	3	D	Jul 19 '84	Victoria	BC	CAN	78	228	R
Streit, Mark	32	D	Dec 11 '77	Englisberg		CHE	72	197	L
Begin, Steve	22	L	Jun 14 '78	Trois-Rivières	QC	CAN	72	187	L
Higgins, Christopher	21	L	Jun 02 '83	Smithtown	NY	USA	72	199	L
Kostitsyn, Andrei	46	L	Feb 03 '85	Novopolotsk		BLR	72	201	L
Kostitsyn, Sergei	74	L	Mar 20 '87	Novopolotsk		BLR	71	196	L
Stewart, Gregory	70	L	May 21 '86	Kitchener	ON	CAN	74	200	L
D'Agostini, Matt	36	R	Oct 23 '86	Sault Ste. Marie	ON	CAN	72	201	R
Dandenault, Mathieu	25	R	Feb 03 '76	Sherbrooke	QC	CAN	72	204	R
Kostopoulos, Tom	6	R	Jan 24 '79	Mississauga	ON	CAN	72	200	R
Kovalev, Alex	27	R	Feb 24 '73	Togliatti		RUS	73	224	L
Latendresse, Guillaume	84	R	May 24 '87	Ste-Catherine	QC	CAN	74	222	L
Ryder, Michael	73	R	Mar 31 '80	Bonavista	NL	CAN	72	186	R

Goalies	#	Pos	DOB	Hometown	S/P	Ctry	Ht	Wt	C
Halak, Jaroslav	41	G	May 13 '85	Bratislava		SVK	71	182	L
Price, Carey	31	G	Aug 16 '87	Vancouver	BC	CAN	75	226	L

Regular Season Schedule

October 2008	Visitor	Home
Fri Oct 10, 2008	Canadiens	Sabres
Sat Oct 11, 2008	Canadiens	Maple Leafs
Mon Oct 13, 2008	Canadiens	Flyers
Wed Oct 15, 2008	Bruins	Canadiens
Sat Oct 18, 2008	Coyotes	Canadiens
Mon Oct 20, 2008	Panthers	Canadiens
Sat Oct 25, 2008	Ducks	Canadiens
Tue Oct 28, 2008	Hurricanes	Canadiens
Thu Oct 30, 2008	Canadiens	Wild

November 2008	Visitor	Home
Sat Nov 1, 2008	Canadiens	Islanders
Fri Nov 7, 2008	Canadiens	Blue Jackets
Sat Nov 8, 2008	Canadiens	Maple Leafs
Tue Nov 11, 2008	Senators	Canadiens
Thu Nov 13, 2008	Canadiens	Bruins
Sat Nov 15, 2008	Flyers	Canadiens
Sun Nov 16, 2008	Canadiens	Blues
Tue Nov 18, 2008	Canadiens	Hurricanes
Thu Nov 20, 2008	Canadiens	Senators
Sat Nov 22, 2008	Bruins	Canadiens
Mon Nov 24, 2008	Islanders	Canadiens
Wed Nov 26, 2008	Canadiens	Red Wings
Fri Nov 28, 2008	Canadiens	Capitals
Sat Nov 29, 2008	Sabres	Canadiens

December 2008	Visitor	Home
Tue Dec 2, 2008	Thrashers	Canadiens
Thu Dec 4, 2008	Rangers	Canadiens
Sat Dec 6, 2008	Devils	Canadiens
Tue Dec 9, 2008	Flames	Canadiens
Thu Dec 11, 2008	Lightning	Canadiens
Sat Dec 13, 2008	Capitals	Canadiens
Tue Dec 16, 2008	Canadiens	Hurricanes
Thu Dec 18, 2008	Flyers	Canadiens
Sat Dec 20, 2008	Sabres	Canadiens
Sun Dec 21, 2008	Hurricanes	Canadiens
Sat Dec 27, 2008	Canadiens	Penguins
Mon Dec 29, 2008	Canadiens	Panthers
Tue Dec 30, 2008	Canadiens	Lightning

January 2009	Visitor	Home
Fri Jan 2, 2009	Canadiens	Devils
Sun Jan 4, 2009	Panthers	Canadiens
Wed Jan 7, 2009	Canadiens	Rangers
Thu Jan 8, 2009	Maple Leafs	Canadiens
Sat Jan 10, 2009	Capitals	Canadiens
Tue Jan 13, 2009	Canadiens	Bruins

January 2009, cont.	Visitor	Home
Thu Jan 15, 2009	Predators	Canadiens
Sat Jan 17, 2009	Canadiens	Senators
Tue Jan 20, 2009	Canadiens	Thrashers
Wed Jan 21, 2009	Canadiens	Devils
Tue Jan 27, 2009	Canadiens	Lightning
Thu Jan 29, 2009	Canadiens	Panthers
Sat Jan 31, 2009	Kings	Canadiens

February 2009	Visitor	Home
Sun Feb 1, 2009	Bruins	Canadiens
Tue Feb 3, 2009	Penguins	Canadiens
Fri Feb 6, 2009	Canadiens	Sabres
Sat Feb 7, 2009	Maple Leafs	Canadiens
Mon Feb 9, 2009	Canadiens	Flames
Wed Feb 11, 2009	Canadiens	Oilers
Fri Feb 13, 2009	Canadiens	Avalanche
Sun Feb 15, 2009	Canadiens	Canucks
Wed Feb 18, 2009	Canadiens	Capitals
Thu Feb 19, 2009	Canadiens	Penguins
Sat Feb 21, 2009	Senators	Canadiens
Tue Feb 24, 2009	Canucks	Canadiens
Fri Feb 27, 2009	Canadiens	Flyers
Sat Feb 28, 2009	Sharks	Canadiens

March 2009	Visitor	Home
Wed Mar 4, 2009	Canadiens	Sabres
Fri Mar 6, 2009	Canadiens	Thrashers
Sun Mar 8, 2009	Canadiens	Stars
Tue Mar 10, 2009	Oilers	Canadiens
Thu Mar 12, 2009	Islanders	Canadiens
Sat Mar 14, 2009	Devils	Canadiens
Tue Mar 17, 2009	Rangers	Canadiens
Thu Mar 19, 2009	Canadiens	Senators
Sat Mar 21, 2009	Maple Leafs	Canadiens
Tue Mar 24, 2009	Thrashers	Canadiens
Thu Mar 26, 2009	Lightning	Canadiens
Sat Mar 28, 2009	Sabres	Canadiens
Tue Mar 31, 2009	Blackhawks	Canadiens

April 2009	Visitor	Home
Thu Apr 2, 2009	Canadiens	Islanders
Sat Apr 4, 2009	Canadiens	Maple Leafs
Mon Apr 6, 2009	Senators	Canadiens
Tue Apr 7, 2009	Canadiens	Rangers
Thu Apr 9, 2009	Canadiens	Bruins
Sat Apr 11, 2009	Penguins	Canadiens

Nashville Predators

Founded in 1998, the Nashville Predators have yet to win a division or conference championship or a Stanley Cup. Plagued by rumors in the 2007–08 season that the team would be moving from Nashville, Tennessee, the Predators are remaining in their home city, ending 2008 with a 4 games to 2 loss against the Detroit Red Wings in the first round of the playoffs. Despite Nashville's poor showing in the playoffs in seasons past, fans of the Predators are notoriously loyal, and Section 303 at the Sommet Center, known as The Cellblock, is where fans of the most raucous nature sit and motivate the home team and heckle the visitors. This group refers to itself as the loudest section of the loudest arena in the NHL and even sells its own merchandise. The Predators' mascot is Gnash, a blue saber-toothed cat, who is famous for his entertaining stunts involving rappels, zip lines and a pendulum swing.

Owner	General Manager	Coach
Predators Holding, LLC	David Poile	Barry Trotz

2008 Record and Rankings

41-32-9, 2nd in Central Division

	Points	GF/G	GA/G	S/G	SA/G	PP %	PK %	PIM/G
	91	2.77	2.73	29.6	29.8	14.8	85.4	12.5
NHL Rank	17	12	16	12	18	27	3	8

Recent Top Draft Picks

Draft	Num.	Round	Player	Pos	Drafted From
2008 Entry	7	1	Colin Wilson	C	Boston University (NCAA)
2008 Entry	18	1	Chet Pickard	G	Tri-City Americans (WHL)
2008 Entry	38	2	Roman Josi	D	Bern (Swiss-A)
2007 Entry	23	1	Jonathan Blum	D	Vancouver Giants (WHL)
2007 Entry	54	2	Jeremy Smith	G	Plymouth Whalers (OHL)
2007 Entry	58	2	Nick Spaling	C	Kitchener Rangers (OHL)
2006 Entry	56	2	Blake Geoffrion	L	US National Under 18 Team
2006 Entry	105	4	Niko Snellman	R	Ilves Jrs (Finland)
2006 Entry	146	5	Mark Dekanich	G	Colgate University (NCAA)

Shootout Record

GP	W	L	G	S	S%	GA	SA	Sv%
8	3	5	6	21	29	9	22	59

Team Leaders

G		A		P	
Jean-Pierre Dumont	29	Jason Arnott	44	Jean-Pierre Dumont	72
Jason Arnott	28	Jean-Pierre Dumont	43	Jason Arnott	72
Alexander Radulov	26	Marek Zidlicky	38	Alexander Radulov	58
Martin Erat	23	Martin Erat	34	Martin Erat	57
David Legwand	15	Alexander Radulov	32	David Legwand	44

PIM		Hits		+/-	
Jordin Tootoo	100	Dam Hamhuis	162	Jason Arnott	19
Scott Nichol	72	Greg Zanon	160	Ville Koistinen	13
Greg De Vries	71	Jerred Smithson	128	Scott Nichol	12
Ryan Suter	71	Shea Weber	115	Greg De Vries	7
Dan Hamhuis	66	Scott Nichol	110	Alexander Radulov	7

PPG		SHG		Sht	
Jason Arnott	13	Scott Nichol	2	Jason Arnott	248
Jean-Pierre Dumont	7	Jerred Smithson	2	Jean-Pierre Dumont	192
Radek Bonk	6	Martin Gelinas	1	Alexander Radulov	183
Shea Weber	5	Vernon Fiddler	1	Martin Erat	163
4 tied with	4	Jed Ortmeyer	1	2 tied with	152

Goalies	GP	W	GAA	Sv%	SO
Chris Mason	51	18	2.90	0.898	4
Dan Ellis	44	23	2.34	0.924	6
Pekka Rinne	1	0	0.00	1.000	0

Roster

Player	#	Pos	DOB	Hometown	S/P	Ctry	Ht	Wt	S
Arnott, Jason	19	C	Oct 11 '74	Collingwood	ON	CAN	76	220	R
Bonk, Radek	14	C	Jan 09 '76	Krnov		CZE	75	213	L
Fiddler, Vernon	38	C	May 09 '80	Edmonton	AB	CAN	71	204	L
Legwand, David	11	C	Aug 17 '80	Detroit	MI	USA	74	190	L
Nichol, Scott	12	C	Dec 31 '74	Edmonton	AB	CAN	69	175	R
Peverley, Rich	37	C	Jul 08 '82	Guelph	ON	CAN	72	185	R
Smithson, Jerred	25	C	Feb 04 '79	Vernon	BC	CAN	75	194	R
De Vries, Greg	7	D	Jan 04 '73	Sundridge	ON	CAN	74	215	L
Hamhuis, Dan	2	D	Dec 13 '82	Smithers	BC	CAN	73	200	L
Klein, Kevin	8	D	Dec 13 '84	Kitchener	ON	CAN	73	195	R
Koistinen, Ville	4	D	Jun 17 '82	Oulu		FIN	71	190	L
Suter, Ryan	20	D	Jan 21 '85	Madison	WI	USA	73	196	L
Weber, Shea	6	D	Aug 14 '85	Sicamous	BC	CAN	75	213	R
Zanon, Greg	5	D	Jun 05 '80	Burnaby	BC	CAN	71	211	L
Zidlicky, Marek	3	D	Feb 03 '77	Most		CZE	71	190	R
Gelinas, Martin	23	L	Jun 05 '70	Shawinigan	QC	CAN	71	202	L
Hlavac, Jan	17	L	Sep 20 '76	Prague		CZE	72	201	L
Hordichuk, Darcy	16	L	Aug 10 '80	Kamsack	SK	CAN	73	215	L
Pihlstrom, Antti	42	L	Oct 22 '84	Vanntaa		FIN	70	181	L
Bochenski, Brandon	24	R	Apr 04 '82	Blaine	MN	USA	73	187	R
Dumont, Jean-Pierre	71	R	Apr 01 '78	Montreal	QC	CAN	73	205	L
Erat, Martin	10	R	Aug 29 '81	Trebic		CZE	72	195	L
Langfeld, Josh	15	R	Jul 17 '77	Fridley	MN	USA	75	215	R
Ortmeyer, Jed	41	R	Sep 03 '78	Omaha	NE	USA	72	197	R
Radulov, Alexander	47	R	Jul 05 '86	Nizhi Tagil		RUS	73	188	L
Tootoo, Jordin	22	R	Feb 02 '83	Churchill	MB	CAN	69	194	R

Goalies	#	Pos	DOB	Hometown	S/P	Ctry	Ht	Wt	C
Ellis, Dan	39	G	Jun 19 '80	Saskatoon	SK	CAN	72	185	L
Mason, Chris	30	G	Apr 20 '76	Red Deer	AB	CAN	72	195	L
Rinne, Pekka	35	G	Nov 03 '82	Kempele		FIN	77	207	L

Regular Season Schedule

October 2008	Visitor	Home
Fri Oct 10, 2008	Predators	Blues
Sat Oct 11, 2008	Stars	Predators
Mon Oct 13, 2008	Predators	Blackhawks
Wed Oct 15, 2008	Predators	Stars
Fri Oct 17, 2008	Predators	Blue Jackets
Sat Oct 18, 2008	Blue Jackets	Predators
Thu Oct 23, 2008	Flames	Predators
Sat Oct 25, 2008	Kings	Predators
Tue Oct 28, 2008	Predators	Capitals
Thu Oct 30, 2008	Oilers	Predators

November 2008	Visitor	Home
Sat Nov 1, 2008	Panthers	Predators
Tue Nov 4, 2008	Predators	Canucks
Thu Nov 6, 2008	Predators	Flames
Sat Nov 8, 2008	Predators	Avalanche
Tue Nov 11, 2008	Predators	Sharks
Fri Nov 14, 2008	Predators	Ducks
Sat Nov 15, 2008	Predators	Kings
Mon Nov 17, 2008	Sharks	Predators
Fri Nov 21, 2008	Predators	Lightning
Sun Nov 23, 2008	Predators	Hurricanes
Tue Nov 25, 2008	Blues	Predators
Fri Nov 28, 2008	Predators	Thrashers
Sat Nov 29, 2008	Wild	Predators

December 2008	Visitor	Home
Mon Dec 1, 2008	Predators	Sabres
Thu Dec 4, 2008	Avalanche	Predators
Sat Dec 6, 2008	Wild	Predators
Mon Dec 8, 2008	Predators	Blues
Tue Dec 9, 2008	Canucks	Predators
Thu Dec 11, 2008	Predators	Blue Jackets
Sat Dec 13, 2008	Stars	Predators
Thu Dec 18, 2008	Predators	Coyotes
Sat Dec 20, 2008	Islanders	Predators
Tue Dec 23, 2008	Predators	Panthers
Fri Dec 26, 2008	Red Wings	Predators
Sun Dec 28, 2008	Predators	Oilers
Mon Dec 29, 2008	Predators	Avalanche

January 2009	Visitor	Home
Thu Jan 1, 2009	Canucks	Predators
Sat Jan 3, 2009	Flames	Predators
Tue Jan 6, 2009	Avalanche	Predators
Thu Jan 8, 2009	Penguins	Predators
Sat Jan 10, 2009	Blackhawks	Predators
Sun Jan 11, 2009	Predators	Blackhawks

January 2009, cont.	Visitor	Home
Tue Jan 13, 2009	Predators	Maple Leafs
Thu Jan 15, 2009	Predators	Canadiens
Sat Jan 17, 2009	Thrashers	Predators
Mon Jan 19, 2009	Devils	Predators
Wed Jan 28, 2009	Predators	Canucks
Fri Jan 30, 2009	Predators	Flames

February 2009	Visitor	Home
Sun Feb 1, 2009	Predators	Oilers
Tue Feb 3, 2009	Coyotes	Predators
Thu Feb 5, 2009	Ducks	Predators
Fri Feb 6, 2009	Predators	Wild
Sun Feb 8, 2009	Predators	Stars
Tue Feb 10, 2009	Red Wings	Predators
Thu Feb 12, 2009	Blues	Predators
Sat Feb 14, 2009	Bruins	Predators
Mon Feb 16, 2009	Senators	Predators
Wed Feb 18, 2009	Predators	Red Wings
Thu Feb 19, 2009	Blues	Predators
Sat Feb 21, 2009	Predators	Blues
Tue Feb 24, 2009	Blackhawks	Predators
Thu Feb 26, 2009	Coyotes	Predators
Sat Feb 28, 2009	Red Wings	Predators

March 2009	Visitor	Home
Tue Mar 3, 2009	Oilers	Predators
Thu Mar 5, 2009	Blue Jackets	Predators
Sat Mar 7, 2009	Predators	Flyers
Tue Mar 10, 2009	Capitals	Predators
Thu Mar 12, 2009	Rangers	Predators
Sat Mar 14, 2009	Predators	Coyotes
Mon Mar 16, 2009	Predators	Kings
Wed Mar 18, 2009	Predators	Ducks
Thu Mar 19, 2009	Predators	Sharks
Tue Mar 24, 2009	Ducks	Predators
Thu Mar 26, 2009	Sharks	Predators
Sat Mar 28, 2009	Kings	Predators
Sun Mar 29, 2009	Predators	Red Wings
Tue Mar 31, 2009	Predators	Blue Jackets

April 2009	Visitor	Home
Fri Apr 3, 2009	Predators	Blackhawks
Sat Apr 4, 2009	Blue Jackets	Predators
Tue Apr 7, 2009	Blackhawks	Predators
Thu Apr 9, 2009	Predators	Red Wings
Fri Apr 10, 2009	Predators	Wild

New York Islanders

Consecutive winners of the Stanley Cup from 1980 to 1983, the New York Islanders also boast six division and conference championship wins. Based in Uniondale, New York, and one of two New York state teams (the other being the New York Rangers), the Islanders were founded in 1972 and have been playing their home games in the Nassau Veterans Memorial Coliseum on Long Island since their inception. The Islanders stayed in the playoff race through to the trade deadline in 2008, but multiple players ending up on the injured list caused them to play to the fifth worst record in the league by the end of the 2007–08 season.

Owner	General Manager	Coach
Charles Wang	Garth Snow	Ted Nolan

2008 Record and Rankings

35-38-9, 5th in Atlantic Division

	Points	GF/G	GA/G	S/G	SA/G	PP %	PK %	PIM/G
	79	2.3	2.93	29.7	30.3	14.6	81.9	12.7
NHL Rank	26	30	23	10	21	29	19	10

Recent Top Draft Picks

Draft	Num.	Round	Player	Pos	Drafted From
2008 Entry	9	1	Joshua Bailey	C	Windsor Spitfires (OHL)
2008 Entry	36	2	Corey Trivino	C	Stouffville Spirit (OPJHL)
2008 Entry	40	2	Aaron Ness	D	Roseau H.S. (Minn.)
2007 Entry	62	3	Mark Katic	D	Sarnia Sting (OHL)
2007 Entry	76	3	Jason Gregoire	L	Lincoln Stars (USHL)
2007 Entry	106	4	Max Gratchev	D	Rimouski Oceanic (QMJHL)
2006 Entry	7	1	Kyle Okposo	R	Des Moines Buccaneers (USHL)
2006 Entry	60	2	Jesse Joensuu	W	Assat Pori (FNL)
2006 Entry	70	3	Robin Figren	L	Vastra Frolunda Juniors (Sweden)

Shootout Record

GP	W	L	G	S	S%	GA	SA	Sv%
8	5	3	11	32	34	10	34	71

Team Leaders

	G		A		P
Bill Guerin	23	Trent Hunter	29	Mike Comrie	49
Mike Comrie	21	Mike Comrie	28	Bill Guerin	44
Miroslav Satan	16	Miroslav Satan	25	Miroslav Satan	41
Josef Vasicek	16	Bill Guerin	21	Trent Hunter	41
Ruslan Fedotenko	16	Richard Park	20	Josef Vasicek	35

	PIM		Hits		+/-
Mike Comrie	87	Trent Hunter	256	Kyle Okposo	3
Andy Sutton	86	Sean Bergenheim	138	Aaron Johnson	2
Bill Guerin	65	Brendan Witt	135	Andy Hilbert	2
Sean Bergenheim	62	Ruslan Fedotenko	104	Freddy Meyer	2
Tim Jackman	57	Freddy Meyer	88	4 tied with	1

	PPG		SHG		Sht
Ruslan Fedotenko	8	Richard Park	4	Bill Guerin	227
Bill Guerin	7	Mike Sillinger	2	Trent Hunter	222
Miroslav Satan	5	Josef Vasicek	2	Mike Comrie	194
Mike Comrie	4	Chris Campoli	1	Miroslav Satan	171
Bryan Berard	4	Rob Davison	1	Sean Bergenheim	155

Goalies	GP	W	GAA	Sv%	SO
Rick Dipietro	63	26	2.82	0.902	3
Wade Dubielewicz	20	9	2.70	0.919	0
Joey MacDonald	2	0	3.00	0.918	0

Roster

Player	#	Pos	DOB	Hometown	S/P	Ctry	Ht	Wt	S
Colliton, Jeremy	72	C	Jan 13 '85	Blackie	AB	CAN	74	195	R
Comrie, Mike	89	C	Sep 11 '80	Edmonton	AB	CAN	70	185	L
Nielsen, Frans	51	C	Apr 24 '84	Herning		DNK	71	172	L
Sillinger, Mike	18	C	Jun 29 '71	Regina	SK	CAN	71	198	R
Vasicek, Josef	63	C	Sep 12 '80	Havlickuv Brod		CZE	77	214	L
Walter, Ben	29	C	May 11 '84	Beaconsfield	QC	CAN	73	195	L
Berard, Bryan	4	D	Mar 05 '77	Woonsocket	RI	USA	74	220	L
Campoli, Chris	14	D	Jul 09 '84	Mississauga	ON	CAN	71	190	L
Davison, Rob	3	D	May 01 '80	St. Catharines	ON	CAN	75	220	L
Fata, Drew	49	D	Jul 28 '83	Sault Ste. Marie	ON	CAN	73	209	L
Gervais, Bruno	8	D	Oct 03 '84	Longueuil	QC	CAN	72	188	R
Hillen, Jack	38	D	Jan 24 '86	Portland	OR	USA	70	190	L
Johnson, Aaron	2	D	Apr 30 '83	Port Hawkesbury	NS	CAN	74	211	L
Martinek, Radek	24	D	Aug 31 '76	Havlicko Brod		CZE	71	200	R
Meyer, Freddy	44	D	Jan 04 '81	Sanbornville	NH	USA	70	192	L
Spiller, Matthew	6	D	Feb 07 '83	Daysland	AB	CAN	77	233	L
Sutton, Andy	25	D	Mar 10 '75	Kingston	ON	CAN	78	245	L
Witt, Brendan	32	D	Feb 20 '75	Humboldt	SK	CAN	74	223	L
Bergenheim, Sean	20	L	Feb 08 '84	Helsinki		FIN	71	205	L
Brennan, Kip	37	L	Aug 27 '80	Kingston	ON	CAN	76	230	L
Fedotenko, Ruslan	26	L	Jan 18 '79	Kiev		UKR	74	195	L
Hilbert, Andy	11	L	Feb 06 '81	Howell	MI	USA	71	194	L
Regier, Steve	48	L	Aug 31 '84	Edmonton	AB	CAN	76	194	L
Sim, Jon	16	L	Sep 29 '77	New Glasgow	NS	CAN	70	195	L
Tambellini, Jeff	15	L	Apr 13 '84	Calgary	AB	CAN	71	186	L
Bootland, Darryl	27	R	Nov 02 '81	Toronto	ON	CAN	73	197	R
Comeau, Blake	57	R	Feb 18 '86	Meadow Lake	SK	CAN	73	207	R
Guerin, Bill	13	R	Nov 09 '70	Worcester	MA	USA	74	220	R
Hunter, Trent	7	R	Jul 05 '80	Red Deer	AB	CAN	75	210	R
Jackman, Tim	28	R	Nov 14 '81	Minot	ND	USA	76	210	R
Keith, Matt	27	R	Apr 11 '83	Edmonton	AB	CAN	74	200	R
Okposo, Kyle	21	R	Apr 16 '88	St. Paul	MN	USA	73	200	R
Park, Richard	10	R	May 27 '76	Seoul		KOR	71	190	R
Satan, Miroslav	81	R	Oct 22 '74	Topolcany		SVK	75	191	L

Goalies	#	Pos	DOB	Hometown	S/P	Ctry	Ht	Wt	C
Dipietro, Rick	39	G	Sep 19 '81	Winthrop	MA	USA	73	210	R
Dubielewicz, Wade	34	G	Jan 30 '79	Invermere	BC	CAN	70	185	L
MacDonald, Joey	35	G	Feb 07 '80	Pictou	NS	CAN	72	197	L

Regular Season Schedule

October 2008	Visitor	Home
Fri Oct 10, 2008	Islanders	Devils
Sat Oct 11, 2008	Blues	Islanders
Mon Oct 13, 2008	Sabres	Islanders
Thu Oct 16, 2008	Islanders	Lightning
Sat Oct 18, 2008	Islanders	Panthers
Thu Oct 23, 2008	Stars	Islanders
Sat Oct 25, 2008	Hurricanes	Islanders
Mon Oct 27, 2008	Rangers	Islanders
Thu Oct 30, 2008	Islanders	Flyers

November 2008	Visitor	Home
Sat Nov 1, 2008	Canadiens	Islanders
Mon Nov 3, 2008	Blue Jackets	Islanders
Tue Nov 4, 2008	Islanders	Rangers
Thu Nov 6, 2008	Islanders	Thrashers
Sat Nov 8, 2008	Penguins	Islanders
Tue Nov 11, 2008	Flyers	Islanders
Thu Nov 13, 2008	Islanders	Senators
Sat Nov 15, 2008	Senators	Islanders
Mon Nov 17, 2008	Canucks	Islanders
Fri Nov 21, 2008	Islanders	Devils
Sat Nov 22, 2008	Islanders	Sabres
Mon Nov 24, 2008	Islanders	Canadiens
Wed Nov 26, 2008	Penguins	Islanders
Fri Nov 28, 2008	Islanders	Bruins
Sat Nov 29, 2008	Senators	Islanders

December 2008	Visitor	Home
Thu Dec 4, 2008	Islanders	Capitals
Sat Dec 6, 2008	Thrashers	Islanders
Mon Dec 8, 2008	Islanders	Maple Leafs
Tue Dec 9, 2008	Islanders	Flyers
Thu Dec 11, 2008	Islanders	Penguins
Sat Dec 13, 2008	Islanders	Blue Jackets
Tue Dec 16, 2008	Capitals	Islanders
Fri Dec 19, 2008	Islanders	Wild
Sat Dec 20, 2008	Islanders	Predators
Tue Dec 23, 2008	Thrashers	Islanders
Fri Dec 26, 2008	Maple Leafs	Islanders
Sat Dec 27, 2008	Islanders	Sabres
Mon Dec 29, 2008	Islanders	Rangers
Wed Dec 31, 2008	Panthers	Islanders

January 2009	Visitor	Home
Fri Jan 2, 2009	Islanders	Coyotes
Sat Jan 3, 2009	Islanders	Sharks
Mon Jan 5, 2009	Islanders	Oilers
Thu Jan 8, 2009	Islanders	Flames

January 2009, cont.	Visitor	Home
Tue Jan 13, 2009	Rangers	Islanders
Thu Jan 15, 2009	Bruins	Islanders
Sat Jan 17, 2009	Devils	Islanders
Mon Jan 19, 2009	Capitals	Islanders
Wed Jan 21, 2009	Ducks	Islanders
Thu Jan 29, 2009	Islanders	Thrashers
Sat Jan 31, 2009	Panthers	Islanders

February 2009	Visitor	Home
Tue Feb 3, 2009	Lightning	Islanders
Thu Feb 5, 2009	Islanders	Panthers
Sat Feb 7, 2009	Islanders	Lightning
Tue Feb 10, 2009	Kings	Islanders
Wed Feb 11, 2009	Islanders	Devils
Sat Feb 14, 2009	Islanders	Flyers
Mon Feb 16, 2009	Penguins	Islanders
Wed Feb 18, 2009	Islanders	Rangers
Thu Feb 19, 2009	Hurricanes	Islanders
Sat Feb 21, 2009	Devils	Islanders
Wed Feb 25, 2009	Islanders	Penguins
Thu Feb 26, 2009	Maple Leafs	Islanders
Sat Feb 28, 2009	Sabres	Islanders

March 2009	Visitor	Home
Mon Mar 2, 2009	Avalanche	Islanders
Thu Mar 5, 2009	Rangers	Islanders
Sat Mar 7, 2009	Devils	Islanders
Sun Mar 8, 2009	Coyotes	Islanders
Tue Mar 10, 2009	Islanders	Maple Leafs
Thu Mar 12, 2009	Islanders	Canadiens
Sat Mar 14, 2009	Islanders	Bruins
Sun Mar 15, 2009	Islanders	Blackhawks
Fri Mar 20, 2009	Islanders	Hurricanes
Sat Mar 21, 2009	Islanders	Senators
Wed Mar 25, 2009	Wild	Islanders
Fri Mar 27, 2009	Islanders	Red Wings
Sat Mar 28, 2009	Flyers	Islanders

April 2009	Visitor	Home
Wed Apr 1, 2009	Islanders	Capitals
Thu Apr 2, 2009	Canadiens	Islanders
Sat Apr 4, 2009	Lightning	Islanders
Tue Apr 7, 2009	Islanders	Hurricanes
Thu Apr 9, 2009	Islanders	Penguins
Sat Apr 11, 2009	Flyers	Islanders
Sun Apr 12, 2009	Bruins	Islanders

New Jersey Devils

Three-time Stanley Cup winners (1995, 2000 and 2003), the New Jersey Devils settled in Newark, New Jersey, in 1982 after previous stints in Kansas City, Mississippi, and Denver, Colorado, in the 1970s and early 1980s. The 2007–08 season saw the opening of the new Prudential Center, where the Devils now play all of their home games. In the last games of 2008 against rivals the New York Rangers, the Devils lost their playoff series 4–1, losing the three games they played on home ice. Longtime Devils player Martin Brodeur was awarded the Vezina Trophy in June 2008 for the fourth time in five years, and he remains the only player with the team who was also with the franchise when it won all three of its Stanley Cup championships.

Owner	General Manager	Coach
Jeffrey Vanderbeek	Lou Lamoriello	Brent Sutter

2008 Record and Rankings

46-29-7, 2nd in Atlantic Division

	Points	GF/G	GA/G	S/G	SA/G	PP %	PK %	PIM/G
	99	2.42	2.35	28.8	27.5	15.6	82.8	11.9
NHL Rank	6	27	5	15	8	25	13	3

Recent Top Draft Picks

Draft	Num.	Round	Player	Pos	Drafted From
2008 Entry	24	1	Mattias Tedenby	L	HV71 Jonkoping (SEL)
2008 Entry	52	2	Brandon Burlon	D	St. Michael's Buzzers (OPJHL)
2008 Entry	54	2	Patrice Cormier	C	Rimouski Oceanic (QMJHL)
2007 Entry	57	2	Mike Hoeffel	W	US National Under 18 Team
2007 Entry	79	3	Nick Palmieri	R	Erie Otters (OHL)
2007 Entry	87	3	Corbin McPherson	D	Cowichan Valley Capitals (BCHL)
2006 Entry	30	1	Matt Corrente	D	Saginaw Spirit (OHL)
2006 Entry	58	2	Alexander Vasyunov	L	Yaroslavl Jrs. (Russia)
2006 Entry	67	3	Kirill Tulupov	D	Almetyevsk Neftyanik (Rus-1)

Shootout Record

GP	W	L	G	S	S%	GA	SA	Sv%
12	8	4	15	42	36	11	43	74

Team Leaders

	G		A			P
Zach Parise	32	Patrik Elias	35	Zach Parise	65
Brian Gionta	22	Zach Parise	33	Patrik Elias	55
Patrik Elias	20	Brian Gionta	31	Brian Gionta	53
John Madden	20	Jamie Langenbrunner	28	John Madden	43
Travis Zajac	14	Paul Martin	27	Jamie Langenbrunner	41

	PIM		Hits		+/-
David Clarkson	183	David Clarkson	150	David-Johnny Oduya	27
Arron Asham	84	Vitaly Vishnevski	140	Paul Martin	20
Sheldon Brookbank	63	Colin White	106	Zach Parise	13
Michael Rupp	58	Michael Rupp	104	Bryce Salvador	12
Bryce Salvador	54	Arron Asham	87	2 tied with	10

	PPG		SHG		Sht
Zach Parise	10	John Madden	3	Zach Parise	266
Brian Gionta	8	Brian Gionta	1	Patrik Elias	263
Patrik Elias	7	Jamie Langenbrunner	1	Brian Gionta	257
Travis Zajac	5	Zach Parise	1	John Madden	185
Jamie Langenbrunner	5			Travis Zajac	155

Goalies	GP	W	GAA	Sv%	SO
Martin Brodeur	77	44	2.17	0.920	4
Kevin Weekes	9	2	2.97	0.894	0

Roster

Player	#	Pos	DOB	Hometown	S/P	Ctry	Ht	Wt	S
Madden, John	11	C	May 04 '73	Barrie	ON	CAN	71	190	L
Pelley, Rod	10	C	Sep 01 '84	Kitimat	BC	CAN	72	200	L
Rupp, Michael	17	C	Jan 13 '80	Cleveland	OH	USA	77	230	L
Zajac, Travis	19	C	May 13 '85	Winnipeg	MB	CAN	74	200	R
Brookbank, Sheldon	8	D	Oct 03 '80	Lanigan	SK	CAN	74	215	R
Greene, Andy	6	D	Oct 30 '82	Trenton	MI	USA	71	195	L
Malmivaara, Olli	24	D	Mar 13 '82	Kajaani		FIN	79	230	L
Martin, Paul	7	D	Mar 05 '81	Minneapolis	MN	USA	73	195	L
Mottau, Mike	27	D	Mar 19 '78	Quincy	MA	USA	72	190	L
Oduya, David-Johnny	29	D	Oct 01 '81	Stockholm		SWE	72	200	L
Rachunek, Karel	28	D	Aug 27 '79	Zlinwaldow		CZE	74	220	R
Salvador, Bryce	24	D	Feb 11 '76	Brandon	MB	CAN	74	220	L
Vishnevski, Vitaly	2	D	Mar 18 '80	Kharkov		UKR	74	215	L
White, Colin	5	D	Dec 12 '77	New Glasgow	NS	CAN	76	220	L
Brylin, Sergei	18	L	Jan 13 '74	Moscow		RUS	70	190	L
Clarke, Noah	12	L	Jun 11 '79	La Verne	CA	USA	69	190	L
Elias, Patrik	26	L	Apr 13 '76	Trebic		CZE	73	195	L
Pandolfo, Jay	20	L	Dec 27 '74	Winchester	MA	USA	73	190	L
Parise, Zach	9	L	Jul 28 '84	Minneapolis	MN	USA	71	190	L
Asham, Arron	22	R	Apr 13 '78	Portage La Prairie	MB	CAN	71	205	R
Bergfors, Nicklas	12	R	Mar 07 '87	Sodertalje		SWE	71	190	R
Clarkson, David	23	R	Mar 31 '84	Toronto	ON	CAN	73	200	R
Gionta, Brian	14	R	Jan 18 '79	Rochester	NY	USA	67	175	R
Langenbrunner, Jamie	15	R	Jul 24 '75	Cloquet	MN	USA	73	205	R
Tallackson, Barry	21	R	Apr 14 '83	Grafton	ND	USA	77	215	R
Zubrus, Dainius	16	R	Jun 16 '78	Elektrenai		LTU	77	225	L

Goalies	#	Pos	DOB	Hometown	S/P	Ctry	Ht	Wt	C
Brodeur, Martin	30	G	May 06 '72	Montreal	QC	CAN	74	215	L
Weekes, Kevin	1	G	Apr 04 '75	Toronto	ON	CAN	74	215	L

Regular Season Schedule

October 2008	Visitor	Home
Fri Oct 10, 2008	Islanders	Devils
Sat Oct 11, 2008	Devils	Penguins
Mon Oct 13, 2008	Devils	Rangers
Thu Oct 16, 2008	Devils	Thrashers
Sat Oct 18, 2008	Devils	Capitals
Wed Oct 22, 2008	Stars	Devils
Fri Oct 24, 2008	Flyers	Devils
Sat Oct 25, 2008	Devils	Flyers
Wed Oct 29, 2008	Maple Leafs	Devils

November 2008	Visitor	Home
Sat Nov 1, 2008	Thrashers	Devils
Mon Nov 3, 2008	Sabres	Devils
Wed Nov 5, 2008	Lightning	Devils
Sat Nov 8, 2008	Devils	Red Wings
Sun Nov 9, 2008	Oilers	Devils
Wed Nov 12, 2008	Rangers	Devils
Fri Nov 14, 2008	Devils	Capitals
Sat Nov 15, 2008	Capitals	Devils
Thu Nov 20, 2008	Panthers	Devils
Fri Nov 21, 2008	Islanders	Devils
Sun Nov 23, 2008	Devils	Lightning
Wed Nov 26, 2008	Devils	Panthers
Sat Nov 29, 2008	Devils	Penguins

December 2008	Visitor	Home
Thu Dec 4, 2008	Devils	Flyers
Sat Dec 6, 2008	Devils	Canadiens
Wed Dec 10, 2008	Penguins	Devils
Fri Dec 12, 2008	Rangers	Devils
Sat Dec 13, 2008	Sabres	Devils
Tue Dec 16, 2008	Devils	Maple Leafs
Wed Dec 17, 2008	Devils	Sabres
Fri Dec 19, 2008	Senators	Devils
Sun Dec 21, 2008	Flyers	Devils
Tue Dec 23, 2008	Bruins	Devils
Fri Dec 26, 2008	Penguins	Devils
Sat Dec 27, 2008	Devils	Rangers
Tue Dec 30, 2008	Devils	Blues
Wed Dec 31, 2008	Devils	Stars

January 2009	Visitor	Home
Fri Jan 2, 2009	Canadiens	Devils
Sun Jan 4, 2009	Senators	Devils
Tue Jan 6, 2009	Devils	Hurricanes
Thu Jan 8, 2009	Thrashers	Devils
Sat Jan 10, 2009	Devils	Kings
Sun Jan 11, 2009	Devils	Ducks

January 2009, cont.	Visitor	Home
Tue Jan 13, 2009	Devils	Canucks
Fri Jan 16, 2009	Devils	Blue Jackets
Sat Jan 17, 2009	Devils	Islanders
Mon Jan 19, 2009	Devils	Predators
Wed Jan 21, 2009	Canadiens	Devils
Tue Jan 27, 2009	Devils	Senators
Thu Jan 29, 2009	Devils	Bruins
Fri Jan 30, 2009	Penguins	Devils

February 2009	Visitor	Home
Tue Feb 3, 2009	Capitals	Devils
Fri Feb 6, 2009	Devils	Thrashers
Sat Feb 7, 2009	Kings	Devils
Mon Feb 9, 2009	Rangers	Devils
Wed Feb 11, 2009	Islanders	Devils
Fri Feb 13, 2009	Bruins	Devils
Sun Feb 15, 2009	Sharks	Devils
Tue Feb 17, 2009	Devils	Panthers
Thu Feb 19, 2009	Devils	Lightning
Sat Feb 21, 2009	Devils	Islanders
Thu Feb 26, 2009	Avalanche	Devils
Sat Feb 28, 2009	Panthers	Devils

March 2009	Visitor	Home
Sun Mar 1, 2009	Flyers	Devils
Tue Mar 3, 2009	Devils	Maple Leafs
Sat Mar 7, 2009	Devils	Islanders
Tue Mar 10, 2009	Flames	Devils
Thu Mar 12, 2009	Coyotes	Devils
Sat Mar 14, 2009	Devils	Canadiens
Tue Mar 17, 2009	Blackhawks	Devils
Wed Mar 18, 2009	Devils	Hurricanes
Fri Mar 20, 2009	Wild	Devils
Sun Mar 22, 2009	Devils	Bruins
Mon Mar 23, 2009	Devils	Flyers
Fri Mar 27, 2009	Devils	Blackhawks
Sat Mar 28, 2009	Hurricanes	Devils
Mon Mar 30, 2009	Devils	Rangers

April 2009	Visitor	Home
Wed Apr 1, 2009	Devils	Penguins
Fri Apr 3, 2009	Lightning	Devils
Sat Apr 4, 2009	Devils	Sabres
Tue Apr 7, 2009	Maple Leafs	Devils
Thu Apr 9, 2009	Devils	Senators
Sat Apr 11, 2009	Hurricanes	Devils

New York Rangers

The first team in the NHL to win the Stanley Cup in 1928, the New York Rangers have won the Cup championship three times since then, with the most recent win in 1994. One of the Original Six, the Rangers are one of the oldest teams in the NHL and have played in Madison Square Garden in New York, New York, since 1925. Six former players on the New York Rangers have had their numbers retired, including Mark Messier (11) and Mike Richter (35), and Adam Graves' (9) is to be retired in the 2008–09 season. The Rangers also have a significant number of former team members in the Hockey Hall of Fame, with 47 earning a spot in this famous institution. With Scott Gomez and Chris Drury joining the Rangers in the 2007–08 season, the team still couldn't quite make the Stanley Cup finals, losing their second-round series 4–1 against the Pittsburgh Penguins.

Owner	General Manager	Coach
Madison Square Garden, L.P.	Glen Sather	Tom Renney

2008 Record and Rankings

42-27-13, 3rd in Atlantic Division

	Points	GF/G	GA/G	S/G	SA/G	PP %	PK %	PIM/G
	97	2.5	2.32	31.5	25.9	16.5	84.6	14.1
NHL Rank	9	25	4	3	3	22	6	18

Recent Top Draft Picks

Draft	Num.	Round	Player	Pos	Drafted From
2008 Entry	20	1	Michael Del Zotto	D	Oshawa Generals (OHL)
2008 Entry	51	2	Derek Stepan	C	Shattuck St. Mary's (Minn.)
2008 Entry	75	3	Evgeny Grachev	C	Yaroslavl Jrs. (Russia)
2007 Entry	17	1	Alexei Cherepanov	R	Omsk Avangard (Russia)
2007 Entry	48	2	Antoine Lafleur	G	Prince Edward Island Rocket (QMJHL)
2007 Entry	138	5	Max Campbell	C	Strathroy (WJRB)
2006 Entry	21	1	Bob Sanguinetti	D	Owen Sound Attack (OHL)
2006 Entry	54	2	Artem Anisimov	C	Yaroslavl Lokomotiv (Russia)
2006 Entry	84	3	Ryan Hillier	L	Halifax Mooseheads (QMJHL)

Shootout Record

GP	W	L	G	S	S%	GA	SA	Sv%
17	8	9	15	53	28	16	53	70

Team Leaders

G		A		P	
Jaromir Jagr	25	Scott Gomez	54	Jaromir Jagr	71
Chris Drury	25	Jaromir Jagr	46	Scott Gomez	70
Brendan Shanahan	23	Chris Drury	33	Chris Drury	58
Scott Gomez	16	Martin Straka	27	Brendan Shanahan	46
Sean Avery	15	Brandon Dubinsky	26	Martin Straka	41

PIM		Hits		+/-	
Colton Orr	159	Fedor Tyutin	218	Nigel Dawes	11
Sean Avery	154	Brandon Dubinsky	196	Jaromir Jagr	8
Ryan Hollweg	96	Daniel Girardi	179	Brandon Dubinsky	8
Michal Rozsival	80	Ryan Hollweg	174	Marek Malik	7
Brandon Dubinsky	79	Colton Orr	146	Ryan Callahan	7

PPG		SHG		Sht	
Chris Drury	12	Fredrik Sjostrom	2	Brendan Shanahan	265
Brendan Shanahan	11	Michal Rozsival	2	Jaromir Jagr	249
Jaromir Jagr	7	Martin Straka	1	Scott Gomez	242
Scott Gomez	7	Ryan Callahan	1	Chris Drury	220
Michal Rozsival	6			Brandon Dubinsky	157

Goalies	GP	W	GAA	Sv%	SO
Henrik Lundqvist	72	37	2.23	0.912	10
Stephen Valiquette	13	5	2.19	0.916	2

Roster

Player	#	Pos	DOB	Hometown	S/P	Ctry	Ht	Wt	S
Betts, Blair	15	C	Feb 16 '80	Edmonton	AB	CAN	75	210	L
Drury, Chris	23	C	Aug 20 '76	Trumbull	CT	USA	70	190	R
Dubinsky, Brandon	17	C	Apr 29 '86	Anchorage	AK	USA	73	210	L
Gomez, Scott	19	C	Dec 23 '79	Anchorage	AK	USA	71	200	L
Straka, Martin	82	C	Sep 03 '72	Plzen		CZE	69	180	L
Backman, Christian	55	D	Apr 28 '80	Gothenburg		SWE	76	210	L
Baranka, Ivan	21	D	May 19 '85	Ilava		SVK	75	205	L
Girardi, Daniel	5	D	Apr 29 '84	Welland	ON	CAN	74	208	R
Malik, Marek	8	D	Jun 24 '75	Ostrava		CZE	78	235	L
Mara, Paul	27	D	Sep 07 '79	Ridgewood	NJ	USA	76	212	L
Pock, Thomas	22	D	Dec 02 '81	Klagenfurt		AUT	73	210	L
Rozsival, Michal	3	D	Sep 03 '78	Vlasim		CZE	74	210	R
Staal, Marc	18	D	Jan 13 '87	Thunder Bay	ON	CAN	76	205	L
Strudwick, Jason	34	D	Jul 17 '75	Edmonton	AB	CAN	76	225	L
Tyutin, Fedor	51	D	Jul 19 '83	Izhevsk		RUS	75	210	L
Avery, Sean	16	L	Apr 10 '80	Pickering	ON	CAN	70	195	L
Byers, Dane	54	L	Feb 21 '86	Nipawin	SK	CAN	75	195	L
Dawes, Nigel	10	L	Feb 09 '85	Winnipeg	MB	CAN	69	190	L
Hollweg, Ryan	44	L	Apr 23 '83	Downey	CA	USA	71	210	L
Prucha, Petr	25	L	Sep 14 '82	Chrudim		CZE	72	175	R
Sjostrom, Fredrik	20	L	May 06 '83	Färgelanda		SWE	73	217	L
Callahan, Ryan	24	R	Mar 21 '85	Rochester	NY	USA	71	188	R
Jagr, Jaromir	68	R	Feb 15 '72	Kladno		CZE	75	240	L
Moore, Greg	49	R	Mar 26 '84	Lisbon	ME	USA	73	210	R
Orr, Colton	28	R	Mar 03 '82	Winnipeg	MB	CAN	75	222	R
Shanahan, Brendan	14	R	Jan 23 '69	Mimico	ON	CAN	75	220	R

Goalies	#	Pos	DOB	Hometown	S/P	Ctry	Ht	Wt	C
Lundqvist, Henrik	30	G	Mar 02 '82	Are		SWE	73	195	L
Valiquette, Stephen	40	G	Aug 20 '77	Etobicoke	ON	CAN	78	210	L

Regular Season Schedule

October 2008	Visitor	Home
Sat Oct 4, 2008	Rangers	Lightning (Prague, CZE)
Sun Oct 5, 2008	Lightning	Rangers (Prague, CZE)
Fri Oct 10, 2008	Blackhawks	Rangers
Sat Oct 11, 2008	Rangers	Flyers
Mon Oct 13, 2008	Devils	Rangers
Wed Oct 15, 2008	Sabres	Rangers
Fri Oct 17, 2008	Maple Leafs	Rangers
Sat Oct 18, 2008	Rangers	Red Wings
Mon Oct 20, 2008	Stars	Rangers
Fri Oct 24, 2008	Rangers	Blue Jackets
Sat Oct 25, 2008	Penguins	Rangers
Mon Oct 27, 2008	Rangers	Islanders
Thu Oct 30, 2008	Thrashers	Rangers

November 2008	Visitor	Home
Sat Nov 1, 2008	Rangers	Maple Leafs
Tue Nov 4, 2008	Islanders	Rangers
Thu Nov 6, 2008	Lightning	Rangers
Sat Nov 8, 2008	Rangers	Capitals
Mon Nov 10, 2008	Oilers	Rangers
Wed Nov 12, 2008	Rangers	Devils
Sat Nov 15, 2008	Bruins	Rangers
Mon Nov 17, 2008	Senators	Rangers
Wed Nov 19, 2008	Canucks	Rangers
Sat Nov 22, 2008	Rangers	Senators
Mon Nov 24, 2008	Coyotes	Rangers
Wed Nov 26, 2008	Rangers	Lightning
Fri Nov 28, 2008	Rangers	Panthers
Sun Nov 30, 2008	Panthers	Rangers

December 2008	Visitor	Home
Wed Dec 3, 2008	Penguins	Rangers
Thu Dec 4, 2008	Rangers	Canadiens
Sun Dec 7, 2008	Flames	Rangers
Wed Dec 10, 2008	Rangers	Thrashers
Fri Dec 12, 2008	Rangers	Devils
Sat Dec 13, 2008	Hurricanes	Rangers
Tue Dec 16, 2008	Rangers	Ducks
Wed Dec 17, 2008	Rangers	Kings
Sat Dec 20, 2008	Rangers	Sharks
Tue Dec 23, 2008	Capitals	Rangers
Sat Dec 27, 2008	Devils	Rangers
Mon Dec 29, 2008	Islanders	Rangers

January 2009	Visitor	Home
Sat Jan 3, 2009	Rangers	Capitals
Mon Jan 5, 2009	Penguins	Rangers

January 2009, cont.	Visitor	Home
Wed Jan 7, 2009	Canadiens	Rangers
Fri Jan 9, 2009	Rangers	Sabres
Sat Jan 10, 2009	Rangers	Senators
Tue Jan 13, 2009	Rangers	Islanders
Fri Jan 16, 2009	Rangers	Blackhawks
Sun Jan 18, 2009	Rangers	Penguins
Tue Jan 20, 2009	Ducks	Rangers
Tue Jan 27, 2009	Hurricanes	Rangers
Wed Jan 28, 2009	Rangers	Penguins
Sat Jan 31, 2009	Rangers	Bruins

February 2009	Visitor	Home
Tue Feb 3, 2009	Thrashers	Rangers
Fri Feb 6, 2009	Rangers	Stars
Mon Feb 9, 2009	Rangers	Devils
Wed Feb 11, 2009	Capitals	Rangers
Fri Feb 13, 2009	Rangers	Panthers
Sun Feb 15, 2009	Flyers	Rangers
Mon Feb 16, 2009	Rangers	Blues
Wed Feb 18, 2009	Islanders	Rangers
Sat Feb 21, 2009	Rangers	Sabres
Sun Feb 22, 2009	Maple Leafs	Rangers
Wed Feb 25, 2009	Rangers	Maple Leafs
Thu Feb 26, 2009	Panthers	Rangers
Sat Feb 28, 2009	Avalanche	Rangers

March 2009	Visitor	Home
Thu Mar 5, 2009	Rangers	Islanders
Sun Mar 8, 2009	Bruins	Rangers
Mon Mar 9, 2009	Rangers	Hurricanes
Thu Mar 12, 2009	Rangers	Predators
Sat Mar 14, 2009	Rangers	Flyers
Sun Mar 15, 2009	Flyers	Rangers
Tue Mar 17, 2009	Rangers	Canadiens
Sat Mar 21, 2009	Sabres	Rangers
Sun Mar 22, 2009	Senators	Rangers
Tue Mar 24, 2009	Wild	Rangers
Thu Mar 26, 2009	Rangers	Thrashers
Sat Mar 28, 2009	Rangers	Penguins
Mon Mar 30, 2009	Devils	Rangers

April 2009	Visitor	Home
Thu Apr 2, 2009	Rangers	Hurricanes
Sat Apr 4, 2009	Rangers	Bruins
Tue Apr 7, 2009	Canadiens	Rangers
Thu Apr 9, 2009	Flyers	Rangers
Sun Apr 12, 2009	Rangers	Flyers

Ottawa Senators

The Ottawa Senators, based in the Ottawa suburb of Nepean, Ontario, have yet to win a Stanley Cup, but are considered one the most successful teams in NHL standings, qualifying for the playoffs for the past 11 seasons. And, most recently, the Senators were the recipients of the Prince of Wales Trophy in 2007. Coming back to life after their NHL demise in 1934, the team got off to a shaky start in 1992 and even filed for bankruptcy in 2003, but now boasts several coveted players and one of the league's top lines—the "CASH" or "Pizza" line of Daniel Alfredsson, Jason Spezza and Dany Heatley. These three players, along with Ray Emery, Chris Phillips and Wade Redden, were named to the All-Star Game ballot in 2007, causing the Senators to lead the NHL in overall number of all-star picks from a single team. Fans of the Senators call themselves the Sens Army and can be found rooting for their home team in the 19,153-capacity Scotiabank Place.

Owner	General Manager	Coach
Eugene Melnyk	Bryan Murray	Craig Hartsburg

2008 Record and Rankings

43-31-8, 2nd in Northeast Division

	Points	GF/G	GA/G	S/G	SA/G	PP %	PK %	PIM/G
	94	3.15	2.95	30.1	30	18.3	81.0	14.3
NHL Rank	12	1	24	9	19	12	22	20

Recent Top Draft Picks

Draft	Num.	Round	Player	Pos	Drafted From
2008 Entry	15	1	Erik Karlsson	D	Frolunda Jrs (Sweden)
2008 Entry	42	2	Patrick Wiercioch	D	Omaha Lancers (USHL)
2008 Entry	79	3	Zack Smith	C	Swift Current Broncos (WHL)
2007 Entry	29	1	Jim O'Brien	C	U. of Minnesota (NCAA)
2007 Entry	60	2	Ruslan Bashkirov	L	Quebec Remparts (QMJHL)
2007 Entry	90	3	Louie Caporusso	F	St. Michael's Buzzers (OPJHL)
2006 Entry	28	1	Nick Foligno	L	Sudbury Wolves (OHL)
2006 Entry	68	3	Eric Gryba	D	Green Bay Gamblers (USHL)
2006 Entry	91	3	Kaspars Daugavins	L	Riga (Lavtia)

Shootout Record

GP	W	L	G	S	S%	GA	SA	Sv%
8	3	5	10	31	32	12	31	61

Team Leaders

	G		A		P
Dany Heatley	41	Jason Spezza	58	Jason Spezza	92
Daniel Alfredsson	40	Daniel Alfredsson	49	Daniel Alfredsson	89
Jason Spezza	34	Dany Heatley	41	Dany Heatley	82
Cory Stillman	24	Cory Stillman	41	Cory Stillman	65
Antoine Vermette	24	Wade Redden	32	Antoine Vermette	53

	PIM		Hits		+/-
Chris Neil	199	Mike Fisher	234	Dany Heatley	33
Mike Commodore	100	Chris Neil	204	Jason Spezza	26
Mike Fisher	82	Christoph Schubert	187	Chris Phillips	15
Dany Heatley	76	Anton Volchenkov	153	Daniel Alfredsson	15
Shean Donovan	73	Mike Commodore	144	Anton Volchenkov	14

	PPG		SHG		Sht
Dany Heatley	13	Daniel Alfredsson	7	Dany Heatley	224
Jason Spezza	11	Antoine Vermette	3	Daniel Alfredsson	217
Cory Stillman	11	Dean McAmmond	3	Mike Fisher	215
Daniel Alfredsson	9	Mike Fisher	2	Jason Spezza	210
2 tied with	6	3 tied with	1	Antoine Vermette	175

Goalies	GP	W	GAA	Sv%	SO
Martin Gerber	57	30	2.72	0.910	2
Ray Emery	31	12	3.13	0.890	0
Brian Elliott	1	1	1.00	0.966	0

Roster

Player	#	Pos	DOB	Hometown	S/P	Ctry	Ht	Wt	S
Bass, Cody	58	C	Jan 07 '87	Owen Sound	ON	CAN	72	211	R
Fisher, Mike	12	C	Jun 05 '80	Peterborough	ON	CAN	73	209	R
Hennessy, Joshua	36	C	Feb 07 '85	Brockton	MA	USA	72	192	L
Kelly, Chris	22	C	Nov 11 '80	Toronto	ON	CAN	72	195	L
McAmmond, Dean	37	C	Jun 15 '73	Grande Cache	AB	CAN	71	195	L
Nikulin, Alexander	41	C	Aug 25 '85	Perm		RUS	73	198	L
Robitaille, Randy	27	C	Oct 12 '75	Ottawa	ON	CAN	71	200	L
Spezza, Jason	19	C	Jun 13 '83	Toronto	ON	CAN	75	214	R
Winchester, Jesse	18	C	Oct 04 '83	Long Sault	ON	CAN	73	215	R
Zubov, Ilja	53	C	Feb 14 '87	Chelyabinsk		RUS	72	197	L
Commodore, Mike	44	D	Nov 07 '79	Fort Saskatchewan	AB	CAN	77	228	R
Lee, Brian	55	D	Mar 26 '87	Moorhead	MN	USA	74	205	R
Meszaros, Andrej	14	D	Oct 13 '85	Povazska Bystrica		SVK	74	218	R
Nycholat, Lawrence	3	D	May 07 '79	Calgary	AB	CAN	72	200	L
Phillips, Chris	4	D	Mar 09 '78	Calgary	AB	CAN	75	219	L
Redden, Wade	6	D	Jun 12 '77	Lloydminster	SK	CAN	74	209	L
Richardson, Luke	2	D	Mar 26 '69	Ottawa	ON	CAN	75	208	L
Schubert, Christoph	5	D	Feb 05 '82	Munich		DEU	75	229	L
Volchenkov, Anton	24	D	Feb 25 '82	Moscow		RUS	73	232	L
Foligno, Nick	71	L	Oct 31 '87	Buffalo	NY	USA	72	201	L
Heatley, Dany	15	L	Jan 21 '81	Freiburg		DEU	75	220	L
Stillman, Cory	61	L	Dec 20 '73	Peterborough	ON	CAN	72	200	L
Vermette, Antoine	20	L	Jul 20 '82	St. Agapi	QC	CAN	73	200	L
Alfredsson, Daniel	11	R	Dec 11 '72	Gothenburg		SWE	71	205	R
Donovan, Shean	10	R	Jan 22 '75	Timmins	ON	CAN	74	215	R
Lapointe, Martin	28	R	Sep 12 '73	Ville St. Pierre	QC	CAN	71	215	R
McGrattan, Brian	16	R	Sep 02 '81	Hamilton	ON	CAN	76	234	R
Neil, Chris	25	R	Jun 18 '79	Markdale	ON	CAN	73	214	R

Goalies	#	Pos	DOB	Hometown	S/P	Ctry	Ht	Wt	C
Elliott, Brian	30	G	Apr 09 '85	Newmarket	ON	CAN	74	202	L
Emery, Ray	1	G	Sep 28 '82	Hamilton	ON	CAN	74	196	L
Gerber, Martin	29	G	Sep 03 '74	Burgdorf		CHE	71	211	L

Regular Season Schedule

October 2008	Visitor	Home
Sat Oct 4, 2008	Penguins	Senators (Stockholm, SWE)
Sun Oct 5, 2008	Senators	Penguins (Stockholm, SWE)
Sat Oct 11, 2008	Red Wings	Senators
Fri Oct 17, 2008	Coyotes	Senators
Sat Oct 18, 2008	Bruins	Senators
Wed Oct 22, 2008	Panthers	Senators
Fri Oct 24, 2008	Ducks	Senators
Sat Oct 25, 2008	Senators	Maple Leafs
Mon Oct 27, 2008	Senators	Sabres
Thu Oct 30, 2008	Senators	Panthers

November 2008	Visitor	Home
Sat Nov 1, 2008	Senators	Lightning
Tue Nov 4, 2008	Capitals	Senators
Thu Nov 6, 2008	Flyers	Senators
Fri Nov 7, 2008	Senators	Hurricanes
Tue Nov 11, 2008	Senators	Canadiens
Thu Nov 13, 2008	Islanders	Senators
Sat Nov 15, 2008	Senators	Islanders
Mon Nov 17, 2008	Senators	Rangers
Thu Nov 20, 2008	Canadiens	Senators
Sat Nov 22, 2008	Rangers	Senators
Thu Nov 27, 2008	Maple Leafs	Senators
Sat Nov 29, 2008	Senators	Islanders

December 2008	Visitor	Home
Wed Dec 3, 2008	Thrashers	Senators
Sat Dec 6, 2008	Penguins	Senators
Mon Dec 8, 2008	Panthers	Senators
Wed Dec 10, 2008	Senators	Blackhawks
Fri Dec 12, 2008	Senators	Capitals
Sat Dec 13, 2008	Lightning	Senators
Tue Dec 16, 2008	Thrashers	Senators
Fri Dec 19, 2008	Senators	Devils
Sat Dec 20, 2008	Stars	Senators
Tue Dec 23, 2008	Senators	Flyers
Sat Dec 27, 2008	Senators	Flames
Sun Dec 28, 2008	Senators	Canucks
Tue Dec 30, 2008	Senators	Oilers

January 2009	Visitor	Home
Sat Jan 3, 2009	Senators	Maple Leafs
Sun Jan 4, 2009	Senators	Devils
Tue Jan 6, 2009	Senators	Sabres
Thu Jan 8, 2009	Senators	Bruins
Sat Jan 10, 2009	Rangers	Senators

January 2009, cont.	Visitor	Home
Tue Jan 13, 2009	Hurricanes	Senators
Wed Jan 14, 2009	Senators	Thrashers
Sat Jan 17, 2009	Canadiens	Senators
Tue Jan 20, 2009	Capitals	Senators
Tue Jan 27, 2009	Devils	Senators
Thu Jan 29, 2009	Senators	Blues
Fri Jan 30, 2009	Senators	Blue Jackets

February 2009	Visitor	Home
Sun Feb 1, 2009	Senators	Capitals
Tue Feb 3, 2009	Kings	Senators
Thu Feb 5, 2009	Bruins	Senators
Sat Feb 7, 2009	Sabres	Senators
Wed Feb 11, 2009	Senators	Sabres
Thu Feb 12, 2009	Senators	Flyers
Sat Feb 14, 2009	Senators	Wild
Mon Feb 16, 2009	Senators	Predators
Tue Feb 17, 2009	Senators	Avalanche
Thu Feb 19, 2009	Canucks	Senators
Sat Feb 21, 2009	Senators	Canadiens
Tue Feb 24, 2009	Hurricanes	Senators
Thu Feb 26, 2009	Sharks	Senators
Sat Feb 28, 2009	Maple Leafs	Senators

March 2009	Visitor	Home
Tue Mar 3, 2009	Flames	Senators
Thu Mar 5, 2009	Oilers	Senators
Sat Mar 7, 2009	Sabres	Senators
Mon Mar 9, 2009	Maple Leafs	Senators
Wed Mar 11, 2009	Lightning	Senators
Thu Mar 12, 2009	Senators	Bruins
Sat Mar 14, 2009	Senators	Penguins
Tue Mar 17, 2009	Sabres	Senators
Thu Mar 19, 2009	Canadiens	Senators
Sat Mar 21, 2009	Islanders	Senators
Sun Mar 22, 2009	Senators	Rangers
Wed Mar 25, 2009	Senators	Hurricanes
Sat Mar 28, 2009	Senators	Thrashers
Sun Mar 29, 2009	Senators	Lightning
Tue Mar 31, 2009	Senators	Panthers

April 2009	Visitor	Home
Thu Apr 2, 2009	Senators	Bruins
Sat Apr 4, 2009	Flyers	Senators
Mon Apr 6, 2009	Senators	Canadiens
Tue Apr 7, 2009	Bruins	Senators
Thu Apr 9, 2009	Devils	Senators
Sat Apr 11, 2009	Senators	Maple Leafs

Philadelphia Flyers

Based in Philadelphia, Pennsylvania, the Philadelphia Flyers made their debut in the NHL in 1967 and have won two Stanley Cup finals since their founding. The Flyers have returned to the Cup championship five times since their last league win in 1975, but have yet to win the trophy for a third time. Throughout their years in the NHL, the Flyers have made their mark in the sport, earning the nickname the Broad Street Bullies in the 1970s due to their brawling tendencies. Broad Street referred to the street their home arena was located on then and still is now (1967–1996, The Spectrum; 1996–present, The Wachovia Center). And although the Flyers once had hockey great Eric Lindros on their team, they are also in the NHL history books for being the first and only one of two league teams to ever wear Cooperalls: hockey pants that extend from the waist to the ankles. They brought in the trend that never caught on in 1981–82 and wore them for only one more season before returning to traditional hockey pants in 1983.

Owner	General Manager	Coach
Comcast-Spectacor	Paul Holmgren	John Stevens

2008 Record and Rankings

42-29-11, 4th in Atlantic Division

	Points	GF/G	GA/G	S/G	SA/G	PP %	PK %	PIM/G
	95	2.99	2.77	28.8	31.8	21.8	83.2	17.9
NHL Rank	10	6	18	16	27	2	10	28

Recent Top Draft Picks

Draft	Num.	Round	Player	Pos	Drafted From
2008 Entry	19	1	Luca Sbisa	D	Lethbridge Hurricanes (WHL)
2008 Entry	67	3	Marc-Andre Bourdon	D	Rouyn-Noranda Huskies (QMJHL)
2008 Entry	84	3	Jacob DeSerres	G	Seattle Thunderbirds (WHL)
2007 Entry	2	1	James Van Riemsdyk	L	US National Under 18 Team
2007 Entry	41	2	Kevin Marshall	D	Lewiston MAINEiacs (QMJHL)
2007 Entry	66	3	Garrett Klotz	L	Saskatoon Blades (WHL)
2006 Entry	22	1	Claude Giroux	R	Gatineau Olympiques (QMJHL)
2006 Entry	39	2	Andreas Nodl	R	Sioux Falls Stampede (USHL)
2006 Entry	42	2	Mike Ratchuk	D	US National Under 18 Team

Shootout Record

GP	W	L	G	S	S%	GA	SA	Sv%
9	3	6	10	25	40	13	23	44

Team Leaders

	G			A			P
Vaclav Prospal	33	Mike Richards	47	Mike Richards	75
Daniel Briere	31	Daniel Briere	41	Daniel Briere	72
Mike Knuble	29	Vaclav Prospal	38	Vaclav Prospal	71
Jeff Carter	29	R.J. Umberger	37	Mike Knuble	55
Mike Richards	28	Kimmo Timonen	36	Jeff Carter	53

	PIM			Hits			+/-
Riley Cote	202	Jason Smith	142	Braydon Coburn	17
Scott Hartnell	159	Scott Hartnell	110	Mike Richards	14
Jason Smith	86	Mike Richards	110	Randy Jones	8
Mike Richards	76	Derian Hatcher	106	Jeff Carter	6
2 tied with	74	Scottie Upshall	86	Stefan Ruzicka	5

	PPG			SHG			Sht
Mike Knuble	15	Mike Richards	5	Jeff Carter	260
Daniel Briere	14	Jeff Carter	2	Vaclav Prospal	215
Vaclav Prospal	10	6 tied with	1	Mike Richards	212
Scott Hartnell	10			Daniel Briere	182
Mike Richards	8			Mike Knuble	177

Goalies	GP	W	GAA	Sv%	SO
Martin Biron	62	30	2.59	0.918	5
Antero Niittymaki	28	12	2.91	0.907	1

Roster

Player	#	Pos	DOB	Hometown	S/P	Ctry	Ht	Wt	S
Briere, Daniel	48	C	Oct 06 '77	Gatineau	QC	CAN	70	179	R
Carter, Jeff	17	C	Jan 01 '85	London	ON	CAN	75	200	R
Dowd, James	34	C	Dec 25 '68	Brick	NJ	USA	72	180	R
Potulny, Ryan	11	C	Sep 05 '84	Grand Forks	ND	USA	72	192	L
Richards, Mike	18	C	Feb 11 '85	Kenora	ON	CAN	71	195	L
Umberger, R.J.	20	C	May 03 '82	Pittsburgh	PA	USA	74	200	L
Coburn, Braydon	5	D	Feb 27 '85	Calgary	AB	CAN	77	220	L
Fitzpatrick, Rory	8	D	Jan 11 '75	Rochester	NY	USA	74	210	R
Guenin, Nathan	29	D	Dec 10 '82	Sewickley	PA	USA	74	210	R
Hatcher, Derian	2	D	Jun 04 '72	Sterling Heights	MI	USA	77	235	L
Jones, Randy	6	D	Jul 23 '81	Quispamsis	NB	CAN	74	200	L
Kukkonen, Lasse	28	D	Sep 18 '81	Oulu		FIN	73	190	L
Modry, Jaroslav	26	D	Feb 27 '71	Ceske-Budejovice		CZE	74	220	L
Parent, Ryan	77	D	Mar 17 '87	Prince Albert	SK	CAN	74	205	L
Smith, Jason	21	D	Nov 02 '73	Calgary	AB	CAN	75	215	R
Timonen, Kimmo	44	D	Mar 18 '75	Kuopio		FIN	70	194	L
Cote, Riley	32	L	Mar 16 '82	Winnipeg	MB	CAN	73	210	L
Gagne, Simon	12	L	Feb 29 '80	Ste. Foy	QC	CAN	72	195	L
Greentree, Kyle	65	L	Nov 15 '83	Victoria	BC	CAN	75	215	L
Hartnell, Scott	19	L	Apr 18 '82	Regina	SK	CAN	74	210	L
Prospal, Vaclav	40	L	Feb 17 '75	Ceske Budejovice		CZE	74	198	L
Thoresen, Patrick	25	L	Nov 07 '83	Oslo		NOR	71	188	L
Boulerice, Jesse	36	R	Aug 10 '78	Plattsburgh	NY	USA	74	215	R
Downie, Steve	27	R	Apr 03 '87	Newmarket	ON	CAN	71	200	R
Giroux, Claude	56	R	Jan 12 '88	Hearst	ON	CAN	71	172	R
Kapanen, Sami	24	R	Jun 14 '73	Vantaa		FIN	70	185	L
Knuble, Mike	22	R	Jul 04 '72	Toronto	ON	CAN	75	230	R
Lupul, Joffrey	15	R	Sep 23 '83	Fort Saskatchewan	AB	CAN	73	205	R
Ruzicka, Stefan	14	R	Feb 17 '85	Nitra		SVK	72	200	R
Tolpeko, Denis	53	R	Jan 29 '85	Moscow		RUS	73	190	L
Upshall, Scottie	9	R	Oct 07 '83	Fort McMurray	AB	CAN	72	197	L

Goalies	#	Pos	DOB	Hometown	S/P	Ctry	Ht	Wt	C
Biron, Martin	43	G	Aug 15 '77	Lac St. Charles	QC	CAN	75	163	L
Niittymaki, Antero	30	G	Jun 18 '80	Turku		FIN	73	215	L

Regular Season Schedule

October 2008	Visitor	Home
Sat Oct 11, 2008	Rangers	Flyers
Mon Oct 13, 2008	Canadiens	Flyers
Tue Oct 14, 2008	Flyers	Penguins
Thu Oct 16, 2008	Flyers	Avalanche
Sat Oct 18, 2008	Flyers	Sharks
Wed Oct 22, 2008	Sharks	Flyers
Fri Oct 24, 2008	Flyers	Devils
Sat Oct 25, 2008	Devils	Flyers
Tue Oct 28, 2008	Flyers	Thrashers
Thu Oct 30, 2008	Islanders	Flyers

November 2008	Visitor	Home
Sun Nov 2, 2008	Oilers	Flyers
Thu Nov 6, 2008	Flyers	Senators
Sat Nov 8, 2008	Lightning	Flyers
Tue Nov 11, 2008	Flyers	Islanders
Thu Nov 13, 2008	Flyers	Penguins
Sat Nov 15, 2008	Flyers	Canadiens
Sun Nov 16, 2008	Thrashers	Flyers
Fri Nov 21, 2008	Flyers	Sabres
Sat Nov 22, 2008	Coyotes	Flyers
Mon Nov 24, 2008	Stars	Flyers
Wed Nov 26, 2008	Flyers	Hurricanes
Fri Nov 28, 2008	Hurricanes	Flyers
Sat Nov 29, 2008	Flyers	Maple Leafs

December 2008	Visitor	Home
Tue Dec 2, 2008	Lightning	Flyers
Thu Dec 4, 2008	Devils	Flyers
Sat Dec 6, 2008	Flyers	Hurricanes
Tue Dec 9, 2008	Islanders	Flyers
Thu Dec 11, 2008	Hurricanes	Flyers
Sat Dec 13, 2008	Penguins	Flyers
Tue Dec 16, 2008	Avalanche	Flyers
Thu Dec 18, 2008	Flyers	Canadiens
Sat Dec 20, 2008	Capitals	Flyers
Sun Dec 21, 2008	Flyers	Devils
Tue Dec 23, 2008	Senators	Flyers
Fri Dec 26, 2008	Flyers	Blackhawks
Sat Dec 27, 2008	Flyers	Blue Jackets
Tue Dec 30, 2008	Flyers	Canucks

January 2009	Visitor	Home
Fri Jan 2, 2009	Flyers	Ducks
Sat Jan 3, 2009	Flyers	Kings
Tue Jan 6, 2009	Flyers	Capitals
Thu Jan 8, 2009	Wild	Flyers
Sat Jan 10, 2009	Maple Leafs	Flyers

January 2009, cont.	Visitor	Home
Tue Jan 13, 2009	Penguins	Flyers
Thu Jan 15, 2009	Flyers	Lightning
Fri Jan 16, 2009	Flyers	Panthers
Wed Jan 21, 2009	Thrashers	Flyers
Tue Jan 27, 2009	Flyers	Panthers
Fri Jan 30, 2009	Flyers	Lightning
Sat Jan 31, 2009	Flyers	Blues

February 2009	Visitor	Home
Wed Feb 4, 2009	Bruins	Flyers
Sat Feb 7, 2009	Flyers	Bruins
Sun Feb 8, 2009	Flyers	Thrashers
Thu Feb 12, 2009	Senators	Flyers
Sat Feb 14, 2009	Islanders	Flyers
Sun Feb 15, 2009	Flyers	Rangers
Thu Feb 19, 2009	Sabres	Flyers
Sat Feb 21, 2009	Penguins	Flyers
Tue Feb 24, 2009	Flyers	Capitals
Wed Feb 25, 2009	Kings	Flyers
Fri Feb 27, 2009	Canadiens	Flyers

March 2009	Visitor	Home
Sun Mar 1, 2009	Flyers	Devils
Tue Mar 3, 2009	Flyers	Bruins
Thu Mar 5, 2009	Flames	Flyers
Sat Mar 7, 2009	Predators	Flyers
Tue Mar 10, 2009	Sabres	Flyers
Thu Mar 12, 2009	Capitals	Flyers
Sat Mar 14, 2009	Rangers	Flyers
Sun Mar 15, 2009	Flyers	Rangers
Tue Mar 17, 2009	Flyers	Red Wings
Fri Mar 20, 2009	Flyers	Sabres
Sun Mar 22, 2009	Flyers	Penguins
Mon Mar 23, 2009	Devils	Flyers
Thu Mar 26, 2009	Panthers	Flyers
Sat Mar 28, 2009	Flyers	Islanders
Sun Mar 29, 2009	Bruins	Flyers

April 2009	Visitor	Home
Wed Apr 1, 2009	Flyers	Maple Leafs
Fri Apr 3, 2009	Maple Leafs	Flyers
Sat Apr 4, 2009	Flyers	Senators
Tue Apr 7, 2009	Panthers	Flyers
Thu Apr 9, 2009	Flyers	Rangers
Sat Apr 11, 2009	Flyers	Islanders
Sun Apr 12, 2009	Rangers	Flyers

97

Phoenix Coyotes

Co-owned and coached by The Great One, Wayne Gretzky, The Phoenix Coyotes are based in Glendale, Arizona, and became the Coyotes in 1996. Previously the WHA's and the NHL's Winnipeg Jets (1972–79 and 1979–96, respectively), the Coyotes have made the playoffs every year except one since '96. The one year they didn't make it, the Coyotes became the first team in NHL history to post 90 points in regular-season play, yet still miss the playoffs. Bobby Hull, who played for the Jets from 1972–80, had his #9 jersey retired in 1989, but it was briefly taken out of retirement at Hull's request for his son Brett in the 2005–06 season. Brett retired himself five games into that same season, but Bobby's #9 still hangs in the Coyotes' arena, Jobing.com Arena, in the Winnipeg Jets colors of blue, white and red.

Owners	General Manager	Coach
Jerry Moyes Wayne Gretzky	Don Maloney	Wayne Gretzky

2008 Record and Rankings

38-37-7, 4th in Pacific Division

	Points	GF/G	GA/G	S/G	SA/G	PP %	PK %	PIM/G
	83	2.55	2.74	30.5	30.7	18.6	80.7	14.5
NHL Rank	24	21	17	7	23	11	24	24

Recent Top Draft Picks

Draft	Num.	Round	Player	Pos	Drafted From
2008 Entry	8	1	Mikkel Boedker	L	Kitchener Rangers (OHL)
2008 Entry	28	1	Viktor Tikhonov	W	Cherepovets Severstal (Russia)
2008 Entry	49	2	Jared Staal	R	Sudbury Wolves (OHL)
2007 Entry	3	1	Kyle Turris	C	Burnaby Express (BCHL)
2007 Entry	30	1	Nick Ross	D	Regina Pats (WHL)
2007 Entry	32	2	Brett MacLean	L	Oshawa Generals (OHL)
2006 Entry	8	1	Peter Mueller	C	Everett Silvertips (WHL)
2006 Entry	29	1	Chris Summers	D	US National Under 18 Team
2006 Entry	88	3	Jonas Ahnelov	D	Vastra Frolunda HC Goteborg (SEL)

Shootout Record

GP	W	L	G	S	S%	GA	SA	Sv%
11	5	6	12	39	31	12	42	71

Team Leaders

	G			A			P	
Shane Doan	28		Shane Doan	50		Shane Doan	78	
Radim Vrbata	27		Ed Jovanovski	39		Radim Vrbata	56	
Peter Mueller	22		Peter Mueller	32		Peter Mueller	54	
Steven Reinprecht	16		Steven Reinprecht	30		Ed Jovanovski	51	
Daniel Carcillo	13		Radim Vrbata	29		Steven Reinprecht	46	

	PIM			Hits			+/-	
Daniel Carcillo	324		Keith Ballard	169		Zbynek Michalek	9	
Nick Boynton	125		Shane Doan	158		Derek Morris	8	
Keith Ballard	85		Craig Weller	123		Keith Ballard	7	
Derek Morris	83		Ed Jovanovski	114		Radim Vrbata	6	
Craig Weller	80		Daniel Carcillo	109		Shane Doan	4	

	PPG			SHG			Sht	
Shane Doan	9		Radim Vrbata	3		Radim Vrbata	246	
Ed Jovanovski	8		Shane Doan	2		Shane Doan	243	
Peter Mueller	7		4 tied with	1		Ed Jovanovski	240	
Radim Vrbata	7					Peter Mueller	201	
2 tied with	5					Derek Morris	135	

Goalies	GP	W	GAA	Sv%	SO
Ilja Bryzgalov	64	28	2.44	0.920	3
Mikael Tellqvist	22	9	2.75	0.908	2
David Aebischer	1	0	3.00	0.909	0

Roster

Player	#	Pos	DOB	Hometown	S/P	Ctry	Ht	Wt	S
Hanzal, Martin	11	C	Feb 20 '87	Pisek		CZE	77	208	L
Kapanen, Niko	39	C	Apr 29 '78	Hameenlinna		FIN	68	180	L
Mueller, Peter	88	C	Apr 14 '88	Bloomington	MN	USA	74	205	R
Perrault, Joel	26	C	Apr 06 '83	Montreal	QC	CAN	73	197	R
Reinprecht, Steven	28	C	May 07 '76	Edmonton	AB	CAN	72	191	L
Turris, Kyle	91	C	Aug 14 '89	New Westminster	BC	CAN	73	180	R
Zigomanis, Michael	15	C	Jan 17 '81	Toronto	ON	CAN	72	200	R
Ballard, Keith	2	D	Nov 26 '82	Baudette	MN	USA	71	208	L
Bell, Brendan	6	D	Mar 31 '83	Ottawa	ON	CAN	73	205	L
Boynton, Nick	44	D	Jan 14 '79	Nobleton	ON	CAN	74	210	R
Caldwell, Ryan	29	D	Jun 15 '81	Deloraine	MB	CAN	74	174	L
Jones, Matt	5	D	Aug 08 '83	Downers Grove	IL	USA	72	215	L
Jovanovski, Ed	55	D	Jun 26 '76	Windsor	ON	CAN	74	210	L
Michalek, Zbynek	4	D	Dec 23 '82	Jindrichuv Hradec		CZE	73	200	L
Morris, Derek	53	D	Aug 24 '78	Edmonton	AB	CAN	72	220	R
Yandle, Keith	3	D	Sep 09 '86	Boston	MA	USA	74	195	L
Carcillo, Daniel	13	L	Jan 28 '85	King City	ON	CAN	71	203	L
Gratton, Josh	24	L	Sep 09 '82	Brantford	ON	CAN	74	214	L
Hossa, Marcel	81	L	Oct 12 '81	Ilava		SVK	75	220	L
Murley, Matt	18	L	Dec 17 '79	Troy	NY	USA	74	206	L
Tjarnqvist, Mathias	22	L	Apr 15 '79	Umeaas		SWE	74	196	L
Vandermeer, Pete	75	L	Oct 14 '75	Red Deer	AB	CAN	72	212	L
Winnik, Daniel	34	L	Mar 06 '85	Toronto	ON	CAN	74	210	R
York, Michael	16	L	Jan 03 '78	Waterford	MI	USA	70	185	R
Doan, Shane	19	R	Oct 10 '76	Halkirk	AB	CAN	74	216	R
Lisin, Enver	18	R	Apr 22 '86	Moscow		RUS	74	190	L
Thomas, William	21	R	Jun 20 '83	Pittsburgh	PA	USA	73	185	R
Vrbata, Radim	17	R	Jun 13 '81	Mlada Boleslav		CZE	73	190	R
Weller, Craig	12	R	Mar 17 '81	Calgary	AB	CAN	76	220	R

Goalies	#	Pos	DOB	Hometown	S/P	Ctry	Ht	Wt	C
Aebischer, David	1	G	Feb 07 '78	Fribourg		CHE	73	187	L
Bryzgalov, Ilja	30	G	Jun 22 '80	Togliatti		RUS	75	210	L
Tellqvist, Mikael	32	G	Sep 19 '79	Sundbyberg		SWE	71	185	L

Regular Season Schedule

October 2008	Visitor	Home
Sat Oct 11, 2008	Blue Jackets	Coyotes
Sun Oct 12, 2008	Coyotes	Ducks
Wed Oct 15, 2008	Coyotes	Blackhawks
Fri Oct 17, 2008	Coyotes	Senators
Sat Oct 18, 2008	Coyotes	Canadiens
Thu Oct 23, 2008	Capitals	Coyotes
Sat Oct 25, 2008	Flames	Coyotes
Thu Oct 30, 2008	Penguins	Coyotes

November 2008	Visitor	Home
Sat Nov 1, 2008	Wild	Coyotes
Tue Nov 4, 2008	Coyotes	Flames
Thu Nov 6, 2008	Coyotes	Canucks
Sat Nov 8, 2008	Panthers	Coyotes
Sun Nov 9, 2008	Sharks	Coyotes
Wed Nov 12, 2008	Coyotes	Blue Jackets
Thu Nov 13, 2008	Coyotes	Wild
Sat Nov 15, 2008	Stars	Coyotes
Tue Nov 18, 2008	Blackhawks	Coyotes
Fri Nov 21, 2008	Coyotes	Hurricanes
Sat Nov 22, 2008	Coyotes	Flyers
Mon Nov 24, 2008	Coyotes	Rangers
Wed Nov 26, 2008	Coyotes	Blue Jackets
Fri Nov 28, 2008	Avalanche	Coyotes
Sat Nov 29, 2008	Sharks	Coyotes

December 2008	Visitor	Home
Tue Dec 2, 2008	Kings	Coyotes
Thu Dec 4, 2008	Maple Leafs	Coyotes
Sat Dec 6, 2008	Coyotes	Blues
Sun Dec 7, 2008	Coyotes	Blackhawks
Wed Dec 10, 2008	Coyotes	Stars
Thu Dec 11, 2008	Wild	Coyotes
Sat Dec 13, 2008	Red Wings	Coyotes
Tue Dec 16, 2008	Coyotes	Stars
Thu Dec 18, 2008	Predators	Coyotes
Sat Dec 20, 2008	Blue Jackets	Coyotes
Mon Dec 22, 2008	Coyotes	Oilers
Tue Dec 23, 2008	Coyotes	Avalanche
Fri Dec 26, 2008	Coyotes	Kings
Sat Dec 27, 2008	Kings	Coyotes
Wed Dec 31, 2008	Avalanche	Coyotes

January 2009	Visitor	Home
Fri Jan 2, 2009	Islanders	Coyotes
Sun Jan 4, 2009	Coyotes	Ducks
Tue Jan 6, 2009	Blackhawks	Coyotes
Thu Jan 8, 2009	Lightning	Coyotes

January 2009, cont.	Visitor	Home
Sat Jan 10, 2009	Stars	Coyotes
Tue Jan 13, 2009	Coyotes	Wild
Thu Jan 15, 2009	Coyotes	Canucks
Sat Jan 17, 2009	Coyotes	Flames
Sun Jan 18, 2009	Coyotes	Oilers
Tue Jan 20, 2009	Red Wings	Coyotes
Tue Jan 27, 2009	Ducks	Coyotes
Thu Jan 29, 2009	Coyotes	Sharks
Sat Jan 31, 2009	Sabres	Coyotes

February 2009	Visitor	Home
Tue Feb 3, 2009	Coyotes	Predators
Wed Feb 4, 2009	Coyotes	Red Wings
Sat Feb 7, 2009	Hurricanes	Coyotes
Wed Feb 11, 2009	Coyotes	Stars
Thu Feb 12, 2009	Canucks	Coyotes
Sat Feb 14, 2009	Flames	Coyotes
Mon Feb 16, 2009	Oilers	Coyotes
Thu Feb 19, 2009	Thrashers	Coyotes
Sat Feb 21, 2009	Coyotes	Kings
Tue Feb 24, 2009	Coyotes	Blues
Thu Feb 26, 2009	Coyotes	Predators
Sat Feb 28, 2009	Blues	Coyotes

March 2009	Visitor	Home
Thu Mar 5, 2009	Coyotes	Bruins
Fri Mar 6, 2009	Coyotes	Sabres
Sun Mar 8, 2009	Coyotes	Islanders
Tue Mar 10, 2009	Coyotes	Red Wings
Thu Mar 12, 2009	Coyotes	Devils
Sat Mar 14, 2009	Predators	Coyotes
Tue Mar 17, 2009	Sharks	Coyotes
Thu Mar 19, 2009	Ducks	Coyotes
Sat Mar 21, 2009	Canucks	Coyotes
Sun Mar 22, 2009	Coyotes	Ducks
Thu Mar 26, 2009	Oilers	Coyotes
Sat Mar 28, 2009	Coyotes	Sharks
Mon Mar 30, 2009	Stars	Coyotes

April 2009	Visitor	Home
Wed Apr 1, 2009	Coyotes	Avalanche
Thu Apr 2, 2009	Kings	Coyotes
Sat Apr 4, 2009	Coyotes	Kings
Tue Apr 7, 2009	Blues	Coyotes
Thu Apr 9, 2009	Coyotes	Sharks
Sat Apr 11, 2009	Ducks	Coyotes

Pittsburgh Penguins

Home team through many seasons in the 1980s, 1990s and new millennium to former player and current co-owner Mario Lemieux, the Penguins are based in Pittsburgh, Pennsylvania, and were founded in 1967. Young hockey phenom Sidney Crosby has been playing in Pittsburgh since 2005 and was awarded the title of captain in the 2007–08 season, making him the youngest full team captain in NHL history at 19 years old. Crosby led his team into the 2008 Stanley Cup finals against the Detroit Red Wings, but the Penguins couldn't rally and lost the series in six games, finishing the playoffs with a 14–6 record. Fans of the Penguins might be interested to know that their team's name comes from the fact that the team was originally set to play in the "Igloo", the nickname of the Pittsburgh Civic Arena. They never did play there, however, and have called the Mellon Arena home ice since their first season. And, as forecasted this year, the Penguins will play their first home game off the Mellon Arena ice in the 2010–11 season when a newly approved rink opens overlooking downtown Pittsburgh.

Owners	General Manager	Coach
Mario Lemieux Ron Burkle	Ray Shero	Michel Therrien

2008 Record and Rankings

47-27-8, 1st in Atlantic Division

	Points	GF/G	GA/G	S/G	SA/G	PP %	PK %	PIM/G
	102	2.93	2.58	27.7	30.8	20.4	81.0	14.4
NHL Rank	5	7	10	23	24	4	23	22

Recent Top Draft Picks

Draft	Num.	Round	Player	Pos	Drafted From
2008 Entry	120	4	Nathan Moon	C	Kingston Frontenacs (OHL)
2008 Entry	150	5	Alexander Pechurski	G	Magnitogorsk Jr. (Russia)
2008 Entry	180	6	Patrick Killeen	G	Brampton Battalion (OHL)
2007 Entry	20	1	Angelo Esposito	C	Quebec Remparts (QMJHL)
2007 Entry	51	2	Keven Veilleux	C	Victoriaville Tigres (QMJHL)
2007 Entry	78	3	Robert Bortuzzo	D	Kitchener Rangers (OHL)
2006 Entry	2	1	Jordan Staal	C	Peterborough Petes (OHL)
2006 Entry	32	2	Carl Sneep	D	Brainerd H.S. (Minn.)
2006 Entry	65	3	Brian Strait	D	US National Under 18 Team

Shootout Record

GP	W	L	G	S	S%	GA	SA	Sv%
11	7	4	17	44	39	13	44	71

Team Leaders

	G		A		P
Evgeni Malkin	47	Evgeni Malkin	59	Evgeni Malkin	106
Marian Hossa	29	Sergei Gonchar	53	Sidney Crosby	72
Petr Sykora	28	Sidney Crosby	48	Marian Hossa	66
Ryan Malone	27	Marian Hossa	37	Sergei Gonchar	65
Sidney Crosby	24	Petr Sykora	35	Petr Sykora	63

	PIM		Hits		+/-
Georges Laraque	141	Brooks Orpik	239	Sidney Crosby	18
Jarkko Ruutu	138	Ryan Malone	138	Evgeni Malkin	16
Ryan Malone	103	Jarkko Ruutu	134	Ryan Malone	14
Evgeni Malkin	78	Hal Gill	127	Sergei Gonchar	13
Hal Gill	68	Georges Laraque	87	Brooks Orpik	11

	PPG		SHG		Sht
Evgeni Malkin	17	Pascal Dupuis	3	Evgeni Malkin	272
Petr Sykora	15	Ryan Malone	2	Marian Hossa	264
Ryan Malone	11	Maxime Talbot	2	Petr Sykora	201
Marian Hossa	8	Marian Hossa	2	Jordan Staal	183
Sergei Gonchar	8	2 tied with	1	2 tied with	173

Goalies	GP	W	GAA	Sv%	SO
Marc-Andre Fleury	35	19	2.33	0.921	4
Ty Conklin	33	18	2.51	0.923	2
Dany Sabourin	24	10	2.75	0.904	2

Roster

Player	#	Pos	DOB	Hometown	S/P	Ctry	Ht	Wt	S
Beech, Kris	24	C	Feb 05 '81	Salmon Arm	BC	CAN	75	211	L
Brent, Tim	47	C	Mar 10 '84	Cambridge	ON	CAN	72	188	R
Crosby, Sidney	87	C	Aug 07 '87	Cole Harbour	NS	CAN	71	200	L
Kennedy, Tyler	48	C	Jul 15 '86	Sault Ste. Marie	ON	CAN	71	183	R
Malkin, Evgeni	71	C	Jul 31 '86	Magnitogorsk		RUS	75	195	L
Smith, Nathan	41	C	Feb 09 '82	Edmonton	AB	CAN	74	206	L
Staal, Jordan	11	C	Sep 10 '88	Thunder Bay	ON	CAN	76	220	L
Stone, Ryan	33	C	Mar 20 '85	Calgary	AB	CAN	74	207	L
Talbot, Maxime	25	C	Feb 11 '84	Lemoyne	QC	CAN	71	190	L
Eaton, Mark	3	D	May 06 '77	Wilmington	DE	USA	74	204	L
Gill, Hal	2	D	Apr 06 '75	Concord	MA	USA	79	250	L
Goligoski, Alex	67	D	Jul 30 '85	Grand Rapids	MN	USA	71	180	R
Gonchar, Sergei	55	D	Apr 13 '74	Chelyabinsk		RUS	74	211	L
Letang, Kristopher	58	D	Apr 24 '87	Montreal	QC	CAN	72	201	R
Nasreddine, Alain	32	D	Jul 10 '75	Montreal	QC	CAN	73	204	L
Orpik, Brooks	44	D	Sep 26 '80	San Francisco	CA	USA	74	219	L
Scuderi, Rob	4	D	Dec 30 '78	Syosset	NY	USA	72	218	L
Sydor, Darryl	5	D	May 13 '72	Edmonton	AB	CAN	73	211	L
Whitney, Ryan	19	D	Feb 19 '83	Boston	MA	USA	76	219	L
James, Connor	36	L	Aug 25 '82	Calgary	AB	CAN	70	180	R
Malone, Ryan	12	L	Dec 01 '79	Pittsburgh	PA	USA	76	224	L
Minard, Christopher	39	L	Nov 18 '81	Owen Sound	ON	CAN	73	190	L
Roberts, Gary	10	L	May 23 '66	North York	ON	CAN	74	215	L
Ruutu, Jarkko	37	L	Aug 23 '75	Helsinki		FIN	73	200	L
Taffe, Jeff	38	L	Feb 19 '81	Hastings	MN	USA	75	207	L
Dupuis, Pascal	9	R	Apr 07 '79	Laval	QC	CAN	73	205	L
Filewich, Jonathan	34	R	Oct 02 '84	Kelowna	BC	CAN	74	208	R
Hall, Adam	28	R	Aug 14 '80	Kalamazoo	MI	USA	75	206	R
Hossa, Marian	18	R	Jan 12 '79	Stara Lubovna		SVK	73	210	L
Laraque, Georges	17	R	Dec 07 '76	Montreal	QC	CAN	75	243	R
Sykora, Petr	17	R	Nov 19 '76	Plzen		CZE	72	190	L

Goalies	#	Pos	DOB	Hometown	S/P	Ctry	Ht	Wt	C
Conklin, Ty	35	G	Mar 30 '76	Anchorage	AK	USA	72	184	L
Fleury, Marc-Andre	29	G	Nov 28 '84	Sorel	QC	CAN	74	180	L
Sabourin, Dany	30	G	Sep 02 '80	Val D'or	QC	CAN	76	200	L

Regular Season Schedule

October 2008	Visitor	Home
Sat Oct 4, 2008	Penguins	Senators (Stockholm, SWE)
Sun Oct 5, 2008	Senators	Penguins (Stockholm, SWE)
Sat Oct 11, 2008	Devils	Penguins
Tue Oct 14, 2008	Flyers	Penguins
Thu Oct 16, 2008	Capitals	Penguins
Sat Oct 18, 2008	Maple Leafs	Penguins
Mon Oct 20, 2008	Penguins	Bruins
Thu Oct 23, 2008	Hurricanes	Penguins
Sat Oct 25, 2008	Penguins	Rangers
Tue Oct 28, 2008	Penguins	Sharks
Thu Oct 30, 2008	Penguins	Coyotes

November 2008	Visitor	Home
Sat Nov 1, 2008	Penguins	Blues
Thu Nov 6, 2008	Oilers	Penguins
Sat Nov 8, 2008	Penguins	Islanders
Tue Nov 11, 2008	Penguins	Red Wings
Thu Nov 13, 2008	Flyers	Penguins
Sat Nov 15, 2008	Sabres	Penguins
Tue Nov 18, 2008	Wild	Penguins
Thu Nov 20, 2008	Penguins	Thrashers
Sat Nov 22, 2008	Canucks	Penguins
Wed Nov 26, 2008	Penguins	Islanders
Fri Nov 28, 2008	Penguins	Sabres
Sat Nov 29, 2008	Devils	Penguins

December 2008	Visitor	Home
Wed Dec 3, 2008	Penguins	Rangers
Thu Dec 4, 2008	Penguins	Hurricanes
Sat Dec 6, 2008	Penguins	Senators
Mon Dec 8, 2008	Sabres	Penguins
Wed Dec 10, 2008	Penguins	Devils
Thu Dec 11, 2008	Islanders	Penguins
Sat Dec 13, 2008	Penguins	Flyers
Thu Dec 18, 2008	Penguins	Thrashers
Sat Dec 20, 2008	Maple Leafs	Penguins
Mon Dec 22, 2008	Penguins	Sabres
Tue Dec 23, 2008	Lightning	Penguins
Fri Dec 26, 2008	Penguins	Devils
Sat Dec 27, 2008	Canadiens	Penguins
Tue Dec 30, 2008	Bruins	Penguins

January 2009	Visitor	Home
Thu Jan 1, 2009	Penguins	Bruins
Sat Jan 3, 2009	Panthers	Penguins
Mon Jan 5, 2009	Penguins	Rangers

January 2009, cont.	Visitor	Home
Tue Jan 6, 2009	Thrashers	Penguins
Thu Jan 8, 2009	Penguins	Predators
Sat Jan 10, 2009	Penguins	Avalanche
Tue Jan 13, 2009	Penguins	Flyers
Wed Jan 14, 2009	Capitals	Penguins
Fri Jan 16, 2009	Ducks	Penguins
Sun Jan 18, 2009	Rangers	Penguins
Tue Jan 20, 2009	Hurricanes	Penguins
Wed Jan 28, 2009	Rangers	Penguins
Fri Jan 30, 2009	Penguins	Devils
Sat Jan 31, 2009	Penguins	Maple Leafs

February 2009	Visitor	Home
Tue Feb 3, 2009	Penguins	Canadiens
Wed Feb 4, 2009	Lightning	Penguins
Fri Feb 6, 2009	Blue Jackets	Penguins
Sun Feb 8, 2009	Red Wings	Penguins
Wed Feb 11, 2009	Sharks	Penguins
Sat Feb 14, 2009	Penguins	Maple Leafs
Mon Feb 16, 2009	Penguins	Islanders
Thu Feb 19, 2009	Canadiens	Penguins
Sat Feb 21, 2009	Penguins	Flyers
Sun Feb 22, 2009	Penguins	Capitals
Wed Feb 25, 2009	Islanders	Penguins
Fri Feb 27, 2009	Penguins	Blackhawks

March 2009	Visitor	Home
Sun Mar 1, 2009	Penguins	Stars
Tue Mar 3, 2009	Penguins	Lightning
Thu Mar 5, 2009	Penguins	Panthers
Sun Mar 8, 2009	Penguins	Capitals
Tue Mar 10, 2009	Panthers	Penguins
Thu Mar 12, 2009	Penguins	Blue Jackets
Sat Mar 14, 2009	Senators	Penguins
Sun Mar 15, 2009	Bruins	Penguins
Tue Mar 17, 2009	Thrashers	Penguins
Fri Mar 20, 2009	Kings	Penguins
Sun Mar 22, 2009	Flyers	Penguins
Wed Mar 25, 2009	Flames	Penguins
Sat Mar 28, 2009	Rangers	Penguins

April 2009	Visitor	Home
Wed Apr 1, 2009	Devils	Penguins
Sat Apr 4, 2009	Penguins	Hurricanes
Sun Apr 5, 2009	Penguins	Panthers
Tue Apr 7, 2009	Penguins	Lightning
Thu Apr 9, 2009	Islanders	Penguins
Sat Apr 11, 2009	Penguins	Canadiens

San Jose Sharks

The San Jose Sharks, three-time division champions (2002, 2004 and 2008), have yet to win a Stanley Cup, but proved themselves to be a team with heart in the recent NHL season. Fans in San Jose, California, saw the Sharks go an entire month without a loss, as well as capture their 2008 division title with 108 points, both a franchise record and a total that placed the team second in the league behind the Detroit Red Wings. San Jose eventually lost in Game 6 to the Dallas Stars in the Western Conference semifinals, a game that went into four overtime periods, marking it as the longest game in Sharks' history. Founded in 1991, San Jose plays in the HP Pavilion, otherwise known as the "The Shark Tank."

Owner	General Manager	Coach
San Jose Sports & Entertainment Enterprises	Doug Wilson	Todd McLellean

2008 Record and Rankings

49-23-10, 1st in Pacific Division

	Points	GF/G	GA/G	S/G	SA/G	PP %	PK %	PIM/G
	108	2.63	2.28	29.6	24.2	18.7	85.8	13.1
NHL Rank	2	19	3	11	2	10	1	12

Recent Top Draft Picks

Draft	Num.	Round	Player	Pos	Drafted From
2008 Entry	62	3	Justin Daniels	C	Kent High School (Conn)
2008 Entry	92	4	Samuel Groulx	D	Quebec Ramparts (QMJHL)
2008 Entry	106	4	Harri Sateri	G	Tappara (Finland Jr.)
2007 Entry	9	1	Logan Couture	C	Ottawa 67's (OHL)
2007 Entry	28	1	Nick Petrecki	D	Omaha Lancers (USHL)
2007 Entry	83	3	Timo Peilmeier	G	Kolner Haie (DEL)
2006 Entry	16	1	Ty Wishart	D	Prince George Cougars (WHL)
2006 Entry	36	2	Jamie McGinn	C	Ottawa 67's (OHL)
2006 Entry	98	4	James Delory	D	Oshawa Generals (OHL)

Shootout Record

GP	W	L	G	S	S%	GA	SA	Sv%
12	6	6	18	41	44	18	40	55

Team Leaders

	G		A		P
Joe Thornton	29	Joe Thornton	67	Joe Thornton	96
Milan Michalek	24	Brian Campbell	54	Brian Campbell	62
Jonathan Cheechoo	23	Milan Michalek	31	Milan Michalek	55
Patrick Marleau	19	Craig Rivet	30	Patrick Marleau	48
Joe Pavelski	19	Patrick Marleau	29	Joe Pavelski	40

	PIM		Hits		+/-
Jody Shelley	135	Kyle McLaren	127	Douglas Murray	20
Craig Rivet	104	Douglas Murray	127	Milan Michalek	19
Douglas Murray	98	Jonathan Cheechoo	123	Joe Thornton	18
Kyle McLaren	84	Mike Grier	119	Jonathan Cheechoo	11
Christian Ehrhoff	72	Torrey Mitchell	113	Christian Ehrhoff	9

	PPG		SHG		Sht
Joe Thornton	11	Mike Grier	3	Milan Michalek	233
Jonathan Cheechoo	10	Torrey Mitchell	2	Jonathan Cheechoo	220
Joe Pavelski	8	Joe Pavelski	1	Joe Pavelski	207
Patrick Marleau	7	Milan Michalek	1	Patrick Marleau	185
Jeremy Roenick	7			Joe Thornton	178

Goalies	GP	W	GAA	Sv%	SO
Evgeni Nabokov	77	46	2.14	0.910	6
Brian Boucher	5	3	1.76	0.932	1
Thomas Greiss	3	0	3.26	0.860	0
Dimitri Patzold	3	0	5.45	0.800	0

Roster

Player	#	Pos	DOB	Hometown	S/P	Ctry	Ht	Wt	S
Brown, Curtis	37	C	Feb 12 '76	Unity	SK	CAN	72	200	L
Goc, Marcel	11	C	Aug 24 '83	Calw		DEU	73	200	L
Iggulden, Mike	46	C	Nov 09 '82	St. Catharines	ON	CAN	75	215	R
Marleau, Patrick	12	C	Sep 15 '79	Aneroid	SK	CAN	74	220	L
Mitchell, Torrey	17	C	Jan 30 '85	Greenfield Park	QC	CAN	71	190	L
Pavelski, Joe	8	C	Jul 11 '84	Stevens Point	WI	USA	71	195	R
Plihal, Tomas	39	C	Mar 28 '83	Frydlant		CZE	73	200	L
Roenick, Jeremy	27	C	Jan 17 '70	Boston	MA	USA	73	205	R
Thornton, Joe	19	C	Jul 02 '79	London	ON	CAN	76	235	L
Campbell, Brian	51	D	May 23 '79	Strathroy	ON	CAN	72	191	L
Carle, Matthew	18	D	Sep 25 '84	Anchorage	AK	USA	72	205	L
Ehrhoff, Christian	10	D	Jul 06 '82	Moers		DEU	74	205	L
McLaren, Kyle	4	D	Jun 18 '77	Coaldale	AB	CAN	76	235	L
Murray, Douglas	3	D	Mar 12 '80	Bromma		SWE	75	240	L
Ozolinsh, Sandis	24	D	Aug 03 '72	Riga		LVA	75	215	L
Rivet, Craig	52	D	Sep 13 '74	North Bay	ON	CAN	74	210	R
Semenov, Alexei	21	D	Apr 10 '81	Murmansk		RUS	78	235	L
Vlasic, Marc-Edouard	44	D	Mar 30 '87	Montreal	QC	CAN	73	200	L
Clowe, Ryane	29	L	Sep 30 '82	Fermeuse	NL	CAN	74	225	R
Kaspar, Lukas	43	L	Sep 23 '85	Most		CZE	74	220	R
Michalek, Milan	9	L	Dec 07 '84	Jindrichuv Hradec		CZE	74	225	L
Rissmiller, Patrick	34	L	Oct 26 '78	Belmont	MA	USA	76	220	L
Shelley, Jody	45	L	Feb 07 '76	Thompson	MB	CAN	76	230	L
Cavanagh, Tom	47	R	Mar 24 '82	Warwick	RI	USA	70	200	L
Cheechoo, Jonathan	14	R	Jul 15 '80	Moose Factory	ON	CAN	73	205	R
Grier, Mike	25	R	Jan 05 '75	Detroit	MI	USA	73	225	R
Setoguchi, Devin	16	R	Jan 01 '87	Taber	AB	CAN	72	205	R

Goalies	#	Pos	DOB	Hometown	S/P	Ctry	Ht	Wt	C
Boucher, Brian	33	G	Jan 02 '77	Woonsocket	RI	USA	74	198	L
Greiss, Thomas	1	G	Jan 29 '86	Koln		DEU	73	200	L
Nabokov, Evgeni	20	G	Jul 25 '75	Kamenogorsk		KAZ	72	200	L
Patzold, Dimitri	30	G	Feb 03 '83	Kamenogorsk		KAZ	72	195	L

Regular Season Schedule

October 2008	Visitor	Home
Thu Oct 9, 2008	Ducks	Sharks
Sat Oct 11, 2008	Kings	Sharks
Sun Oct 12, 2008	Sharks	Kings
Tue Oct 14, 2008	Blue Jackets	Sharks
Fri Oct 17, 2008	Sharks	Ducks
Sat Oct 18, 2008	Flyers	Sharks
Wed Oct 22, 2008	Sharks	Flyers
Fri Oct 24, 2008	Sharks	Panthers
Sat Oct 25, 2008	Sharks	Lightning
Tue Oct 28, 2008	Penguins	Sharks
Thu Oct 30, 2008	Red Wings	Sharks

November 2008	Visitor	Home
Sun Nov 2, 2008	Sharks	Avalanche
Tue Nov 4, 2008	Wild	Sharks
Thu Nov 6, 2008	Blues	Sharks
Sat Nov 8, 2008	Stars	Sharks
Sun Nov 9, 2008	Sharks	Coyotes
Tue Nov 11, 2008	Predators	Sharks
Thu Nov 13, 2008	Flames	Sharks
Sun Nov 16, 2008	Sharks	Blackhawks
Mon Nov 17, 2008	Sharks	Predators
Sat Nov 22, 2008	Capitals	Sharks
Wed Nov 26, 2008	Blackhawks	Sharks
Fri Nov 28, 2008	Sharks	Stars
Sat Nov 29, 2008	Sharks	Coyotes

December 2008	Visitor	Home
Tue Dec 2, 2008	Maple Leafs	Sharks
Thu Dec 4, 2008	Blue Jackets	Sharks
Sat Dec 6, 2008	Oilers	Sharks
Thu Dec 11, 2008	Ducks	Sharks
Sat Dec 13, 2008	Blues	Sharks
Mon Dec 15, 2008	Sharks	Kings
Wed Dec 17, 2008	Sharks	Blue Jackets
Thu Dec 18, 2008	Sharks	Red Wings
Sat Dec 20, 2008	Rangers	Sharks
Tue Dec 23, 2008	Canucks	Sharks
Sat Dec 27, 2008	Sharks	Blues
Mon Dec 29, 2008	Sharks	Stars
Wed Dec 31, 2008	Sharks	Wild

January 2009	Visitor	Home
Sat Jan 3, 2009	Islanders	Sharks
Tue Jan 6, 2009	Sharks	Flames
Fri Jan 9, 2009	Sharks	Oilers
Sat Jan 10, 2009	Sharks	Canucks
Tue Jan 13, 2009	Lightning	Sharks

January 2009, cont.	Visitor	Home
Thu Jan 15, 2009	Flames	Sharks
Sat Jan 17, 2009	Red Wings	Sharks
Tue Jan 20, 2009	Canucks	Sharks
Tue Jan 27, 2009	Sharks	Avalanche
Thu Jan 29, 2009	Coyotes	Sharks
Sat Jan 31, 2009	Blackhawks	Sharks

February 2009	Visitor	Home
Thu Feb 5, 2009	Hurricanes	Sharks
Sat Feb 7, 2009	Sharks	Blue Jackets
Tue Feb 10, 2009	Sharks	Bruins
Wed Feb 11, 2009	Sharks	Penguins
Fri Feb 13, 2009	Sharks	Sabres
Sun Feb 15, 2009	Sharks	Devils
Tue Feb 17, 2009	Oilers	Sharks
Thu Feb 19, 2009	Kings	Sharks
Sat Feb 21, 2009	Thrashers	Sharks
Mon Feb 23, 2009	Sharks	Stars
Wed Feb 25, 2009	Sharks	Red Wings
Thu Feb 26, 2009	Sharks	Senators
Sat Feb 28, 2009	Sharks	Canadiens

March 2009	Visitor	Home
Tue Mar 3, 2009	Stars	Sharks
Thu Mar 5, 2009	Wild	Sharks
Sat Mar 7, 2009	Sharks	Canucks
Tue Mar 10, 2009	Sharks	Wild
Thu Mar 12, 2009	Sharks	Blues
Sat Mar 14, 2009	Kings	Sharks
Sun Mar 15, 2009	Sharks	Ducks
Tue Mar 17, 2009	Sharks	Coyotes
Thu Mar 19, 2009	Predators	Sharks
Sat Mar 21, 2009	Stars	Sharks
Sun Mar 22, 2009	Avalanche	Sharks
Wed Mar 25, 2009	Sharks	Blackhawks
Thu Mar 26, 2009	Sharks	Predators
Sat Mar 28, 2009	Coyotes	Sharks
Mon Mar 30, 2009	Sharks	Flames

April 2009	Visitor	Home
Thu Apr 2, 2009	Sharks	Oilers
Sat Apr 4, 2009	Ducks	Sharks
Sun Apr 5, 2009	Sharks	Ducks
Tue Apr 7, 2009	Avalanche	Sharks
Thu Apr 9, 2009	Coyotes	Sharks
Sat Apr 11, 2009	Sharks	Kings

St. Louis Blues

Despite boasting former captains such as Wayne Gretzky, Chris Pronger and Brett Hull, the St. Louis Blues are winless in conference and Stanley Cup championships. Finishing the 2007–08 season fifth in the Central Division, the St. Louis, Missouri-based Blues have been in the NHL since 1967 and currently play in the Scottrade Center. The Blues introduced a new mascot in 2007, and fans now see Louie, a big blue bear, on the ice and mingling in the stands. With a name honoring W.C. Handy's famous *St. Louis Blues* song, the team and its fans keep the music theme alive today and traditionally play an organ version of *When the Saints Go Marching In* before every Blues home game.

Owner	General Manager	Coach
Dave Checketts	Larry Pleau	Andy Murray

2008 Record and Rankings

33-36-13, 5th in Central Division

	Points	GF/G	GA/G	S/G	SA/G	PP %	PK %	PIM/G
	79	2.46	2.83	26.1	27.4	14.1	84.4	14.1
NHL Rank	27	26	21	29	7	30	7	17

Recent Top Draft Picks

Draft	Num.	Round	Player	Pos	Drafted From
2008 Entry	4	1	Alex Pietrangelo	D	Niagara IceDogs (OHL)
2008 Entry	33	2	Philip McRae	C	London Knights (OHL)
2008 Entry	34	2	Jake Allen	G	St. John's Fog Devils (QMJHL)
2007 Entry	13	1	Lars Eller	F	Frolunda Jrs (Sweden)
2007 Entry	18	1	Ian Cole	D	US National Under 18 Team
2007 Entry	26	1	David Perron	C	Lewiston MAINEiacs (QMJHL)
2006 Entry	1	1	Erik Johnson	D	US National Under 18 Team
2006 Entry	25	1	Patrik Berglund	C	Vasteras IK (Swe-1)
2006 Entry	31	2	Tomas Kana	C	Vitkovice HC (Czech)

Shootout Record

GP	W	L	G	S	S%	GA	SA	Sv%
8	3	5	5	27	19	6	26	77

Team Leaders

	G			A			P
Brad Boyes	43	Paul Kariya	49	Brad Boyes	65
Keith Tkachuk	27	Andy McDonald	34	Paul Kariya	65
Andy McDonald	18	Keith Tkachuk	31	Keith Tkachuk	58
Paul Kariya	16	Erik Johnson	28	Andy McDonald	52
2 tied with	13	Lee Stempniak	25	Lee Stempniak	38

	PIM			Hits			+/-
Dwayne King	100	David Backes	240	David Perron	16
David Backes	99	Barret Jackman	135	Jeff Woywitka	2
Barret Jackman	93	Dan Hinote	114	Jay McKee	2
Jamal Mayers	91	Lee Stempniak	103	3 tied with	1
Eric Brewer	91	Jamal Mayers	101		

	PPG			SHG			Sht
Keith Tkachuk	12	Keith Tkachuk	1	Paul Kariya	223
Brad Boyes	11	Ryan Johnson	1	Brad Boyes	207
Paul Kariya	5	Jamal Mayers	1	Andy McDonald	182
Erik Johnson	4			Keith Tkachuk	177
4 tied with	3			Lee Stempniak	162

Goalies	GP	W	GAA	Sv%	SO
Manny Legace	66	27	2.41	0.911	5
Hannu Toivonen	23	6	3.44	0.878	0
Marek Schwarz	2	0	7.20	0.647	0
Chris Beckford-Tseu	1	0	2.22	0.889	0

Roster

Player	#	Pos	DOB	Hometown	S/P	Ctry	Ht	Wt	S
Backes, David	42	C	May 01 '84	Minneapolis	MN	USA	75	216	R
Johnson, Ryan	17	C	Jun 14 '76	Thunder Bay	ON	CAN	73	202	L
McClement, Jay	18	C	Mar 02 '83	Kingston	ON	CAN	73	201	L
McDonald, Andy	10	C	Aug 25 '77	Strathroy	ON	CAN	71	183	L
Stastny, Yan	25	C	Sep 30 '82	Quebec City	QC	CAN	70	191	L
Tkachuk, Keith	7	C	Mar 28 '72	Melrose	MA	USA	74	232	L
Brewer, Eric	4	D	Apr 17 '79	Vernon	BC	CAN	75	222	L
Dupont, Micki	36	D	Apr 15 '80	Calgary	AB	CAN	70	186	R
Jackman, Barret	5	D	Mar 05 '81	Trail	BC	CAN	72	203	L
Johnson, Erik	6	D	Mar 21 '88	Bloomington	MN	USA	76	219	R
McKee, Jay	77	D	Sep 08 '77	Kingston	ON	CAN	76	203	L
Polak, Roman	46	D	Apr 28 '86	Ostrava		CZE	73	227	R
Wagner, Steve	49	D	Mar 06 '84	Grand Rapids	MN	USA	74	200	L
Walker, Matt	28	D	Apr 07 '80	Beaverlodge	AB	CAN	75	213	R
Woywitka, Jeff	29	D	Sep 01 '83	Vermilion	AB	CAN	74	217	L
Kariya, Paul	9	L	Oct 16 '74	Vancouver	BC	CAN	70	180	L
King, Dwayne	19	L	Jun 27 '84	Meadow Lake	SK	CAN	74	228	L
Perron, David	57	L	May 28 '88	Sherbrooke	QC	CAN	72	180	R
Rucinsky, Martin	26	L	Mar 11 '71	Most		CZE	73	205	L
Boyes, Brad	22	R	Apr 17 '82	Mississauga	ON	CAN	72	195	R
Glumac, Mike	15	R	Apr 05 '80	Niagara Falls	ON	CAN	74	200	R
Hinote, Dan	13	R	Jan 30 '77	Leesburg	FL	USA	72	187	R
Janssen, Cam	55	R	Apr 15 '84	St. Louis	MO	USA	72	210	R
Johnson, Mike	20	R	Oct 03 '74	Scarborough	ON	CAN	74	202	R
Mayers, Jamal	21	R	Oct 24 '74	Toronto	ON	CAN	73	214	R
Stempniak, Lee	12	R	Feb 04 '83	West Seneca	NY	USA	72	195	R

Goalies	#	Pos	DOB	Hometown	S/P	Ctry	Ht	Wt	C
Beckford-Tseu, Chris	45	G	Jun 22 '84	Toronto	ON	CAN	75	201	L
Legace, Manny	34	G	Feb 04 '73	Toronto	ON	CAN	70	200	L
Schwarz, Marek	40	G	Apr 01 '86	Mlada Boleslav		CZE	72	180	R
Toivonen, Hannu	35	G	May 18 '84	Kalvola		FIN	74	200	L

Regular Season Schedule

October 2008	Visitor	Home
Fri Oct 10, 2008	Predators	Blues
Sat Oct 11, 2008	Blues	Islanders
Mon Oct 13, 2008	Blues	Maple Leafs
Thu Oct 16, 2008	Stars	Blues
Sat Oct 18, 2008	Blackhawks	Blues
Wed Oct 22, 2008	Red Wings	Blues
Fri Oct 24, 2008	Kings	Blues
Sat Oct 25, 2008	Panthers	Blues
Thu Oct 30, 2008	Hurricanes	Blues

November 2008	Visitor	Home
Sat Nov 1, 2008	Penguins	Blues
Wed Nov 5, 2008	Blues	Ducks
Thu Nov 6, 2008	Blues	Sharks
Sat Nov 8, 2008	Blues	Kings
Wed Nov 12, 2008	Blues	Sabres
Fri Nov 14, 2008	Blues	Blackhawks
Sun Nov 16, 2008	Canadiens	Blues
Fri Nov 21, 2008	Ducks	Blues
Sat Nov 22, 2008	Blues	Wild
Tue Nov 25, 2008	Blues	Predators
Wed Nov 26, 2008	Blues	Avalanche
Sat Nov 29, 2008	Oilers	Blues
Sun Nov 30, 2008	Blues	Thrashers

December 2008	Visitor	Home
Wed Dec 3, 2008	Blues	Wild
Fri Dec 5, 2008	Flames	Blues
Sat Dec 6, 2008	Coyotes	Blues
Mon Dec 8, 2008	Predators	Blues
Wed Dec 10, 2008	Blues	Ducks
Thu Dec 11, 2008	Blues	Kings
Sat Dec 13, 2008	Blues	Sharks
Tue Dec 16, 2008	Flames	Blues
Thu Dec 18, 2008	Blues	Capitals
Sat Dec 20, 2008	Wild	Blues
Sun Dec 21, 2008	Bruins	Blues
Tue Dec 23, 2008	Blues	Red Wings
Sat Dec 27, 2008	Sharks	Blues
Sun Dec 28, 2008	Ducks	Blues
Tue Dec 30, 2008	Devils	Blues

January 2009	Visitor	Home
Fri Jan 2, 2009	Blues	Hurricanes
Sat Jan 3, 2009	Blue Jackets	Blues
Fri Jan 9, 2009	Blues	Canucks
Sun Jan 11, 2009	Blues	Oilers
Tue Jan 13, 2009	Blues	Flames

January 2009, cont.	Visitor	Home
Thu Jan 15, 2009	Avalanche	Blues
Sat Jan 17, 2009	Blackhawks	Blues
Mon Jan 19, 2009	Blues	Bruins
Wed Jan 21, 2009	Blues	Blackhawks
Thu Jan 29, 2009	Senators	Blues
Sat Jan 31, 2009	Flyers	Blues

February 2009	Visitor	Home
Mon Feb 2, 2009	Blues	Red Wings
Tue Feb 3, 2009	Blues	Blue Jackets
Thu Feb 5, 2009	Oilers	Blues
Sat Feb 7, 2009	Avalanche	Blues
Tue Feb 10, 2009	Canucks	Blues
Thu Feb 12, 2009	Blues	Predators
Fri Feb 13, 2009	Blackhawks	Blues
Mon Feb 16, 2009	Rangers	Blues
Wed Feb 18, 2009	Blues	Blue Jackets
Thu Feb 19, 2009	Blues	Predators
Sat Feb 21, 2009	Predators	Blues
Tue Feb 24, 2009	Coyotes	Blues
Thu Feb 26, 2009	Blues	Stars
Sat Feb 28, 2009	Blues	Coyotes

March 2009	Visitor	Home
Tue Mar 3, 2009	Red Wings	Blues
Fri Mar 6, 2009	Blues	Lightning
Sat Mar 7, 2009	Blues	Panthers
Tue Mar 10, 2009	Stars	Blues
Thu Mar 12, 2009	Sharks	Blues
Sat Mar 14, 2009	Red Wings	Blues
Sun Mar 15, 2009	Wild	Blues
Tue Mar 17, 2009	Blues	Oilers
Thu Mar 19, 2009	Blues	Canucks
Fri Mar 20, 2009	Blues	Flames
Tue Mar 24, 2009	Kings	Blues
Thu Mar 26, 2009	Canucks	Blues
Sat Mar 28, 2009	Blue Jackets	Blues
Sun Mar 29, 2009	Blues	Blue Jackets

April 2009	Visitor	Home
Wed Apr 1, 2009	Blues	Blackhawks
Thu Apr 2, 2009	Blues	Red Wings
Sat Apr 4, 2009	Blues	Stars
Tue Apr 7, 2009	Blues	Coyotes
Fri Apr 10, 2009	Blue Jackets	Blues
Sun Apr 12, 2009	Blues	Avalanche

Tampa Bay Lightning

Based in Tampa, Florida, the Tampa Bay Lightning, or "Bolts," have one Stanley Cup to their name (2004), as well as one conference championship (2004) and two division championships (2003 and 2004). Boasting the "Big 3" players—Vincent Lecavalier, Martin St. Louis and Brad Richards—the Lightning couldn't pull it together for the 2007–08 season. Finishing with a 31–42–9 record, the Lightning earned the unfortunate season record of the worst NHL team on the road, winning only 11 of their away games. Tampa Bay has remained consistent, however, in their colors of blue, black and white and logo of a lightning bolt that is instantly recognizable around the league. The Lightning play in the St. Pete Times Forum, where their biggest team supporters, the Lightning Girls, cheer them on at every home game.

Owners	General Manager	Coach
Oren Koules Len Barrie	Jay Feaster	John Tortorella

2008 Record and Rankings

31-42-9, 5th in Southeast Division

	Points	GF/G	GA/G	S/G	SA/G	PP %	PK %	PIM/G
	71	2.7	3.24	28.7	28.2	19.3	82.0	12.7
NHL Rank	29	16	30	17	11	5	18	9

Recent Top Draft Picks

Draft	Num.	Round	Player	Pos	Drafted From
2008 Entry	1	1	Steven Stamkos	C	Sarnia Sting (OHL)
2008 Entry	117	4	James Wright	C	Vancouver Giants (WHL)
2008 Entry	122	5	Dustin Tokarski	G	Spokane Chiefs (WHL)
2007 Entry	47	2	Dana Tyrell	C	Prince George Cougars (WHL)
2007 Entry	75	3	Luca Cunti	F	Dubendorf (Switzerland)
2007 Entry	77	3	Alexander Killorn	C	Deerfield Academy (Mass H.S.)
2006 Entry	15	1	Riku Helenius	G	Ilves Tampere (FNL)
2006 Entry	78	3	Kevin Quick	D	Salisbury School (Conn. H.S.)
2006 Entry	168	6	Dane Crowley	D	Swift Current Broncos (WHL)

Shootout Record

GP	W	L	G	S	S%	GA	SA	Sv%
3	2	1	4	10	40	3	9	67

Team Leaders

G		A		P	
Vincent Lecavalier	40	Martin St. Louis	58	Vincent Lecavalier	92
Martin St. Louis	25	Vincent Lecavalier	52	Martin St. Louis	83
Jeff Halpern	20	Jussi Jokinen	26	Jeff Halpern	42
Michel Ouellet	17	Filip Kuba	25	Jussi Jokinen	42
Jussi Jokinen	16	Jeff Halpern	22	Michel Ouellet	36

PIM		Hits		+/-	
Shane O'Brien	154	Brad Lukowich	153	Michel Ouellet	11
Andre Roy	108	Shane O'Brien	128	Mike Lundin	3
Vincent Lecavalier	89	Mathieu Darche	125	Blair Jones	0
Nick Tarnasky	78	Nick Tarnasky	119	Jeff Halpern	0
Chris Gratton	77	Vincent Lecavalier	112	4 tied with	-1

PPG		SHG		Sht	
Vincent Lecavalier	10	Martin St. Louis	2	Vincent Lecavalier	318
Martin St. Louis	10	5 tied with	1	Martin St. Louis	241
Jussi Jokinen	6			Michel Ouellet	132
Michel Ouellet	5			Jeff Halpern	132
Jeff Halpern	4			Jussi Jokinen	131

Goalies	GP	W	GAA	Sv%	SO
Mike Smith	34	15	2.59	0.901	3
Karri Ramo	22	7	3.03	0.899	0
Marc Denis	10	1	4.05	0.859	0

Roster

Player	#	Pos	DOB	Hometown	S/P	Ctry	Ht	Wt	S
Craig, Ryan	34	C	Jan 06 '82	Abbotsford	BC	CAN	74	212	L
Gratton, Chris	77	C	Jul 05 '75	Brantford	ON	CAN	76	226	L
Halpern, Jeff	11	C	May 03 '76	Potomac	MD	USA	72	203	R
Jones, Blair	49	C	Sep 27 '86	Central Butte	SK	CAN	75	210	R
Karlsson, Andreas	24	C	Aug 19 '75	Luvika		SWE	76	201	L
Lecavalier, Vincent	4	C	Apr 21 '80	Ile Bizard	QC	CAN	76	219	L
MacDonald, Craig	29	C	Apr 07 '77	Antigonish	NS	CAN	73	201	L
Tarnasky, Nick	74	C	Nov 25 '84	Rocky Mountain House	AB	CAN	74	224	L
Boyle, Dan	22	D	Jul 12 '76	Ottawa	ON	CAN	71	184	R
Janik, Doug	3	D	Mar 26 '80	Agawam	MA	USA	74	209	L
Kuba, Filip	71	D	Dec 29 '76	Ostrava		CZE	77	225	L
Leach, Jay	38	D	Sep 02 '79	Syracuse	NY	USA	76	220	L
Lukowich, Brad	37	D	Aug 12 '76	Cranbrook	BC	CAN	73	201	L
Lundin, Mike	39	D	Sep 24 '84	Burnsville	MN	USA	74	188	L
O'Brien, Shane	55	D	Aug 09 '83	Port Hope	ON	CAN	75	224	L
Picard, Alexandre	2	D	Jul 05 '85	Gatineau	QC	CAN	74	220	L
Ranger, Paul	54	D	Sep 12 '84	Whitby	ON	CAN	75	208	L
Smaby, Matt	32	D	Oct 14 '84	Minneapolis	MN	USA	77	222	L
Darche, Mathieu	21	L	Nov 26 '76	Montreal	QC	CAN	73	217	L
Jokinen, Jussi	10	L	Apr 01 '83	Kalajoki		FIN	71	190	L
Stewart, Karl	61	L	Jun 30 '83	Scarborough	ON	CAN	71	185	L
Lessard, Junior	42	R	May 26 '80	St. Joseph De Beauce	QC	CAN	71	191	R
Ouellet, Michel	7	R	Mar 05 '82	Rimouski	QC	CAN	73	193	R
Roy, Andre	36	R	Feb 08 '75	Port Chester	NY	USA	76	229	L
St. Louis, Martin	26	R	Jun 18 '75	Laval	QC	CAN	69	177	L
Wanvig, Kyle	46	R	Jan 29 '81	Calgary	AB	CAN	74	210	R
Ward, Jason	16	R	Jan 16 '79	Chapleau	ON	CAN	74	208	R

Goalies	#	Pos	DOB	Hometown	S/P	Ctry	Ht	Wt	C
Denis, Marc	38	G	Aug 01 '77	Montreal	QC	CAN	73	193	L
Ramo, Karri	31	G	Jul 01 '86	Asikkala		FIN	74	201	L
Smith, Mike	41	G	Mar 22 '82	Kingston	ON	CAN	75	211	L

Regular Season Schedule

October 2008

October 2008	Visitor	Home
Sat Oct 4, 2008	Rangers	Lightning (Prague, CZE)
Sun Oct 5, 2008	Lightning	Rangers (Prague, CZE)
Sat Oct 11, 2008	Hurricanes	Lightning
Thu Oct 16, 2008	Islanders	Lightning
Sat Oct 18, 2008	Wild	Lightning
Tue Oct 21, 2008	Thrashers	Lightning
Sat Oct 25, 2008	Sharks	Lightning
Tue Oct 28, 2008	Lightning	Maple Leafs
Thu Oct 30, 2008	Lightning	Sabres

November 2008

November 2008	Visitor	Home
Sat Nov 1, 2008	Senators	Lightning
Wed Nov 5, 2008	Lightning	Devils
Thu Nov 6, 2008	Lightning	Rangers
Sat Nov 8, 2008	Lightning	Flyers
Mon Nov 10, 2008	Lightning	Capitals
Wed Nov 12, 2008	Lightning	Panthers
Thu Nov 13, 2008	Red Wings	Lightning
Sun Nov 16, 2008	Lightning	Hurricanes
Tue Nov 18, 2008	Panthers	Lightning
Fri Nov 21, 2008	Predators	Lightning
Sun Nov 23, 2008	Devils	Lightning
Wed Nov 26, 2008	Rangers	Lightning
Fri Nov 28, 2008	Lightning	Wild
Sat Nov 29, 2008	Lightning	Avalanche

December 2008

December 2008	Visitor	Home
Tue Dec 2, 2008	Lightning	Flyers
Thu Dec 4, 2008	Bruins	Lightning
Sat Dec 6, 2008	Sabres	Lightning
Mon Dec 8, 2008	Lightning	Bruins
Wed Dec 10, 2008	Lightning	Sabres
Thu Dec 11, 2008	Lightning	Canadiens
Sat Dec 13, 2008	Lightning	Senators
Thu Dec 18, 2008	Avalanche	Lightning
Sat Dec 20, 2008	Lightning	Thrashers
Tue Dec 23, 2008	Lightning	Penguins
Fri Dec 26, 2008	Lightning	Panthers
Sat Dec 27, 2008	Panthers	Lightning
Tue Dec 30, 2008	Canadiens	Lightning

January 2009

January 2009	Visitor	Home
Thu Jan 1, 2009	Lightning	Capitals
Sat Jan 3, 2009	Hurricanes	Lightning
Sun Jan 4, 2009	Lightning	Thrashers
Thu Jan 8, 2009	Lightning	Coyotes

January 2009, cont.	Visitor	Home
Fri Jan 9, 2009	Lightning	Ducks
Mon Jan 12, 2009	Lightning	Kings
Tue Jan 13, 2009	Lightning	Sharks
Thu Jan 15, 2009	Flyers	Lightning
Sat Jan 17, 2009	Panthers	Lightning
Mon Jan 19, 2009	Stars	Lightning
Wed Jan 21, 2009	Sabres	Lightning
Tue Jan 27, 2009	Canadiens	Lightning
Thu Jan 29, 2009	Lightning	Hurricanes
Fri Jan 30, 2009	Flyers	Lightning

February 2009

February 2009	Visitor	Home
Tue Feb 3, 2009	Lightning	Islanders
Wed Feb 4, 2009	Lightning	Penguins
Sat Feb 7, 2009	Islanders	Lightning
Tue Feb 10, 2009	Thrashers	Lightning
Thu Feb 12, 2009	Maple Leafs	Lightning
Sat Feb 14, 2009	Capitals	Lightning
Tue Feb 17, 2009	Blackhawks	Lightning
Thu Feb 19, 2009	Devils	Lightning
Fri Feb 20, 2009	Lightning	Hurricanes
Sun Feb 22, 2009	Bruins	Lightning
Tue Feb 24, 2009	Lightning	Oilers
Fri Feb 27, 2009	Lightning	Canucks

March 2009

March 2009	Visitor	Home
Sun Mar 1, 2009	Lightning	Flames
Tue Mar 3, 2009	Penguins	Lightning
Fri Mar 6, 2009	Blues	Lightning
Sat Mar 7, 2009	Hurricanes	Lightning
Wed Mar 11, 2009	Lightning	Senators
Thu Mar 12, 2009	Lightning	Maple Leafs
Sat Mar 14, 2009	Lightning	Panthers
Tue Mar 17, 2009	Maple Leafs	Lightning
Thu Mar 19, 2009	Capitals	Lightning
Sat Mar 21, 2009	Thrashers	Lightning
Tue Mar 24, 2009	Blue Jackets	Lightning
Thu Mar 26, 2009	Lightning	Canadiens
Fri Mar 27, 2009	Lightning	Capitals
Sun Mar 29, 2009	Senators	Lightning
Tue Mar 31, 2009	Lightning	Bruins

April 2009

April 2009	Visitor	Home
Fri Apr 3, 2009	Lightning	Devils
Sat Apr 4, 2009	Lightning	Islanders
Tue Apr 7, 2009	Penguins	Lightning
Thu Apr 9, 2009	Capitals	Lightning
Sat Apr 11, 2009	Lightning	Thrashers

Toronto Maple Leafs

One of the Original Six teams and winner of 13 Stanley Cups, the Toronto Maple Leafs have been Toronto, Ontario's home team since 1917. As of 2007, the Leafs were the most valuable team in the NHL at $413 million and have had many dynasty years, but the team has yet to win another Cup since its last in 1967. However, despite their failure to perform on the ice in recent years, Maple Leafs fans are among the most loyal in the league and Leafs home games have proved to be some of the hardest tickets to buy in Canada. Calling themselves the Leaf Nation, a name that the franchise also now uses officially for the fans, they have given Toronto one of the longest sellout streaks in the NHL. And, in the 2007–08 season, fans packed into the Air Canada Centre produced the highest average ticket revenue per game, with $1.9 million. Toronto fans also love to hate when the Montreal Canadiens are in town because these two historical Canadian hockey teams have developed a rivalry so strong as to have a title: the Forever Rivals. The Canadiens remain in first place in Stanley Cup wins with 24, while the Maple Leafs come in second with their 13.

Owner	General Manager	Coach
Maple Leafs Sports & Entertainment Ltd.	Cliff Fletcher	Paul Maurice

2008 Record and Rankings

36-35-11, 5th in Northeast Division

	Points	GF/G	GA/G	S/G	SA/G	PP %	PK %	PIM/G
	83	2.78	3.12	31	29.3	17.8	78.1	13.3
NHL Rank	23	11	27	5	17	15	29	14

Recent Top Draft Picks

Draft	Num.	Round	Player	Pos	Drafted From
2008 Entry	5	1	Luke Schenn	D	Kelowna Rockets (WHL)
2008 Entry	60	2	Jimmy Hayes	R	Lincoln Stars (USHL)
2008 Entry	98	4	Mikhail Stefanovich	C	Quebec Remparts (QMJHL)
2007 Entry	74	3	Dale Mitchell	R	Oshawa Generals (OHL)
2007 Entry	99	4	Matt Frattin	R	Fort Saskatchewan Traders (AJHL)
2007 Entry	104	4	Ben Winnett	L	Salmon Arm Silverbacks (BCHL)
2006 Entry	13	1	Jiri Tlusty	L	Kladno (Czech)
2006 Entry	44	2	Nikolai Kulemin	W	Magnitogorsk Metallurg (Russia)
2006 Entry	99	4	James Reimer	G	Red Deer Rebels (WHL)

Shootout Record

GP	W	L	G	S	S%	GA	SA	Sv%
7	3	4	8	24	33	9	24	63

Team Leaders

	G		A		P
Mats Sundin	32	Mats Sundin	46	Mats Sundin	78
Nik Antropov	26	Tomas Kaberle	45	Nik Antropov	56
Alexei Ponikarovsky	18	Jason Blake	37	Tomas Kaberle	53
Darcy Tucker	18	Nik Antropov	30	Jason Blake	52
Matt Stajan	16	Pavel Kubina	29	Alexander Steen	42

	PIM		Hits		+/-
Pavel Kubina	116	Chad Kilger	137	Mats Sundin	17
Darcy Tucker	100	Darcy Tucker	126	Nik Antropov	10
Nik Antropov	92	Pavel Kubina	121	Andy Wozniewski	5
Bryan McCabe	81	Bryan McCabe	109	Pavel Kubina	5
Mats Sundin	76	Nik Antropov	102	Alexei Ponikarovsky	3

	PPG		SHG		Sht
Nik Antropov	12	Mats Sundin	1	Jason Blake	332
Mats Sundin	10	Matt Stajan	1	Mats Sundin	259
Darcy Tucker	7	Boyd Devereaux	1	Alexander Steen	169
Pavel Kubina	6	Alexander Steen	1	Nik Antropov	165
Tomas Kaberle	6			Tomas Kaberle	155

Goalies	GP	W	GAA	Sv%	SO
Vesa Toskala	66	33	2.74	0.904	3
Andrew Raycroft	19	2	3.92	0.876	1
Scott Clemmensen	3	1	3.90	0.839	0

Roster

Player	#	Pos	DOB	Hometown	S/P	Ctry	Ht	Wt	S
Boyce, Darryl	50	C	Jul 07 '84	Summerside	PE	CAN	72	200	L
Devereaux, Boyd	22	C	Apr 16 '78	Seaforth	ON	CAN	74	195	L
Foster, Alex	32	C	Aug 26 '84	Canton	MI	USA	71	195	L
Moore, Dominic	19	C	Aug 03 '80	Thornhill	ON	CAN	72	188	L
Newbury, Kris	54	C	Feb 19 '82	Brampton	ON	CAN	70	200	L
Pohl, John	21	C	Jun 29 '79	Rochester	MN	USA	73	196	R
Stajan, Matt	14	C	Dec 19 '83	Mississauga	ON	CAN	73	200	L
Sundin, Mats	13	C	Feb 13 '71	Bromma		SWE	77	231	R
Tlusty, Jiri	11	C	Mar 16 '88	Slany		CZE	72	209	L
Wellwood, Kyle	42	C	May 16 '83	Windsor	ON	CAN	70	180	R
Colaiacovo, Carlo	8	D	Jan 27 '83	Toronto	ON	CAN	73	200	L
Kaberle, Tomas	15	D	Mar 02 '78	Rakovnik		CZE	73	198	L
Kronwall, Staffan	44	D	Sep 10 '82	Järfälla		SWE	75	209	L
Kubina, Pavel	31	D	Apr 15 '77	Celadna		CZE	76	244	R
McCabe, Bryan	24	D	Jun 08 '75	St. Catharines	ON	CAN	74	220	L
Stralman, Anton	36	D	Aug 01 '86	Tibro		SWE	73	180	R
White, Ian	7	D	Jun 04 '84	Steinbach	MB	CAN	70	185	R
Wozniewski, Andy	56	D	May 25 '80	Buffalo Grove	IL	USA	77	225	L
Battaglia, Bates	33	L	Dec 13 '75	Chicago	IL	USA	74	205	L
Bell, Mark	9	L	Aug 05 '80	St. Pauls	ON	CAN	76	220	L
Blake, Jason	55	L	Sep 02 '73	Moorhead	MN	USA	70	180	L
Earl, Robert	52	L	Jun 02 '85	Chicago	IL	USA	73	195	L
Gamache, Simon	39	L	Jan 03 '81	Thetford Mines	QC	CAN	70	186	L
Kilger, Chad	19	L	Nov 27 '76	Cornwall	ON	CAN	76	224	L
Ponikarovsky, Alexei	23	L	Apr 09 '80	Kiev		UKR	76	220	L
Steen, Alexander	10	L	Mar 01 '84	Winnipeg	MB	CAN	73	205	L
Antropov, Nik	80	R	Feb 18 '80	Ust-Kamenog		KAZ	78	230	L
Ondrus, Benjamin	26	R	Jun 25 '82	Sherwood Park	AB	CAN	72	194	R
Tucker, Darcy	16	R	Mar 15 '75	Castor	AB	CAN	70	178	L
Williams, Jeremy	48	R	Jan 26 '84	Regina	SK	CAN	71	188	R

Goalies	#	Pos	DOB	Hometown	S/P	Ctry	Ht	Wt	C
Clemmensen, Scott	30	G	Jul 23 '77	Des Moines	IA	USA	75	205	L
Raycroft, Andrew	1	G	May 04 '80	Belleville	ON	CAN	72	185	L
Toskala, Vesa	35	G	May 20 '77	Tampere		FIN	70	195	L

Regular Season Schedule

October 2008	Visitor	Home
Thu Oct 9, 2008	Maple Leafs	Red Wings
Sat Oct 11, 2008	Canadiens	Maple Leafs
Mon Oct 13, 2008	Blues	Maple Leafs
Fri Oct 17, 2008	Maple Leafs	Rangers
Sat Oct 18, 2008	Maple Leafs	Penguins
Tue Oct 21, 2008	Ducks	Maple Leafs
Thu Oct 23, 2008	Maple Leafs	Bruins
Sat Oct 25, 2008	Senators	Maple Leafs
Tue Oct 28, 2008	Lightning	Maple Leafs
Wed Oct 29, 2008	Maple Leafs	Devils

November 2008	Visitor	Home
Sat Nov 1, 2008	Rangers	Maple Leafs
Sun Nov 2, 2008	Maple Leafs	Hurricanes
Tue Nov 4, 2008	Hurricanes	Maple Leafs
Thu Nov 6, 2008	Maple Leafs	Bruins
Sat Nov 8, 2008	Canadiens	Maple Leafs
Tue Nov 11, 2008	Maple Leafs	Flames
Thu Nov 13, 2008	Maple Leafs	Oilers
Sat Nov 15, 2008	Maple Leafs	Canucks
Mon Nov 17, 2008	Bruins	Maple Leafs
Sat Nov 22, 2008	Blackhawks	Maple Leafs
Tue Nov 25, 2008	Thrashers	Maple Leafs
Thu Nov 27, 2008	Maple Leafs	Senators
Sat Nov 29, 2008	Flyers	Maple Leafs

December 2008	Visitor	Home
Mon Dec 1, 2008	Maple Leafs	Kings
Tue Dec 2, 2008	Maple Leafs	Sharks
Thu Dec 4, 2008	Maple Leafs	Coyotes
Sat Dec 6, 2008	Capitals	Maple Leafs
Mon Dec 8, 2008	Islanders	Maple Leafs
Fri Dec 12, 2008	Maple Leafs	Sabres
Tue Dec 16, 2008	Devils	Maple Leafs
Thu Dec 18, 2008	Maple Leafs	Bruins
Sat Dec 20, 2008	Maple Leafs	Penguins
Mon Dec 22, 2008	Maple Leafs	Thrashers
Tue Dec 23, 2008	Stars	Maple Leafs
Fri Dec 26, 2008	Maple Leafs	Islanders
Sun Dec 28, 2008	Maple Leafs	Capitals
Tue Dec 30, 2008	Thrashers	Maple Leafs

January 2009	Visitor	Home
Thu Jan 1, 2009	Sabres	Maple Leafs
Sat Jan 3, 2009	Senators	Maple Leafs
Tue Jan 6, 2009	Panthers	Maple Leafs
Thu Jan 8, 2009	Maple Leafs	Canadiens
Sat Jan 10, 2009	Maple Leafs	Flyers

January 2009, cont.	Visitor	Home
Tue Jan 13, 2009	Predators	Maple Leafs
Thu Jan 15, 2009	Maple Leafs	Hurricanes
Fri Jan 16, 2009	Maple Leafs	Thrashers
Mon Jan 19, 2009	Hurricanes	Maple Leafs
Wed Jan 21, 2009	Bruins	Maple Leafs
Tue Jan 27, 2009	Maple Leafs	Wild
Thu Jan 29, 2009	Maple Leafs	Avalanche
Sat Jan 31, 2009	Penguins	Maple Leafs

February 2009	Visitor	Home
Tue Feb 3, 2009	Panthers	Maple Leafs
Wed Feb 4, 2009	Maple Leafs	Sabres
Sat Feb 7, 2009	Maple Leafs	Canadiens
Tue Feb 10, 2009	Maple Leafs	Panthers
Thu Feb 12, 2009	Maple Leafs	Lightning
Sat Feb 14, 2009	Penguins	Maple Leafs
Tue Feb 17, 2009	Sabres	Maple Leafs
Thu Feb 19, 2009	Blue Jackets	Maple Leafs
Sat Feb 21, 2009	Canucks	Maple Leafs
Sun Feb 22, 2009	Maple Leafs	Rangers
Wed Feb 25, 2009	Rangers	Maple Leafs
Thu Feb 26, 2009	Maple Leafs	Islanders
Sat Feb 28, 2009	Maple Leafs	Senators

March 2009	Visitor	Home
Tue Mar 3, 2009	Devils	Maple Leafs
Thu Mar 5, 2009	Maple Leafs	Capitals
Sat Mar 7, 2009	Oilers	Maple Leafs
Mon Mar 9, 2009	Maple Leafs	Senators
Tue Mar 10, 2009	Islanders	Maple Leafs
Thu Mar 12, 2009	Lightning	Maple Leafs
Sat Mar 14, 2009	Flames	Maple Leafs
Tue Mar 17, 2009	Maple Leafs	Lightning
Thu Mar 19, 2009	Maple Leafs	Panthers
Sat Mar 21, 2009	Maple Leafs	Canadiens
Tue Mar 24, 2009	Capitals	Maple Leafs
Fri Mar 27, 2009	Maple Leafs	Sabres
Sat Mar 28, 2009	Bruins	Maple Leafs

April 2009	Visitor	Home
Wed Apr 1, 2009	Flyers	Maple Leafs
Fri Apr 3, 2009	Maple Leafs	Flyers
Sat Apr 4, 2009	Canadiens	Maple Leafs
Tue Apr 7, 2009	Maple Leafs	Devils
Wed Apr 8, 2009	Sabres	Maple Leafs
Sat Apr 11, 2009	Senators	Maple Leafs

Vancouver Canucks

Playing their home games out of General Motors Place in Vancouver, British Columbia, the Canucks have yet to win a Stanley Cup since joining the league in 1970. The team did manage to make the Stanley Cup finals two times, but lost both series to New York teams—the Islanders in 1982 and the Rangers in 1994. Analysts had high hopes for the Canucks coming out of the 2005 NHL lockout, many placing the team on the short list of Stanley Cup favorites. However, the team underachieved, missing the playoffs altogether and finishing ninth overall in their conference. This marked the end of the "West Coast Express" days, as previous high-scoring forwards Markus Naslund, Todd Bertuzzi and Brendan Morrison failed to produce as expected under the new league rules. After replacing coach Marc Crawford, the Canucks regrouped around newly acquired goaltending phenom Roberto Luongo, winning the 2006–07 Northwest Division title for the second time in three years, eventually losing to the Anaheim Ducks in the second round of the playoffs. Although the team was hot out of the gate in 2007–08, the Canucks failed to make the playoffs, finishing last in their division.

Owner	General Manager	Coach
Canucks Sports and Entertainment	Dave Nonnis	Alain Vigneault

2008 Record and Rankings

39-33-10, 5th in Northwest Division

	Points	GF/G	GA/G	S/G	SA/G	PP %	PK %	PIM/G
	88	2.52	2.51	27.5	28.9	17.1	82.6	18
NHL Rank	19	23	7	24	15	18	14	29

Recent Top Draft Picks

Draft	Num.	Round	Player	Pos	Drafted From
2008 Entry	10	1	Cody Hodgson	C	Brampton Battalion (OHL)
2008 Entry	41	2	Yann Sauve	D	Saint John Sea Dogs (QMJHL)
2008 Entry	131	5	Prabh Rai	C	Seattle Thunderbirds (WHL)
2007 Entry	25	1	Patrick White	C	Tri-City Storm (USHL)
2007 Entry	33	2	Taylor Ellington	D	Everett Silvertips (WHL)
2007 Entry	145	5	Charles-Antoine Messier	C	Baie-Comeau Drakkar (QMJHL)
2006 Entry	14	1	Michael Grabner	R	Spokane Chiefs (WHL)
2006 Entry	82	3	Daniel Rahimi	D	Bjorkloven Jr. (Sweden)
2006 Entry	163	6	Sergei Shirokov	W	CSKA Moscow (Russia)

Shootout Record

GP	W	L	G	S	S%	GA	SA	Sv%
15	6	9	13	56	23	17	58	71

Team Leaders

G		A		P	
Daniel Sedin	29	Henrik Sedin	61	Henrik Sedin	76
Markus Naslund	25	Daniel Sedin	45	Daniel Sedin	74
Ryan Kesler	21	Markus Naslund	30	Markus Naslund	55
Taylor Pyatt	16	Taylor Pyatt	21	Ryan Kesler	37
Henrik Sedin	15	Alex Burrows	19	Taylor Pyatt	37

PIM		Hits		+/-	
Alex Burrows	179	Byron Ritchie	89	Alex Burrows	11
Jeff Cowan	110	Alex Burrows	80	Taylor Pyatt	9
Kevin Bieksa	90	Ryan Kesler	78	Sami Salo	8
Willie Mitchell	81	Taylor Pyatt	76	Luc Bourdon	7
Byron Ritchie	80	Matt Pettinger	75	4 tied with	6

PPG		SHG		Sht	
Daniel Sedin	12	Alex Burrows	3	Daniel Sedin	247
Markus Naslund	9	Ryan Kesler	2	Markus Naslund	237
Taylor Pyatt	7	Trevor Linden	2	Ryan Kesler	177
Sami Salo	6	Henrik Sedin	1	Taylor Pyatt	167
5 tied with	4			Henrik Sedin	141

Goalies	GP	W	GAA	Sv%	SO
Roberto Luongo	73	35	2.38	0.917	6
Curtis Sanford	16	4	2.83	0.898	0
Drew MacIntyre	2	0	2.95	0.864	0

Roster

Player	#	Pos	DOB	Hometown	S/P	Ctry	Ht	Wt	S
Kesler, Ryan	17	C	Aug 31 '84	Livonia	MI	USA	74	205	R
Linden, Trevor	16	C	Apr 11 '70	Medicine Hat	AB	CAN	76	220	R
Morrison, Brendan	7	C	Aug 15 '75	Pitt Meadows	BC	CAN	71	181	L
Ritchie, Byron	15	C	Apr 24 '77	Burnaby	BC	CAN	70	190	L
Rypien, Rick	37	C	May 16 '84	Coleman	AB	CAN	71	170	R
Sedin, Henrik	33	C	Sep 26 '80	Ornskoldsvik		SWE	74	190	L
Bieksa, Kevin	3	D	Jun 16 '81	Grimsby	ON	CAN	72	205	R
Bourdon, Luc	28	D	Feb 16 '87	Shippagan	NB	CAN	75	211	L
Edler, Alexander	23	D	Apr 21 '86	Ostersund		SWE	75	220	L
Fitzgerald, Zach	49	D	Jun 16 '85	Two Harbors	MN	USA	74	205	L
Krajicek, Lukas	5	D	Mar 11 '83	Prostejov		CZE	74	196	L
McIver, Nathan	45	D	Jan 06 '85	Summerside	PE	CAN	75	205	L
Miller, Aaron	4	D	Aug 11 '71	Buffalo	NY	USA	75	210	R
Mitchell, Willie	8	D	Apr 23 '77	Port McNeill	BC	CAN	75	210	L
Ohlund, Mattias	2	D	Sep 09 '76	Pitea		SWE	75	220	L
Salo, Sami	6	D	Sep 02 '74	Turku		FIN	75	215	R
Weaver, Mike	18	D	May 02 '78	Bramalea	ON	CAN	69	182	R
Burrows, Alex	14	L	Apr 11 '81	Pointe-Claire	QC	CAN	73	190	L
Cowan, Jeff	20	L	Sep 27 '76	Scarborough	ON	CAN	74	205	L
Isbister, Brad	27	L	May 07 '77	Edmonton	AB	CAN	76	225	R
Jaffray, Jason	29	L	Jun 30 '81	Rimbey	AB	CAN	73	195	L
Naslund, Markus	19	L	Jul 30 '73	Ornskoldsvik		SWE	72	195	L
Pettinger, Matt	25	L	Oct 22 '80	Edmonton	AB	CAN	73	205	L
Pyatt, Taylor	9	L	Aug 19 '81	Thunder Bay	ON	CAN	76	230	L
Raymond, Mason	21	L	Sep 17 '85	Calgary	AB	CAN	72	182	L
Sedin, Daniel	22	L	Sep 26 '80	Ornskoldsvik		SWE	73	185	L
Brown, Mike	13	R	Jun 24 '85	Northbrook	IL	USA	72	210	R
Hansen, Jannik	36	R	Mar 15 '86	Herlev		DNK	73	201	R
Shannon, Ryan	26	R	Mar 02 '83	Darien	CT	USA	69	173	R

Goalies	#	Pos	DOB	Hometown	S/P	Ctry	Ht	Wt	C
Luongo, Roberto	1	G	Apr 04 '79	Montreal	QC	CAN	75	205	L
MacIntyre, Drew	31	G	Jun 24 '83	Charlottetown	PE	CAN	72	185	L
Sanford, Curtis	41	G	Oct 05 '79	Owen Sound	ON	CAN	70	187	L

Regular Season Schedule

October 2008	Visitor	Home
Thu Oct 9, 2008	Flames	Canucks
Sat Oct 11, 2008	Canucks	Flames
Mon Oct 13, 2008	Canucks	Capitals
Thu Oct 16, 2008	Canucks	Red Wings
Fri Oct 17, 2008	Canucks	Sabres
Sun Oct 19, 2008	Canucks	Blackhawks
Tue Oct 21, 2008	Canucks	Blue Jackets
Sat Oct 25, 2008	Oilers	Canucks
Tue Oct 28, 2008	Bruins	Canucks
Thu Oct 30, 2008	Canucks	Kings
Fri Oct 31, 2008	Canucks	Ducks

November 2008	Visitor	Home
Sun Nov 2, 2008	Red Wings	Canucks
Tue Nov 4, 2008	Predators	Canucks
Thu Nov 6, 2008	Coyotes	Canucks
Sat Nov 8, 2008	Wild	Canucks
Wed Nov 12, 2008	Avalanche	Canucks
Sat Nov 15, 2008	Maple Leafs	Canucks
Mon Nov 17, 2008	Canucks	Islanders
Wed Nov 19, 2008	Canucks	Rangers
Thu Nov 20, 2008	Canucks	Wild
Sat Nov 22, 2008	Canucks	Penguins
Mon Nov 24, 2008	Red Wings	Canucks
Thu Nov 27, 2008	Flames	Canucks
Sat Nov 29, 2008	Canucks	Flames

December 2008	Visitor	Home
Mon Dec 1, 2008	Canucks	Blue Jackets
Thu Dec 4, 2008	Canucks	Red Wings
Fri Dec 5, 2008	Canucks	Wild
Sun Dec 7, 2008	Canucks	Avalanche
Tue Dec 9, 2008	Canucks	Predators
Sat Dec 13, 2008	Canucks	Oilers
Sun Dec 14, 2008	Panthers	Canucks
Wed Dec 17, 2008	Oilers	Canucks
Sat Dec 20, 2008	Blackhawks	Canucks
Mon Dec 22, 2008	Ducks	Canucks
Tue Dec 23, 2008	Canucks	Sharks
Fri Dec 26, 2008	Oilers	Canucks
Sun Dec 28, 2008	Senators	Canucks
Tue Dec 30, 2008	Flyers	Canucks

January 2009	Visitor	Home
Thu Jan 1, 2009	Canucks	Predators
Fri Jan 2, 2009	Canucks	Thrashers
Sun Jan 4, 2009	Stars	Canucks
Wed Jan 7, 2009	Canucks	Oilers

January 2009, cont.	Visitor	Home
Fri Jan 9, 2009	Blues	Canucks
Sat Jan 10, 2009	Sharks	Canucks
Tue Jan 13, 2009	Devils	Canucks
Thu Jan 15, 2009	Coyotes	Canucks
Sun Jan 18, 2009	Blue Jackets	Canucks
Tue Jan 20, 2009	Canucks	Sharks
Wed Jan 28, 2009	Predators	Canucks
Sat Jan 31, 2009	Wild	Canucks

February 2009	Visitor	Home
Tue Feb 3, 2009	Hurricanes	Canucks
Sat Feb 7, 2009	Blackhawks	Canucks
Tue Feb 10, 2009	Canucks	Blues
Thu Feb 12, 2009	Canucks	Coyotes
Fri Feb 13, 2009	Canucks	Stars
Sun Feb 15, 2009	Canadiens	Canucks
Tue Feb 17, 2009	Canucks	Flames
Thu Feb 19, 2009	Canucks	Senators
Sat Feb 21, 2009	Canucks	Maple Leafs
Tue Feb 24, 2009	Canucks	Canadiens
Fri Feb 27, 2009	Lightning	Canucks

March 2009	Visitor	Home
Sun Mar 1, 2009	Blue Jackets	Canucks
Tue Mar 3, 2009	Wild	Canucks
Sat Mar 7, 2009	Sharks	Canucks
Mon Mar 9, 2009	Canucks	Kings
Wed Mar 11, 2009	Canucks	Ducks
Fri Mar 13, 2009	Kings	Canucks
Sun Mar 15, 2009	Avalanche	Canucks
Tue Mar 17, 2009	Stars	Canucks
Thu Mar 19, 2009	Blues	Canucks
Sat Mar 21, 2009	Canucks	Coyotes
Tue Mar 24, 2009	Canucks	Stars
Thu Mar 26, 2009	Canucks	Blues
Fri Mar 27, 2009	Canucks	Avalanche
Sun Mar 29, 2009	Canucks	Blackhawks
Tue Mar 31, 2009	Canucks	Wild

April 2009	Visitor	Home
Thu Apr 2, 2009	Ducks	Canucks
Sat Apr 4, 2009	Canucks	Oilers
Sun Apr 5, 2009	Avalanche	Canucks
Tue Apr 7, 2009	Flames	Canucks
Thu Apr 9, 2009	Kings	Canucks
Sat Apr 11, 2009	Canucks	Avalanche

125

Washington Capitals

Founded in 1974, the Washington Capitals are winless in Stanley Cup championships, but have four division (1989, 2000, 2001 and 2008) and conference (1998) wins to their name. Based in Washington, D.C., the start of the Capitals' season in 2007–08 was rocky, but ended with the division title win, as well as various accolades for the team and its players. Alexander Ovechkin won the Art Ross Trophy, the Maurice "Rocket" Richard Trophy, the Hart Trophy and the Lester B. Pearson Award—making him the first player in NHL history to win all four awards. Ovechkin also holds the franchise record for most goals in a season (2007–08) with 65. The Capitals play on home ice in the Verizon Center, nicknamed the Phone Booth, and during the Capitals' last game against the Florida Panthers in this year's bout for the division title, the entire crowd was clothed in red in support of their hometown red, white and blue.

Owner	General Manager	Coach
Ted Leonsis	George McPhee	Bruce Boudreau

2008 Record and Rankings

43-31-8, 1st in Southeast Division

	Points	GF/G	GA/G	S/G	SA/G	PP %	PK %	PIM/G
	94	2.9	2.77	31	27.5	18.8	80.5	11.9
NHL Rank	13	8	19	6	9	9	25	4

Recent Top Draft Picks

Draft	Num.	Round	Player	Pos	Drafted From
2008 Entry	21	1	Anton Gustafsson	C	Frolunda Jr. (SWE-JR.)
2008 Entry	27	1	John Carlson	D	Indiana Ice (USHL)
2008 Entry	57	2	Eric Mestery	D	Tri-City Americans (WHL)
2007 Entry	5	1	Karl Alzner	D	Calgary Hitmen (WHL)
2007 Entry	34	2	Josh Godfrey	D	Sault Ste. Marie Greyhounds (OHL)
2007 Entry	46	2	Ted Ruth	D	US National Under 18 Team
2006 Entry	4	1	Nicklas Backstrom	C	Brynas IF Gavle (SEL)
2006 Entry	23	1	Semen Varlamov	G	Yaroslavl-2 (Russia)
2006 Entry	34	2	Michal Neuvirth	G	Sparta Jrs. (Czech Rep)

Shootout Record

GP	W	L	G	S	S%	GA	SA	Sv%
8	4	4	10	39	26	11	39	72

Team Leaders

	G			A			P	
Alexander Ovechkin	65		Nicklas Backstrom	55		Alexander Ovechkin	112	
Alexander Semin	26		Alexander Ovechkin	47		Nicklas Backstrom	69	
Brooks Laich	21		Mike Green	38		Mike Green	56	
Mike Green	18		Viktor Kozlov	38		Viktor Kozlov	54	
Viktor Kozlov	16		Sergei Fedorov	30		Alexander Semin	42	

	PIM			Hits			+/-	
Donald Brashear	119		Alexander Ovechkin	220		Alexander Ovechkin	28	
John Erskine	96		Matt Cooke	198		Viktor Kozlov	28	
Matt Cooke	91		Milan Jurcina	151		Nicklas Backstrom	13	
Matt Bradley	74		Donald Brashear	133		Jeff Schultz	12	
Shaone Morrisonn	63		Matt Bradley	126		Tom Poti	9	

	PPG			SHG			Sht	
Alexander Ovechkin	22		Brooks Laich	2		Alexander Ovechkin	446	
Alexander Semin	10		Boyd Gordon	1		Mike Green	234	
Brooks Laich	8		Matt Cooke	1		Viktor Kozlov	219	
Mike Green	8		Matt Bradley	1		Alexander Semin	185	
Sergei Fedorov	6					Nicklas Backstrom	153	

Goalies	GP	W	GAA	Sv%	SO
Olaf Kolzig	54	25	2.91	0.892	1
Cristobal Huet	52	32	2.32	0.920	4
Brent Johnson	19	7	2.67	0.908	0

Roster

Player	#	Pos	DOB	Hometown	S/P	Ctry	Ht	Wt	S
Backstrom, Nicklas	19	C	Nov 23 '87	Gavle		SWE	72	203	L
Fedorov, Sergei	91	C	Dec 13 '69	Pskov		RUS	74	207	L
Gordon, Boyd	15	C	Oct 19 '83	Unity	SK	CAN	72	201	R
Kozlov, Viktor	25	C	Feb 14 '75	Togliatti		RUS	76	224	R
Laich, Brooks	21	C	Jun 23 '83	Wawota	SK	CAN	74	205	L
Nylander, Michael	92	C	Oct 03 '72	Stockholm		SWE	73	195	L
Steckel, David	39	C	Mar 15 '82	Milwaukee	WI	USA	77	218	L
Eminger, Steve	44	D	Oct 31 '83	Woodbridge	ON	CAN	74	212	R
Erskine, John	4	D	Jun 26 '80	Kingston	ON	CAN	76	218	L
Green, Mike	52	D	Oct 12 '85	Calgary	AB	CAN	74	201	R
Jurcina, Milan	23	D	Jun 07 '83	Liptovsky		SVK	76	235	R
Lepisto, Sami	42	D	Oct 17 '84	Espoo		FIN	73	195	L
Morrisonn, Shaone	26	D	Dec 23 '82	Vancouver	BC	CAN	76	212	L
Pothier, Brian	2	D	Apr 15 '77	New Bedford	MA	USA	72	200	L
Poti, Tom	3	D	Mar 22 '77	Worcester	MA	USA	75	210	L
Schultz, Jeff	55	D	Feb 25 '86	Calgary	AB	CAN	78	221	L
Bourque, Christopher	56	L	Jan 29 '86	Boston	MA	USA	67	173	L
Brashear, Donald	87	L	Jan 07 '72	Bedford	IN	USA	75	239	L
Cooke, Matt	24	L	Sep 07 '78	Belleville	ON	CAN	71	205	L
Fleischmann, Tomas	43	L	May 16 '84	Koprivnice		CZE	73	192	L
Laing, Quintin	53	L	Jun 08 '79	Harris	SK	CAN	74	200	L
Ovechkin, Alexander	8	L	Sep 17 '85	Moscow		RUS	74	217	R
Semin, Alexander	28	L	Mar 03 '84	Krasjonarsk		RUS	74	205	L
Bradley, Matt	10	R	Jun 13 '78	Stittsville	ON	CAN	75	210	R
Clark, Chris	17	R	Mar 08 '76	South Windsor	CT	USA	72	202	R
Fehr, Eric	14	R	Sep 07 '85	Winkler	MB	CAN	76	212	R
Motzko, Joe	50	R	Mar 14 '80	Bemidji	MN	USA	72	184	R

Goalies	#	Pos	DOB	Hometown	S/P	Ctry	Ht	Wt	C
Huet, Cristobal	38	G	Sep 03 '75	St-Martin-d'Hères		FRA	73	204	L
Johnson, Brent	1	G	Mar 12 '77	Farmington	MI	USA	75	210	L
Kolzig, Olaf	37	G	Apr 06 '70	Johannesburg		ZAF	75	224	L

Regular Season Schedule

October 2008	Visitor	Home
Fri Oct 10, 2008	Capitals	Thrashers
Sat Oct 11, 2008	Blackhawks	Capitals
Mon Oct 13, 2008	Canucks	Capitals
Thu Oct 16, 2008	Capitals	Penguins
Sat Oct 18, 2008	Devils	Capitals
Tue Oct 21, 2008	Capitals	Flames
Thu Oct 23, 2008	Capitals	Coyotes
Sat Oct 25, 2008	Capitals	Stars
Tue Oct 28, 2008	Predators	Capitals

November 2008	Visitor	Home
Sat Nov 1, 2008	Capitals	Sabres
Tue Nov 4, 2008	Capitals	Senators
Thu Nov 6, 2008	Hurricanes	Capitals
Sat Nov 8, 2008	Rangers	Capitals
Mon Nov 10, 2008	Lightning	Capitals
Wed Nov 12, 2008	Capitals	Hurricanes
Fri Nov 14, 2008	Devils	Capitals
Sat Nov 15, 2008	Capitals	Devils
Wed Nov 19, 2008	Capitals	Ducks
Thu Nov 20, 2008	Capitals	Kings
Sat Nov 22, 2008	Capitals	Sharks
Mon Nov 24, 2008	Capitals	Wild
Wed Nov 26, 2008	Thrashers	Capitals
Fri Nov 28, 2008	Canadiens	Capitals
Sat Nov 29, 2008	Capitals	Blue Jackets

December 2008	Visitor	Home
Tue Dec 2, 2008	Panthers	Capitals
Thu Dec 4, 2008	Islanders	Capitals
Sat Dec 6, 2008	Capitals	Maple Leafs
Sun Dec 7, 2008	Capitals	Hurricanes
Wed Dec 10, 2008	Bruins	Capitals
Fri Dec 12, 2008	Senators	Capitals
Sat Dec 13, 2008	Capitals	Canadiens
Tue Dec 16, 2008	Capitals	Islanders
Thu Dec 18, 2008	Blues	Capitals
Sat Dec 20, 2008	Capitals	Flyers
Tue Dec 23, 2008	Capitals	Rangers
Fri Dec 26, 2008	Sabres	Capitals
Sun Dec 28, 2008	Maple Leafs	Capitals
Tue Dec 30, 2008	Capitals	Sabres

January 2009	Visitor	Home
Thu Jan 1, 2009	Lightning	Capitals
Sat Jan 3, 2009	Rangers	Capitals
Tue Jan 6, 2009	Flyers	Capitals
Fri Jan 9, 2009	Blue Jackets	Capitals

January 2009, cont.	Visitor	Home
Sat Jan 10, 2009	Capitals	Canadiens
Tue Jan 13, 2009	Oilers	Capitals
Wed Jan 14, 2009	Capitals	Penguins
Sat Jan 17, 2009	Bruins	Capitals
Mon Jan 19, 2009	Capitals	Islanders
Tue Jan 20, 2009	Capitals	Senators
Tue Jan 27, 2009	Capitals	Bruins
Sat Jan 31, 2009	Red Wings	Capitals

February 2009	Visitor	Home
Sun Feb 1, 2009	Senators	Capitals
Tue Feb 3, 2009	Capitals	Devils
Thu Feb 5, 2009	Kings	Capitals
Sat Feb 7, 2009	Panthers	Capitals
Wed Feb 11, 2009	Capitals	Rangers
Sat Feb 14, 2009	Capitals	Lightning
Sun Feb 15, 2009	Capitals	Panthers
Wed Feb 18, 2009	Canadiens	Capitals
Fri Feb 20, 2009	Avalanche	Capitals
Sun Feb 22, 2009	Penguins	Capitals
Tue Feb 24, 2009	Flyers	Capitals
Thu Feb 26, 2009	Thrashers	Capitals
Sat Feb 28, 2009	Capitals	Bruins

March 2009	Visitor	Home
Sun Mar 1, 2009	Panthers	Capitals
Tue Mar 3, 2009	Hurricanes	Capitals
Thu Mar 5, 2009	Maple Leafs	Capitals
Sun Mar 8, 2009	Penguins	Capitals
Tue Mar 10, 2009	Capitals	Predators
Thu Mar 12, 2009	Capitals	Flyers
Sat Mar 14, 2009	Hurricanes	Capitals
Mon Mar 16, 2009	Capitals	Thrashers
Tue Mar 17, 2009	Capitals	Panthers
Thu Mar 19, 2009	Capitals	Lightning
Sat Mar 21, 2009	Capitals	Hurricanes
Tue Mar 24, 2009	Capitals	Maple Leafs
Fri Mar 27, 2009	Lightning	Capitals

April 2009	Visitor	Home
Wed Apr 1, 2009	Islanders	Capitals
Fri Apr 3, 2009	Sabres	Capitals
Sun Apr 5, 2009	Thrashers	Capitals
Tue Apr 7, 2009	Capitals	Thrashers
Thu Apr 9, 2009	Capitals	Lightning
Sat Apr 11, 2009	Capitals	Panthers

Team Statistics

Team	GP	W	L	OL	PTS	PTS%	GF
Detroit Red Wings*	82	54	21	7	115	0.701	257
San Jose Sharks*	82	49	23	10	108	0.659	222
Montreal Canadiens*	82	47	25	10	104	0.634	262
Pittsburgh Penguins*	82	47	27	8	102	0.622	247
Anaheim Ducks*	82	47	27	8	102	0.622	205
New Jersey Devils*	82	46	29	7	99	0.604	206
Minnesota Wild*	82	44	28	10	98	0.598	223
New York Rangers*	82	42	27	13	97	0.591	213
Dallas Stars*	82	45	30	7	97	0.591	242
Philadelphia Flyers*	82	42	29	11	95	0.579	248
Colorado Avalanche*	82	44	31	7	95	0.579	231
Ottawa Senators*	82	43	31	8	94	0.573	261
Boston Bruins*	82	41	29	12	94	0.573	212
Calgary Flames*	82	42	30	10	94	0.573	229
Washington Capitals*	82	43	31	8	94	0.573	242
Carolina Hurricanes	82	43	33	6	92	0.561	252
Nashville Predators*	82	41	32	9	91	0.555	230
Buffalo Sabres	82	39	31	12	90	0.549	255
Vancouver Canucks	82	39	33	10	88	0.537	213
Chicago Blackhawks	82	40	34	8	88	0.537	239
Edmonton Oilers	82	41	35	6	88	0.537	235
Florida Panthers	82	38	35	9	85	0.518	216
Phoenix Coyotes	82	38	37	7	83	0.506	214
Toronto Maple Leafs	82	36	35	11	83	0.506	231
Columbus Blue Jackets	82	34	36	12	80	0.488	193
St. Louis Blues	82	33	36	13	79	0.482	205
New York Islanders	82	35	38	9	79	0.482	194
Atlanta Thrashers	82	34	40	8	76	0.463	216
Los Angeles Kings	82	32	43	7	71	0.433	231
Tampa Bay Lightning	82	31	42	9	71	0.433	223
League Average	**82**	**41**	**32**	**9**	**91**	**0.555**	**228**

GA	PP	PPO	PP%	PPGA	PPOA	PK%	SH	SHGA
184	74	356	20.8	52	324	84.0	5	7
193	60	344	17.4	42	285	85.3	7	7
222	83	346	24.0	58	308	81.2	7	3
216	70	339	20.7	63	326	80.7	5	9
191	57	344	16.6	66	393	83.2	8	7
197	48	299	16.1	50	293	82.9	6	7
218	57	313	18.2	46	307	85.0	2	10
199	54	337	16.0	52	316	83.5	4	5
207	58	320	18.1	45	323	86.1	12	7
233	79	359	22.0	59	352	83.2	13	6
219	44	317	13.9	52	277	81.2	2	5
247	57	297	19.2	65	350	81.4	14	4
222	51	295	17.3	66	314	79.0	7	6
227	54	325	16.6	66	354	81.4	9	8
231	60	309	19.4	64	326	80.4	4	8
249	68	379	17.9	69	320	78.4	3	11
229	52	339	15.3	49	319	84.6	6	9
242	60	336	17.9	53	315	83.2	9	6
215	59	331	17.8	56	340	83.5	8	7
235	52	332	15.7	63	350	82.0	14	6
251	54	323	16.7	53	344	84.6	7	9
226	58	289	20.1	63	344	81.7	3	3
231	61	324	18.8	59	319	81.5	9	11
260	57	323	17.7	70	324	78.4	4	7
218	49	325	15.1	55	345	84.1	8	4
237	42	305	13.8	52	327	84.1	2	10
243	46	302	15.2	60	340	82.4	8	14
272	52	296	17.6	68	323	79.0	12	9
266	62	349	17.8	61	283	78.5	10	4
267	52	269	19.3	53	281	81.1	7	6
228	**58**	**324**	**17.8**	**58**	**324**	**82.2**	**7**	**7**

Season Standings

EASTERN CONFERENCE

	GP	W	L	OL	PTS	PTS%	GF	GA
ATLANTIC DIVISION								
Pittsburgh Penguins*	82	47	27	8	102	0.622	247	216
New Jersey Devils*	82	46	29	7	99	0.604	206	197
New York Rangers*	82	42	27	13	97	0.591	213	199
Philadelphia Flyers*	82	42	29	11	95	0.579	248	233
New York Islanders	82	35	38	9	79	0.482	194	243
NORTHEAST DIVISION								
Montreal Canadiens*	82	47	25	10	104	0.634	262	222
Ottawa Senators*	82	43	31	8	94	0.573	261	247
Boston Bruins*	82	41	29	12	94	0.573	212	222
Buffalo Sabres	82	39	31	12	90	0.549	255	242
Toronto Maple Leafs	82	36	35	11	83	0.506	231	260
SOUTHEAST DIVISION								
Washington Capitals*	82	43	31	8	94	0.573	242	231
Carolina Hurricanes	82	43	33	6	92	0.561	252	249
Florida Panthers	82	38	35	9	85	0.518	216	226
Atlanta Thrashers	82	34	40	8	76	0.463	216	272
Tampa Bay Lightning	82	31	42	9	71	0.433	223	267

WESTERN CONFERENCE

	GP	W	L	OL	PTS	PTS%	GF	GA
CENTRAL DIVISION								
Detroit Red Wings*	82	54	21	7	115	0.701	257	184
Nashville Predators*	82	41	32	9	91	0.555	230	229
Chicago Blackhawks	82	40	34	8	88	0.537	239	235
Columbus Blue Jackets	82	34	36	12	80	0.488	193	218
St. Louis Blues	82	33	36	13	79	0.482	205	237
NORTHWEST DIVISION								
Minnesota Wild*	82	44	28	10	98	0.598	223	218
Colorado Avalanche*	82	44	31	7	95	0.579	231	219
Calgary Flames*	82	42	30	10	94	0.573	229	227
Edmonton Oilers	82	41	35	6	88	0.537	235	251
Vancouver Canucks	82	39	33	10	88	0.537	213	215
PACIFIC DIVISION								
San Jose Sharks*	82	49	23	10	108	0.659	222	193
Anaheim Ducks*	82	47	27	8	102	0.622	205	191
Dallas Stars*	82	45	30	7	97	0.591	242	207
Phoenix Coyotes	82	38	37	7	83	0.506	214	231
Los Angeles Kings	82	32	43	7	71	0.433	231	266

Regular Season League Leaders

Goals

1	Alexander Ovechkin	WSH	65
2	Ilya Kovalchuk	ATL	52
3	Jarome Iginla	CGY	50
4	Evgeni Malkin	PIT	47
5	Brad Boyes	STL	43
	Henrik Zetterberg	DET	43

Goals per Game

1	Alexander Ovechkin	WSH	0.79
2	Ilya Kovalchuk	ATL	0.66
3	Jarome Iginla	CGY	0.61
4	Dany Heatley	OTT	0.58
5	3 tied with		0.57

Power-play Goals

1	Alexander Ovechkin	WSH	22
2	Thomas Vanek	BUF	19
3	Olli Jokinen	FLA	18
4	Evgeni Malkin	PIT	17
	Alex Kovalev	MTL	17

Short-handed Goals

1	Patrick Sharp	CHI	7
	Daniel Alfredsson	OTT	7
3	Mike Richards	PHI	5
	Rene Bourque	CHI	5
5	3 tied with		4

Even-strength Goals

1	Alexander Ovechkin	WSH	43
2	Jarome Iginla	CGY	35
3	Ilya Kovalchuk	ATL	34
4	Brad Boyes	STL	32
5	Marian Gaborik	MIN	30

Game-winning Goals

1	Alexander Ovechkin	WSH	11
2	Jeremy Roenick	SJS	10
3	Jarome Iginla	CGY	9
	Brad Boyes	STL	9
	Thomas Vanek	BUF	9

Assists

1	Joe Thornton	SJS	67
2	Pavel Datsyuk	DET	66
3	Marc Savard	BOS	63
4	Henrik Sedin	VAN	61
5	Nicklas Lidstrom	DET	60

Assists per Game

1	Sidney Crosby	PIT	0.91
2	Marc Savard	BOS	0.85
3	Joe Thornton	SJS	0.82
4	Pavel Datsyuk	DET	0.80
5	Nicklas Lidstrom	DET	0.79

Regular Season League Leaders

Points

1	Alexander Ovechkin	WSH	112
2	Evgeni Malkin	PIT	106
3	Jarome Iginla	CGY	98
4	Pavel Datsyuk	DET	97
5	Joe Thornton	SJS	96

Points per Game

1	Alexander Ovechkin	WSH	1.37
2	Sidney Crosby	PIT	1.36
3	Evgeni Malkin	PIT	1.29
4	Daniel Alfredsson	OTT	1.27
5	Henrik Zetterberg	DET	1.23

Total Goals For

1	Alexander Ovechkin	WSH	150
2	Pavel Datsyuk	DET	144
3	Andrei Markov	MTL	140
	Nicklas Lidstrom	DET	140
5	Evgeni Malkin	PIT	137

Total Goals Against

1	Paul Ranger	TBL	113
	Martin St. Louis	TBL	113
3	Jay Bouwmeester	FLA	111
4	Filip Kuba	TBL	107
5	Niclas Havelid	ATL	106

Shots on Goal

1	Alexander Ovechkin	WSH	446
2	Henrik Zetterberg	DET	358
3	Olli Jokinen	FLA	341
4	Jarome Iginla	CGY	338
5	Jason Blake	TOR	332

Shooting Percentage

1	Mike Ribeiro	DAL	25.2
2	Brad Boyes	STL	20.8
3	Marek Svatos	COL	18.6
4	Daniel Alfredsson	OTT	18.4
5	Ilya Kovalchuk	ATL	18.4

Penalty Minutes

1	Daniel Carcillo	PHX	324
2	Jared Boll	CBJ	226
3	Adam Burish	CHI	214
4	Riley Cote	PHI	202
5	Zack Stortini	EDM	201

Fighting Majors

1	Jared Boll	CBJ	27
2	Riley Cote	PHI	24
3	George Parros	ANA	23
	Zack Stortini	EDM	23
5	David Clarkson	NJD	21

Time on Ice per Game

1	Jay Bouwmeester	FLA	27:28
2	Dan Boyle	TBL	27:24
3	Zdeno Chara	BOS	26:50
4	Nicklas Lidstrom	DET	26:43
5	Dion Phaneuf	CGY	26:25

Power-play Time on Ice

1	Tobias Enstrom	ATL	470:45
2	Alexander Ovechkin	WSH	465:11
3	Ilya Kovalchuk	ATL	452:01
4	Tomas Kaberle	TOR	439:55
5	Sergei Gonchar	PIT	439:11

Shifts per Game

1	Brett Clark	COL	31.3
2	Kim Johnsson	MIN	31.2
3	Jay Bouwmeester	FLA	31.1
4	Brent Burns	MIN	30.9
5	Derek Morris	PHX	30.2

Average Shift Length

1	Alexander Ovechkin	WSH	1:05
2	Ilya Kovalchuk	ATL	1:04
3	Sergei Zubov	DAL	1:03
4	Brad Richards	DAL	1:00
	Dan Boyle	TBL	1:00

Hits

1	Dustin Brown	LAK	311
2	Michael Komisarek	MTL	266
3	Brenden Morrow	DAL	260
4	Trent Hunter	NYI	256
5	David Backes	STL	240

Blocked Shots

1	Michael Komisarek	MTL	227
2	Anton Volchenkov	OTT	209
3	Jason Smith	PHI	204
4	Roman Hamrlik	MTL	187
	Steve Staios	EDM	187

Face-off Percentage

1	Scott Nichol	NSH	59.8
2	Manny Malhotra	CBJ	59.0
3	Kris Draper	DET	58.6
4	Bobby Holik	ATL	58.4
5	Rod Brind'Amour	CAR	58.3

Plus / Minus

1	Pavel Datsyuk	DET	41
2	Nicklas Lidstrom	DET	40
3	Dany Heatley	OTT	33
4	Ryan Getzlaf	ANA	32
5	Duncan Keith	CHI	30
	Henrik Zetterberg	DET	30

Regular Season League Leaders

GOALIES

Wins

1	Evgeni Nabokov	SJS	46
2	Martin Brodeur	NJD	44
3	Miikka Kiprusoff	CGY	39
4	Henrik Lundqvist	NYR	37
	Cam Ward	CAR	37

Shots Against

1	Tomas Vokoun	FLA	2213
2	Ryan Miller	BUF	2104
3	Miikka Kiprusoff	CGY	2096
4	Martin Brodeur	NJD	2089
5	Roberto Luongo	VAN	2029

Goals Against Average

1	Chris Osgood	DET	2.09
2	Jean-Sebastien Giguere	ANA	2.12
3	Evgeni Nabokov	SJS	2.14
4	Dominik Hasek	DET	2.14
5	Martin Brodeur	NJD	2.17

Save Percentage

1	Dan Ellis	NSH	0.924
2	Ty Conklin	PIT	0.923
3	Jean-Sebastien Giguere	ANA	0.922
4	Tim Thomas	BOS	0.921
5	Marc-Andre Fleury	PIT	0.921

Shutouts

1	Henrik Lundqvist	NYR	10
2	Pascal Leclaire	CBJ	9
3	Evgeni Nabokov	SJS	6
	Roberto Luongo	VAN	6
	Dan Ellis	NSH	6

Points Percentage

1	Chris Osgood	DET	0.725
2	Dominik Hasek	DET	0.713
3	Niklas Backstrom	MIN	0.685
4	Dan Ellis	NSH	0.681
5	Cristobal Huet	2Tm	0.673

Saves

1	Tomas Vokoun	FLA	2033
2	Martin Brodeur	NJD	1921
3	Ryan Miller	BUF	1907
4	Miikka Kiprusoff	CGY	1899
5	Roberto Luongo	VAN	1861

Assists

1	Rick Dipietro	NYI	6
	Tomas Vokoun	FLA	6
3	Vesa Toskala	TOR	5
4	Martin Brodeur	NJD	4
5	Chris Osgood	DET	3

2008 Playoff Results

Stanley Cup Finals

Game 1	May 24	Detroit Red Wings	4	Pittsburgh Penguins	0	
Game 2	May 26	Detroit Red Wings	3	Pittsburgh Penguins	0	
Game 3	May 28	Pittsburgh Penguins	3	Detroit Red Wings	2	
Game 4	May 31	Pittsburgh Penguins	1	Detroit Red Wings	2	
Game 5	June 02	Detroit Red Wings	3	Pittsburgh Penguins	4	(OT)
Game 6	June 04	Pittsburgh Penguins	2	Detroit Red Wings	3	

Western Conference Finals

Game 1	May 08	Detroit Red Wings	4	Dallas Stars	1	
Game 2	May 10	Detroit Red Wings	2	Dallas Stars	1	
Game 3	May 12	Dallas Stars	2	Detroit Red Wings	5	
Game 4	May 14	Dallas Stars	3	Detroit Red Wings	1	
Game 5	May 17	Detroit Red Wings	1	Dallas Stars	2	
Game 6	May 19	Dallas Stars	1	Detroit Red Wings	4	

Eastern Conference Finals

Game 1	May 09	Pittsburgh Penguins	4	Philadelphia Flyers	2	
Game 2	May 11	Pittsburgh Penguins	4	Philadelphia Flyers	2	
Game 3	May 13	Philadelphia Flyers	1	Pittsburgh Penguins	4	
Game 4	May 15	Philadelphia Flyers	4	Pittsburgh Penguins	2	
Game 5	May 18	Pittsburgh Penguins	6	Philadelphia Flyers	0	

Western Conference Semifinals

Game 1	April 25	San Jose Sharks	2	Dallas Stars	3	(OT)
Game 2	April 27	San Jose Sharks	2	Dallas Stars	5	
Game 3	April 29	Dallas Stars	2	San Jose Sharks	1	(OT)
Game 4	April 30	Dallas Stars	1	San Jose Sharks	2	
Game 5	May 02	San Jose Sharks	3	Dallas Stars	2	(OT)
Game 6	May 04	Dallas Stars	2	San Jose Sharks	1	(OT)

Western Conference Semifinals

Game 1	April 24	Detroit Red Wings	4	Colorado Avalanche	3
Game 2	April 26	Detroit Red Wings	5	Colorado Avalanche	1
Game 3	April 29	Colorado Avalanche	3	Detroit Red Wings	4
Game 4	May 01	Colorado Avalanche	2	Detroit Red Wings	8

Eastern Conference Semifinals

Game 1	April 25	Pittsburgh Penguins	5	New York Rangers	4	
Game 2	April 27	Pittsburgh Penguins	2	New York Rangers	0	
Game 3	April 29	New York Rangers	3	Pittsburgh Penguins	5	
Game 4	May 01	New York Rangers	3	Pittsburgh Penguins	0	
Game 5	May 04	Pittsburgh Penguins	3	New York Rangers	2	(OT)

Eastern Conference Semifinals

Game 1	April 24	Montreal Canadiens	4	Philadelphia Flyers	3	(OT)
Game 2	April 26	Montreal Canadiens	2	Philadelphia Flyers	4	
Game 3	April 28	Philadelphia Flyers	3	Montreal Canadiens	2	
Game 4	April 30	Philadelphia Flyers	4	Montreal Canadiens	2	
Game 5	May 03	Montreal Canadiens	4	Philadelphia Flyers	6	

Western Conference Quarterfinals

Game 1	April 10	Anaheim Ducks	0	Dallas Stars	4
Game 2	April 12	Anaheim Ducks	2	Dallas Stars	5
Game 3	April 15	Dallas Stars	2	Anaheim Ducks	4
Game 4	April 17	Dallas Stars	3	Anaheim Ducks	1

2008 Playoff Leaders

Goals

1	Johan Franzen	DET	13
	Henrik Zetterberg	DET	13
3	Marian Hossa	PIT	12
4	Pavel Datsyuk	DET	10
	Evgeni Malkin	PIT	10
	R.J. Umberger	PHI	10
7	Brenden Morrow	DAL	9
	Daniel Briere	PHI	9
9	Mike Richards	PHI	7
10	Jeff Carter	PHI	6
	Sidney Crosby	PIT	6
	Ryan Malone	PIT	6
	Jordan Staal	PIT	6
	Petr Sykora	PIT	6

Points

1	Sidney Crosby	PIT	27
	Henrik Zetterberg	DET	27
3	Marian Hossa	PIT	26
4	Pavel Datsyuk	DET	23
5	Evgeni Malkin	PIT	22
6	Johan Franzen	DET	18
7	Mike Ribeiro	DAL	17
8	Ryan Malone	PIT	16
	Daniel Briere	PHI	16
10	Jaromir Jagr	NYR	15
	Niklas Kronwall	DET	15
	Brenden Morrow	DAL	15
	Brad Richards	DAL	15
	R.J. Umberger	PHI	15

Assists

1	Sidney Crosby	PIT	21
2	Niklas Kronwall	DET	15
3	Marian Hossa	PIT	14
	Mike Ribeiro	DAL	14
	Henrik Zetterberg	DET	14
6	Pavel Datsyuk	DET	13
	Sergei Gonchar	PIT	13
8	Brad Richards	DAL	12
	Evgeni Malkin	PIT	12
10	Jaromir Jagr	NYR	10
	Nicklas Lidstrom	DET	10
	Ryan Malone	PIT	10
	Vaclav Prospal	PHI	10
	Brian Rafalski	DET	10

Plus / Minus

1	Niklas Kronwall	DET	16
	Henrik Zetterberg	DET	16
3	Brad Stuart	DET	15
4	Pavel Datsyuk	DET	13
	Johan Franzen	DET	13
6	Ryan Whitney	PIT	8
	Mikael Samuelsson	DET	8
	Nicklas Lidstrom	DET	8
	Marian Hossa	PIT	8
10	Sidney Crosby	PIT	7
	Valtteri Filppula	DET	7
	R.J. Umberger	PHI	7

Shots on Goal

1	Henrik Zetterberg	DET	116
2	Mikael Samuelsson	DET	79
3	Marian Hossa	PIT	76
4	Evgeni Malkin	PIT	75
5	Pavel Datsyuk	DET	74
6	Jeff Carter	PHI	72
7	Johan Franzen	DET	70
8	Sidney Crosby	PIT	59
9	Brian Rafalski	DET	58
10	Daniel Cleary	DET	54
	Brad Richards	DAL	54

Penalty Minutes

1	Scottie Upshall	PHI	44
2	Derian Hatcher	PHI	40
3	Maxime Talbot	PIT	36
4	Gary Roberts	PIT	32
5	Stephane Veilleux	MIN	27
6	Jarkko Ruutu	PIT	26
	Cody McLeod	COL	26
	Tomas Holmstrom	DET	26
	Francois Beauchemin	ANA	26
10	Ryan Malone	PIT	25
	Ryan Whitney	PIT	25

GOALIES

Games Played

1	Marc-Andre Fleury	PIT	20
2	Chris Osgood	DET	19
3	Marty Turco	DAL	18
4	Martin Biron	PHI	17
5	Evgeni Nabokov	SJS	13
6	Carey Price	MTL	11
7	Henrik Lundqvist	NYR	10
	Jose Theodore	COL	10
9	Cristobal Huet	WSH	7
	Miikka Kiprusoff	CGY	7
	Tim Thomas	BOS	7

Shots Against

1	Marc-Andre Fleury	PIT	610
2	Martin Biron	PHI	540
3	Marty Turco	DAL	511
4	Chris Osgood	DET	430
5	Evgeni Nabokov	SJS	333
6	Carey Price	MTL	304
7	Henrik Lundqvist	NYR	287
8	Jose Theodore	COL	286
9	Cristobal Huet	WSH	242
10	Dan Ellis	NSH	240

Goals Against Average

1	Chris Osgood	DET	1.55
2	Marc-Andre Fleury	PIT	1.97
3	Marty Turco	DAL	2.08
4	Evgeni Nabokov	SJS	2.18
5	Dan Ellis	NSH	2.52
6	Henrik Lundqvist	NYR	2.57
7	Tim Thomas	BOS	2.65
8	Carey Price	MTL	2.78
9	Niklas Backstrom	MIN	2.83
10	Cristobal Huet	WSH	2.93

Save Percentage

1	Dan Ellis	NSH	0.938
2	Marc-Andre Fleury	PIT	0.933
3	Chris Osgood	DET	0.93
4	Marty Turco	DAL	0.922
5	Tim Thomas	BOS	0.914
6	Henrik Lundqvist	NYR	0.909
7	Cristobal Huet	WSH	0.909
8	Miikka Kiprusoff	CGY	0.908
9	Evgeni Nabokov	SJS	0.907
10	Jose Theodore	COL	0.906

NHL Annual Awards

Art Ross Trophy

Awarded to the NHL player who leads the league in points at the end of the regular season.

Season	Player	Age	Team	Pos	GP	G	A	PTS	+/-	PIM
2007–08	Alexander Ovechkin	22	Washington Capitals	LW	82	65	47	112	28	40
2006–07	Sidney Crosby	19	Pittsburgh Penguins	C	79	36	84	120	10	60
2005–06	Joe Thornton	26	2 Teams	C	81	29	96	125	31	61
2003–04	Martin St. Louis	28	Tampa Bay Lightning	RW	82	38	56	94	35	24
2002–03	Peter Forsberg	29	Colorado Avalanche	C	75	29	77	106	52	70
2001–02	Jarome Iginla	24	Calgary Flames	RW	82	52	44	96	27	77
2000–01	Jaromir Jagr	28	Pittsburgh Penguins	RW	81	52	69	121	19	42
1999–00	Jaromir Jagr	27	Pittsburgh Penguins	RW	63	42	54	96	25	50
1998–99	Jaromir Jagr	26	Pittsburgh Penguins	RW	81	44	83	127	17	66
1997–98	Jaromir Jagr	25	Pittsburgh Penguins	RW	77	35	67	102	17	64
1996–97	Mario Lemieux	31	Pittsburgh Penguins	C	76	50	72	122	27	65
1995–96	Mario Lemieux	30	Pittsburgh Penguins	C	70	69	92	161	10	54
1994–95	Jaromir Jagr	22	Pittsburgh Penguins	RW	48	32	38	70	23	37
1993–94	Wayne Gretzky	33	Los Angeles Kings	C	81	38	92	130	-25	20
1992–93	Mario Lemieux	27	Pittsburgh Penguins	C	60	69	91	160	55	38
1991–92	Mario Lemieux	26	Pittsburgh Penguins	C	64	44	87	131	27	94
1990–91	Wayne Gretzky	30	Los Angeles Kings	C	78	41	122	163	30	16
1989–90	Wayne Gretzky	29	Los Angeles Kings	C	73	40	102	142	8	42
1988–89	Mario Lemieux	23	Pittsburgh Penguins	C	76	85	114	199	41	100
1987–88	Mario Lemieux	22	Pittsburgh Penguins	C	77	70	98	168	23	92

Hart Memorial Trophy

Awarded to the "player adjudged most valuable to his team," voted by the Professional Hockey Writers' Association.

| | | | Goalie Stats | | GP | W | L | T/OT | GAA | Sv% |
| | | | Scoring Stats | | GP | G | A | P | +/- | PIM |
Season	Player	Age	Team	Pos						
2007–08	Alexander Ovechkin	22	Washington Capitals	LW	82	65	47	112	28	40
2006–07	Sidney Crosby	19	Pittsburgh Penguins	C	79	36	84	120	10	60
2005–06	Joe Thornton	26	2 Teams	C	81	29	96	125	31	61
2003–04	Martin St. Louis	28	Tampa Bay Lightning	RW	82	38	56	94	35	24
2002–03	Peter Forsberg	29	Colorado Avalanche	C	75	29	77	106	52	70
2001–02	Jose Theodore	25	Montreal Canadiens	G	67	30	24	10	2.11	0.931
2000–01	Joe Sakic	31	Colorado Avalanche	C	82	54	64	118	45	30
1999–00	Chris Pronger	25	St. Louis Blues	D	79	14	48	62	52	92
1998–99	Jaromir Jagr	26	Pittsburgh Penguins	RW	81	44	83	127	17	66
1997–98	Dominik Hasek	33	Buffalo Sabres	G	72	33	23	13	2.09	0.932
1996–97	Dominik Hasek	32	Buffalo Sabres	G	67	37	20	10	2.27	0.930
1995–96	Mario Lemieux	30	Pittsburgh Penguins	C	70	69	92	161	10	54
1994–95	Eric Lindros	21	Philadelphia Flyers	C	46	29	41	70	27	60
1993–94	Sergei Fedorov	24	Detroit Red Wings	C	82	56	64	120	48	34
1992–93	Mario Lemieux	27	Pittsburgh Penguins	C	60	69	91	160	55	38
1991–92	Mark Messier	31	New York Rangers	C	79	35	72	107	31	76
1990–91	Brett Hull	26	St. Louis Blues	RW	78	86	45	131	23	22
1989–90	Mark Messier	29	Edmonton Oilers	C	79	45	84	129	19	79
1988–89	Wayne Gretzky	28	Los Angeles Kings	C	78	54	114	168	15	26
1987–88	Mario Lemieux	22	Pittsburgh Penguins	C	77	70	98	168	23	92

Lady Byng Memorial Trophy

Awarded to the "player adjudged to have exhibited the best type of sportsmanship and gentlemanly conduct combined with a high standard of playing ability," voted by the Professional Hockey Writers' Association.

Season	Player	Age	Team	Pos	GP	G	A	PTS	+/-	PIM
2007–08	Pavel Datsyuk	29	Detroit Red Wings	C	82	31	66	97	41	20
2006–07	Pavel Datsyuk	28	Detroit Red Wings	C	79	27	60	87	36	20
2005–06	Pavel Datsyuk	27	Detroit Red Wings	C	75	28	59	87	26	22
2003–04	Brad Richards	23	Tampa Bay Lightning	C	82	26	53	79	14	12
2002–03	Alexander Mogilny	33	Toronto Maple Leafs	RW	73	33	46	79	4	12
2001–02	Ron Francis	38	Carolina Hurricanes	C	80	27	50	77	4	18
2000–01	Joe Sakic	31	Colorado Avalanche	C	82	54	64	118	45	30
1999–00	Pavol Demitra	25	St. Louis Blues	LW	71	28	47	75	34	8
1998–99	Wayne Gretzky	38	New York Rangers	C	70	9	53	62	-23	14
1997–98	Ron Francis	34	Pittsburgh Penguins	C	81	25	62	87	12	20
1996–97	Paul Kariya	22	Mighty Ducks of Anaheim	LW	69	44	55	99	36	6
1995–96	Paul Kariya	21	Mighty Ducks of Anaheim	LW	82	50	58	108	9	20
1994–95	Ron Francis	31	Pittsburgh Penguins	C	44	11	48	59	30	18
1993–94	Wayne Gretzky	33	Los Angeles Kings	C	81	38	92	130	-25	20
1992–93	Pierre Turgeon	23	New York Islanders	C	83	58	74	132	-1	26
1991–92	Wayne Gretzky	31	Los Angeles Kings	C	74	31	90	121	-12	34
1990–91	Wayne Gretzky	30	Los Angeles Kings	C	78	41	122	163	30	16
1989–90	Brett Hull	25	St. Louis Blues	RW	80	72	41	113	-1	24
1988–89	Joe Mullen	31	Calgary Flames	RW	79	51	59	110	51	16
1987–88	Mats Naslund	28	Montreal Canadiens	LW	78	24	59	83	17	14

Calder Memorial Trophy

Awarded to the "most proficient" player in his first year of NHL competition, voted by the Professional Hockey Writers' Association.

						Goalie Stats	GP	W	L	T/OT	GAA	Sv%
						Scoring Stats	GP	G	A	PTS	+/-	PIM
Season	Player	Age	Team			Pos						
2007–08	Patrick Kane	19	Chicago Blackhawks			RW	82	21	51	72	-5	52
2006–07	Evgeni Malkin	20	Pittsburgh Penguins			C	78	33	52	85	2	80
2005–06	Alexander Ovechkin	20	Washington Capitals			LW	81	52	54	106	2	52
2003–04	Andrew Raycroft	23	Boston Bruins			G	57	29	18	9	2.05	0.926
2002–03	Barret Jackman	21	St. Louis Blues			D	82	3	16	19	23	190
2001–02	Dany Heatley	21	Atlanta Thrashers			LW	82	26	41	67	-19	56
2000–01	Evgeni Nabokov	25	San Jose Sharks			G	66	32	21	7	2.19	0.915
1999–00	Scott Gomez	20	New Jersey Devils			C	82	19	51	70	14	78
1998–99	Chris Drury	22	Colorado Avalanche			C	79	20	24	44	9	62
1997–98	Sergei Samsonov	19	Boston Bruins			LW	81	22	25	47	9	8
1996–97	Bryan Berard	19	New York Islanders			D	82	8	40	48	1	86
1995–96	Daniel Alfredsson	23	Ottawa Senators			RW	82	26	35	61	-18	28
1994–95	Peter Forsberg	21	Quebec Nordiques			C	47	15	35	50	17	16
1993–94	Martin Brodeur	21	New Jersey Devils			G	47	27	11	8	2.4	0.915
1992–93	Teemu Selanne	22	Winnipeg Jets			RW	84	76	56	132	8	45
1991–92	Pavel Bure	20	Vancouver Canucks			RW	65	34	26	60	0	30
1990–91	Ed Belfour	25	Chicago Blackhawks			G	74	43	19	7	2.47	0.910
1989–90	Sergei Makarov	31	Calgary Flames			RW	80	24	62	86	33	55
1988–89	Brian Leetch	20	New York Rangers			D	68	23	48	71	8	50
1987–88	Joe Nieuwendyk	21	Calgary Flames			C	75	51	41	92	20	23

James Norris Memorial Trophy

Awarded to the NHL's top defense player, voted by the Professional Hockey Writers' Association

Season	Player	Age	Team	Pos	GP	G	A	PTS	+/-	PIM
2007–08	Nicklas Lidstrom	37	Detroit Red Wings	D	76	10	60	70	40	40
2006–07	Nicklas Lidstrom	36	Detroit Red Wings	D	80	13	49	62	40	46
2005–06	Nicklas Lidstrom	35	Detroit Red Wings	D	80	16	64	80	21	50
2003–04	Scott Niedermayer	30	New Jersey Devils	D	81	14	40	54	20	44
2002–03	Nicklas Lidstrom	32	Detroit Red Wings	D	82	18	44	62	40	38
2001–02	Nicklas Lidstrom	31	Detroit Red Wings	D	78	9	50	59	13	20
2000–01	Nicklas Lidstrom	30	Detroit Red Wings	D	82	15	56	71	9	18
1999–00	Chris Pronger	25	St. Louis Blues	D	79	14	48	62	52	92
1998–99	Al MacInnis	35	St. Louis Blues	D	82	20	42	62	33	70
1997–98	Rob Blake	28	Los Angeles Kings	D	81	23	27	50	-3	94
1996–97	Brian Leetch	28	New York Rangers	D	82	20	58	78	31	40
1995–96	Chris Chelios	34	Chicago Blackhawks	D	81	14	58	72	25	140
1994–95	Paul Coffey	33	Detroit Red Wings	D	45	14	44	58	18	72
1993–94	Raymond Bourque	33	Boston Bruins	D	72	20	71	91	26	58
1992–93	Chris Chelios	31	Chicago Blackhawks	D	84	15	58	73	14	282
1991–92	Brian Leetch	23	New York Rangers	D	80	22	80	102	25	26
1990–91	Raymond Bourque	30	Boston Bruins	D	76	21	73	94	33	75
1989–90	Raymond Bourque	29	Boston Bruins	D	76	19	65	84	31	50
1988–89	Chris Chelios	27	Montreal Canadiens	D	80	15	58	73	35	185
1987–88	Raymond Bourque	27	Boston Bruins	D	78	17	64	81	34	72

Bill Masterton Memorial Trophy

Awarded to the NHL player who best exemplifies the qualities of perseverance, sportsmanship and dedication to ice hockey, voted by the Professional Hockey Writers' Association.

			Goalie Stats		GP	W	L	T/OT	GAA	Sv%
			Scoring Stats		GP	G	A	PTS	+/-	PIM
Season	Player	Age	Team	Pos						
2007–08	Jason Blake	34	Toronto Maple Leafs	C	82	15	37	52	-4	28
2006–07	Phil Kessel	19	Boston Bruins	C	70	11	18	29	-12	12
2005–06	Teemu Selanne	35	Mighty Ducks of Anaheim	RW	80	40	50	90	28	44
2003–04	Bryan Berard	26	Chicago Blackhawks	D	58	13	34	47	-24	53
2002–03	Steve Yzerman	37	Detroit Red Wings	C	16	2	6	8	6	8
2001–02	Saku Koivu	27	Montreal Canadiens	C	3	0	2	2	0	0
2000–01	Adam Graves	32	New York Rangers	LW	82	10	16	26	-16	77
1999–00	Ken Daneyko	35	New Jersey Devils	D	78	0	6	6	13	98
1998–99	John Cullen	34	Tampa Bay Lightning	C	4	0	0	0	-2	2
1997–98	Jamie McLennan	26	St. Louis Blues	G	30	16	8	2	2.17	0.903
1996–97	Tony Granato	32	San Jose Sharks	RW	76	25	15	40	-7	159
1995–96	Gary Roberts	29	Calgary Flames	LW	35	22	20	42	15	78
1994–95	Pat LaFontaine	29	Buffalo Sabres	C	22	12	15	27	2	4
1993–94	Cam Neely	28	Boston Bruins	RW	49	50	24	74	12	54
1992–93	Mario Lemieux	27	Pittsburgh Penguins	C	60	69	91	160	55	38
1991–92	Mark Fitzpatrick	23	New York Islanders	G	30	11	13	5	3.2	0.902
1990–91	Dave Taylor	35	Los Angeles Kings	RW	73	23	30	53	27	148
1989–90	Gord Kluzak	25	Boston Bruins	D	8	0	2	2	4	11
1988–89	Tim Kerr	29	Philadelphia Flyers	C/RW	69	48	40	88	-4	73
1987–88	Bob Bourne	33	Los Angeles Kings	C	72	7	11	18	-31	28

Frank J. Selke Trophy

Awarded to the NHL forward who demonstrates the most skill in the defensive component of the game, voted by the Professional Hockey Writers' Association.

Season	Player	Age	Team	Pos	GP	G	A	PTS	+/-	PIM
2007–08	Pavel Datsyuk	29	Detroit Red Wings	C	82	31	66	97	41	20
2006–07	Rod Brind'Amour	36	Carolina Hurricanes	C	78	26	56	82	7	46
2005–06	Rod Brind'Amour	35	Carolina Hurricanes	C	78	31	39	70	8	68
2003–04	Kris Draper	32	Detroit Red Wings	C	67	24	16	40	22	31
2002–03	Jere Lehtinen	29	Dallas Stars	RW	80	31	17	48	39	20
2001–02	Michael Peca	27	New York Islanders	C	80	25	35	60	19	62
2000–01	John Madden	27	New Jersey Devils	C	80	23	15	38	24	12
1999–00	Steve Yzerman	34	Detroit Red Wings	C	78	35	44	79	28	34
1998–99	Jere Lehtinen	25	Dallas Stars	RW	74	20	32	52	29	18
1997–98	Jere Lehtinen	24	Dallas Stars	RW	72	23	19	42	19	20
1996–97	Michael Peca	22	Buffalo Sabres	C	79	20	29	49	26	80
1995–96	Sergei Fedorov	26	Detroit Red Wings	C	78	39	68	107	49	48
1994–95	Ron Francis	31	Pittsburgh Penguins	C	44	11	48	59	30	18
1993–94	Sergei Fedorov	24	Detroit Red Wings	C	82	56	64	120	48	34
1992–93	Doug Gilmour	29	Toronto Maple Leafs	C	83	32	95	127	32	100
1991–92	Guy Carbonneau	31	Montreal Canadiens	C	72	18	21	39	2	39
1990–91	Dirk Graham	31	Chicago Blackhawks	W	80	24	21	45	12	88
1989–90	Rick Meagher	36	St. Louis Blues	C	76	8	17	25	4	47
1988–89	Guy Carbonneau	28	Montreal Canadiens	C	79	26	30	56	37	44
1987–88	Guy Carbonneau	27	Montreal Canadiens	C	80	17	21	38	14	61

Lester B. Pearson Award

Awarded to the most outstanding player, voted by the NHL Players' Association.

| | | | | | Goalie Stats | GP | W | L | T/OT | GAA | Sv% |
					Scoring Stats	GP	G	A	PTS	+/-	PIM
Season	Player	Age	Team		Pos						
2007–08	Alexander Ovechkin	22	Washington Capitals		LW	82	65	47	112	28	40
2006–07	Sidney Crosby	19	Pittsburgh Penguins		C	79	36	84	120	10	60
2005–06	Jaromir Jagr	33	New York Rangers		RW	82	54	69	123	34	72
2003–04	Martin St. Louis	28	Tampa Bay Lightning		RW	82	38	56	94	35	24
2002–03	Markus Naslund	29	Vancouver Canucks		LW	82	48	56	104	6	52
2001–02	Jarome Iginla	24	Calgary Flames		RW	82	52	44	96	27	77
2000–01	Joe Sakic	31	Colorado Avalanche		C	82	54	64	118	45	30
1999–00	Jaromir Jagr	27	Pittsburgh Penguins		RW	63	42	54	96	25	50
1998–99	Jaromir Jagr	26	Pittsburgh Penguins		RW	81	44	83	127	17	66
1997–98	Dominik Hasek	33	Buffalo Sabres		G	72	33	23	13	2.09	0.932
1996–97	Dominik Hasek	32	Buffalo Sabres		G	67	37	20	10	2.27	0.930
1995–96	Mario Lemieux	30	Pittsburgh Penguins		C	70	69	92	161	10	54
1994–95	Eric Lindros	21	Philadelphia Flyers		C	46	29	41	70	27	60
1993–94	Sergei Fedorov	24	Detroit Red Wings		C	82	56	64	120	48	34
1992–93	Mario Lemieux	27	Pittsburgh Penguins		C	60	69	91	160	55	38
1991–92	Mark Messier	31	New York Rangers		C	79	35	72	107	31	76
1990–91	Brett Hull	26	St. Louis Blues		RW	78	86	45	131	23	22
1989–90	Mark Messier	29	Edmonton Oilers		C	79	45	84	129	19	79
1988–89	Steve Yzerman	23	Detroit Red Wings		C	80	65	90	155	17	61
1987–88	Mario Lemieux	22	Pittsburgh Penguins		C	77	70	98	168	23	92

King Clancy Memorial Trophy

Awarded to the NHL player who best exemplifies leadership qualities on and off the ice and who has made a significant humanitarian contribution in his community. Selected by "a special panel of representatives" from the Professional Hockey Writers' Association and the NHL Broadcasters' Association.

| | | | Goalie Stats | | GP | W | L | T/OT | GAA | Sv% |
| | | | Scoring Stats | | GP | G | A | P | +/- | PIM |
Season	Player	Age	Team	Pos						
2007–08	Vincent Lecavalier	27	Tampa Bay Lightning	C	81	40	52	92	-17	89
2006–07	Saku Koivu	32	Montreal Canadiens	C	81	22	53	75	-21	74
2005–06	Olaf Kolzig	35	Washington Capitals	G	59	20	28	11	3.53	0.896
2003–04	Jarome Iginla	26	Calgary Flames	RW	81	41	32	73	21	84
2002–03	Brendan Shanahan	34	Detroit Red Wings	LW	78	30	38	68	5	103
2001–02	Ron Francis	38	Carolina Hurricanes	C	80	27	50	77	4	18
2000–01	Shjon Podein	32	Colorado Avalanche	LW	82	15	17	32	7	68
1999–00	Curtis Joseph	32	Toronto Maple Leafs	G	63	36	20	7	2.49	0.915
1998–99	Rob Ray	30	Buffalo Sabres	RW	76	0	4	4	-2	261
1997–98	Kelly Chase	30	St. Louis Blues	RW	67	4	3	7	10	231
1996–97	Trevor Linden	26	Vancouver Canucks	RW	49	9	31	40	5	27
1995–96	Kris King	29	Winnipeg Jets	LW	81	9	11	20	-7	151
1994–95	Joe Nieuwendyk	28	Calgary Flames	C	46	21	29	50	11	33
1993–94	Adam Graves	25	New York Rangers	LW	84	52	27	79	27	127
1992–93	Dave Poulin	34	Boston Bruins	C	84	16	33	49	29	62
1991–92	Raymond Bourque	31	Boston Bruins	D	80	21	60	81	11	56
1990–91	Dave Taylor	35	Los Angeles Kings	RW	73	23	30	53	27	148
1989–90	Kevin Lowe	30	Edmonton Oilers	D	78	7	26	33	18	140
1988–89	Bryan Trottier	32	New York Islanders	C	73	17	28	45	-7	44
1987–88	Lanny McDonald	34	Calgary Flames	RW	60	10	13	23	2	57

Maurice Richard Trophy

Awarded to the NHL's leading goal scorer.

Season	Player	Age	Team	Pos	GP	G	A	PTS	+/-	PIM
2007–08	Alexander Ovechkin	22	Washington Capitals	LW	82	65	47	112	28	40
2006–07	Vincent Lecavalier	26	Tampa Bay Lightning	C	82	52	56	108	2	44
2005–06	Jonathan Cheechoo	25	San Jose Sharks	RW	82	56	37	93	23	58
2003–04	Rick Nash	19	Columbus Blue Jackets	LW	80	41	16	57	-35	87
2003–04	Ilya Kovalchuk	20	Atlanta Thrashers	LW	81	41	46	87	-10	63
2002–03	Milan Hejduk	26	Colorado Avalanche	RW	82	50	48	98	52	32
2001–02	Jarome Iginla	24	Calgary Flames	RW	82	52	44	96	27	77
2000–01	Pavel Bure	29	Florida Panthers	RW	82	59	33	92	-2	58
1999–00	Pavel Bure	28	Florida Panthers	RW	74	58	36	94	25	16
1998–99	Teemu Selanne	28	Mighty Ducks of Anaheim	RW	75	47	60	107	18	30

Conn Smythe Trophy

Awarded to the NHL player judged most valuable to his team during the NHL playoffs, voted by the Professional Hockey Writers' Association.

| | | | | | Goalie Stats | GP | W | L | T/OT | GAA | Sv% |
| | | | | | Scoring Stats | GP | G | A | PTS | +/- | PIM |
Season	Player	Age	Team	Pos							
2007–08	Henrik Zetterberg	27	Detroit Red Wings	LW		22	13	14	27	16	16
2006–07	Scott Niedermayer	33	Anaheim Ducks	D		21	3	8	11	2	26
2005–06	Cam Ward	21	Carolina Hurricanes	G		23	15	8		2.14	0.920
2003–04	Brad Richards	23	Tampa Bay Lightning	C		23	12	14	26	5	4
2002–03	Jean–Sebastien Giguere	25	Mighty Ducks of Anaheim	G		21	15	6		1.62	0.945
2001–02	Nicklas Lidstrom	31	Detroit Red Wings	D		23	5	11	16	6	2
2000–01	Patrick Roy	35	Colorado Avalanche	G		23	16	7		1.7	0.934
1999–00	Scott Stevens	35	New Jersey Devils	D		23	3	8	11	9	6
1998–99	Joe Nieuwendyk	32	Dallas Stars	C		23	11	10	21	7	19
1997–98	Steve Yzerman	32	Detroit Red Wings	C		22	6	18	24	10	22
1996–97	Mike Vernon	33	Detroit Red Wings	G		20	16	4		1.76	0.927
1995–96	Joe Sakic	26	Colorado Avalanche	C		22	18	16	34	10	14
1994–95	Claude Lemieux	29	New Jersey Devils	RW		20	13	3	16	12	20
1993–94	Brian Leetch	25	New York Rangers	D		23	11	23	34	19	6
1992–93	Patrick Roy	27	Montreal Canadiens	G		20	16	4		2.13	0.929
1991–92	Mario Lemieux	26	Pittsburgh Penguins	C		15	16	18	34	6	2
1990–91	Mario Lemieux	25	Pittsburgh Penguins	C		23	16	28	44	14	16
1989–90	Bill Ranford	23	Edmonton Oilers	G		22	16	6		2.53	0.912
1988–89	Al MacInnis	25	Calgary Flames	D		22	7	24	31	6	46
1987–88	Wayne Gretzky	27	Edmonton Oilers	C		19	12	31	43	9	16

Vezina Trophy

Awarded to the NHL's most valuable goalie, voted by the 30 team General Managers.

Season	Player	Age	Team	Pos	GP	W	L	T/OT	GAA	Sv%
2007–08	Martin Brodeur	35	New Jersey Devils	G	77	44	27	6	2.17	0.92
2006–07	Martin Brodeur	34	New Jersey Devils	G	78	48	23	7	2.18	0.922
2005–06	Miikka Kiprusoff	29	Calgary Flames	G	74	42	20	11	2.07	0.923
2003–04	Martin Brodeur	31	New Jersey Devils	G	75	38	26	11	2.03	0.917
2002–03	Martin Brodeur	30	New Jersey Devils	G	73	41	23	9	2.02	0.914
2001–02	Jose Theodore	25	Montreal Canadiens	G	67	30	24	10	2.11	0.931
2000–01	Dominik Hasek	36	Buffalo Sabres	G	67	37	24	4	2.11	0.921
1999–00	Olaf Kolzig	29	Washington Capitals	G	73	41	20	11	2.24	0.917
1998–99	Dominik Hasek	34	Buffalo Sabres	G	64	30	18	14	1.87	0.937
1997–98	Dominik Hasek	33	Buffalo Sabres	G	72	33	23	13	2.09	0.932
1996–97	Dominik Hasek	32	Buffalo Sabres	G	67	37	20	10	2.27	0.93
1995–96	Jim Carey	21	Washington Capitals	G	71	35	24	9	2.26	0.906
1994–95	Dominik Hasek	30	Buffalo Sabres	G	41	19	14	7	2.11	0.93
1993–94	Dominik Hasek	29	Buffalo Sabres	G	58	30	20	6	1.95	0.93
1992–93	Ed Belfour	27	Chicago Blackhawks	G	71	41	18	11	2.59	0.906
1991–92	Patrick Roy	26	Montreal Canadiens	G	67	36	22	8	2.36	0.914
1990–91	Ed Belfour	25	Chicago Blackhawks	G	74	43	19	7	2.47	0.91
1989–90	Patrick Roy	24	Montreal Canadiens	G	54	31	16	5	2.53	0.912
1988–89	Patrick Roy	23	Montreal Canadiens	G	48	33	5	6	2.47	0.908
1987–88	Grant Fuhr	25	Edmonton Oilers	G	75	40	24	9	3.43	0.881

William M. Jennings Trophy

Awarded "to the goalkeeper(s) having played a minimum of 25 games for the team with the fewest goals scored against it."

Season	Player	Age	Team	Pos	GP	W	L	T/OT	GAA	Sv%
2007–08	Chris Osgood	35	Detroit Red Wings	G	43	27	9	4	2.09	0.914
2007–08	Dominik Hasek	43	Detroit Red Wings	G	41	27	10	3	2.14	0.902
2006–07	Manny Fernandez	32	Minnesota Wild	G	44	22	16	1	2.55	0.911
2006–07	Niklas Backstrom	28	Minnesota Wild	G	41	23	8	6	1.97	0.929
2003–04	Martin Brodeur	31	New Jersey Devils	G	75	38	26	11	2.03	0.917
2002–03	Martin Brodeur	30	New Jersey Devils	G	73	41	23	9	2.02	0.914
2002–03	Roman Cechmanek	31	Philadelphia Flyers	G	58	33	15	10	1.83	0.925
2002–03	Robert Esche	25	Philadelphia Flyers	G	30	12	9	3	2.2	0.907
2001–02	Patrick Roy	36	Colorado Avalanche	G	63	32	23	8	1.94	0.925
2000–01	Dominik Hasek	36	Buffalo Sabres	G	67	37	24	4	2.11	0.921
1999–00	Roman Turek	29	St. Louis Blues	G	67	42	15	9	1.95	0.912
1998–99	Roman Turek	28	Dallas Stars	G	26	16	3	3	2.08	0.915
1998–99	Ed Belfour	33	Dallas Stars	G	61	35	15	9	1.99	0.915
1997–98	Martin Brodeur	25	New Jersey Devils	G	70	43	17	8	1.89	0.917
1996–97	Mike Dunham	24	New Jersey Devils	G	26	8	7	1	2.55	0.906
1996–97	Martin Brodeur	24	New Jersey Devils	G	67	37	14	13	1.88	0.927
1995–96	Mike Vernon	32	Detroit Red Wings	G	32	21	7	2	2.26	0.903
1995–96	Chris Osgood	23	Detroit Red Wings	G	50	39	6	5	2.17	0.911
1994–95	Ed Belfour	29	Chicago Blackhawks	G	42	22	15	3	2.28	0.906
1993–94	Dominik Hasek	29	Buffalo Sabres	G	58	30	20	6	1.95	0.93
1992–93	Ed Belfour	27	Chicago Blackhawks	G	71	41	18	11	2.59	0.906
1991–92	Patrick Roy	26	Montreal Canadiens	G	67	36	22	8	2.36	0.914
1990–91	Ed Belfour	25	Chicago Blackhawks	G	74	43	19	7	2.47	0.91
1989–90	Andy Moog	29	Boston Bruins	G	46	24	10	7	2.89	0.893
1988–89	Patrick Roy	23	Montreal Canadiens	G	48	33	5	6	2.47	0.908
1987–88	Patrick Roy	22	Montreal Canadiens	G	45	23	12	9	2.9	0.9

First and Second Team All-Stars

2008 First Team

Pos	Name	Team
LW	Alexander Ovechkin	WSH
C	Evgeni Malkin	PIT
RW	Jerome Iginla	CGY
D	Nicklas Lidstrom	DET
D	Dion Phaneuf	CGY
G	Evgeni Nabokov	SJS

Second Team

Pos	Name	Team
LW	Henrik Zetterberg	DET
C	Joe Thornton	SJS
RW	Alex Kovalev	MTL
D	Brian Campbell	SJS
D	Zdeno Chara	BOS
G	Martin Brodeur	NJD

2007 First Team

Pos	Name	Team
LW	Alexander Ovechkin	WSH
C	Sidney Crosby	PIT
RW	Dany Heatley	OTT
D	Nicklas Lidstrom	DET
D	Scott Niedermayer	ANA
G	Martin Brodeur	NJD

Second Team

Pos	Name	Team
LW	Thomas Vanek	BUF
C	Vincent Lecavalier	TB
RW	Martin St. Louis	TB
D	Dan Boyle	TB
D	Chris Pronger	ANA
G	Roberto Luongo	FLA

2006 First Team

Pos	Name	Team
LW	Alexander Ovechkin	WSH
C	Joe Thornton	SJS
RW	Jaromir Jagr	NYR
D	Nicklas Lidstrom	DET
D	Scott Niedermayer	ANA
G	Miikka Kiprusoff	CGY

Second Team

Pos	Name	Team
LW	Dany Heatley	OTT
C	Eric Staal	CAR
RW	Daniel Alfredsson	OTT
D	Zdeno Chara	OTT
D	Sergei Zubov	DAL
G	Martin Brodeur	NJD

2004 First Team

Pos	Name	Team
LW	Markus Naslund	VAN
C	Joe Sakic	COL
RW	Martin St. Louis	TB
D	Zdeno Chara	OTT
D	Scott Niedermayer	NJD
G	Martin Brodeur	NJD

Second Team

Pos	Name	Team
LW	Ilya Kovalchuk	ATL
C	Mats Sundin	TOR
RW	Jarome Iginla	CGY
D	Bryan McCabe	TOR
D	Chris Pronger	STL
G	Roberto Luongo	FLA

2003

Pos	First Team Name	Team
LW	Markus Naslund	VAN
C	Peter Forsberg	COL
RW	Todd Bertuzzi	VAN
D	Nicklas Lidstrom	DET
D	Al MacInnis	STL
G	Martin Brodeur	NJD

Pos	Second Team Name	Team
LW	Paul Kariya	ANA
C	Joe Thornton	BOS
RW	Milan Hedjuk	COL
D	Sergei Gonchar	WSH
D	Derian Hatcher	DAL
G	Marty Turco	DAL

2002

Pos	First Team Name	Team
LW	Markus Naslund	VAN
C	Joe Sakic	COL
RW	Jarome Iginla	CGY
D	Chris Chelios	DET
D	Nicklas Lidstrom	DET
G	Patrick Roy	COL

Pos	Second Team Name	Team
LW	Brendan Shanahan	DET
C	Mats Sundin	TOR
RW	Bill Guerin	BOS
D	Rob Blake	COL
D	Sergei Gonchar	WSH
G	Jose Theodore	MTL

2001

Pos	First Team Name	Team
LW	Patrik Elias	NJD
C	Joe Sakic	COL
RW	Jaromir Jagr	PIT
D	Raymond Bourque	COL
D	Nicklas Lidstrom	DET
G	Dominik Hasek	BUF

Pos	Second Team Name	Team
LW	Luc Robitaille	LA
C	Mario Lemieux	PIT
RW	Pavel Bure	NYR
D	Rob Blake	COL
D	Scott Stevens	NJD
G	Roman Cechmanek	PHI

2000

Pos	First Team Name	Team
LW	Brendan Shanahan	DET
C	Steve Yzerman	DET
RW	Jaromir Jagr	PIT
D	Nicklas Lidstrom	DET
D	Chris Pronger	STL
G	Olaf Kolzig	WSH

Pos	Second Team Name	Team
LW	Paul Kariya	ANA
C	Mike Modano	DAL
RW	Pavel Bure	FLA
D	Rob Blake	LA
D	Eric Desjardins	PHI
G	Roman Turek	STL

1999 First Team		
Pos	Name	Team
LW	Paul Kariya	ANA
C	Peter Forsberg	COL
RW	Jaromir Jagr	PIT
D	Nicklas Lidstrom	DET
D	Al MacInnis	STL
G	Dominik Hasek	BUF

Second Team		
Pos	Name	Team
LW	John Leclair	PHI
C	Alexei Yashin	OTT
RW	Teemu Selanne	ANA
D	Raymond Bourque	BOS
D	Eric Desjardins	PHI
G	Byron Dafoe	BOS

All-Rookie Teams

2008

Pos	Name	Team
F	Nicklas Backstrom	WSH
F	Patrick Kane	CHI
F	Jonathan Toews	CHI
D	Tobias Enstrom	ATL
D	Tom Gilbert	EDM
G	Carey Price	MTL

2007

Pos	Name	Team
F	Evgeni Malkin	PIT
F	Jordan Staal	PIT
F	Paul Statsny	COL
D	Matt Carle	SJS
D	Marc-Edouard Vlasic	SJS
G	Mike Smith	DAL

2006

Pos	Name	Team
F	Brad Boyes	BOS
F	Sidney Crosby	PIT
F	Alexander Ovechkin	WSH
D	Andrej Meszaros	OTT
D	Dion Phaneuf	CGY
G	Henrik Lundqvist	NYR

2004

Pos	Name	Team
F	Trent Hunter	NYI
F	Ryan Malone	PIT
F	Michael Ryder	MTL
D	John-Michael Liles	COL
D	Joni Pitkanen	PHI
G	Andrew Raycroft	BOS

2003

Pos	Name	Team
F	Tyler Arnason	CHI
F	Rick Nash	CBJ
F	Henrik Zetterberg	DET
D	Jay Bouwmeester	FLA
D	Barret Jackman	STL
G	Sebastien Caron	PIT

2002

Pos	Name	Team
F	Dany Heatley	ATL
F	Kristian Huselius	FLA
F	Ilya Kovalchuk	ATL
D	Nick Boynton	BOS
D	Rostislav Klesla	CBJ
G	Dan Blackburn	NYR

2001

Pos	Name	Team
F	Martin Havlat	OTT
F	Brad Richards	TB
F	Shane Willis	CAR
D	Lubomir Visnovsky	LA
D	Colin White	NJD
G	Evgeni Nabokov	SJS

2000

Pos	Name	Team
F	Simon Gagne	PHI
F	Scott Gomez	NJD
F	Mike York	NYR
D	Brian Rafalski	NJD
D	Brad Stuart	SJS
G	Brian Boucher	PHI

1999

Pos	Name	Team
F	Chris Drury	COL
F	Milan Hedjuk	COL
F	Marian Hossa	OTT
D	Tom Poti	EDM
D	Sami Salo	OTT
G	Jamie Storr	LA

Hall of Fame Inductees

Year	Name	Category	GP	G	A	PTS	+/-	PIM	W	L	T/OT	GAA	Sv%
			\<span\>Skater Statistics\</span\>							\<span\>Goalie Statistics\</span\>			
2007	Ron Francis	Player	1731	549	1249	1798	-10	979					
2007	Al MacInnis	Player	1416	340	934	1274	373	1511					
2007	Mark Messier	Player	1756	694	1193	1887	210	1910					
2007	Scott Stevens	Player	1635	196	712	908	393	2785					
2006	Dick Duff	Player	1030	283	289	572	-47	743					
2006	Patrick Roy	Player	1029	0	45	45	0	262	551	315	131	2.54	0.910
2005	Murray Costello	Builder	162	13	19	32		54					
2005	Valeri Kharlamov	Player											
2005	Cam Neely	Player	726	395	299	694	82	1241					
2004	Raymond Bourque	Player	1612	410	1169	1579	528	1141					
2004	Paul Coffey	Player	1409	396	1135	1531	294	1802					
2004	Larry Murphy	Player	1615	287	929	1216	200	1084					
2003	Grant Fuhr	Player	868	0	40	40	0	114	403	295	114	3.38	0.887
2003	Brian Kilrea	Builder	26	3	5	8	-4	12					
2003	Pat LaFontaine	Player	865	468	545	1013	-4	552					
2002	Bernie Federko	Player	1000	369	761	1130	-132	487					
2002	Clark Gillies	Player	958	319	378	697	241	1023					
2002	Rod Langway	Player	994	51	278	329	277	849					
2001	Viacheslav Fetisov	Player	546	36	192	228	114	656					
2001	Mike Gartner	Player	1432	708	627	1335	67	1159					
2001	Dale Hawerchuk	Player	1188	518	891	1409	-92	730					
2001	Jari Kurri	Player	1251	601	797	1398	282	545					
2001	Craig Patrick	Builder	401	72	91	163	-131	61					
2000	Joe Mullen	Player	1062	502	561	1063	163	241					
2000	Denis Savard	Player	1196	473	865	1338	97	1336					
1999	Wayne Gretzky	Player	1487	894	1963	2857	518	577					
1998	Roy Conacher	Player	490	226	200	426		90					
1998	Michel Goulet	Player	1089	548	604	1152	97	825					
1998	Peter Stastny	Player	977	450	789	1239	-12	824					

2008 Statistical Registry

Player	Team	Pos	GP	G	A	P	PIM	+/-	PP	SH	GW	OT	S
Abdelkader, Justin	DET	L	2	0	0	0	2	0	0	0	0	0	6
NHL Totals			2	0	0	0	2						
Adams, Craig	CHI	R	75	4	7	11	58	-16	0	1	1	0	63
NHL Totals			462	35	48	83	361						
Adams, Kevyn	CHI	C	27	0	2	2	13	-7	0	0	0	0	32
NHL Totals			540	59	77	136	317						
Afinogenov, Maxim	BUF	R	56	10	18	28	42	-16	1	0	1	0	114
NHL Totals			521	128	186	314	420						
Alberts, Andrew	BOS	D	35	0	2	2	39	4	0	0	0	0	25
NHL Totals			184	1	18	19	231						
Alfredsson, Daniel	OTT	R	70	40	49	89	34	15	9	7	5	1	217
NHL Totals			853	331	516	847	385						
Allen, Bobby	BOS	D	19	0	0	0	2	-2	0	0	0	0	10
NHL Totals			51	0	3	3	12						
Allen, Bryan	FLA	D	73	2	14	16	67	5	0	0	0	0	67
NHL Totals			371	20	53	73	467						
Antropov, Nik	TOR	R	72	26	30	56	92	10	12	0	5	1	165
NHL Totals			446	104	141	245	453						
Armstrong, Colby	ATL	R	72	13	22	35	56	4	1	0	3	0	113
NHL Totals			199	41	68	109	181						
Armstrong, Derek	LAK	C	77	8	27	35	63	4	1	0	2	0	118
NHL Totals			415	67	145	212	290						
Arnason, Tyler	COL	C	70	10	21	31	16	-1	3	0	1	0	179
NHL Totals			416	83	140	223	126						
Arnott, Jason	NSH	C	79	28	44	72	54	19	13	0	3	0	248
NHL Totals			971	331	439	770	1101						
Asham, Arron	NJD	R	77	6	4	10	84	-6	0	0	2	0	68
NHL Totals			498	64	71	135	537						
Aucoin, Adrian	CGY	D	76	10	25	35	37	13	5	0	1	0	121
NHL Totals			770	98	204	302	581						
Aucoin, Keith	CAR	R	38	5	8	13	10	3	0	0	0	0	65
NHL Totals			53	5	10	15	14						
Avery, Sean	NYR	L	57	15	18	33	154	6	2	0	4	0	125
NHL Totals			379	65	102	167	1067						
Axelsson, P.J.	BOS	L	75	13	16	29	15	11	0	2	2	0	100
NHL Totals			722	97	160	257	260						
Backes, David	STL	C	72	13	18	31	99	-11	3	0	2	0	129
NHL Totals			121	23	31	54	136						
Backman, Christian	NYR	D	63	3	15	18	50	-2	1	0	0	0	51
NHL Totals			246	21	51	72	150						

S%	TOI/G	Sft/G	Hits	BkS	MsS	GvA	TkA	FOW	FOL	Tot	FO%	%Tm	S/G	PS
0	12:13	16.5	5	0	2	0	1	5	7	12	41.7	10.4	3	0
6.3	10:47	15.8	117	43	26	9	22	19	22	41	46.3	0.9	0.8	0
0	10:56	15.8	13	11	7	3	9	103	104	207	49.8	14.5	1.2	0
8.8	16:03	17.9	25	6	47	44	17	1	4	5	20	0.1	2	0
0	20:37	24.9	53	52	14	15	5	1	1	2	50	0.1	0.7	0
18.4	22:17	24.4	55	30	70	60	72	21	18	39	53.8	0.9	3.1	1
0	9:53	13.9	15	6	3	5	0	0	0	0	0	0	0.5	0
3	21:17	25.7	112	119	35	25	27	0	0	0	0	0	0.9	0
15.8	20:06	26.4	102	51	75	53	30	114	157	271	42.1	6.6	2.3	0
11.5	16:03	21.4	85	31	41	13	42	3	12	15	20	0.3	1.6	0
6.8	13:16	18.9	106	29	41	43	19	380	370	750	50.7	17.2	1.5	0
5.6	15:15	19.6	6	17	38	41	61	375	417	792	47.3	20.4	2.6	0
11.3	18:59	22.3	42	23	96	30	50	614	646	1260	48.7	27.4	3.1	0
8.8	8:33	12.3	87	5	12	18	21	0	3	3	0	0	0.9	0
8.3	20:57	25	69	55	74	35	35	0	0	0	0	0	1.6	0
7.7	13:27	17.3	34	8	26	7	22	124	203	327	37.9	14.3	1.7	0
12	15:50	19.6	119	11	65	29	18	11	17	28	39.3	0.9	2.2	0
13	17:36	23.5	44	37	46	30	40	17	28	45	37.8	1	1.3	0
10.1	14:40	20.3	240	13	45	14	20	30	37	67	44.8	1.6	1.8	0
5.9	19:12	23.9	34	51	29	25	13	0	0	0	0	0	0.8	0

Player	Team	Pos	GP	G	A	P	PIM	+/-	PP	SH	GW	OT	S
Backstrom, Nicklas	WSH	C	82	14	55	69	24	13	3	0	4	1	153
NHL Totals			82	14	55	69	24						
Ballard, Keith	PHX	D	82	6	15	21	85	7	2	1	1	0	105
NHL Totals			233	19	68	87	243						
Baranka, Ivan	NYR	D	1	0	1	1	0	1	0	0	0	0	1
NHL Totals			1	0	1	1	0						
Barch, Krystofer	DAL	R	48	1	2	3	105	-3	0	0	0	0	23
NHL Totals			74	4	4	8	212						
Barker, Cameron	CHI	D	45	6	12	18	52	-3	2	0	0	0	42
NHL Totals			81	7	19	26	96						
Barnes, Stu	DAL	C	79	12	11	23	26	-3	0	2	4	0	71
NHL Totals			1136	261	336	597	438						
Bass, Cody	OTT	C	21	2	2	4	19	-1	0	1	1	0	12
NHL Totals			21	2	2	4	19						
Bates, Shawn	NYI	C	2	0	0	0	0	-2	0	0	0	0	0
NHL Totals			465	72	126	198	266						
Battaglia, Bates	TOR	L	13	0	0	0	7	-6	0	0	0	0	6
NHL Totals			580	80	118	198	385						
Bayda, Ryan	CAR	L	31	3	3	6	28	-2	0	0	0	0	58
NHL Totals			109	11	17	28	68						
Beauchemin, Francois	ANA	D	82	2	19	21	59	-9	0	0	2	1	144
NHL Totals			226	17	68	85	160						
Beech, Kris	PIT	C	25	6	5	11	4	3	2	0	0	0	36
NHL Totals			198	25	42	67	113						
Begin, Steve	MTL	L	44	3	5	8	48	0	0	0	0	0	67
NHL Totals			347	40	34	74	440						
Belak, Wade	FLA	R	47	1	0	1	78	-2	0	0	0	0	17
NHL Totals			442	8	21	29	1108						
Belanger, Eric	MIN	C	75	13	24	37	30	-6	7	1	3	0	115
NHL Totals			478	93	129	222	225						
Bell, Brendan	PHX	D	2	0	0	0	0	-2	0	0	0	0	0
NHL Totals			48	1	6	7	27						
Bell, Mark	TOR	L	35	4	6	10	60	-2	0	0	0	0	42
NHL Totals			445	87	95	182	597						
Berard, Bryan	NYI	D	54	5	17	22	48	-17	4	0	2	0	87
NHL Totals			619	76	247	323	500						
Bergenheim, Sean	NYI	L	78	10	12	22	62	-3	1	0	1	0	155
NHL Totals			124	15	18	33	66						
Bergeron, Marc-Andre	ANA	D	55	9	10	19	20	-16	8	0	1	0	108
NHL Totals			297	48	80	128	131						
Bergeron, Patrice	BOS	C	10	3	4	7	2	2	2	0	0	0	24
NHL Totals			239	72	117	189	72						

S%	TOI/G	Sft/G	Hits	BkS	MsS	GvA	TkA	FOW	FOL	Tot	FO%	%Tm	S/G	PS
9.2	18:59	20	34	34	75	50	72	405	469	874	46.3	18.4	1.9	0
5.7	21:15	29.7	169	162	39	38	34	0	0	0	0	0	1.3	0
0	12:44	17	1	1	0	0	0	0	0	0	0	0	1	0
4.3	6:30	8.8	72	6	9	10	10	0	2	2	0	0	0.5	0
14.3	17:11	22.1	46	33	19	8	5	0	0	0	0	0	0.9	0
16.9	13:37	17.4	14	25	38	29	62	343	284	627	54.7	15	0.9	0
16.7	5:18	8.3	19	7	2	2	0	32	41	73	43.8	5.9	0.6	0
0	7	10.5	2	1	0	0	0	1	3	4	25	3.7	0	0
0	4:45	7.3	1	0	1	1	0	0	1	1	0	0.1	0.5	0
5.2	12:35	16.9	38	2	15	4	11	0	2	2	0	0.1	1.9	0
1.4	25:31	26.4	97	71	83	46	36	0	1	1	0	0	1.8	0
16.7	11:30	17.1	33	3	3	5	6	144	132	276	52.2	19.2	1.4	0
4.5	11:38	16.3	119	27	22	11	8	24	45	69	34.8	2.6	1.5	0
5.9	4:04	6.3	41	5	1	4	4	0	1	1	0	0	0.4	0
11.3	17:13	27.3	51	46	65	35	40	587	608	1195	49.1	28.1	1.5	0
0	14:49	19.5	0	2	1	0	0	0	0	0	0	0	0	0
9.5	9:44	13.9	28	9	21	10	13	74	105	179	41.3	9.1	1.2	0
5.7	17:38	19.1	37	59	37	37	19	0	0	0	0	0	1.6	0
6.5	11:15	14	138	20	51	28	42	9	6	15	60	0.3	2	0
8.3	17:23	19.2	27	46	36	43	24	0	0	0	0	0	2	0
12.5	18:10	24.3	6	5	11	3	10	88	87	175	50.3	32	2.4	0

Player	Team	Pos	GP	G	A	P	PIM	+/-	PP	SH	GW	OT	S
Bergfors, Nicklas	NJD	R	1	0	0	0	0	-1	0	0	0	0	3
NHL Totals			1	0	0	0	0						
Bernier, Steve	BUF	R	76	16	16	32	64	-1	4	0	0	0	131
NHL Totals			177	45	45	90	128						
Berti, Adam	CHI	L	2	0	0	0	0	0	0	0	0	0	1
NHL Totals			2	0	0	0	0						
Bertuzzi, Todd	ANA	R	68	14	26	40	97	8	4	0	2	0	121
NHL Totals			793	240	340	580	1147						
Betts, Blair	NYR	C	75	2	5	7	20	-4	0	0	0	0	85
NHL Totals			258	22	16	38	80						
Bickell, Bryan	CHI	L	4	0	0	0	2	-1	0	0	0	0	3
NHL Totals			7	2	0	2	2						
Bieksa, Kevin	VAN	D	34	2	10	12	90	-11	1	0	1	0	64
NHL Totals			154	14	46	60	301						
Blake, Jason	TOR	L	82	15	37	52	28	-4	2	0	0	0	332
NHL Totals			590	149	189	338	332						
Blake, Rob	LAK	D	71	9	22	31	98	-19	5	0	2	0	144
NHL Totals			1127	223	479	702	1509						
Blunden, Michael	CHI	R	1	0	0	0	0	-1	0	0	0	0	1
NHL Totals			10	0	0	0	10						
Bochenski, Brandon	NSH	R	40	3	10	13	12	6	1	0	0	0	56
NHL Totals			121	24	30	54	50						
Boll, Jared	CBJ	R	75	5	5	10	226	-4	0	0	3	0	63
NHL Totals			75	5	5	10	226						
Bolland, Dave	CHI	C	39	4	13	17	28	6	0	0	0	0	49
NHL Totals			40	4	13	17	28						
Bonk, Radek	NSH	C	79	14	15	29	40	-31	6	0	1	0	138
NHL Totals			903	185	287	472	547						
Boogaard, Derek	MIN	L	34	0	0	0	74	-5	0	0	0	0	6
NHL Totals			147	2	5	7	352						
Booth, David	FLA	L	73	22	18	40	26	13	1	0	6	0	228
NHL Totals			121	25	25	50	38						
Bootland, Darryl	NYI	R	4	0	1	1	2	0	0	0	0	0	3
NHL Totals			32	1	2	3	85						
Borer, Casey	CAR	D	11	1	2	3	4	-3	0	0	0	0	5
NHL Totals			11	1	2	3	4						
Bouchard, Pierre-Marc	MIN	C	81	13	50	63	34	11	6	0	4	0	129
NHL Totals			354	61	160	221	116						
Boucher, Philippe	DAL	D	38	2	12	14	26	3	0	1	0	0	72
NHL Totals			707	91	200	291	663						
Bouillon, Francis	MTL	D	74	2	6	8	61	9	0	0	0	0	60
NHL Totals			431	16	77	93	318						

S%	TOI/G	Sft/G	Hits	BkS	MsS	GvA	TkA	FOW	FOL	Tot	FO%	%Tm	S/G	PS
0	11:17	19	0	1	0	0	0	0	1	1	0	2	3	0
12.2	13:20	17	157	34	40	25	17	6	9	15	40	0.3	1.7	0
0	10:07	13	1	1	1	0	0	0	0	0	0	0	0.5	0
11.6	16:27	20.9	66	21	30	50	20	50	60	110	45.4	2.8	1.8	0
2.4	11:51	18.3	91	49	23	11	32	388	383	771	50.3	19	1.1	0
0	9:08	13.5	7	1	2	0	1	0	0	0	0	0	0.8	0
3.1	23:23	27	52	33	38	39	16	0	0	0	0	0	1.9	0
4.5	17:49	22.2	55	14	91	63	42	14	14	28	50	0.6	4	0
6.3	22:44	27.2	93	143	55	58	21	4	4	8	50	0.2	2	0
0	7:51	13	0	1	0	0	0	0	0	0	0	0	1	0
5.4	11:56	16.1	13	5	22	8	19	2	5	7	28.6	0.3	1.4	0
7.9	8	12.3	135	13	16	9	12	2	4	6	33.3	0.1	0.8	0
8.2	13:43	19.6	55	21	13	6	18	179	206	385	46.5	17.6	1.3	0
10.1	15:55	20.7	39	25	42	28	28	457	422	879	52	19.1	1.7	0
0	3:55	7.3	32	3	4	3	0	0	0	0	0	0	0.2	0
9.6	16:10	21.5	113	29	72	26	30	13	25	38	34.2	0.8	3.1	0
0	4:42	7.8	1	0	0	0	0	0	0	0	0	0	0.8	0
20	15:17	23.4	17	12	1	4	3	0	0	0	0	0	0.5	0
10.1	16:50	23	10	15	52	37	31	4	6	10	40	0.2	1.6	0
2.8	21:30	23.5	65	67	29	25	14	0	0	0	0	0	1.9	0
3.3	17:21	22.5	168	116	21	36	22	0	0	0	0	0	0.8	0

Player	Team	Pos	GP	G	A	P	PIM	+/-	PP	SH	GW	OT	S
Boulerice, Jesse	PHI	R	5	0	0	0	29	-2	0	0	0	0	1
NHL Totals			170	8	2	10	333						
Boulton, Eric	ATL	L	74	4	5	9	127	-10	0	0	0	0	64
NHL Totals			342	16	26	42	774						
Bourdon, Luc	VAN	D	27	2	0	2	20	7	1	0	0	0	26
NHL Totals			36	2	0	2	24						
Bourque, Christopher	WSH	L	4	0	0	0	2	0	0	0	0	0	4
NHL Totals			4	0	0	0	2						
Bourque, Rene	CHI	L	62	10	14	24	42	6	0	5	2	0	103
NHL Totals			183	33	42	75	136						
Bouwmeester, Jay	FLA	D	82	15	22	37	72	-5	4	0	0	0	182
NHL Totals			389	38	123	161	261						
Boyce, Darryl	TOR	C	1	0	0	0	0	0	0	0	0	0	0
NHL Totals			1	0	0	0	0						
Boychuk, Johnny	COL	D	4	0	0	0	0	1	0	0	0	0	3
NHL Totals			4	0	0	0	0						
Boyd, Dustin	CGY	C	48	7	5	12	6	-11	0	0	1	0	46
NHL Totals			61	9	7	16	10						
Boyes, Brad	STL	R	82	43	22	65	20	1	11	0	9	1	207
NHL Totals			246	86	94	180	81						
Boyle, Brian	LAK	C	8	4	1	5	4	4	0	0	0	0	19
NHL Totals			8	4	1	5	4						
Boyle, Dan	TBL	D	37	4	21	25	57	-29	2	0	1	1	74
NHL Totals			523	76	216	292	338						
Boynton, Nick	PHX	D	79	3	9	12	125	-9	0	1	0	0	94
NHL Totals			437	27	80	107	660						
Bradley, Matt	WSH	R	77	7	11	18	74	1	1	1	2	0	111
NHL Totals			411	37	58	95	357						
Brashear, Donald	WSH	L	80	5	3	8	119	-7	0	0	0	0	59
NHL Totals			926	84	116	200	2440						
Brassard, Derick	CBJ	C	17	1	1	2	6	-4	0	0	0	0	13
NHL Totals			17	1	1	2	6						
Brennan, Kip	NYI	L	3	0	0	0	12	0	0	0	0	0	0
NHL Totals			61	1	1	2	222						
Brent, Tim	PIT	C	1	0	0	0	0	-1	0	0	0	0	0
NHL Totals			16	1	0	1	6						
Brewer, Eric	STL	D	77	1	21	22	91	-18	0	0	0	0	101
NHL Totals			595	47	126	173	467						
Briere, Daniel	PHI	C	79	31	41	72	68	-22	14	0	3	0	182
NHL Totals			562	193	255	448	433						
Brind'Amour, Rod	CAR	C	59	19	32	51	38	0	6	0	4	1	151
NHL Totals			1324	427	687	1114	1028						

S%	TOI/G	Sft/G	Hits	BkS	MsS	GvA	TkA	FOW	FOL	Tot	FO%	%Tm	S/G	PS
0	3:52	6.8	4	0	0	0	1	0	0	0	0	0	0.2	0
6.3	7:26	10.6	56	19	20	6	16	1	3	4	25	0	0.9	0
7.7	12:52	17.9	18	30	9	10	3	0	0	0	0	0	1	0
0	8:41	11.8	4	1	1	0	0	0	1	1	0	0.4	1	0
9.7	15:16	21.2	72	22	39	6	23	2	6	8	25	0.2	1.7	0
8.2	27:28	31.1	105	118	62	65	19	0	0	0	0	0	2.2	0
0	3:20	5	1	0	0	1	0	2	0	2	100	3.7	0	0
0	8:56	12.5	9	1	0	1	1	0	1	1	0	0.5	0.8	0
15.2	9:49	14.6	39	14	15	11	20	65	64	129	50.4	4.6	1	0
20.8	17:56	22.3	55	20	100	33	33	105	131	236	44.5	5.1	2.5	0
21.1	13:37	17.9	10	2	1	0	1	37	43	80	46.2	16.7	2.4	0
5.4	27:24	27.3	49	68	36	23	18	0	0	0	0	0	2	0
3.2	17	24.2	93	93	36	20	16	0	0	0	0	0	1.2	0
6.3	9:59	13.5	126	17	28	20	21	14	18	32	43.8	0.7	1.4	0
8.5	7:51	10	133	12	28	24	14	0	1	1	0	0	0.7	0
7.7	9:03	12.6	11	0	4	3	4	34	46	80	42.5	8.2	0.8	0
0	4:21	6.7	9	1	0	1	0	0	0	0	0	0	0	0
0	4:34	6	0	0	0	0	0	3	2	5	60	7.3	0	0
1	24:37	29.9	92	123	50	47	27	0	0	0	0	0	1.3	0
17	18:51	22.1	29	17	47	43	28	631	619	1250	50.5	26.3	2.3	0
12.6	22:27	26.7	55	38	37	26	31	851	609	1460	58.3	40.1	2.6	0

Player	Team	Pos	GP	G	A	P	PIM	+/-	PP	SH	GW	OT	S
Brine, David	FLA	C	9	0	1	1	4	-1	0	0	0	0	3
NHL Totals			9	0	1	1	4						
Brisebois, Patrice	MTL	D	43	3	8	11	26	-2	2	0	0	0	42
NHL Totals			947	93	309	402	604						
Brodziak, Kyle	EDM	C	80	14	17	31	33	-6	0	1	3	0	125
NHL Totals			96	15	17	32	39						
Brookbank, Sheldon	NJD	D	44	0	8	8	63	0	0	0	0	0	43
NHL Totals			47	0	9	9	75						
Brookbank, Wade	CAR	L	32	1	1	2	76	4	0	0	0	0	12
NHL Totals			100	5	3	8	305						
Brouwer, Troy	CHI	R	2	0	1	1	0	1	0	0	0	0	0
NHL Totals			12	0	1	1	7						
Brown, Curtis	SJS	C	33	5	4	9	10	4	0	0	0	0	38
NHL Totals			736	129	171	300	398						
Brown, Dustin	LAK	L	78	33	27	60	55	-13	12	2	4	1	219
NHL Totals			269	65	74	139	205						
Brown, Mike	VAN	R	19	1	0	1	55	-2	0	0	0	0	9
NHL Totals			19	1	0	1	55						
Brule, Gilbert	CBJ	C	61	1	8	9	24	-4	0	0	1	0	74
NHL Totals			146	12	20	32	52						
Brunette, Andrew	COL	L	82	19	40	59	14	5	7	0	2	0	125
NHL Totals			788	191	358	549	264						
Brylin, Sergei	NJD	L	82	6	10	16	20	-5	0	0	1	0	65
NHL Totals			765	129	179	308	273						
Burish, Adam	CHI	R	81	4	4	8	214	-13	0	1	1	0	69
NHL Totals			90	4	4	8	216						
Burns, Brent	MIN	D	82	15	28	43	80	12	8	0	4	1	158
NHL Totals			267	27	63	90	150						
Burrows, Alex	VAN	L	82	12	19	31	179	11	1	3	3	0	126
NHL Totals			206	22	30	52	333						
Byers, Dane	NYR	L	1	0	0	0	0	-1	0	0	0	0	0
NHL Totals			1	0	0	0	0						
Byfuglien, Dustin	CHI	R	67	19	17	36	59	-7	7	0	4	0	163
NHL Totals			101	23	21	44	93						
Calder, Kyle	LAK	L	65	7	13	20	18	-11	3	0	0	0	70
NHL Totals			502	106	159	265	260						
Caldwell, Ryan	PHX	D	2	0	0	0	2	0	0	0	0	0	1
NHL Totals			4	0	0	0	4						
Callahan, Ryan	NYR	R	52	8	5	13	31	7	0	1	1	0	92
NHL Totals			66	12	7	19	40						
Cammalleri, Mike	LAK	C	63	19	28	47	30	-16	10	0	1	0	210
NHL Totals			283	93	112	205	170						

S%	TOI/G	Sft/G	Hits	BkS	MsS	GvA	TkA	FOW	FOL	Tot	FO%	%Tm	S/G	PS
0	6:02	8.9	3	4	1	1	2	17	27	44	38.6	7.9	0.3	0
7.1	16:49	21.6	29	40	30	37	15	0	0	0	0	0	1	0
11.2	12:55	17.2	40	38	52	31	30	153	144	297	51.5	6.6	1.6	0
0	15:08	19.2	28	41	32	15	5	0	0	0	0	0	1	0
8.3	3:48	6.2	19	10	1	3	1	1	3	4	25	0.2	0.4	0
0	11:56	17.5	3	0	1	0	0	0	0	0	0	0	0	0
13.2	10:48	15.5	30	20	11	8	7	106	73	179	59.2	10.5	1.2	0
15.1	20:17	25.7	311	23	80	62	26	20	20	40	50	0.9	2.8	0
11.1	6:18	9.7	44	1	6	1	1	0	0	0	0	0	0.5	0
1.4	9:53	13.6	73	11	23	10	14	40	38	78	51.3	2.2	1.2	0
15.2	15:32	20.2	14	21	33	27	24	3	5	8	37.5	0.1	1.5	0
9.2	13:32	18.5	58	26	20	13	25	88	104	192	45.8	4.4	0.8	0
5.8	11:44	18	89	66	11	7	11	111	153	264	42	6	0.9	0
9.5	23:05	30.9	99	73	73	65	61	1	0	1	100	0	1.9	0
9.5	15:05	22	80	45	51	31	50	13	24	37	35.1	0.8	1.5	0
0	5:05	9	3	0	0	0	0	0	0	0	0	0	0	0
11.7	17:01	20.6	137	30	63	28	30	0	1	1	0	0	2.4	0
10	12:59	17.2	26	13	29	38	11	7	11	18	38.9	0.4	1.1	0
0	6:07	10.5	1	2	0	0	0	0	0	0	0	0	0.5	0
8.7	12:22	17	139	25	24	12	18	1	4	5	20	0.1	1.8	0
9	18:34	22.7	31	14	98	54	15	206	174	380	54.2	10.7	3.3	0

Player	Team	Pos	GP	G	A	P	PIM	+/-	PP	SH	GW	OT	S
Campbell, Brian	SJS	D	83	8	54	62	20	8	5	0	0	0	142
NHL Totals			411	35	160	195	121						
Campbell, Gregory	FLA	C	81	5	13	18	72	-12	0	2	1	0	113
NHL Totals			226	14	22	36	183						
Campoli, Chris	NYI	D	46	4	14	18	16	-1	2	1	0	0	68
NHL Totals			177	14	52	66	85						
Carcillo, Daniel	PHX	L	57	13	11	24	324	1	3	0	1	0	106
NHL Totals			75	17	14	31	398						
Carle, Matthew	SJS	D	62	2	13	15	26	-8	2	0	1	0	63
NHL Totals			151	16	47	63	70						
Carney, Keith	MIN	D	61	1	10	11	42	8	0	0	0	0	27
NHL Totals			1018	45	183	228	904						
Carter, Jeff	PHI	C	82	29	24	53	55	6	7	2	5	0	260
NHL Totals			225	66	66	132	143						
Carter, Ryan	ANA	C	34	4	4	8	36	-2	0	0	1	0	56
NHL Totals			34	4	4	8	36						
Cavanagh, Tom	SJS	R	1	0	1	1	0	1	0	0	0	0	0
NHL Totals			1	0	1	1	0						
Chara, Zdeno	BOS	D	77	17	34	51	114	14	9	1	0	0	207
NHL Totals			687	85	184	269	1115						
Cheechoo, Jonathan	SJS	R	69	23	14	37	46	11	10	0	4	0	220
NHL Totals			374	153	109	262	245						
Chelios, Chris	DET	D	69	3	9	12	36	11	0	0	1	0	60
NHL Totals			1616	185	763	948	2873						
Chimera, Jason	CBJ	L	81	14	17	31	98	-5	1	1	3	1	198
NHL Totals			373	65	68	133	377						
Chipchura, Kyle	MTL	C	36	4	7	11	10	-1	0	0	0	0	36
NHL Totals			36	4	7	11	10						
Christensen, Erik	ATL	C	59	11	13	24	30	-10	2	0	0	0	132
NHL Totals			153	35	35	70	90						
Clark, Brett	COL	D	57	5	16	21	33	5	1	0	0	0	87
NHL Totals			377	29	78	107	199						
Clark, Chris	WSH	R	18	5	4	9	43	0	1	0	1	0	29
NHL Totals			448	90	83	173	582						
Clarke, Noah	NJD	L	1	1	0	1	0	0	0	0	0	0	3
NHL Totals			21	3	1	4	4						
Clarkson, David	NJD	R	81	9	13	22	183	1	0	0	1	0	151
NHL Totals			88	12	14	26	189						
Cleary, Daniel	DET	R	63	20	22	42	33	21	5	0	3	0	177
NHL Totals			540	84	125	209	290						
Clowe, Ryane	SJS	L	15	3	5	8	22	-1	2	0	0	0	22
NHL Totals			91	19	25	44	109						

S%	TOI/G	Sft/G	Hits	BkS	MsS	GvA	TkA	FOW	FOL	Tot	FO%	%Tm	S/G	PS
5.6	25:06	27.1	61	96	77	62	22	0	0	0	0	0	1.7	0
4.4	12:26	17.5	156	35	37	18	12	235	225	460	51.1	9.5	1.4	0
5.9	19:09	20.3	51	47	25	21	19	0	0	0	0	0	1.5	0
12.3	12:43	17.1	109	10	43	15	13	4	1	5	80	0.1	1.9	0
3.2	16:32	21.9	29	62	24	43	17	1	0	1	100	0	1	0
3.7	13:22	19.9	39	37	17	17	6	0	0	0	0	0	0.4	0
11.2	18:50	24.2	52	53	107	60	56	657	721	1378	47.7	28.1	3.2	0
7.1	10:29	15.8	40	7	27	8	8	184	115	299	61.5	15.9	1.6	0
0	13:54	16	0	1	2	0	0	1	2	3	33.3	6.1	0	0
8.2	26:50	28.2	223	78	79	50	30	0	0	0	0	0	2.7	0
10.5	16:35	20.3	123	26	73	44	24	4	16	20	20	0.5	3.2	0
5	16:57	21.5	56	46	46	44	15	0	0	0	0	0	0.9	0
7.1	17:29	24.3	73	15	52	22	19	16	19	35	45.7	0.7	2.4	0
11.1	11:22	15.7	21	18	6	13	24	139	178	317	43.8	15.1	1	0
8.3	13:20	17.9	35	2	51	14	20	277	197	474	58.4	13.8	2.2	0
5.7	23:09	31.3	70	143	25	30	23	0	0	0	0	0	1.5	0
17.2	16:54	20.3	24	7	19	7	4	6	7	13	46.2	1.2	1.6	0
33.3	10:39	14	0	1	0	0	1	0	0	0	0	0	3	0
6	12:01	16.2	150	12	61	14	13	6	9	15	40	0.3	1.9	0
11.3	17:23	24.3	82	14	60	25	25	56	54	110	50.9	3.1	2.8	0
13.6	14:17	18	31	5	7	11	7	5	9	14	35.7	1.6	1.5	0

Player	Team	Pos	GP	G	A	P	PIM	+/-	PP	SH	GW	OT	S
Clutterbuck, Cal	MIN	R	2	0	0	0	0	0	0	0	0	0	0
NHL Totals			2	0	0	0	0						
Coburn, Braydon	PHI	D	78	9	27	36	74	17	5	0	2	0	113
NHL Totals			136	12	36	48	124						
Cogliano, Andrew	EDM	C	82	18	27	45	20	1	1	2	5	3	98
NHL Totals			82	18	27	45	20						
Colaiacovo, Carlo	TOR	D	28	2	4	6	10	-4	0	0	1	0	30
NHL Totals			101	12	20	32	51						
Cole, Erik	CAR	L	73	22	29	51	76	5	10	0	4	0	216
NHL Totals			418	129	151	280	406						
Colliton, Jeremy	NYI	C	16	0	0	0	8	-4	0	0	0	0	16
NHL Totals			36	1	1	2	14						
Comeau, Blake	NYI	R	51	8	7	15	22	1	1	0	1	0	67
NHL Totals			54	8	7	15	22						
Commodore, Mike	OTT	D	67	3	11	14	100	-7	0	0	0	0	97
NHL Totals			296	14	49	63	439						
Comrie, Mike	NYI	C	76	21	28	49	87	-21	4	0	3	1	194
NHL Totals			462	144	167	311	363						
Conboy, Tim	CAR	D	19	0	5	5	60	1	0	0	0	0	16
NHL Totals			19	0	5	5	60						
Conner, Chris	DAL	R	22	3	2	5	6	0	0	0	0	0	27
NHL Totals			33	4	4	8	10						
Connolly, Tim	BUF	C	48	7	33	40	8	4	3	1	3	0	111
NHL Totals			438	70	171	241	190						
Conroy, Craig	CGY	C	79	12	22	34	71	6	1	0	4	0	116
NHL Totals			846	165	312	477	542						
Cooke, Matt	WSH	L	78	10	13	23	91	1	0	1	1	0	86
NHL Totals			583	86	124	210	652						
Corvo, Joseph	CAR	D	74	13	35	48	26	17	6	0	3	0	167
NHL Totals			353	48	114	162	156						
Cote, Riley	PHI	L	70	1	3	4	202	2	0	0	0	0	17
NHL Totals			78	1	3	4	213						
Cowan, Jeff	VAN	L	46	0	1	1	110	-5	0	0	0	0	35
NHL Totals			413	47	34	81	695						
Craig, Ryan	TBL	C	7	1	1	2	0	-1	1	0	0	0	8
NHL Totals			127	30	27	57	61						
Crombeen, Brandon	DAL	R	8	0	2	2	39	1	0	0	0	0	9
NHL Totals			8	0	2	2	39						
Crosby, Sidney	PIT	C	53	24	48	72	39	18	6	0	4	0	173
NHL Totals			213	99	195	294	209						
Cullen, Matt	CAR	C	59	13	36	49	32	2	8	0	1	0	137
NHL Totals			730	131	239	370	338						

S%	TOI/G	Sft/G	Hits	BkS	MsS	GvA	TkA	FOW	FOL	Tot	FO%	%Tm	S/G	PS
0	7:05	15.5	4	1	2	0	1	1	0	1	100	0.8	0	0
8	21:14	28.6	79	79	60	53	36	0	0	0	0	0	1.4	0
18.4	13:39	17.8	25	31	32	49	35	214	328	542	39.5	11.7	1.2	0
6.7	17:26	23.4	57	37	8	25	7	0	0	0	0	0	1.1	0
10.2	19:21	24.3	186	24	84	32	35	9	29	38	23.7	0.8	3	0
0	8:46	11.8	12	2	5	1	6	54	50	104	51.9	11.8	1	0
11.9	11:40	14.5	60	6	22	16	28	8	19	27	29.6	0.9	1.3	0
3.1	18:12	24.9	144	95	41	28	23	0	0	0	0	0	1.4	0
10.8	19:11	20.8	47	23	43	62	47	564	663	1227	46	28.5	2.6	0
0	6:58	11.6	25	4	5	2	3	0	0	0	0	0	0.8	0
11.1	11:59	15	17	7	7	5	5	1	0	1	100	0	1.2	0
6.3	18:40	23	18	36	34	33	16	222	241	463	47.9	16.8	2.3	0
10.3	17:09	26	98	55	44	55	53	726	685	1411	51.4	30.7	1.5	0
11.6	13:09	18.5	198	38	48	23	26	12	16	28	42.8	0.6	1.1	0
7.8	18:38	22.1	31	41	51	33	24	0	0	0	0	0	2.3	0
5.9	4:16	7	60	4	4	2	5	1	1	2	50	0	0.2	0
0	8:44	12.4	67	10	10	8	13	0	1	1	0	0	0.8	0
12.5	13:03	17.6	8	4	1	1	1	1	0	1	100	0.2	1.1	0
0	6:37	9.1	7	1	0	1	3	0	1	1	0	0.2	1.1	0
13.9	20:50	24.4	50	40	60	37	35	567	536	1103	51.4	36.5	3.3	0
9.5	16:52	21	33	30	57	28	27	364	285	649	56.1	17.9	2.3	0

Player	Team	Pos	GP	G	A	P	PIM	+/-	PP	SH	GW	OT	S
Cullimore, Jassen	FLA	D	65	3	10	13	38	21	0	0	1	1	55
NHL Totals			708	24	69	93	659						
Cumiskey, Kyle	COL	D	38	0	5	5	16	-3	0	0	0	0	19
NHL Totals			47	1	6	7	18						
D'Agostini, Matt	MTL	R	1	0	0	0	2	0	0	0	0	0	0
NHL Totals			1	0	0	0	2						
Daley, Trevor	DAL	D	82	5	19	24	85	-1	0	0	1	0	87
NHL Totals			264	13	43	56	249						
Dallman, Kevin	LAK	D	34	3	4	7	4	4	0	0	1	0	41
NHL Totals			154	8	23	31	45						
Dandenault, Mathieu	MTL	R	61	9	5	14	34	-11	0	1	0	0	69
NHL Totals			827	64	127	191	499						
Darche, Mathieu	TBL	L	73	7	15	22	20	-14	1	1	0	0	120
NHL Totals			101	8	16	24	26						
Datsyuk, Pavel	DET	C	82	31	66	97	20	41	10	1	6	0	264
NHL Totals			445	139	286	425	117						
Davison, Rob	NYI	D	34	1	1	2	53	-6	0	1	0	0	32
NHL Totals			195	3	13	16	270						
Dawes, Nigel	NYR	L	61	14	15	29	10	11	3	0	4	0	121
NHL Totals			69	15	15	30	10						
Demitra, Pavol	MIN	R	68	15	39	54	24	9	2	0	1	0	126
NHL Totals			750	281	418	699	264						
Devereaux, Boyd	TOR	C	62	7	11	18	24	-6	0	1	1	0	81
NHL Totals			604	61	107	168	203						
DeVries, Greg	NSH	D	77	4	11	15	71	7	0	0	1	0	66
NHL Totals			807	47	142	189	715						
Dipenta, Joe	ANA	D	23	1	4	5	16	3	0	0	0	0	5
NHL Totals			174	6	17	23	110						
Doan, Shane	PHX	R	80	28	50	78	59	4	9	2	5	1	243
NHL Totals			883	227	323	550	843						
Doell, Kevin	ATL	C	8	0	1	1	4	-2	0	0	0	0	6
NHL Totals			8	0	1	1	4						
Donovan, Shean	OTT	R	82	5	7	12	73	-3	0	0	3	0	91
NHL Totals			856	105	121	226	631						
Dowd, James	PHI	C	73	5	5	10	41	0	0	1	0	0	41
NHL Totals			728	71	168	239	390						
Dowell, Jacob	CHI	C	19	2	1	3	10	1	0	1	0	0	19
NHL Totals			19	2	1	3	10						
Downey, Aaron	DET	R	56	0	3	3	116	0	0	0	0	0	15
NHL Totals			239	7	9	16	487						
Downie, Steve	PHI	R	32	6	6	12	73	2	0	1	1	0	25
NHL Totals			32	6	6	12	73						

S%	TOI/G	Sft/G	Hits	BkS	MsS	GvA	TkA	FOW	FOL	Tot	FO%	%Tm	S/G	PS
5.5	18:04	23.5	77	68	12	31	11	1	0	1	100	0	0.8	0
0	12:07	18.4	7	25	8	7	21	0	0	0	0	0	0.5	0
0	8:49	13	1	0	0	0	1	0	0	0	0	0	0	0
5.7	19:48	23.5	32	63	51	34	24	1	0	1	100	0	1.1	0
7.3	12:53	17.8	42	26	32	14	6	0	2	2	0	0.1	1.2	0
13	11:08	14.6	70	26	30	19	17	0	1	1	0	0	1.1	0
5.8	14:25	18	125	39	39	12	33	43	46	89	48.3	2.1	1.6	0
11.7	21:23	26	40	42	97	68	144	453	380	833	54.4	18.2	3.2	0
3.1	13:51	16.6	69	39	9	17	14	0	0	0	0	0	0.9	0
11.6	12:59	16.9	86	26	44	16	22	1	1	2	50	0	2	0
11.9	19:42	27.6	72	94	24	24	27	0	0	0	0	0	0.9	0
8.6	13:58	19.2	17	48	61	42	26	403	487	890	45.3	23.5	1.9	0
6.1	18:51	23.6	47	20	31	28	23	2	4	6	33.3	0.1	1.3	0
20	10:39	15.8	10	8	4	2	6	0	0	0	0	0	0.2	0
11.5	20:45	25.7	158	17	66	30	64	77	110	187	41.2	4	3	0
0	9:39	13.5	7	5	0	1	7	25	28	53	47.2	10.9	0.8	0
5.5	9:34	12.8	68	15	28	16	24	11	18	29	37.9	0.6	1.1	0
12.2	8:26	14.1	32	17	9	15	14	240	206	446	53.8	10.2	0.6	0
10.5	11:55	18.5	24	10	4	6	4	79	91	170	46.5	16.6	1	0
0	4:35	7.5	79	6	4	4	3	0	0	0	0	0	0.3	0
24	9:50	13.7	29	7	7	9	14	5	10	15	33.3	0.8	0.8	0

Player	Team	Pos	GP	G	A	P	PIM	+/-	PP	SH	GW	OT	S
Drake, Dallas	DET	R	65	3	3	6	41	-12	0	1	0	0	46
NHL Totals			1009	177	300	477	885						
Draper, Kris	DET	C	65	9	8	17	68	-2	0	2	2	0	97
NHL Totals			950	141	173	314	710						
Drury, Chris	NYR	C	82	25	33	58	45	-3	12	0	7	1	220
NHL Totals			710	218	304	522	397						
Dubinsky, Brandon	NYR	C	82	14	26	40	79	8	1	0	0	0	157
NHL Totals			88	14	26	40	81						
Dumont, Jean-Pierre	NSH	R	80	29	43	72	34	5	7	0	8	1	192
NHL Totals			596	171	223	394	308						
Dupont, Micki	STL	D	2	0	0	0	2	1	0	0	0	0	3
NHL Totals			23	1	3	4	12						
Dupuis, Pascal	PIT	R	78	12	15	27	32	0	0	3	1	0	143
NHL Totals			435	83	91	174	198						
Dvorak, Radek	FLA	R	67	8	9	17	16	-1	0	1	1	0	146
NHL Totals			895	179	287	466	308						
Eager, Ben	CHI	L	32	0	2	2	89	-9	0	0	0	0	16
NHL Totals			120	9	12	21	340						
Earl, Robert	TOR	L	9	0	1	1	0	-2	0	0	0	0	9
NHL Totals			9	0	1	1	0						
Eaton, Mark	PIT	D	36	0	3	3	4	6	0	0	0	0	28
NHL Totals			384	16	37	53	158						
Eaves, Patrick	CAR	R	37	5	10	15	10	-2	2	0	1	0	81
NHL Totals			168	39	37	76	68						
Ebbett, Andrew	ANA	C	3	0	0	0	2	3	0	0	0	0	3
NHL Totals			3	0	0	0	2						
Edler, Alexander	VAN	D	75	8	12	20	42	6	4	0	0	0	124
NHL Totals			97	9	14	23	48						
Ehrhoff, Christian	SJS	D	77	1	21	22	72	9	1	0	1	0	97
NHL Totals			264	17	73	90	181						
Elias, Patrik	NJD	L	74	20	35	55	38	10	7	0	8	3	263
NHL Totals			745	264	364	628	371						
Ellis, Matt	LAK	L	54	3	5	8	26	3	0	1	1	0	66
NHL Totals			70	3	5	8	32						
Eminger, Steve	WSH	D	20	0	2	2	8	-4	0	0	0	0	14
NHL Totals			212	6	37	43	221						
Enstrom, Tobias	ATL	D	82	5	33	38	42	-5	4	0	0	0	105
NHL Totals			82	5	33	38	42						
Erat, Martin	NSH	R	76	23	34	57	40	-3	4	0	6	1	163
NHL Totals			407	85	168	253	250						
Ericsson, Jonathan	DET	D	8	1	0	1	4	-3	1	0	0	0	19
NHL Totals			8	1	0	1	4						

S%	TOI/G	Sft/G	Hits	BkS	MsS	GvA	TkA	FOW	FOL	Tot	FO%	%Tm	S/G	PS
6.5	10:42	17.1	92	25	17	11	17	29	41	70	41.4	1.9	0.7	0
9.3	15:37	22.9	90	25	40	17	19	553	391	944	58.6	26.1	1.5	0
11.4	19:47	25.2	46	76	73	40	64	746	613	1359	54.9	30.7	2.7	0
8.9	14:29	18	196	30	55	23	40	512	483	995	51.4	22.5	1.9	0
15.1	18:29	22	44	11	83	54	47	3	10	13	23.1	0.2	2.4	0
0	12:34	16	2	0	1	2	0	0	0	0	0	0	1.5	0
8.4	15:11	20.1	85	33	43	20	51	5	11	16	31.2	0.3	1.8	0
5.5	15:06	20.4	50	36	45	15	36	2	10	12	16.7	0.3	2.2	0
0	5:48	8.6	32	0	7	4	2	1	4	5	20	0.2	0.5	0
0	9:14	12.2	3	5	3	3	2	2	0	2	100	0.4	1	0
0	19:40	24.9	17	89	8	7	2	0	0	0	0	0	0.8	0
6.2	12:46	16.2	42	12	31	11	18	1	2	3	33.3	0.1	2.2	0
0	13:18	20	0	2	2	1	1	17	12	29	58.6	15.2	1	0
6.5	21:20	27.1	58	76	56	42	23	1	0	1	100	0	1.7	0
1	21:43	28.2	92	108	86	43	22	0	0	0	0	0	1.3	0
7.6	18:28	24	51	20	80	40	38	354	422	776	45.6	20	3.6	0
4.5	7:56	11.7	28	16	21	9	17	53	61	114	46.5	3.8	1.2	0
0	11:08	15.9	17	8	1	6	5	0	0	0	0	0	0.7	0
4.8	24:28	25.5	21	106	37	52	30	0	0	0	0	0	1.3	0
14.1	18:39	23	49	16	53	52	50	15	26	41	36.6	0.9	2.1	0
5.3	15:58	22.6	9	3	5	9	0	0	0	0	0	0	2.4	0

Player	Team	Pos	GP	G	A	P	PIM	+/-	PP	SH	GW	OT	S
Eriksson, Anders	CGY	D	61	1	17	18	36	-5	1	0	0	0	50
NHL Totals			552	22	149	171	240						
Eriksson, Loui	DAL	L	69	14	17	31	28	5	4	0	0	0	120
NHL Totals			128	20	30	50	46						
Erskine, John	WSH	D	51	2	7	9	96	1	0	0	1	0	48
NHL Totals			221	6	15	21	501						
Exelby, Garnet	ATL	D	79	2	5	7	85	-21	0	0	0	0	37
NHL Totals			298	6	33	39	391						
Fata, Drew	NYI	D	5	0	1	1	4	-1	0	0	0	0	4
NHL Totals			8	1	1	2	9						
Fedorov, Sergei	WSH	C	68	11	30	41	38	-5	6	0	2	0	128
NHL Totals			1196	472	674	1146	789						
Fedoruk, Todd	MIN	L	69	6	7	13	139	2	2	0	0	0	57
NHL Totals			423	23	55	78	924						
Fedotenko, Ruslan	NYI	L	67	16	17	33	40	-9	8	0	2	0	121
NHL Totals			532	123	116	239	325						
Fehr, Eric	WSH	R	23	1	5	6	6	4	0	0	0	0	40
NHL Totals			48	3	6	9	16						
Ference, Andrew	BOS	D	59	1	14	15	50	-14	0	0	0	0	71
NHL Totals			472	23	94	117	448						
Fiddler, Vernon	NSH	C	79	11	21	32	47	-4	2	1	1	0	97
NHL Totals			227	34	42	76	166						
Filewich, Jonathan	PIT	R	5	0	0	0	0	-2	0	0	0	0	3
NHL Totals			5	0	0	0	0						
Filppula, Valtteri	DET	C	78	19	17	36	28	16	3	0	3	0	122
NHL Totals			155	29	25	54	50						
Finger, Jeff	COL	D	72	8	11	19	40	12	1	1	1	0	93
NHL Totals			94	9	15	24	51						
Fisher, Mike	OTT	C	79	23	24	47	82	-10	6	2	4	1	215
NHL Totals			463	115	124	239	396						
Fistric, Mark	DAL	D	37	0	2	2	24	3	0	0	0	0	17
NHL Totals			37	0	2	2	24						
Fitzgerald, Zach	VAN	D	1	0	0	0	0	0	0	0	0	0	1
NHL Totals			1	0	0	0	0						
Fitzpatrick, Rory	PHI	D	19	0	1	1	11	-12	0	0	0	0	10
NHL Totals			287	10	25	35	201						
Fleischmann, Tomas	WSH	L	75	10	20	30	18	-7	1	0	1	1	107
NHL Totals			118	14	26	40	26						
Foligno, Nick	OTT	L	45	6	3	9	20	0	0	0	0	0	44
NHL Totals			45	6	3	9	20						
Foote, Adam	COL	D	75	1	15	16	107	2	0	1	0	0	66
NHL Totals			998	65	219	284	1407						

S%	TOI/G	Sft/G	Hits	BkS	MsS	GvA	TkA	FOW	FOL	Tot	FO%	%Tm	S/G	PS
2	20:47	27.1	63	70	34	44	28	0	0	0	0	0	0.8	0
11.7	14:01	16.5	24	14	45	22	58	2	11	13	15.4	0.3	1.7	0
4.2	15:42	21.3	102	60	16	35	20	0	0	0	0	0	0.9	0
5.4	18:53	23.7	176	137	16	39	30	0	0	0	0	0	0.5	0
0	17:30	20.2	3	3	3	7	4	0	0	0	0	0	0.8	0
8.6	17:40	22.7	41	22	64	44	37	562	449	1011	55.6	26	1.9	0
10.5	10:18	15.6	76	16	16	19	5	0	4	4	0	0.1	0.8	0
13.2	16:41	19.5	104	35	50	24	49	11	17	28	39.3	0.7	1.8	0
2.5	10:30	13.6	11	8	18	6	6	0	2	2	0	0.1	1.7	0
1.4	22:14	26.8	79	65	34	29	10	1	0	1	100	0	1.2	0
11.3	13:56	20.6	52	23	39	17	51	193	191	384	50.3	8.3	1.2	0
0	8:41	13.2	2	1	1	1	1	0	0	0	0	0	0.6	0
15.6	16:57	22.9	35	26	33	32	31	314	307	621	50.6	14.2	1.6	2
8.6	19:57	28	121	117	37	26	29	1	0	1	100	0	1.3	0
10.7	19:45	24.5	234	73	81	45	47	618	612	1230	50.2	27.1	2.7	0
0	12:44	17	79	30	10	13	16	0	0	0	0	0	0.5	0
0	13:20	17	1	0	1	0	1	0	0	0	0	0	1	0
0	12:43	18.8	19	18	3	6	0	0	0	0	0	0	0.5	0
9.3	12:37	15.7	26	11	43	21	29	15	15	30	50	0.6	1.4	0
13.6	9:09	11.6	51	11	9	12	14	22	27	49	44.9	1.9	1	0
1.5	23:23	29.4	93	148	30	18	18	0	0	0	0	0	0.9	0

Player	Team	Pos	GP	G	A	P	PIM	+/-	PP	SH	GW	OT	S
Forsberg, Peter	COL	C	9	1	13	14	8	7	0	0	0	0	15
NHL Totals			706	249	636	885	686						
Foster, Alex	TOR	C	3	0	0	0	0	0	0	0	0	0	1
NHL Totals			3	0	0	0	0						
Foster, Kurtis	MIN	D	56	7	12	19	37	0	3	0	2	0	118
NHL Totals			176	20	51	71	149						
Foy, Matt	MIN	R	28	4	4	8	28	-1	0	0	1	0	38
NHL Totals			56	6	7	13	48						
Franzen, Johan	DET	R	72	27	11	38	51	12	14	0	8	1	199
NHL Totals			221	49	35	84	124						
Fraser, Colin	CHI	C	5	0	0	0	7	-2	0	0	0	0	4
NHL Totals			6	0	0	0	9						
Fritsche, Dan	CBJ	C	69	10	12	22	22	2	1	1	4	0	109
NHL Totals			206	29	34	63	91						
Frolov, Alexander	LAK	L	71	23	44	67	22	1	5	0	7	0	160
NHL Totals			378	117	154	271	154						
Funk, Michael	BUF	D	4	0	0	0	0	-3	0	0	0	0	1
NHL Totals			9	0	2	2	0						
Gaborik, Marian	MIN	R	77	42	41	83	63	17	11	1	8	3	278
NHL Totals			485	206	208	414	299						
Gagne, Simon	PHI	L	25	7	11	18	4	-8	5	0	2	1	76
NHL Totals			527	208	202	410	189						
Gagner, Sam	EDM	C	79	13	36	49	23	-21	4	0	1	0	135
NHL Totals			79	13	36	49	23						
Gamache, Simon	TOR	L	11	2	2	4	6	-1	1	0	0	0	11
NHL Totals			48	6	7	13	18						
Gaustad, Paul	BUF	C	82	10	26	36	85	-4	5	0	2	1	136
NHL Totals			215	28	54	82	224						
Gauthier, Gabe	LAK	L	3	0	0	0	0	0	0	0	0	0	2
NHL Totals			8	0	0	0	2						
Gelinas, Martin	NSH	L	57	9	11	20	20	5	0	1	1	0	110
NHL Totals			1273	309	351	660	820						
Gervais, Bruno	NYI	D	60	0	13	13	34	-5	0	0	0	0	59
NHL Totals			138	3	23	26	70						
Getzlaf, Ryan	ANA	C	77	24	58	82	94	32	4	1	2	0	185
NHL Totals			216	63	116	179	182						
Gilbert, Tom	EDM	D	82	13	20	33	20	-6	3	0	1	0	98
NHL Totals			94	14	25	39	20						
Gill, Hal	PIT	D	81	3	21	24	68	6	0	0	0	0	86
NHL Totals			789	29	112	141	747						
Gionta, Brian	NJD	R	82	22	31	53	46	1	8	1	4	1	257
NHL Totals			392	132	120	252	195						

S%	TOI/G	Sft/G	Hits	BkS	MsS	GvA	TkA	FOW	FOL	Tot	FO%	%Tm	S/G	PS
6.7	19:14	23.8	9	0	2	15	10	4	0	4	100	0.8	1.7	0
0	3:32	4.7	1	0	0	0	1	0	1	1	0	0.6	0.3	0
5.9	16:24	24.6	60	39	45	21	11	2	1	3	66.7	0	2.1	0
10.5	7:49	14.2	11	0	9	3	4	2	5	7	28.6	0.4	1.4	0
13.6	17:43	23.7	89	24	70	28	39	189	201	390	48.5	9.7	2.8	0
0	10:18	14.6	4	3	0	0	3	14	24	38	36.8	13.4	0.8	0
9.2	12:20	17.5	65	27	24	13	21	59	62	121	48.8	3.1	1.6	0
14.4	18:47	22.8	22	18	64	70	45	2	9	11	18.2	0.2	2.3	0
0	11:36	13	3	3	1	2	0	0	0	0	0	0	0.2	0
15.1	19:35	26.8	59	18	99	55	41	6	15	21	28.6	0.4	3.6	0
9.2	18:08	21.4	4	5	26	22	10	1	1	2	50	0.1	3	0
9.6	15:40	18.2	18	31	57	45	27	125	174	299	41.8	6.7	1.7	0
18.2	9:35	13.8	10	1	7	2	3	0	0	0	0	0	1	0
7.4	17:09	21.6	199	48	39	24	19	640	525	1165	54.9	24.8	1.7	0
0	7:07	11.3	3	1	0	1	0	8	9	17	47	9.4	0.7	0
8.2	14:06	18.8	50	12	40	22	35	11	11	22	50	0.6	1.9	0
0	20	22.8	35	72	25	29	37	0	0	0	0	0	1	0
13	19:38	23.6	126	46	70	67	44	545	607	1152	47.3	26.4	2.4	0
13.3	22:11	25.5	27	159	35	74	33	0	0	0	0	0	1.2	0
3.5	19:59	23.8	127	143	41	78	24	0	0	0	0	0	1.1	0
8.6	18:16	22.8	52	14	107	37	37	30	25	55	54.5	1.2	3.1	0

Player	Team	Pos	GP	G	A	P	PIM	+/-	PP	SH	GW	OT	S
Girardi, Daniel	NYR	D	82	10	18	28	14	0	5	0	1	0	147
NHL Totals			116	10	24	34	22						
Giroux, Claude	PHI	R	2	0	0	0	0	-2	0	0	0	0	2
NHL Totals			2	0	0	0	0						
Giuliano, Jeff	LAK	L	53	0	6	6	14	-9	0	0	0	0	30
NHL Totals			101	3	10	13	40						
Glass, Tanner	FLA	L	41	1	1	2	39	-5	0	0	0	0	11
NHL Totals			41	1	1	2	39						
Gleason, Tim	CAR	D	80	3	16	19	84	5	0	0	0	0	98
NHL Totals			262	7	46	53	239						
Glencross, Curtis	EDM	L	62	15	10	25	53	8	1	0	1	1	104
NHL Totals			71	16	10	26	55						
Globke, Rob	FLA	R	9	0	0	0	2	-3	0	0	0	0	4
NHL Totals			46	1	1	2	8						
Glumac, Mike	STL	R	4	0	0	0	5	-1	0	0	0	0	3
NHL Totals			40	7	6	13	38						
Goc, Marcel	SJS	C	51	5	3	8	12	-15	0	0	0	0	87
NHL Totals			210	18	25	43	58						
Godard, Eric	CGY	R	74	1	1	2	171	-8	0	0	1	0	14
NHL Totals			200	3	5	8	481						
Goligoski, Alex	PIT	D	3	0	2	2	2	2	0	0	0	0	2
NHL Totals			3	0	2	2	2						
Gomez, Scott	NYR	C	81	16	54	70	36	3	7	0	3	0	242
NHL Totals			629	132	388	520	398						
Gonchar, Sergei	PIT	D	78	12	53	65	66	13	8	0	2	1	173
NHL Totals			904	185	430	615	767						
Gordon, Boyd	WSH	C	67	7	9	16	12	5	0	1	0	0	100
NHL Totals			204	15	37	52	38						
Gorges, Josh	MTL	D	62	0	9	9	32	0	0	0	0	0	41
NHL Totals			165	1	18	19	89						
Grabovski, Mikhail	MTL	C	24	3	6	9	8	-4	0	0	1	0	23
NHL Totals			27	3	6	9	8						
Gragnani, Marc-Andre	BUF	L	2	0	0	0	4	-2	0	0	0	0	1
NHL Totals			2	0	0	0	4						
Gratton, Chris	TBL	C	60	10	11	21	77	-7	1	0	1	0	92
NHL Totals			1068	214	351	565	1626						
Gratton, Josh	PHX	L	1	0	0	0	5	1	0	0	0	0	0
NHL Totals			67	2	1	3	237						
Grebeshkov, Denis	EDM	D	71	3	15	18	22	2	1	0	0	0	34
NHL Totals			104	3	21	24	42						
Green, Mike	WSH	D	82	18	38	56	62	6	8	0	4	3	234
NHL Totals			174	21	50	71	116						

S%	TOI/G	Sft/G	Hits	BkS	MsS	GvA	TkA	FOW	FOL	Tot	FO%	%Tm	S/G	PS
6.8	21:11	28.3	179	123	56	43	51	0	1	1	0	0	1.8	0
0	9:34	13	0	1	1	0	0	0	0	0	0	0	1	0
0	11:49	17.3	69	27	14	11	11	108	131	239	45.2	8.1	0.6	0
9.1	4:25	6.7	29	5	3	0	1	0	2	2	0	0	0.3	0
3.1	18:38	25.2	151	107	46	39	30	0	0	0	0	0	1.2	0
14.4	11:21	15	94	12	33	22	12	13	12	25	52	0.7	1.7	0
0	7:43	10.9	7	2	4	3	1	0	1	1	0	0.1	0.4	0
0	10:08	15	6	2	1	0	3	1	2	3	33.3	1.3	0.8	0
5.7	10:41	15.2	45	16	25	12	19	107	101	208	51.4	7.9	1.7	0
7.1	4:42	7.6	36	6	11	13	1	0	1	1	0	0	0.2	0
0	13:56	19	1	4	0	0	1	0	0	0	0	0	0.7	0
6.6	19:53	22.8	48	24	68	62	77	612	553	1165	52.5	26.6	3	0
6.9	25:54	27.7	56	126	91	43	33	0	0	0	0	0	2.2	0
7	15:44	21.8	19	50	38	15	28	504	400	904	55.8	23.1	1.5	0
0	16:20	21.1	76	101	27	31	18	0	0	0	0	0	0.7	0
13	11:13	13.9	7	9	15	7	12	51	103	154	33.1	10.5	1	0
0	6:17	9.5	2	0	0	0	0	0	0	0	0	0	0.5	0
10.9	12:42	16.7	88	16	29	18	30	337	281	618	54.5	18.1	1.5	0
0	9:40	14	4	0	1	0	0	0	0	0	0	0	0	0
8.8	16:52	20.3	41	55	26	54	18	0	0	0	0	0	0.5	0
7.7	23:38	25.7	94	68	99	85	53	0	1	1	0	0	2.9	0

Player	Team	Pos	GP	G	A	P	PIM	+/-	PP	SH	GW	OT	S
Greene, Andy	NJD	D	59	2	8	10	22	0	2	0	0	0	50
NHL Totals			82	3	13	16	28						
Greene, Matt	EDM	D	46	0	1	1	53	-3	0	0	0	0	28
NHL Totals			151	1	12	13	205						
Greentree, Kyle	PHI	L	2	0	0	0	0	-1	0	0	0	0	3
NHL Totals			2	0	0	0	0						
Grier, Mike	SJS	R	78	9	13	22	24	-8	1	3	4	0	132
NHL Totals			852	137	185	322	459						
Grossman, Nicklas	DAL	D	62	0	7	7	22	10	0	0	0	0	34
NHL Totals			70	0	7	7	26						
Guenin, Nathan	PHI	D	2	0	0	0	2	2	0	0	0	0	0
NHL Totals			11	0	2	2	6						
Guerin, Bill	NYI	R	81	23	21	44	65	-15	7	0	5	1	227
NHL Totals			1107	387	376	763	1504						
Guite, Ben	COL	C	79	11	11	22	47	1	0	0	2	0	103
NHL Totals			119	14	19	33	63						
Hagman, Niklas	DAL	L	82	27	14	41	51	4	4	4	8	0	178
NHL Totals			481	80	85	165	153						
Hainsey, Ron	CBJ	D	78	8	24	32	25	-7	8	0	0	0	161
NHL Totals			245	20	65	85	143						
Hale, David	CGY	D	58	0	2	2	46	0	0	0	0	0	35
NHL Totals			215	0	11	11	175						
Hall, Adam	PIT	R	46	2	4	6	24	-2	0	0	0	0	39
NHL Totals			352	51	57	108	158						
Halpern, Jeff	TBL	C	83	20	22	42	54	0	4	1	2	0	132
NHL Totals			597	115	166	281	483						
Hamhuis, Dan	NSH	D	80	4	23	27	66	-4	1	0	1	0	127
NHL Totals			323	24	87	111	259						
Hamilton, Jeffrey	CAR	C	58	9	15	24	10	-8	7	0	1	0	116
NHL Totals			142	29	42	71	40						
Hamrlik, Roman	MTL	D	77	5	21	26	38	7	3	0	3	0	129
NHL Totals			1076	136	395	531	1167						
Handzus, Michal	LAK	C	82	7	14	21	45	-21	0	3	0	0	89
NHL Totals			599	121	199	320	358						
Hannan, Scott	COL	D	82	2	19	21	55	-5	0	0	0	0	79
NHL Totals			590	27	121	148	384						
Hansen, Jannik	VAN	R	5	0	0	0	2	0	0	0	0	0	3
NHL Totals			5	0	0	0	2						
Hanzal, Martin	PHX	C	72	8	27	35	28	-7	1	1	3	1	111
NHL Totals			72	8	27	35	28						
Harrold, Peter	LAK	D	25	2	3	5	2	3	0	0	0	0	16
NHL Totals			37	2	5	7	10						

S%	TOI/G	Sft/G	Hits	BkS	MsS	GvA	TkA	FOW	FOL	Tot	FO%	%Tm	S/G	PS
4	19:30	22.6	30	77	25	12	20	0	0	0	0	0	0.8	0
0	16:41	20	64	78	25	32	6	0	0	0	0	0	0.6	0
0	9:11	12.5	2	1	3	1	1	0	0	0	0	0	1.5	0
6.8	16:12	21.4	119	58	35	34	33	22	64	86	25.6	2.1	1.7	0
0	15:33	20.1	87	43	14	26	8	0	0	0	0	0	0.5	0
0	9:56	15	1	4	1	1	0	0	0	0	0	0	0	0
10.1	17:22	20.2	62	20	80	54	44	12	6	18	66.7	0.3	2.8	0
10.7	13:04	19.5	115	66	36	14	35	386	419	805	48	18.6	1.3	0
15.2	15:35	19.6	40	13	61	52	40	2	17	19	10.5	0.4	2.2	0
5	22:33	28	51	91	79	33	13	0	0	0	0	0	2.1	0
0	13:53	18.9	86	25	24	22	14	0	0	0	0	0	0.6	0
5.1	11:52	17.6	45	30	16	2	7	146	144	290	50.3	11	0.8	0
15.2	16:46	21.6	81	46	46	32	40	381	352	733	52	16.6	1.6	0
3.1	22:43	26.1	162	69	44	43	50	0	0	0	0	0	1.6	0
7.8	10:47	12.7	17	12	46	15	8	38	41	79	48.1	2.2	2	0
3.9	23:08	27	138	187	48	70	36	0	0	0	0	0	1.7	0
7.9	15:14	20.8	69	55	20	41	25	532	635	1167	45.6	25.4	1.1	0
2.5	22:40	29.3	58	153	33	48	33	1	0	1	100	0	1	0
0	11:33	14.2	0	0	5	3	0	1	0	1	100	0.3	0.6	0
7.2	16:44	22	98	35	41	23	38	470	549	1019	46.1	24.7	1.5	0
12.5	16:23	21.8	7	13	4	15	6	1	1	2	50	0.1	0.6	0

Player	Team	Pos	GP	G	A	P	PIM	+/-	PP	SH	GW	OT	S
Hartigan, Mark	DET	C	23	3	1	4	16	-2	0	0	0	0	19
NHL Totals			102	19	11	30	58						
Hartnell, Scott	PHI	L	80	24	19	43	159	2	10	1	6	1	176
NHL Totals			516	117	137	254	703						
Hatcher, Derian	PHI	D	44	2	5	7	33	4	0	0	1	0	27
NHL Totals			1045	80	251	331	1581						
Havelid, Niclas	ATL	D	81	1	13	14	42	2	0	0	0	0	54
NHL Totals			550	32	120	152	294						
Havlat, Martin	CHI	R	35	10	17	27	22	4	3	0	2	0	87
NHL Totals			389	140	179	319	216						
Haydar, Darren	ATL	R	16	1	7	8	2	4	0	0	0	0	14
NHL Totals			22	1	7	8	2						
Heatley, Dany	OTT	L	71	41	41	82	76	33	13	0	8	1	224
NHL Totals			425	221	250	471	368						
Hecht, Jochen	BUF	C	75	22	27	49	38	1	3	1	2	0	229
NHL Totals			548	132	211	343	326						
Hedican, Bret	CAR	D	66	2	15	17	70	17	0	0	0	0	80
NHL Totals			988	54	234	288	857						
Hejda, Jan	CBJ	D	81	0	13	13	61	20	0	0	0	0	71
NHL Totals			120	1	21	22	81						
Hejduk, Milan	COL	R	77	29	25	54	36	8	8	1	4	0	205
NHL Totals			701	285	313	598	258						
Helm, Darren	DET	C	7	0	0	0	2	-2	0	0	0	0	7
NHL Totals			7	0	0	0	2						
Hemsky, Ales	EDM	R	74	20	51	71	34	-9	8	0	2	0	184
NHL Totals			349	70	195	265	166						
Hendry, Jordan	CHI	D	40	1	3	4	22	0	0	0	0	0	32
NHL Totals			40	1	3	4	22						
Hennessy, Joshua	OTT	C	5	0	0	0	0	-1	0	0	0	0	2
NHL Totals			15	1	0	1	4						
Hensick, T.J.	COL	C	31	6	5	11	2	-4	4	0	1	0	52
NHL Totals			31	6	5	11	2						
Higgins, Christopher	MTL	L	82	27	25	52	22	0	12	0	5	1	241
NHL Totals			225	72	56	128	74						
Hilbert, Andy	NYI	L	70	8	8	16	18	2	0	0	0	0	127
NHL Totals			236	31	46	77	108						
Hill, Sean	MIN	D	35	2	7	9	32	-16	1	0	1	0	18
NHL Totals			876	62	236	298	1008						
Hillen, Jack	NYI	D	2	0	1	1	4	1	0	0	0	0	3
NHL Totals			2	0	1	1	4						
Hinote, Dan	STL	R	58	5	5	10	42	-3	0	0	0	0	42
NHL Totals			452	37	48	85	319						

S%	TOI/G	Sft/G	Hits	BkS	MsS	GvA	TkA	FOW	FOL	Tot	FO%	%Tm	S/G	PS
15.8	7:09	11.8	25	0	5	2	1	60	54	114	52.6	8.5	0.8	0
13.6	16:10	21.4	110	32	51	32	31	13	19	32	40.6	0.6	2.2	0
7.4	21:05	26.3	106	72	8	33	12	0	0	0	0	0	0.6	0
1.9	20:30	25	35	184	17	45	28	0	0	0	0	0	0.7	0
11.5	18:35	22.9	5	9	17	7	19	0	3	3	0	0.1	2.5	0
7.1	11:45	14.8	1	5	1	6	6	0	2	2	0	0.2	0.9	0
18.3	21:44	23	58	31	84	60	44	15	11	26	57.7	0.6	3.2	0
9.6	19:19	23.8	47	40	80	41	36	380	525	905	42	21.1	3.1	0
2.5	19:17	26.1	65	108	23	20	26	0	0	0	0	0	1.2	0
0	21:07	27.6	148	90	30	24	18	0	0	0	0	0	0.9	0
14.1	19:20	24.8	17	10	57	33	41	54	82	136	39.7	3.2	2.7	0
0	7	10.6	3	0	3	0	2	5	18	23	21.7	5.7	1	0
10.9	18:34	22.6	24	29	63	64	42	1	4	5	20	0.1	2.5	0
3.1	17:12	22.3	46	46	9	9	6	0	0	0	0	0	0.8	0
0	3:45	5.2	1	1	0	0	0	5	7	12	41.7	4.3	0.4	0
11.5	11:59	16.4	4	6	11	11	15	108	148	256	42.2	15.3	1.7	0
11.2	17:57	21	76	65	84	18	50	22	40	62	35.5	1.3	2.9	0
6.3	13:28	17.7	39	50	40	24	46	99	121	220	45	5.5	1.8	0
11.1	15:12	21.7	68	43	8	11	1	0	0	0	0	0	0.5	0
0	15:32	20	1	4	0	0	2	0	0	0	0	0	1.5	0
11.9	10:30	17.1	114	18	11	3	9	14	19	33	42.4	1	0.7	0

Player	Team	Pos	GP	G	A	P	PIM	+/-	PP	SH	GW	OT	S
Hjalmarsson, Niklas	CHI	D	13	0	1	1	13	-2	0	0	0	0	5
NHL Totals			13	0	1	1	13						
Hlavac, Jan	NSH	L	80	12	23	35	40	-1	0	0	2	0	152
NHL Totals			436	90	134	224	138						
Hlinka, Jaroslav	COL	C	63	8	20	28	16	6	0	0	1	0	90
NHL Totals			63	8	20	28	16						
Hnidy, Shane	BOS	D	76	2	6	8	71	-2	0	1	0	0	49
NHL Totals			412	11	34	45	520						
Hoggan, Jeff	BOS	R	1	0	0	0	0	0	0	0	0	0	0
NHL Totals			99	2	8	10	67						
Holik, Bobby	ATL	C	82	15	19	34	90	-14	3	0	3	0	140
NHL Totals			1252	322	416	738	1355						
Hollweg, Ryan	NYR	L	70	2	2	4	96	-12	0	0	0	0	59
NHL Totals			200	5	7	12	311						
Holmstrom, Tomas	DET	L	59	20	20	40	58	9	11	0	5	0	137
NHL Totals			758	175	212	387	569						
Horcoff, Shawn	EDM	C	53	21	29	50	30	1	6	0	2	0	115
NHL Totals			480	103	182	285	327						
Hordichuk, Darcy	NSH	L	45	1	2	3	60	-1	0	0	1	0	18
NHL Totals			302	13	13	26	747						
Horton, Nathan	FLA	R	82	27	35	62	85	15	9	0	3	2	212
NHL Totals			290	100	93	193	292						
Hossa, Marcel	PHX	L	50	1	7	8	28	2	0	0	0	0	66
NHL Totals			237	31	30	61	106						
Hossa, Marian	PIT	R	72	29	37	66	36	-14	8	2	4	2	264
NHL Totals			701	299	349	648	395						
Hudler, Jiri	DET	C	81	13	29	42	26	11	3	0	2	0	131
NHL Totals			173	29	41	70	74						
Hunter, Trent	NYI	R	82	12	29	41	43	-17	2	0	1	1	222
NHL Totals			326	73	93	166	119						
Hunwick, Matt	BOS	D	13	0	1	1	4	-1	0	0	0	0	6
NHL Totals			13	0	1	1	4						
Huselius, Kristian	CGY	L	81	25	41	66	40	10	6	0	5	0	202
NHL Totals			473	132	177	309	164						
Huskins, Kent	ANA	D	76	4	15	19	59	23	1	0	2	0	46
NHL Totals			109	4	18	22	73						
Iggulden, Mike	SJS	C	1	0	0	0	0	-1	0	0	0	0	1
NHL Totals			1	0	0	0	0						
Iginla, Jarome	CGY	R	82	50	48	98	83	27	15	0	9	2	338
NHL Totals			860	374	388	762	631						
Isbister, Brad	VAN	L	55	6	5	11	38	-4	0	0	1	0	71
NHL Totals			541	106	116	222	615						

S%	TOI/G	Sft/G	Hits	BkS	MsS	GvA	TkA	FOW	FOL	Tot	FO%	%Tm	S/G	PS
0	13:37	18.5	8	9	5	1	0	0	0	0	0	0	0.4	0
7.9	15:08	17.9	68	21	68	35	42	1	7	8	12.5	0.1	1.9	0
8.9	13:55	19.2	16	17	26	22	17	167	216	383	43.6	11	1.4	0
4.1	14:01	17.9	66	82	25	21	9	0	0	0	0	0	0.6	0
0	7:57	11	3	0	0	1	0	0	0	0	0	0	0	0
10.7	15:58	21.2	147	41	47	30	65	877	625	1502	58.4	31.5	1.7	0
3.4	8:17	12.4	174	18	20	8	10	18	21	39	46.2	1	0.8	0
14.6	17:32	21.4	58	7	70	32	13	0	1	1	0	0	2.3	0
18.3	22:13	26	15	30	43	31	28	487	476	963	50.6	31.8	2.2	0
5.6	5:09	7.3	64	3	9	2	4	0	0	0	0	0	0.4	0
12.7	18:44	24.5	81	24	82	36	27	29	44	73	39.7	1.4	2.6	1
1.5	13:46	19	94	15	24	12	27	3	12	15	20	0.5	1.3	0
11	21:21	23.5	65	19	64	36	66	4	11	15	26.7	0.3	3.7	0
9.9	13:10	17.3	25	8	47	17	21	10	16	26	38.5	0.5	1.6	0
5.4	18:12	22.7	256	50	79	30	58	6	23	29	20.7	0.6	2.7	0
0	10:36	14.3	8	6	3	3	2	0	0	0	0	0	0.5	0
12.4	17:41	21.2	9	11	54	58	53	1	3	4	25	0	2.5	0
8.7	16:04	20.1	65	49	26	21	29	0	0	0	0	0	0.6	0
0	6:40	12	0	0	0	0	0	0	0	0	0	0	1	0
14.8	21:26	24.6	98	10	117	64	47	245	200	445	55	9.4	4.1	0
8.5	10:49	15.9	26	10	19	11	8	8	9	17	47	0.5	1.3	0

Player	Team	Pos	GP	G	A	P	PIM	+/-	PP	SH	GW	OT	S
Ivanans, Raitis	LAK	L	73	6	2	8	134	-10	0	0	0	0	48
NHL Totals			143	10	6	16	283						
Jackman, Barret	STL	D	78	2	14	16	93	-12	1	0	0	0	80
NHL Totals			309	13	62	75	562						
Jackman, Tim	NYI	R	36	1	3	4	57	-3	0	0	0	0	36
NHL Totals			68	2	5	7	104						
Jacques, J-F	EDM	L	9	0	0	0	2	-3	0	0	0	0	2
NHL Totals			53	0	0	0	35						
Jaffray, Jason	VAN	L	19	2	4	6	19	4	1	0	1	0	15
NHL Totals			19	2	4	6	19						
Jagr, Jaromir	NYR	R	82	25	46	71	58	8	7	0	5	0	249
NHL Totals			1273	646	953	1599	907						
James, Connor	PIT	L	13	1	0	1	2	-2	1	0	0	0	9
NHL Totals			15	1	0	1	2						
Jancevski, Dan	DAL	D	4	0	0	0	2	-1	0	0	0	0	3
NHL Totals			6	0	0	0	2						
Janik, Doug	TBL	D	61	1	3	4	45	-3	0	0	0	0	23
NHL Totals			146	3	12	15	119						
Janssen, Cam	STL	R	12	0	1	1	18	-1	0	0	0	0	9
NHL Totals			107	1	1	2	223						
Jensen, Joe	CAR	C	6	1	0	1	2	1	0	0	1	0	6
NHL Totals			6	1	0	1	2						
Johansson, Magnus	FLA	D	45	0	14	14	18	-5	0	0	0	0	37
NHL Totals			45	0	14	14	18						
Johnson, Aaron	NYI	D	30	0	2	2	30	2	0	0	0	0	16
NHL Totals			146	7	21	28	123						
Johnson, Erik	STL	D	69	5	28	33	28	-9	4	0	3	0	105
NHL Totals			69	5	28	33	28						
Johnson, Jack	LAK	D	74	3	8	11	76	-19	0	0	0	0	81
NHL Totals			79	3	8	11	94						
Johnson, Mike	STL	R	21	2	3	5	8	-4	0	0	0	0	21
NHL Totals			661	129	246	375	315						
Johnson, Ryan	STL	C	79	5	13	18	22	-2	0	1	1	0	85
NHL Totals			547	34	68	102	218						
Johnsson, Kim	MIN	D	80	4	23	27	42	-4	2	0	0	0	87
NHL Totals			598	58	185	243	332						
Jokinen, Jussi	TBL	L	72	16	26	42	18	-14	6	0	2	0	131
NHL Totals			235	47	98	145	66						
Jokinen, Olli	FLA	C	82	34	37	71	67	-19	18	0	5	1	341
NHL Totals			723	208	253	461	727						
Jones, Blair	TBL	C	4	0	0	0	0	0	0	0	0	0	1
NHL Totals			24	1	2	3	2						

S%	TOI/G	Sft/G	Hits	BkS	MsS	GvA	TkA	FOW	FOL	Tot	FO%	%Tm	S/G	PS
12.5	7:30	11.5	139	11	6	19	4	0	0	0	0	0	0.7	0
2.5	22:24	28	135	124	32	40	31	0	0	0	0	0	1	0
2.8	6:36	9.4	41	9	7	1	9	2	0	2	100	0.1	1	0
0	6:09	9.1	15	2	1	2	1	0	0	0	0	0	0.2	0
13.3	12:35	17.4	14	5	6	3	2	84	92	176	47.7	17.2	0.8	0
10	20:28	22.5	27	16	107	69	40	1	2	3	33.3	0	3	0
11.1	7:25	11.2	3	0	1	0	1	0	0	0	0	0	0.7	0
0	5:50	7.8	0	3	0	0	0	0	0	0	0	0	0.8	0
4.3	9:19	12.4	33	44	13	17	8	0	0	0	0	0	0.4	0
0	7:07	10.4	26	1	3	0	1	0	0	0	0	0	0.8	0
16.7	6:30	9.8	3	1	1	0	1	6	8	14	42.8	3.8	1	0
0	15:45	19.6	23	37	15	15	7	0	0	0	0	0	0.8	0
0	13:51	17.1	41	28	6	16	18	0	0	0	0	0	0.5	0
4.8	18:11	22.4	87	64	47	37	27	0	1	1	0	0	1.5	0
3.7	21:41	25.9	84	136	32	62	23	3	2	5	60	0.1	1.1	0
9.5	13:01	19.3	13	3	5	1	5	2	6	8	25	0.6	1	0
5.9	14:21	21.5	74	105	29	14	23	438	365	803	54.5	18	1.1	0
4.6	23:26	31.2	42	121	48	47	28	0	0	0	0	0	1.1	0
12.2	14:27	17.7	16	21	38	34	23	178	163	341	52.2	8.8	1.8	0
10	19:54	23.7	78	25	114	43	30	404	534	938	43.1	19.1	4.2	0
0	1:55	3	1	0	1	0	0	1	7	8	12.5	3.7	0.2	0

Player	Team	Pos	GP	G	A	P	PIM	+/-	PP	SH	GW	OT	S
Jones, David	COL	R	27	2	4	6	8	-5	1	0	0	0	37
NHL Totals			27	2	4	6	8						
Jones, Matt	PHX	D	45	0	2	2	10	-13	0	0	0	0	25
NHL Totals			106	1	10	11	63						
Jones, Randy	PHI	D	71	5	26	31	58	8	1	0	0	0	103
NHL Totals			170	9	52	61	112						
Jovanovski, Ed	PHX	D	80	12	39	51	73	-13	8	0	2	0	240
NHL Totals			821	109	288	397	1221						
Jurcina, Milan	WSH	D	75	1	8	9	30	4	1	0	0	0	58
NHL Totals			196	11	21	32	128						
Kaberle, Frantisek	CAR	D	80	0	22	22	30	-4	0	0	0	0	89
NHL Totals			493	28	157	185	210						
Kaberle, Tomas	TOR	D	82	8	45	53	22	-8	6	0	1	1	155
NHL Totals			681	69	333	402	198						
Kaleta, Patrick	BUF	R	40	3	2	5	41	1	0	0	0	0	26
NHL Totals			47	3	4	7	62						
Kalinin, Dmitri	BUF	D	46	1	7	8	32	-7	1	0	0	0	60
NHL Totals			466	34	111	145	289						
Kane, Patrick	CHI	R	82	21	51	72	52	-5	7	0	4	1	191
NHL Totals			82	21	51	72	52						
Kapanen, Niko	PHX	C	79	10	18	28	34	-1	5	0	5	0	85
NHL Totals			397	36	90	126	160						
Kapanen, Sami	PHI	R	74	5	3	8	16	-12	0	1	1	0	76
NHL Totals			831	189	269	458	175						
Kariya, Paul	STL	L	82	16	49	65	50	-10	5	0	1	0	223
NHL Totals			903	382	549	931	361						
Karlsson, Andreas	TBL	C	58	2	2	4	10	-7	0	0	1	0	31
NHL Totals			264	16	35	51	72						
Kaspar, Lukas	SJS	L	3	0	0	0	0	-2	0	0	0	0	5
NHL Totals			3	0	0	0	0						
Keith, Duncan	CHI	D	82	12	20	32	56	30	1	1	0	0	148
NHL Totals			245	23	61	84	211						
Keith, Matt	NYI	R	3	0	0	0	0	-1	0	0	0	0	3
NHL Totals			27	2	3	5	14						
Kelly, Chris	OTT	C	75	11	19	30	30	3	0	1	1	0	124
NHL Totals			243	36	62	98	146						
Kelly, Steve	MIN	C	2	0	0	0	0	0	0	0	0	0	1
NHL Totals			149	9	12	21	83						
Kennedy, Tyler	PIT	C	55	10	9	19	35	2	1	0	4	0	104
NHL Totals			55	10	9	19	35						
Kesler, Ryan	VAN	C	80	21	16	37	79	1	4	2	2	1	177
NHL Totals			238	39	42	81	214						

S%	TOI/G	Sft/G	Hits	BkS	MsS	GvA	TkA	FOW	FOL	Tot	FO%	%Tm	S/G	PS
5.4	11:21	16	40	9	12	7	2	3	5	8	37.5	0.5	1.4	0
0	14:33	20.4	80	53	14	6	4	0	0	0	0	0	0.6	0
4.9	19:23	26.4	35	82	41	49	26	0	0	0	0	0	1.5	0
5	22:32	28.2	114	63	77	42	31	0	0	0	0	0	3	0
1.7	16:38	22.4	151	107	27	46	15	0	0	0	0	0	0.8	0
0	17:08	23.4	28	82	22	17	26	0	0	0	0	0	1.1	0
5.2	24:52	27.5	41	99	40	84	24	1	1	2	50	0	1.9	0
11.5	6:19	8.8	112	12	3	1	3	1	5	6	16.7	0.2	0.6	0
1.7	17:20	20	24	52	25	25	9	0	0	0	0	0	1.3	0
11	18:21	22.4	16	7	56	22	49	16	10	26	61.5	0.5	2.3	0
11.8	13:48	18.5	23	26	32	20	25	420	386	806	52.1	17.6	1.1	0
6.6	13:19	18.9	51	44	31	17	25	13	18	31	41.9	0.7	1	0
7.2	18:43	23.6	18	21	62	30	18	0	6	6	0	0.1	2.7	0
6.5	9:39	13	34	30	16	2	14	182	151	333	54.6	10.2	0.5	0
0	12:14	14.3	3	1	0	1	1	0	1	1	0	0.6	1.7	0
8.1	25:33	27.9	67	115	38	41	52	0	0	0	0	0	1.8	0
0	10:41	15.7	2	2	1	0	0	0	0	0	0	0	1	0
8.9	16:36	21.8	64	35	44	35	50	86	76	162	53.1	3.7	1.7	0
0	3:43	6	0	0	0	0	0	2	1	3	66.7	3.1	0.5	0
9.6	12:13	16.7	48	10	34	12	20	2	6	8	25	0.2	1.9	0
11.9	19:03	26.1	78	71	56	27	59	720	638	1358	53	30.5	2.2	0

Player	Team	Pos	GP	G	A	P	PIM	+/-	PP	SH	GW	OT	S
Kessel, Phil	BOS	C	82	19	18	37	28	-6	5	0	3	0	213
NHL Totals			152	30	36	66	40						
Kilger, Chad	TOR	L	53	10	7	17	18	1	0	0	0	0	74
NHL Totals			714	107	111	218	363						
King, Dwayne	STL	L	61	3	3	6	100	-4	0	0	1	0	36
NHL Totals			88	4	4	8	152						
King, Jason	ANA	R	4	0	0	0	0	-3	0	0	0	0	2
NHL Totals			59	12	11	23	8						
Klee, Ken	ATL	D	72	1	9	10	60	-5	0	0	0	0	56
NHL Totals			863	54	130	184	852						
Klein, Kevin	NSH	D	13	0	2	2	6	-3	0	0	0	0	14
NHL Totals			18	1	2	3	6						
Klemm, Jon	LAK	D	22	0	0	0	10	-5	0	0	0	0	6
NHL Totals			773	42	100	142	436						
Klesla, Rostislav	CBJ	D	82	6	12	18	60	7	3	0	1	0	130
NHL Totals			410	35	71	106	418						
Knuble, Mike	PHI	R	82	29	26	55	72	-3	15	1	3	0	177
NHL Totals			738	188	194	382	432						
Kobasew, Chuck	BOS	R	73	22	17	39	29	6	6	3	3	0	147
NHL Totals			293	57	55	112	214						
Koci, David	CHI	L	18	0	0	0	68	-4	0	0	0	0	2
NHL Totals			27	0	0	0	156						
Koistinen, Ville	NSH	D	48	4	13	17	18	13	2	0	1	0	60
NHL Totals			48	4	13	17	18						
Koivu, Mikko	MIN	C	57	11	31	42	42	13	2	0	2	0	144
NHL Totals			203	37	80	117	140						
Koivu, Saku	MTL	C	77	16	40	56	93	-4	8	0	3	1	150
NHL Totals			727	175	416	591	579						
Komisarek, Michael	MTL	D	75	4	13	17	101	9	0	0	1	1	75
NHL Totals			295	10	37	47	375						
Kondratiev, Maxim	ANA	D	4	0	0	0	0	-2	0	0	0	0	1
NHL Totals			40	1	2	3	24						
Konopka, Zenon	CBJ	C	3	0	0	0	15	0	0	0	0	0	4
NHL Totals			32	4	3	7	83						
Kontiola, Petri	CHI	C	12	0	5	5	6	5	0	0	0	0	13
NHL Totals			12	0	5	5	6						
Kopecky, Tomas	DET	C	77	5	7	12	43	2	0	0	1	0	87
NHL Totals			104	6	7	13	67						
Kopitar, Anze	LAK	C	82	32	45	77	22	-15	12	2	3	1	201
NHL Totals			154	52	86	138	46						
Kostitsyn, Andrei	MTL	L	78	26	27	53	29	15	12	0	5	0	156
NHL Totals			112	29	38	67	37						

S%	TOI/G	Sft/G	Hits	BkS	MsS	GvA	TkA	FOW	FOL	Tot	FO%	%Tm	S/G	PS
8.9	15:13	19.4	11	17	82	30	38	138	188	326	42.3	6.9	2.6	0
13.5	11:38	16.3	137	22	40	15	9	34	36	70	48.6	2.3	1.4	0
8.3	5:36	9	75	3	3	0	4	2	5	7	28.6	0.2	0.6	0
0	10:56	16.3	1	0	2	2	1	1	0	1	100	0.4	0.5	0
1.8	20:02	25.6	78	136	19	37	24	0	0	0	0	0	0.8	0
0	14:24	18.8	7	15	6	2	2	0	0	0	0	0	1.1	0
0	10:57	15.1	34	22	2	6	2	2	0	2	100	0.1	0.3	0
4.6	23:12	30.2	107	110	48	17	20	4	1	5	80	0.1	1.6	0
16.4	18:54	23.1	58	47	73	36	36	10	15	25	40	0.5	2.2	0
15	17:40	23.5	86	29	31	21	29	28	42	70	40	1.6	2	0
0	3:38	5.9	17	2	0	0	0	0	0	0	0	0	0.1	0
6.7	16:47	19.8	37	30	29	14	7	0	0	0	0	0	1.2	0
7.6	20:53	29.8	40	21	43	21	59	542	490	1032	52.5	32.3	2.5	0
10.7	18:07	21.4	41	29	48	43	49	701	640	1341	52.3	30.2	1.9	0
5.3	21:09	25.8	266	227	41	68	40	0	1	1	0	0	1	0
0	7:30	9.3	3	1	1	2	1	0	0	0	0	0	0.2	0
0	7:54	11	5	2	0	0	0	11	10	21	52.4	12.8	1.3	0
0	14:33	20.5	13	0	3	5	6	31	14	45	68.9	6.6	1.1	0
5.7	9:36	14.1	111	17	60	13	11	44	65	109	40.4	2.5	1.1	0
15.9	20:41	25.3	47	40	81	85	52	566	584	1150	49.2	25	2.5	0
16.7	15:41	17.9	102	22	68	26	22	4	2	6	66.7	0.1	2	0

Player	Team	Pos	GP	G	A	P	PIM	+/-	PP	SH	GW	OT	S
Kostitsyn, Sergei	MTL	L	52	9	18	27	51	9	3	1	0	0	49
NHL Totals			52	9	18	27	51						
Kostopoulos, Tom	MTL	R	67	7	6	13	113	-3	0	3	1	0	98
NHL Totals			298	32	51	83	362						
Kotalik, Ales	BUF	R	79	23	20	43	58	-5	12	0	1	0	207
NHL Totals			370	101	107	208	239						
Kovalchuk, Ilya	ATL	L	79	52	35	87	52	-12	16	2	4	1	283
NHL Totals			466	254	212	466	334						
Kovalev, Alex	MTL	R	82	35	49	84	70	18	17	0	5	1	230
NHL Totals			1073	368	508	876	1126						
Kozlov, Viktor	WSH	C	81	16	38	54	18	28	2	0	2	0	219
NHL Totals			830	185	311	496	232						
Kozlov, Vyacheslav	ATL	L	82	17	24	41	26	-10	5	0	4	0	161
NHL Totals			1045	322	429	751	627						
Krajicek, Lukas	VAN	D	39	2	9	11	36	-3	1	0	0	0	28
NHL Totals			207	8	42	50	162						
Krejci, David	BOS	C	56	6	21	27	20	-3	1	1	0	0	73
NHL Totals			62	6	21	27	22						
Kreps, Kamil	FLA	C	76	8	17	25	29	10	1	0	2	0	99
NHL Totals			90	9	18	27	35						
Kronvall, Niklas	DET	D	65	7	28	35	44	25	0	0	0	0	108
NHL Totals			180	10	61	71	142						
Kronvall, Staffan	TOR	D	18	0	0	0	7	-2	0	0	0	0	9
NHL Totals			52	0	1	1	21						
Kuba, Filip	TBL	D	75	6	25	31	40	-8	2	0	0	0	113
NHL Totals			531	55	152	207	239						
Kubina, Pavel	TOR	D	72	11	29	40	116	5	6	0	4	2	136
NHL Totals			664	83	187	270	827						
Kukkonen, Lasse	PHI	D	53	1	4	5	38	3	0	0	0	0	31
NHL Totals			137	6	14	20	80						
Kunitz, Chris	ANA	L	82	21	29	50	80	8	7	1	6	0	196
NHL Totals			253	65	92	157	244						
Kwiatkowski, Joel	ATL	D	18	0	5	5	20	-5	0	0	0	0	24
NHL Totals			282	16	29	45	245						
Ladd, Andrew	CHI	L	63	14	16	30	35	13	1	0	1	0	131
NHL Totals			157	31	31	62	85						
Laich, Brooks	WSH	C	82	21	16	37	35	-3	8	2	4	0	122
NHL Totals			233	36	41	77	92						
Laing, Quintin	WSH	L	39	1	5	6	10	4	0	0	1	0	48
NHL Totals			42	1	6	7	10						
Lang, Robert	CHI	C	76	21	33	54	50	9	7	0	3	0	172
NHL Totals			875	234	401	635	358						

S%	TOI/G	Sft/G	Hits	BkS	MsS	GvA	TkA	FOW	FOL	Tot	FO%	%Tm	S/G	PS
18.4	14:21	17.4	54	23	20	19	17	8	15	23	34.8	0.7	0.9	1
7.1	11:16	15.5	128	34	27	16	11	8	20	28	28.6	0.7	1.5	0
11.1	15:20	19	139	18	59	32	13	98	122	220	44.5	4.8	2.6	0
18.4	21:30	20.1	40	25	111	66	49	14	18	32	43.8	0.7	3.6	1
15.2	19:33	21.1	88	39	60	67	47	32	26	58	55.2	1.2	2.8	0
7.3	17:34	19.6	51	32	74	47	46	203	239	442	45.9	9.4	2.7	0
10.6	15:56	18.4	27	16	59	46	47	31	37	68	45.6	1.4	2	0
7.1	18:10	24.8	27	54	19	14	4	0	0	0	0	0	0.7	0
8.2	14:55	18.9	47	27	15	8	18	306	329	635	48.2	20.2	1.3	0
8.1	12:58	18.5	45	30	20	23	32	411	352	763	53.9	16.8	1.3	0
6.5	21:06	27.6	93	79	38	30	11	0	0	0	0	0	1.7	0
0	11:07	16.8	14	14	4	9	4	0	0	0	0	0	0.5	0
5.3	24:57	28.9	69	131	59	60	23	0	2	2	0	0	1.5	0
8.1	23:55	28.8	121	166	57	48	34	0	1	1	0	0	1.9	0
3.2	15:44	23.2	40	111	17	20	14	0	0	0	0	0	0.6	0
10.7	16:54	22.2	159	19	66	32	32	16	33	49	32.6	1	2.4	0
0	16:44	21.4	9	18	9	7	6	0	0	0	0	0	1.3	0
10.7	12:46	17.7	138	14	35	11	19	4	4	8	50	0.2	2.1	0
17.2	14:02	19.4	83	56	33	26	22	281	315	596	47.1	12.5	1.5	0
2.1	11:33	17.8	49	52	20	12	12	2	4	6	33.3	0.2	1.2	0
12.2	18:25	23.2	25	22	45	33	28	593	524	1117	53.1	27	2.3	0

Player	Team	Pos	GP	G	A	P	PIM	+/-	PP	SH	GW	OT	S
Langenbrunner, Jamie	NJD	R	64	13	28	41	30	-1	5	1	2	0	152
NHL Totals			803	180	296	476	660						
Langfeld, Josh	NSH	R	2	0	0	0	0	0	0	0	0	0	5
NHL Totals			143	9	23	32	60						
Langkow, Daymond	CGY	C	80	30	35	65	19	16	14	1	4	0	201
NHL Totals			868	224	331	555	483						
Laperriere, Ian	COL	R	70	4	15	19	140	-5	0	0	1	0	68
NHL Totals			927	111	186	297	1631						
Lapierre, Maxim	MTL	C	53	7	11	18	60	5	0	0	0	0	68
NHL Totals			100	13	17	30	84						
Lapointe, Martin	OTT	R	70	6	7	13	70	-5	1	0	0	0	63
NHL Totals			991	181	200	381	1417						
Laraque, Georges	PIT	R	71	4	9	13	141	0	0	0	2	0	29
NHL Totals			634	52	96	148	1037						
Larman, Drew	FLA	C	6	0	1	1	2	1	0	0	0	0	1
NHL Totals			22	2	1	3	4						
Larose, Chad	CAR	C	58	11	12	23	46	6	0	1	2	0	117
NHL Totals			187	18	36	54	91						
Larsen, Brad	ATL	L	62	1	3	4	12	-17	0	0	0	0	35
NHL Totals			294	19	29	48	134						
Lashoff, Matt	BOS	D	18	1	4	5	0	-2	1	0	0	0	11
NHL Totals			30	1	6	7	12						
Latendresse, Guillaume	MTL	R	73	16	11	27	41	-2	2	0	3	1	116
NHL Totals			153	32	24	56	88						
Lavallee-Smotherman, Jordan	ATL	L	2	1	1	2	0	2	0	0	0	0	1
NHL Totals			2	1	1	2	0						
Leach, Jay	TBL	D	2	0	0	0	0	-1	0	0	0	0	0
NHL Totals			4	0	0	0	7						
Lebda, Brett	DET	D	78	3	11	14	48	-1	0	0	1	1	110
NHL Totals			198	11	33	44	129						
Lecavalier, Vincent	TBL	C	81	40	52	92	89	-17	10	1	7	0	318
NHL Totals			710	273	329	602	507						
Lee, Brian	OTT	D	6	0	1	1	4	1	0	0	0	0	6
NHL Totals			6	0	1	1	4						
Legwand, David	NSH	C	65	15	29	44	38	-4	4	0	1	0	144
NHL Totals			549	121	206	327	318						
Lehtinen, Jere	DAL	R	48	15	22	37	14	9	9	0	1	0	118
NHL Totals			769	231	242	473	194						
Leopold, Jordan	COL	D	43	5	8	13	20	5	2	0	1	0	35
NHL Totals			272	22	63	85	138						
Lepisto, Sami	WSH	D	7	0	1	1	12	-1	0	0	0	0	8
NHL Totals			7	0	1	1	12						

S%	TOI/G	Sft/G	Hits	BkS	MsS	GvA	TkA	FOW	FOL	Tot	FO%	%Tm	S/G	PS
8.6	18:17	23.3	58	15	63	26	24	10	8	18	55.6	0.5	2.4	0
0	9:47	13	2	0	1	0	0	0	0	0	0	0	2.5	0
14.9	18:49	22.5	75	37	70	43	52	357	460	817	43.7	17.7	2.5	0
5.9	13:39	19.5	101	49	21	13	34	64	77	141	45.4	3.6	1	0
10.3	13:09	16.7	101	35	20	21	12	259	268	527	49.1	17.2	1.3	0
9.5	9:24	14.4	79	12	13	22	11	9	14	23	39.1	0.5	0.9	0
13.8	7:42	11.3	87	9	11	10	9	0	1	1	0	0	0.4	0
0	5:59	8.8	5	1	2	0	1	10	16	26	38.5	6.9	0.2	0
9.4	14:03	19.1	73	15	33	14	24	6	13	19	31.6	0.5	2	1
2.9	9:01	13	44	10	8	8	19	34	47	81	42	2.2	0.6	0
9.1	13:34	15.7	4	12	6	2	1	0	0	0	0	0	0.6	0
13.8	12:15	15.1	134	27	49	21	22	2	6	8	25	0.1	1.6	0
100	11:27	15	6	0	1	2	1	0	0	0	0	0	0.5	0
0	4:37	8	1	2	0	0	0	0	0	0	0	0	0	0
2.7	16:28	21.9	46	38	50	26	8	0	1	1	0	0	1.4	0
12.6	22:57	24.9	112	21	97	67	52	815	856	1671	48.8	36.7	3.9	2
0	16:49	21	3	7	3	4	1	0	0	0	0	0	1	0
10.4	18	22.8	7	21	30	26	52	305	395	700	43.6	18.4	2.2	0
12.7	18:55	23.1	19	31	42	18	36	1	10	11	9.1	0.4	2.5	0
14.3	15:59	22.5	26	40	16	16	8	0	0	0	0	0	0.8	0
0	13:17	18.6	6	3	2	4	2	0	0	0	0	0	1.1	0

Player	Team	Pos	GP	G	A	P	PIM	+/-	PP	SH	GW	OT	S
Lessard, Junior	TBL	R	21	1	1	2	11	-6	0	0	0	0	21
NHL Totals			27	3	1	4	23						
Letang, Kristopher	PIT	D	63	6	11	17	23	-1	1	0	3	0	68
NHL Totals			70	8	11	19	27						
Letowski, Trevor	CAR	R	75	9	9	18	30	-10	0	1	1	0	67
NHL Totals			616	84	117	201	209						
Lidstrom, Nicklas	DET	D	76	10	60	70	40	40	5	0	4	0	188
NHL Totals			1252	212	726	938	412						
Liles, John-Michael	COL	D	81	6	26	32	26	2	5	0	1	0	163
NHL Totals			313	44	115	159	122						
Lilja, Andreas	DET	D	79	2	10	12	93	-2	0	0	2	0	72
NHL Totals			398	12	47	59	431						
Linden, Trevor	VAN	C	59	7	5	12	15	0	0	2	1	0	45
NHL Totals			1382	375	492	867	895						
Lindstrom, Joakim	CBJ	C	25	3	4	7	14	0	2	0	1	0	25
NHL Totals			37	4	4	8	18						
Lisin, Enver	PHX	R	13	4	1	5	6	-5	1	0	0	0	27
NHL Totals			30	5	2	7	22						
Little, Bryan	ATL	C	48	6	10	16	18	-2	2	0	1	0	76
NHL Totals			48	6	10	16	18						
Locke, Corey	MTL	C	1	0	0	0	0	-1	0	0	0	0	1
NHL Totals			1	0	0	0	0						
Lojek, Martin	FLA	D	2	0	0	0	0	-1	0	0	0	0	2
NHL Totals			5	0	1	1	0						
Lombardi, Matthew	CGY	C	82	14	22	36	67	-6	2	2	4	1	181
NHL Totals			297	56	81	137	195						
Lucic, Milan	BOS	L	77	8	19	27	89	-2	1	0	4	0	88
NHL Totals			77	8	19	27	89						
Lukowich, Brad	TBL	D	59	1	6	7	20	-15	0	0	0	0	28
NHL Totals			582	22	81	103	353						
Lundin, Mike	TBL	D	81	0	6	6	16	3	0	0	0	0	33
NHL Totals			81	0	6	6	16						
Lundqvist, Joel	DAL	C	55	3	11	14	22	-3	0	0	0	0	48
NHL Totals			91	6	14	20	36						
Lupul, Joffrey	PHI	R	56	20	26	46	35	2	7	0	3	0	176
NHL Totals			293	77	84	161	156						
Lydman, Toni	BUF	D	82	4	22	26	74	1	3	0	0	0	86
NHL Totals			513	26	129	155	351						
MacArthur, Clarke	BUF	L	37	8	7	15	20	3	0	0	1	1	51
NHL Totals			56	11	11	22	24						
MacDonald, Craig	TBL	C	65	2	9	11	16	-10	0	0	0	0	84
NHL Totals			225	10	23	33	91						

S%	TOI/G	Sft/G	Hits	BkS	MsS	GvA	TkA	FOW	FOL	Tot	FO%	%Tm	S/G	PS
4.8	9:52	13.4	40	1	10	2	2	0	0	0	0	0	1	0
8.8	18:09	21.3	79	75	38	39	16	0	0	0	0	0	1.1	0
13.4	10:16	15.8	26	37	17	8	13	269	333	602	44.7	13	0.9	0
5.3	26:43	29.2	23	70	89	39	23	0	0	0	0	0	2.5	0
3.7	19:40	24.4	59	121	58	54	31	0	0	0	0	0	2	0
2.8	18:13	24.5	133	114	27	38	17	0	1	1	0	0	0.9	0
15.6	11:18	16.2	48	16	12	14	11	158	158	316	50	9.6	0.8	0
12	9:26	14	9	1	13	0	5	2	5	7	28.6	0.5	1	0
14.8	14:27	19.8	8	1	24	2	2	1	1	2	50	0.2	2.1	0
7.9	15:36	18.1	15	8	19	12	26	228	277	505	45.1	18	1.6	0
0	5:59	9	0	0	0	0	0	2	3	5	40	8	1	0
0	6:08	9.5	1	0	0	1	0	0	0	0	0	0	1	0
7.7	17:18	24.5	72	53	68	29	40	455	500	955	47.6	20.1	2.2	0
9.1	12:07	15.2	181	28	41	15	21	4	4	8	50	0.1	1.1	0
3.6	16:36	22.5	153	108	13	11	18	0	0	0	0	0	0.5	0
0	13:47	18.1	18	65	18	18	16	0	0	0	0	0	0.4	0
6.3	10:52	13.7	88	9	21	23	20	107	117	224	47.8	7.7	0.9	0
11.4	18:12	22.3	79	20	52	17	18	3	1	4	75	0.1	3.1	1
4.7	21:39	25.5	159	146	32	83	18	0	1	1	0	0	1	0
15.7	14:33	18.3	36	11	15	13	9	4	10	14	28.6	0.6	1.4	0
2.4	10:52	15	54	33	27	4	21	202	204	406	49.8	11.4	1.3	0

Player	Team	Pos	GP	G	A	P	PIM	+/-	PP	SH	GW	OT	S
MacKenzie, Derek	CBJ	C	17	2	0	2	8	-2	0	0	0	0	19
NHL Totals			45	2	2	4	28						
Madden, John	NJD	C	80	20	23	43	26	1	3	3	3	1	185
NHL Totals			636	133	141	274	167						
Mair, Adam	BUF	C	72	5	12	17	66	-2	0	0	2	0	62
NHL Totals			406	23	54	77	616						
Malhotra, Manny	CBJ	C	71	11	18	29	34	-3	2	0	2	0	112
NHL Totals			557	65	97	162	316						
Malik, Marek	NYR	D	42	2	8	10	48	7	0	0	0	0	34
NHL Totals			649	33	130	163	584						
Malkin, Evgeni	PIT	C	82	47	59	106	78	16	17	0	5	0	272
NHL Totals			160	80	111	191	158						
Malmivaara, Olli	NJD	D	2	0	0	0	0	2	0	0	0	0	0
NHL Totals			2	0	0	0	0						
Malone, Ryan	PIT	L	77	27	24	51	103	14	11	2	6	0	159
NHL Totals			299	87	82	169	301						
Maltby, Kirk	DET	L	61	6	4	10	32	-8	0	0	1	0	70
NHL Totals			942	119	124	243	807						
Mara, Paul	NYR	D	61	1	16	17	52	1	0	0	0	0	80
NHL Totals			563	58	160	218	546						
Marchant, Todd	ANA	C	75	9	7	16	48	-3	0	0	0	0	93
NHL Totals			966	171	279	450	682						
Markov, Andrei	MTL	D	82	16	42	58	63	1	10	1	2	0	145
NHL Totals			493	62	203	265	289						
Marleau, Patrick	SJS	C	78	19	29	48	33	-19	7	0	2	1	185
NHL Totals			795	238	301	539	285						
Martin, Paul	NJD	D	73	5	27	32	22	20	2	0	2	0	93
NHL Totals			305	19	100	119	76						
Martinek, Radek	NYI	D	69	0	15	15	40	-9	0	0	0	0	98
NHL Totals			322	10	64	74	197						
Matthias, Shawn	FLA	C	4	2	0	2	2	-2	1	0	0	0	5
NHL Totals			4	2	0	2	2						
May, Brad	ANA	L	61	3	1	4	53	2	0	0	2	0	34
NHL Totals			943	126	154	280	2093						
Mayers, Jamal	STL	R	80	12	15	27	91	-19	0	1	3	0	153
NHL Totals			595	71	87	158	756						
McAmmond, Dean	OTT	C	68	9	13	22	12	1	0	3	1	0	67
NHL Totals			872	173	242	415	426						
McCabe, Bryan	TOR	D	54	5	18	23	81	-2	4	0	2	0	107
NHL Totals			917	115	303	418	1574						
McCarthy, Steve	ATL	D	55	1	6	7	48	-23	0	0	0	0	41
NHL Totals			302	17	38	55	168						

S%	TOI/G	Sft/G	Hits	BkS	MsS	GvA	TkA	FOW	FOL	Tot	FO%	%Tm	S/G	PS
10.5	7:46	12.3	12	4	7	2	7	25	48	73	34.2	7.7	1.1	0
10.8	19:26	25.2	49	50	62	36	76	786	677	1463	53.7	34.9	2.3	0
8.1	8:51	12.1	112	16	18	16	13	164	197	361	45.4	8.7	0.9	0
9.8	16:27	24	64	40	31	19	29	683	475	1158	59	29.1	1.6	0
5.9	19:14	25.9	40	45	19	27	19	0	0	0	0	0	0.8	0
17.3	21:19	24.2	49	40	86	76	69	350	540	890	39.3	18.9	3.3	0
0	8:48	15	1	1	0	0	0	0	0	0	0	0	0	0
17	19:04	24.5	138	34	57	32	50	12	26	38	31.6	0.8	2.1	0
8.6	12:03	19	92	17	16	15	17	3	4	7	42.8	0.2	1.1	0
1.3	17:53	24.3	74	74	55	18	11	0	1	1	0	0	1.3	0
9.7	14:49	21	82	52	38	16	28	331	342	673	49.2	16	1.2	0
11	24:58	28	59	127	83	92	60	0	0	0	0	0	1.8	0
10.3	18:13	21.5	83	10	57	72	44	317	288	605	52.4	14.9	2.4	1
5.4	23:53	25.8	52	76	41	35	33	0	0	0	0	0	1.3	0
0	22:52	24.2	80	134	22	48	66	0	0	0	0	0	1.4	0
40	13:07	16.3	1	1	5	1	1	17	21	38	44.7	14.6	1.2	0
8.8	6:37	9.7	39	3	13	7	5	0	3	3	0	0	0.6	0
7.8	15:55	23.5	101	38	49	18	42	384	299	683	56.2	15.1	1.9	0
13.4	11:32	15.4	43	18	25	28	33	112	147	259	43.2	6.6	1	0
4.7	25:55	28.6	109	96	45	52	8	0	0	0	0	0	2	0
2.4	15:47	19.7	101	69	16	14	10	0	0	0	0	0	0.7	0

Player	Team	Pos	GP	G	A	P	PIM	+/-	PP	SH	GW	OT	S
McCarty, Darren	DET	R	3	0	1	1	2	2	0	0	0	0	3
NHL Totals			745	126	161	287	1452						
McClement, Jay	STL	C	81	9	13	22	26	-17	0	0	2	0	110
NHL Totals			229	23	62	85	111						
McCormick, Cody	COL	R	40	2	2	4	50	5	0	0	1	0	45
NHL Totals			135	8	10	18	158						
McDonald, Andy	STL	C	82	18	34	52	62	-21	3	0	1	0	182
NHL Totals			440	106	189	295	194						
McGrattan, Brian	OTT	R	38	0	3	3	46	0	0	0	0	0	11
NHL Totals			143	2	8	10	287						
McIver, Nathan	VAN	D	17	0	0	0	52	-8	0	0	0	0	9
NHL Totals			18	0	0	0	59						
McKee, Jay	STL	D	66	2	7	9	42	2	0	0	2	0	42
NHL Totals			671	19	88	107	524						
McLaren, Kyle	SJS	D	61	3	8	11	84	3	0	0	0	0	39
NHL Totals			719	46	161	207	671						
McLean, Brett	FLA	C	67	14	23	37	34	-5	3	1	1	0	140
NHL Totals			305	49	94	143	175						
McLeod, Cody	COL	L	49	4	5	9	120	-6	0	0	0	0	60
NHL Totals			49	4	5	9	120						
Meech, Derek	DET	D	32	0	3	3	6	-5	0	0	0	0	44
NHL Totals			36	0	3	3	8						
Meszaros, Andrej	OTT	D	82	9	27	36	50	5	6	1	1	0	160
NHL Totals			246	26	84	110	213						
Methot, Marc	CBJ	D	9	0	0	0	8	-1	0	0	0	0	9
NHL Totals			29	0	4	4	20						
Metropolit, Glen	BOS	C	82	11	22	33	36	-3	1	0	5	0	141
NHL Totals			262	35	78	113	96						
Meyer, Freddy	NYI	D	57	3	9	12	22	2	0	0	2	0	51
NHL Totals			175	11	36	47	93						
Meyer, Stefan	FLA	L	4	0	0	0	0	-1	0	0	0	0	0
NHL Totals			4	0	0	0	0						
Mezei, Branislav	FLA	D	57	2	2	4	64	-13	0	0	0	0	38
NHL Totals			240	5	19	24	311						
Michalek, Milan	SJS	L	79	24	31	55	47	19	5	1	8	0	233
NHL Totals			240	68	89	157	132						
Michalek, Zbynek	PHX	D	75	4	13	17	34	9	0	0	2	1	92
NHL Totals			261	18	53	71	134						
Miettinen, Antti	DAL	R	69	15	19	34	34	4	5	0	3	0	136
NHL Totals			238	38	53	91	118						
Miller, Aaron	VAN	D	57	1	8	9	32	-1	0	0	1	0	27
NHL Totals			677	25	94	119	422						

S%	TOI/G	Sft/G	Hits	BkS	MsS	GvA	TkA	FOW	FOL	Tot	FO%	%Tm	S/G	PS
0	7:46	12.7	4	1	0	0	0	0	0	0	0	0	1	0
8.2	13:55	20.2	62	41	34	14	35	366	334	700	52.3	15.3	1.4	1
4.4	10:58	16.2	81	9	17	4	16	6	11	17	35.3	0.7	1.1	0
9.9	17:52	22.7	46	20	61	33	31	527	421	948	55.6	20.3	2.2	0
0	2:52	4.1	18	2	4	2	4	0	0	0	0	0	0.3	0
0	10:27	15.8	19	20	3	0	0	0	0	0	0	0	0.5	0
4.8	17:53	23.5	73	164	16	11	5	0	0	0	0	0	0.6	0
7.7	18:21	26.9	127	75	21	29	11	0	0	0	0	0	0.6	0
10	16:14	22.8	22	30	34	22	25	296	328	624	47.4	15.6	2.1	0
6.7	10:07	15.4	98	7	19	4	13	0	3	3	0	0.1	1.2	0
0	12:08	17.1	22	18	14	14	8	0	0	0	0	0	1.4	0
5.6	21:02	26.1	101	100	75	48	33	0	1	1	0	0	2	0
0	14:13	19.4	16	2	3	1	0	0	0	0	0	0	1	0
7.8	16:25	23.2	65	34	39	22	37	613	629	1242	49.4	26.4	1.7	0
5.9	18:44	21.9	88	72	26	27	38	0	0	0	0	0	0.9	0
0	2:25	4	6	0	0	0	0	3	3	6	50	2.5	0	0
5.3	14:27	19.1	115	56	15	20	9	0	0	0	0	0	0.7	0
10.3	18:04	22.3	70	31	74	34	37	6	4	10	60	0.2	2.9	0
4.3	21:35	29	53	124	40	29	30	0	0	0	0	0	1.2	0
11	13:59	17.1	65	8	62	37	29	14	9	23	60.9	0.6	2	0
3.7	17:20	23.5	37	80	18	29	15	0	0	0	0	0	0.5	0

Player	Team	Pos	GP	G	A	P	PIM	+/-	PP	SH	GW	OT	S
Miller, Drew	ANA	L	26	2	3	5	6	-1	0	0	0	0	30
NHL Totals			26	2	3	5	6						
Minard, Christopher	PIT	L	15	1	1	2	10	-1	0	0	0	0	9
NHL Totals			15	1	1	2	10						
Mitchell, Torrey	SJS	C	82	10	10	20	50	-3	1	2	0	0	110
NHL Totals			82	10	10	20	50						
Mitchell, Willie	VAN	D	72	2	10	12	81	6	0	0	1	0	65
NHL Totals			456	12	72	84	514						
Modano, Mike	DAL	C	82	21	36	57	48	-11	5	1	4	1	200
NHL Totals			1320	528	755	1283	850						
Modin, Fredrik	CBJ	L	23	6	6	12	20	1	2	0	1	0	41
NHL Totals			764	211	205	416	385						
Modry, Jaroslav	PHI	D	80	1	8	9	50	-9	0	0	0	0	56
NHL Totals			725	49	201	250	510						
Moen, Travis	ANA	L	77	3	5	8	81	-10	0	1	1	0	98
NHL Totals			280	22	18	40	396						
Montador, Steve	FLA	D	73	8	15	23	73	1	2	0	0	0	96
NHL Totals			290	14	33	47	461						
Moore, Dominic	TOR	C	68	5	12	17	24	-4	1	0	0	0	100
NHL Totals			224	22	33	55	108						
Moore, Greg	NYR	R	6	0	0	0	0	-2	0	0	0	0	13
NHL Totals			6	0	0	0	0						
Moreau, Ethan	EDM	L	25	5	4	9	39	-4	1	0	0	0	54
NHL Totals			710	122	111	233	871						
Mormina, Joey	CAR	D	1	0	0	0	0	0	0	0	0	0	1
NHL Totals			1	0	0	0	0						
Morris, Derek	PHX	D	82	8	17	25	83	8	2	0	0	0	135
NHL Totals			718	71	249	320	754						
Morrison, Brendan	VAN	C	39	9	16	25	18	-3	3	0	3	0	54
NHL Totals			674	159	315	474	352						
Morrisonn, Shaone	WSH	D	76	1	9	10	63	4	0	0	1	0	47
NHL Totals			278	6	39	45	278						
Morrow, Brenden	DAL	L	82	32	42	74	105	23	12	2	7	1	207
NHL Totals			573	168	206	374	894						
Moss, David	CGY	L	41	4	7	11	10	-4	0	0	0	0	60
NHL Totals			82	14	15	29	22						
Mottau, Mike	NJD	D	76	4	13	17	48	-11	1	0	1	0	68
NHL Totals			99	4	16	20	61						
Motzko, Joe	WSH	R	8	2	2	4	0	1	0	0	0	0	10
NHL Totals			19	3	2	5	0						
Moulson, Matt	LAK	L	22	5	4	9	4	2	0	0	0	0	35
NHL Totals			22	5	4	9	4						

S%	TOI/G	Sft/G	Hits	BkS	MsS	GvA	TkA	FOW	FOL	Tot	FO%	%Tm	S/G	PS
6.7	11:11	16.4	12	11	12	4	6	3	6	9	33.3	0.6	1.2	0
11.1	3:52	6.4	16	0	3	0	2	0	0	0	0	0	0.6	0
9.1	14:18	20.7	113	66	42	41	43	342	350	692	49.4	16.2	1.3	0
3.1	23:11	28.2	49	109	29	41	37	0	0	0	0	0	0.9	0
10.5	19:14	22.4	10	28	93	82	86	563	582	1145	49.2	26.4	2.4	0
14.6	16:50	24.3	16	11	20	7	11	46	57	103	44.7	7.8	1.8	0
1.8	19:03	24.5	45	134	21	56	12	0	1	1	0	0	0.7	0
3.1	15:49	21.9	154	28	38	23	19	8	17	25	32	0.5	1.3	0
8.3	11:39	15.4	95	21	27	24	10	0	0	0	0	0	1.3	0
5	13:17	19.1	40	29	38	22	24	362	342	704	51.4	18.2	1.5	0
0	11:49	16.8	7	1	3	0	3	3	5	8	37.5	2.4	2.2	0
9.3	15:55	20.8	49	13	17	16	6	10	13	23	43.5	1.6	2.2	0
0	7:45	11	4	0	1	0	0	0	0	0	0	0	1	0
5.9	21:42	30.2	81	115	57	22	24	0	1	1	0	0	1.6	0
16.7	15:22	20.2	17	13	22	20	15	167	203	370	45.1	17	1.4	0
2.1	20:16	26.4	94	89	26	48	32	1	0	1	100	0	0.6	0
15.5	19:59	21.3	260	29	85	70	56	16	25	41	39	0.9	2.5	0
6.7	12:23	18.9	42	18	26	11	9	7	10	17	41.2	0.7	1.5	0
5.9	20:39	24.2	41	84	18	24	20	0	0	0	0	0	0.9	0
20	12:27	15.4	4	0	2	7	3	0	3	3	0	0.7	1.2	0
14.3	12:04	16.7	14	21	5	3	5	1	3	4	25	0.3	1.6	0

Player	Team	Pos	GP	G	A	P	PIM	+/-	PP	SH	GW	OT	S
Mowers, Mark	ANA	R	17	1	0	1	8	0	0	0	0	0	6
NHL Totals			278	18	44	62	70						
Mueller, Peter	PHX	C	81	22	32	54	32	-13	7	0	3	0	201
NHL Totals			81	22	32	54	32						
Murley, Matt	PHX	L	3	0	1	1	0	1	0	0	0	0	3
NHL Totals			62	2	7	9	38						
Murphy, Cory	FLA	D	47	2	15	17	22	0	1	0	0	0	65
NHL Totals			47	2	15	17	22						
Murray, Andrew	CBJ	C	39	6	4	10	12	0	0	0	0	0	45
NHL Totals			39	6	4	10	12						
Murray, Brady	LAK	L	4	1	0	1	6	-2	0	0	0	0	2
NHL Totals			4	1	0	1	6						
Murray, Douglas	SJS	D	66	1	9	10	98	20	0	0	0	0	48
NHL Totals			135	1	13	14	156						
Murray, Garth	FLA	C	7	0	0	0	19	0	0	0	0	0	3
NHL Totals			106	8	2	10	119						
Murray, Glen	BOS	R	63	17	13	30	50	-4	7	0	2	0	158
NHL Totals			1009	337	314	651	679						
Nagy, Ladislav	LAK	L	38	9	17	26	18	-2	2	0	1	0	78
NHL Totals			435	115	196	311	358						
Nash, Rick	CBJ	L	80	38	31	69	95	2	10	4	6	0	329
NHL Totals			363	154	122	276	384						
Naslund, Markus	VAN	L	82	25	30	55	46	-7	9	0	2	0	237
NHL Totals			1035	371	452	823	679						
Nasreddine, Alain	PIT	D	6	0	0	0	4	-4	0	0	0	0	3
NHL Totals			74	1	4	5	84						
Neil, Chris	OTT	R	68	6	14	20	199	-3	0	0	1	0	78
NHL Totals			451	58	66	124	1152						
Newbury, Kris	TOR	C	28	1	1	2	32	-7	0	0	0	0	14
NHL Totals			43	3	3	6	58						
Nichol, Scott	NSH	C	73	10	8	18	72	12	0	2	1	0	101
NHL Totals			374	40	42	82	645						
Niedermayer, Rob	ANA	C	78	8	8	16	54	1	0	1	1	0	111
NHL Totals			932	157	250	407	795						
Niedermayer, Scott	ANA	D	48	8	17	25	16	-2	7	0	3	0	87
NHL Totals			1101	148	485	633	676						
Nielsen, Frans	NYI	C	16	2	1	3	0	1	0	0	0	0	17
NHL Totals			31	3	2	5	0						
Nikulin, Alexander	OTT	C	2	0	0	0	0	-2	0	0	0	0	0
NHL Totals			2	0	0	0	0						
Nilson, Marcus	CGY	L	47	3	2	5	4	2	0	0	0	0	47
NHL Totals			521	67	101	168	270						

S%	TOI/G	Sft/G	Hits	BkS	MsS	GvA	TkA	FOW	FOL	Tot	FO%	%Tm	S/G	PS
16.7	9:02	13.2	6	3	2	1	0	22	23	45	48.9	4.5	0.4	0
10.9	17:15	20.9	30	12	95	19	21	105	146	251	41.8	5.3	2.5	0
0	11:43	17.3	3	0	1	1	1	2	1	3	66.7	1.6	1	0
3.1	15:23	18.1	11	39	29	16	7	0	0	0	0	0	1.4	0
13.3	11:42	17.5	47	16	16	2	8	15	17	32	46.9	1.4	1.2	0
50	11:18	14.8	6	2	1	2	0	16	15	31	51.6	12.8	0.5	0
2.1	17:28	25.8	127	83	28	39	24	1	1	2	50	0	0.7	0
0	6:13	8.9	13	0	0	1	0	0	3	3	0	0.6	0.4	0
10.8	18:12	21.9	42	10	57	13	24	6	13	19	31.6	0.5	2.5	0
11.5	13:47	18.8	28	11	30	13	7	44	39	83	53	3.8	2.1	0
11.6	20:29	28.6	67	30	96	30	56	14	30	44	31.8	0.9	4.1	0
10.5	17:23	22.7	13	24	79	39	40	0	1	1	0	0	2.9	0
0	12:53	18	5	4	1	1	0	0	0	0	0	0	0.5	0
7.7	12:45	16.8	204	10	39	20	21	0	0	0	0	0	1.1	0
7.1	4:22	6.4	23	2	2	5	4	22	33	55	40	3.3	0.5	0
9.9	13:15	19.2	110	35	38	11	39	441	297	738	59.8	17.3	1.4	0
7.2	17:42	24.6	61	28	40	45	33	23	46	69	33.3	1.5	1.4	0
9.2	23:54	25.5	35	46	44	39	37	0	0	0	0	0	1.8	0
11.8	8:42	12.1	4	8	7	1	6	54	57	111	48.6	12.3	1.1	0
0	4:55	7	0	0	0	0	0	1	0	1	100	0.7	0	0
6.4	9:48	15.1	6	17	11	6	9	21	20	41	51.2	1.5	1	0

Player	Team	Pos	GP	G	A	P	PIM	+/-	PP	SH	GW	OT	S
Nilsson, Robert	EDM	C	71	10	31	41	22	8	3	0	0	0	102
NHL Totals			128	17	45	62	52						
Niskanen, Matt	DAL	D	78	7	19	26	36	22	2	0	0	0	99
NHL Totals			78	7	19	26	36						
Nokelainen, Petteri	BOS	C	57	7	3	10	19	0	0	0	1	0	40
NHL Totals			72	8	4	12	23						
Nolan, Brandon	CAR	C	6	0	1	1	0	-2	0	0	0	0	2
NHL Totals			6	0	1	1	0						
Nolan, Owen	CGY	R	77	16	16	32	71	6	1	1	3	0	163
NHL Totals			1068	381	426	807	1727						
Norstrom, Mattias	DAL	D	66	2	11	13	40	3	1	0	1	0	54
NHL Totals			903	18	146	164	661						
Novotny, Jiri	CBJ	C	65	8	14	22	24	-10	1	0	0	0	91
NHL Totals			147	16	28	44	52						
Nummelin, Petteri	MIN	D	27	2	7	9	2	-2	1	0	1	1	31
NHL Totals			139	9	36	45	34						
Numminen, Teppo	BUF	D	1	0	0	0	0	0	0	0	0	0	1
NHL Totals			1315	115	505	620	491						
Nycholat, Lawrence	OTT	D	3	0	0	0	0	1	0	0	0	0	4
NHL Totals			31	2	6	8	18						
Nylander, Michael	WSH	C	40	11	26	37	24	-19	5	0	1	0	77
NHL Totals			848	200	446	646	436						
Nystrom, Eric	CGY	L	44	3	7	10	48	-5	0	0	0	0	42
NHL Totals			46	3	7	10	48						
O'Brien, Shane	TBL	D	77	4	17	21	154	-2	0	0	1	0	69
NHL Totals			157	6	31	37	330						
O'Byrne, Ryan	MTL	D	33	1	6	7	45	7	0	0	0	0	10
NHL Totals			33	1	6	7	45						
O'Donnell, Sean	ANA	D	82	2	7	9	84	9	0	1	0	0	25
NHL Totals			932	27	150	177	1558						
Oduya, David Johnny	NJD	D	75	6	20	26	46	27	2	0	0	0	63
NHL Totals			151	8	29	37	107						
Ohlund, Mattias	VAN	D	53	9	15	24	79	-1	4	0	2	0	128
NHL Totals			688	87	213	300	651						
Okposo, Kyle	NYI	R	9	2	3	5	2	3	1	0	1	0	15
NHL Totals			9	2	3	5	2						
Olesz, Rostislav	FLA	L	56	14	12	26	16	3	5	0	2	0	139
NHL Totals			190	33	44	77	68						
Ondrus, Benjamin	TOR	R	3	0	0	0	5	-1	0	0	0	0	4
NHL Totals			41	0	2	2	43						
Orpik, Brooks	PIT	D	78	1	10	11	57	11	0	0	0	0	50
NHL Totals			297	4	32	36	392						

S%	TOI/G	Sft/G	Hits	BkS	MsS	GvA	TkA	FOW	FOL	Tot	FO%	%Tm	S/G	PS
9.8	13:55	17.5	20	14	33	57	35	7	8	15	46.7	0.3	1.4	0
7.1	20:29	22.7	47	62	39	57	27	0	0	0	0	0	1.3	0
17.5	8:16	11.8	54	19	11	7	4	152	136	288	52.8	8.8	0.7	0
0	7:15	11.3	8	1	2	0	3	0	0	0	0	0	0.3	0
9.8	16:33	23.3	86	22	66	50	44	181	165	346	52.3	7.7	2.1	0
3.7	19:30	23	77	91	18	43	21	0	0	0	0	0	0.8	0
8.8	17:43	23.4	103	39	27	13	13	375	416	791	47.4	21.5	1.4	0
6.5	15:20	21	4	12	6	4	5	0	1	1	0	0	1.1	0
0	16:03	18	0	2	0	0	0	0	0	0	0	0	1	0
0	11:56	17.7	4	2	0	1	0	0	0	0	0	0	1.3	0
14.3	19:09	19.3	4	10	16	27	26	263	272	535	49.2	23.4	1.9	0
7.1	11:29	17.7	68	17	14	9	16	7	7	14	50	0.5	1	0
5.8	21:13	26.1	128	100	30	57	42	0	0	0	0	0	0.9	0
10	13:23	16.4	65	50	6	19	10	0	0	0	0	0	0.3	0
8	17:14	22.5	54	51	13	35	43	2	0	2	100	0	0.3	0
9.5	19:01	23.1	71	79	34	38	16	0	0	0	0	0	0.8	0
7	23:46	29.6	64	96	61	34	9	0	0	0	0	0	2.4	0
13.3	16:27	18.3	5	3	4	1	4	0	0	0	0	0	1.7	0
10.1	17:03	23.5	69	25	39	19	35	7	3	10	70	0.3	2.5	0
0	5:07	8	2	0	0	0	0	1	2	3	33.3	1.7	1.3	0
2	16:57	20.8	239	125	38	25	10	0	0	0	0	0	0.6	0

Player	Team	Pos	GP	G	A	P	PIM	+/-	PP	SH	GW	OT	S
Orr, Colton	NYR	R	74	1	1	2	159	-13	0	0	1	0	24
NHL Totals			163	3	3	6	356						
Ortmeyer, Jed	NSH	R	51	4	4	8	32	-8	0	1	0	0	68
NHL Totals			228	13	19	32	108						
O'Sullivan, Patrick	LAK	C	82	22	31	53	36	-8	3	3	2	0	220
NHL Totals			126	27	45	72	50						
Ott, Steve	DAL	C	73	11	11	22	147	2	0	1	2	0	89
NHL Totals			273	21	46	67	543						
Ouellet, Michel	TBL	R	64	17	19	36	12	11	5	0	0	0	132
NHL Totals			187	52	64	116	58						
Ovechkin, Alexander	WSH	L	82	65	47	112	40	28	22	0	11	2	446
NHL Totals			245	163	147	310	144						
Ozolinsh, Sandis	SJS	D	39	3	13	16	24	-11	2	0	0	0	39
NHL Totals			875	167	397	564	638						
Paetsch, Nathan	BUF	D	59	2	7	9	27	3	0	0	0	0	49
NHL Totals			123	4	30	34	77						
Pahlsson, Samuel	ANA	C	56	6	9	15	34	-2	0	3	3	1	94
NHL Totals			492	47	81	128	226						
Paille, Daniel	BUF	L	77	19	16	35	14	9	0	3	2	0	110
NHL Totals			120	23	26	49	34						
Pandolfo, Jay	NJD	L	54	12	12	24	22	10	0	0	1	0	78
NHL Totals			706	90	114	204	138						
Parent, Ryan	PHI	D	22	0	0	0	6	-4	0	0	0	0	9
NHL Totals			23	0	0	0	6						
Parise, Zach	NJD	L	81	32	33	65	25	13	10	1	8	2	266
NHL Totals			244	77	82	159	83						
Park, Richard	NYI	R	82	12	20	32	20	-4	1	4	2	1	132
NHL Totals			532	72	93	165	192						
Parker, Scott	COL	R	25	0	0	0	70	0	0	0	0	0	5
NHL Totals			308	7	14	21	699						
Parrish, Mark	MIN	R	66	16	14	30	16	2	7	0	0	0	95
NHL Totals			660	208	164	372	224						
Parros, George	ANA	R	69	1	4	5	183	3	0	0	0	0	30
NHL Totals			158	4	7	11	423						
Pavelski, Joe	SJS	C	82	19	21	40	28	1	8	1	4	0	207
NHL Totals			128	33	35	68	46						
Peca, Michael	CBJ	C	65	8	26	34	64	-1	3	0	3	0	86
NHL Totals			793	172	271	443	740						
Peckham, Theo	EDM	D	1	0	0	0	2	0	0	0	0	0	0
NHL Totals			1	0	0	0	2						
Pelletier, Pascal	BOS	L	6	0	0	0	0	-2	0	0	0	0	8
NHL Totals			6	0	0	0	0						

S%	TOI/G	Sft/G	Hits	BkS	MsS	GvA	TkA	FOW	FOL	Tot	FO%	%Tm	S/G	PS
4.2	7:49	11.8	146	25	14	4	14	1	1	2	50	0	0.3	0
5.9	12:27	19.3	63	23	33	12	31	6	6	12	50	0.4	1.3	0
10	18:42	23.8	95	45	97	61	38	203	258	461	44	10	2.7	0
12.4	14:27	18.7	182	26	45	41	35	183	128	311	58.8	8.1	1.2	0
12.9	13:37	17	57	19	63	8	19	19	23	42	45.2	1.1	2.1	0
14.6	23:06	21.3	220	44	199	93	68	7	11	18	38.9	0.3	5.4	0
7.7	16:58	20.6	28	32	25	28	6	0	0	0	0	0	1	0
4.1	13:37	17.1	35	52	10	20	4	0	0	0	0	0	0.8	0
6.4	18:46	25.4	114	24	32	22	33	586	480	1066	55	33.7	1.7	1
17.3	13:16	17.2	61	26	34	25	18	15	26	41	36.6	0.9	1.4	0
15.4	17:16	23.8	32	32	23	12	21	3	4	7	42.8	0.2	1.4	0
0	14:58	21.6	23	17	5	12	1	0	0	0	0	0	0.4	0
12	18:03	21.9	76	30	98	30	45	50	54	104	48.1	2.4	3.3	0
9.1	15:13	19.5	43	62	42	29	54	314	312	626	50.2	13.5	1.6	0
0	3:41	5.9	18	1	1	5	1	0	0	0	0	0	0.2	0
16.8	14:56	23.4	32	43	41	17	13	4	6	10	40	0.2	1.4	0
3.3	5:56	8.7	91	9	11	7	9	3	7	10	30	0.2	0.4	0
9.2	14:06	18.1	67	59	63	26	37	268	233	501	53.5	11.7	2.5	0
9.3	18:34	25.8	74	57	34	18	28	571	513	1084	52.7	29.5	1.3	0
0	13:22	18	1	2	2	0	0	0	0	0	0	0	0	0
0	11:03	16.8	12	2	8	0	0	1	0	1	100	0.3	1.3	0

Player	Team	Pos	GP	G	A	P	PIM	+/-	PP	SH	GW	OT	S
Pelley, Rod	NJD	C	58	2	4	6	19	-3	0	0	1	0	59
NHL Totals			67	2	4	6	19						
Peltonen, Ville	FLA	L	56	5	15	20	20	-2	1	0	0	0	108
NHL Totals			303	40	77	117	88						
Penner, Dustin	EDM	L	82	23	24	47	45	-12	13	0	4	1	201
NHL Totals			183	56	43	99	117						
Perrault, Joel	PHX	C	49	7	10	17	48	-11	3	0	2	0	87
NHL Totals			80	9	13	22	64						
Perreault, Yanic	CHI	C	53	9	5	14	24	-1	0	0	0	0	58
NHL Totals			859	247	269	516	402						
Perrin, Eric	ATL	C	81	12	33	45	26	-5	2	2	0	0	121
NHL Totals			167	25	56	81	56						
Perron, David	STL	L	62	13	14	27	38	16	3	0	1	0	68
NHL Totals			62	13	14	27	38						
Perry, Corey	ANA	R	70	29	25	54	108	12	11	0	4	0	200
NHL Totals			208	59	64	123	213						
Peters, Andrew	BUF	L	44	1	1	2	100	-4	0	0	0	0	18
NHL Totals			172	4	2	6	476						
Petersen, Toby	DAL	C	8	0	3	3	4	0	0	0	0	0	6
NHL Totals			163	16	28	44	16						
Pettinger, Matt	VAN	L	76	6	7	13	36	-11	1	0	3	0	127
NHL Totals			354	56	49	105	180						
Peverley, Rich	NSH	C	33	5	5	10	8	4	0	0	2	1	43
NHL Totals			46	5	6	11	8						
Phaneuf, Dion	CGY	D	82	17	43	60	182	12	10	1	4	0	263
NHL Totals			243	54	105	159	373						
Phillips, Chris	OTT	D	81	5	13	18	56	15	1	0	1	0	80
NHL Totals			699	45	137	182	512						
Picard, Alexandre	CBJ	L	3	0	0	0	2	0	0	0	0	0	1
NHL Totals			43	0	1	1	22						
Picard, Alexandre	TBL	D	24	3	3	6	10	-12	1	0	1	0	24
NHL Totals			92	6	22	28	31						
Pihlstrom, Antti	NSH	L	1	0	0	0	0	-1	0	0	0	0	1
NHL Totals			1	0	0	0	0						
Pineault, Adam	CBJ	R	3	0	0	0	0	-2	0	0	0	0	5
NHL Totals			3	0	0	0	0						
Pisani, Fernando	EDM	R	56	13	9	22	28	-5	4	0	3	0	96
NHL Totals			324	69	61	130	166						
Pitkanen, Joni	EDM	D	63	8	18	26	56	-5	1	1	1	0	101
NHL Totals			269	33	109	142	266						
Platt, Geoff	ANA	C	5	0	0	0	2	2	0	0	0	0	4
NHL Totals			46	4	10	14	28						

S%	TOI/G	Sft/G	Hits	BkS	MsS	GvA	TkA	FOW	FOL	Tot	FO%	%Tm	S/G	PS
3.4	9:18	13.6	73	12	25	4	13	150	171	321	46.7	10.6	1	0
4.6	15:49	20.8	33	31	33	28	23	3	13	16	18.8	0.4	1.9	0
11.4	17:12	21	99	37	80	55	44	104	85	189	55	4.1	2.5	0
8	14:26	19.6	42	16	26	15	14	294	305	599	49.1	20.6	1.8	0
15.5	11:30	16.7	17	12	12	15	12	294	163	457	64.3	15.9	1.1	0
9.9	17:49	21.6	52	31	42	36	58	380	337	717	53	15.2	1.5	1
19.1	12:33	16.8	65	7	30	12	24	5	9	14	35.7	0.4	1.1	0
14.5	17:57	21.7	95	11	85	43	29	3	13	16	18.8	0.4	2.9	0
5.6	3:08	5	22	3	3	6	2	0	1	1	0	0	0.4	0
0	7:50	10.6	9	3	3	1	5	22	22	44	50	10.3	0.8	0
4.7	14:18	19.5	75	35	37	12	25	11	8	19	57.9	0.4	1.7	0
11.6	10:19	13.4	12	5	17	6	10	61	71	132	46.2	6.9	1.3	0
6.5	26:25	29.6	194	88	109	51	52	0	0	0	0	0	3.2	0
6.3	22:28	27.3	126	151	20	57	25	0	1	1	0	0	1	0
0	6:46	11	10	0	0	0	0	0	0	0	0	0	0.3	0
12.5	20:25	25.2	35	38	11	10	5	0	0	0	0	0	1	0
0	9:08	13	1	0	1	0	0	0	0	0	0	0	1	0
0	11:02	16.3	1	0	1	0	1	0	1	1	0	0.6	1.7	0
13.5	16:31	21.8	41	14	29	22	20	2	5	7	28.6	0.2	1.7	0
7.9	24:07	25.1	32	59	40	71	20	0	0	0	0	0	1.6	0
0	11:17	17.4	3	1	3	2	0	2	5	7	28.6	2.3	0.8	0

Player	Team	Pos	GP	G	A	P	PIM	+/-	PP	SH	GW	OT	S
Plekanec, Tomas	MTL	C	81	29	40	69	42	15	12	2	6	0	186
NHL Totals			231	58	87	145	110						
Plihal, Tomas	SJS	C	22	2	1	3	4	4	0	0	0	0	34
NHL Totals			25	2	1	3	4						
Pock, Thomas	NYR	D	1	0	0	0	0	-2	0	0	0	0	2
NHL Totals			59	7	7	14	20						
Pohl, John	TOR	C	33	1	4	5	10	-4	0	0	1	0	23
NHL Totals			115	17	21	38	24						
Polak, Roman	STL	D	6	0	1	1	0	1	0	0	0	0	2
NHL Totals			25	0	1	1	6						
Pominville, Jason	BUF	R	82	27	53	80	20	16	2	1	1	0	232
NHL Totals			222	79	89	168	72						
Ponikarovsky, Alexei	TOR	L	66	18	17	35	36	3	1	0	1	0	150
NHL Totals			334	72	83	155	236						
Popovic, Mark	ATL	D	33	0	2	2	10	-4	0	0	0	0	25
NHL Totals			44	0	3	3	10						
Pothier, Brian	WSH	D	38	5	9	14	20	5	1	0	1	0	65
NHL Totals			292	20	80	100	177						
Poti, Tom	WSH	D	71	2	27	29	46	9	0	0	0	0	99
NHL Totals			665	60	221	281	508						
Potulny, Ryan	PHI	C	7	0	1	1	4	0	0	0	0	0	5
NHL Totals			44	7	7	14	26						
Pouliot, Benoit	MIN	L	11	2	1	3	0	-1	0	0	0	0	10
NHL Totals			14	2	1	3	0						
Pouliot, Marc-Antoine	EDM	C	24	1	6	7	12	-1	0	0	0	0	32
NHL Totals			78	6	13	19	30						
Pratt, Nolan	BUF	D	55	1	6	7	30	1	0	0	0	0	21
NHL Totals			592	9	56	65	537						
Preissing, Tom	LAK	D	77	8	16	24	16	-6	6	0	1	0	93
NHL Totals			300	28	96	124	72						
Primeau, Wayne	CGY	C	43	3	7	10	26	-3	0	0	0	0	39
NHL Totals			691	66	116	182	740						
Pronger, Chris	ANA	D	72	12	31	43	128	-1	8	0	4	1	182
NHL Totals			940	131	427	558	1369						
Prospal, Vaclav	PHI	L	80	33	38	71	45	0	10	0	5	1	215
NHL Totals			792	179	375	554	421						
Prucha, Petr	NYR	L	62	7	10	17	22	3	2	0	1	0	89
NHL Totals			209	59	45	104	84						
Purcell, Edward	LAK	C	10	1	2	3	0	2	0	0	0	0	10
NHL Totals			10	1	2	3	0						
Pyatt, Taylor	VAN	L	79	16	21	37	60	9	7	0	2	0	167
NHL Totals			463	81	91	172	272						

S%	TOI/G	Sft/G	Hits	BkS	MsS	GvA	TkA	FOW	FOL	Tot	FO%	%Tm	S/G	PS
15.6	18:04	21.7	32	28	63	40	51	683	698	1381	49.4	29.5	2.3	0
5.9	10:49	15.5	20	5	12	10	12	5	14	19	26.3	1.6	1.5	1
0	18:53	26	1	3	0	1	1	0	0	0	0	0	2	0
4.3	7:05	10.8	28	3	11	4	6	41	53	94	43.6	4.8	0.7	0
0	11:32	16.5	6	6	1	2	1	0	0	0	0	0	0.3	0
11.6	19:58	23.6	30	38	83	45	38	25	42	67	37.3	1.4	2.8	0
12	15:57	21.5	77	21	72	28	22	1	3	4	25	0.1	2.3	0
0	14:28	18.3	22	35	9	11	9	0	0	0	0	0	0.8	0
7.7	18:41	23.7	25	34	16	27	18	0	0	0	0	0	1.7	0
2	23:28	28	42	119	27	58	32	0	0	0	0	0	1.4	0
0	6:30	8.1	6	2	3	0	0	14	18	32	43.8	7.1	0.7	0
20	8:49	15.3	6	1	6	2	7	26	39	65	40	10.6	0.9	0
3.1	10:20	13.2	23	3	17	9	3	21	23	44	47.7	3.3	1.3	0
4.8	13:31	16.8	55	76	15	20	11	0	0	0	0	0	0.4	0
8.6	17:52	23.8	22	42	44	45	16	2	7	9	22.2	0.2	1.2	0
7.7	11:02	16.1	36	20	15	6	9	51	43	94	54.2	3.8	0.9	0
6.6	26	28.2	74	99	65	37	39	4	3	7	57.1	0.1	2.5	0
15.3	19:22	22.1	76	37	65	36	42	146	116	262	55.7	5.7	2.7	0
7.9	11:38	15	81	17	37	21	31	2	1	3	66.7	0	1.4	0
10	11:59	17.3	2	0	8	5	1	0	0	0	0	0	1	0
9.6	15:47	21	76	45	49	25	39	12	24	36	33.3	0.8	2.1	0

Player	Team	Pos	GP	G	A	P	PIM	+/-	PP	SH	GW	OT	S
Quincey, Kyle	DET	D	6	0	0	0	4	-3	0	0	0	0	5
NHL Totals			13	1	0	1	4						
Rachunek, Karel	NJD	D	47	4	9	13	40	3	0	0	0	0	68
NHL Totals			371	22	118	140	227						
Radivojevic, Branko	MIN	R	73	7	10	17	48	-14	1	0	3	0	91
NHL Totals			393	52	68	120	252						
Radulov, Alexander	NSH	R	81	26	32	58	44	7	4	0	2	1	183
NHL Totals			145	44	51	95	70						
Rafalski, Brian	DET	D	73	13	42	55	34	27	10	0	1	0	175
NHL Totals			614	57	309	366	214						
Ramholt, Tim	CGY	D	1	0	0	0	0	-1	0	0	0	0	0
NHL Totals			1	0	0	0	0						
Ranger, Paul	TBL	D	72	10	21	31	56	-13	0	1	0	0	105
NHL Totals			220	15	62	77	156						
Raymond, Mason	VAN	L	49	9	12	21	2	1	1	0	0	0	80
NHL Totals			49	9	12	21	2						
Reasoner, Marty	EDM	C	82	11	14	25	50	-17	0	0	0	0	113
NHL Totals			465	64	112	176	259						
Recchi, Mark	ATL	R	72	14	34	48	32	-18	7	0	0	0	121
NHL Totals			1410	522	859	1381	942						
Redden, Wade	OTT	D	80	6	32	38	60	11	4	0	1	0	136
NHL Totals			838	101	309	410	576						
Reddox, Liam	EDM	L	1	0	0	0	0	-1	0	0	0	0	1
NHL Totals			1	0	0	0	0						
Regehr, Robyn	CGY	D	82	5	15	20	79	11	1	1	0	0	93
NHL Totals			591	25	96	121	591						
Regier, Steve	NYI	L	8	0	0	0	4	-1	0	0	0	0	7
NHL Totals			10	0	0	0	4						
Reich, Jeremy	BOS	C	58	2	2	4	78	-5	0	0	1	0	39
NHL Totals			99	2	4	6	161						
Reinprecht, Steven	PHX	C	81	16	30	46	26	-3	5	1	0	0	105
NHL Totals			479	106	187	293	142						
Ribeiro, Mike	DAL	C	76	27	56	83	46	21	7	0	5	1	107
NHL Totals			433	95	200	295	160						
Richards, Brad	DAL	C	74	20	42	62	15	-27	9	2	4	0	249
NHL Totals			564	152	348	500	133						
Richards, Mike	PHI	C	73	28	47	75	76	14	8	5	6	1	212
NHL Totals			211	49	92	141	193						
Richardson, Brad	COL	C	22	2	3	5	8	-3	0	0	0	0	32
NHL Totals			136	19	21	40	48						
Richardson, Luke	OTT	D	76	2	7	9	41	1	0	0	0	0	41
NHL Totals			1415	35	166	201	2053						

S%	TOI/G	Sft/G	Hits	BkS	MsS	GvA	TkA	FOW	FOL	Tot	FO%	%Tm	S/G	PS
0	13:58	19.8	12	7	3	4	1	0	0	0	0	0	0.8	0
5.9	19:23	22.7	62	47	32	16	13	0	0	0	0	0	1.4	0
7.7	14:54	23.6	98	31	45	18	21	15	24	39	38.5	0.9	1.2	0
14.2	16:23	19.8	17	36	50	52	58	0	1	1	0	0	2.3	0
7.4	24:04	27.7	38	70	52	52	27	0	0	0	0	0	2.4	0
0	0:45	2	0	0	0	0	0	0	0	0	0	0	0	0
9.5	25:13	29.9	106	118	42	53	38	0	0	0	0	0	1.5	0
11.3	12:31	16.9	23	8	24	16	12	24	39	63	38.1	2.3	1.6	0
9.7	14:57	20.1	23	53	54	34	45	478	428	906	52.8	19.6	1.4	0
11.6	17:52	20	71	22	30	44	34	27	31	58	46.6	1.3	1.7	0
4.4	22:12	25.5	88	94	78	66	23	0	0	0	0	0	1.7	0
0	5:55	12	1	0	0	1	0	0	0	0	0	0	1	0
5.4	21:20	28.5	154	88	57	34	22	0	0	0	0	0	1.1	0
0	7:59	11.3	9	4	2	1	1	0	1	1	0	0.2	0.9	0
5.1	8:15	12.5	51	13	19	1	8	15	16	31	48.4	0.9	0.7	0
15.2	15:42	20.3	28	42	43	26	41	516	504	1020	50.6	21.8	1.3	0
25.2	18:25	18.8	53	23	35	88	43	397	486	883	45	22	1.4	0
8	23:27	23.4	13	22	100	46	48	527	547	1074	49.1	26	3.4	0
13.2	21:30	25.6	110	46	91	68	46	698	683	1381	50.5	31.6	2.9	0
6.3	13:28	19.2	13	3	10	2	5	26	34	60	43.3	4.9	1.5	0
4.9	12:19	17.1	65	55	17	22	13	0	0	0	0	0	0.5	0

Player	Team	Pos	GP	G	A	P	PIM	+/-	PP	SH	GW	OT	S
Richmond, Danny	CHI	D	7	0	0	0	2	-5	0	0	0	0	2
NHL Totals			49	0	3	3	75						
Rissmiller, Patrick	SJS	L	79	8	9	17	30	-8	0	0	2	0	119
NHL Totals			180	18	27	45	60						
Ritchie, Byron	VAN	C	71	3	8	11	80	-10	0	0	0	0	73
NHL Totals			324	25	33	58	373						
Ritola, Mattias	DET	C	2	0	1	1	0	0	0	0	0	0	2
NHL Totals			2	0	1	1	0						
Rivet, Craig	SJS	D	74	5	30	35	104	3	2	0	0	0	105
NHL Totals			744	45	149	194	911						
Roberts, Gary	PIT	L	38	3	12	15	40	-3	1	0	0	0	41
NHL Totals			1194	434	469	903	2533						
Robidas, Stephane	DAL	D	82	9	17	26	85	0	7	0	2	0	153
NHL Totals			489	27	82	109	342						
Robitaille, Randy	OTT	C	68	10	19	29	18	4	1	0	1	0	99
NHL Totals			531	84	172	256	201						
Roenick, Jeremy	SJS	C	69	14	19	33	26	-8	7	0	10	0	89
NHL Totals			1321	509	694	1203	1439						
Rolston, Brian	MIN	R	81	31	28	59	53	-1	11	1	8	0	289
NHL Totals			977	286	348	634	372						
Rome, Aaron	CBJ	D	977	286	348	634	372	-4	0	0	0	0	15
NHL Totals			18	1	1	2	33						
Rourke, Allan	EDM	D	13	0	0	0	5	-1	0	0	0	0	4
NHL Totals			55	1	4	5	31						
Roy, Andre	TBL	R	63	4	3	7	108	-1	0	0	0	0	38
NHL Totals			471	32	33	65	1086						
Roy, Derek	BUF	C	78	32	49	81	46	13	6	3	4	0	218
NHL Totals			272	80	129	209	175						
Roy, Mathieu	EDM	D	13	0	1	1	27	0	0	0	0	0	8
NHL Totals			30	2	1	3	57						
Rozsival, Michal	NYR	D	80	13	25	38	80	0	6	2	0	0	127
NHL Totals			479	46	127	173	383						
Rucinsky, Martin	STL	L	40	5	11	16	40	-9	1	0	0	0	67
NHL Totals			961	241	371	612	821						
Rupp, Michael	NJD	C	64	3	6	9	58	-8	1	0	0	0	69
NHL Totals			263	24	20	44	276						
Russell, Kris	CBJ	D	67	2	8	10	14	-12	1	0	1	0	90
NHL Totals			67	2	8	10	14						
Ruutu, Jarkko	PIT	L	71	6	10	16	138	3	0	1	1	0	55
NHL Totals			419	36	47	83	716						
Ruutu, Tuomo	CAR	C	77	10	22	32	91	4	4	0	1	0	100
NHL Totals			245	52	67	119	275						

S%	TOI/G	Sft/G	Hits	BkS	MsS	GvA	TkA	FOW	FOL	Tot	FO%	%Tm	S/G	PS
0	9:24	12.9	7	2	1	5	0	0	0	0	0	0.3	0	
6.7	13:09	18.9	111	35	51	24	22	109	105	214	50.9	5.2	1.5	0
4.1	12:19	17.7	89	34	17	21	18	262	253	515	50.9	13	1	0
0	5:46	9	0	0	0	0	0	0	0	0	0	0	1	0
4.8	21:11	28	73	79	36	44	21	0	0	0	0	0	1.4	0
7.3	13:20	17.6	43	5	13	9	11	5	2	7	71.4	0.3	1.1	0
5.9	20:38	23.4	220	109	58	35	33	0	0	0	0	0	1.9	0
10.1	13:33	16.8	23	13	35	27	21	82	60	142	57.7	3.6	1.5	0
15.7	13:44	17.7	96	22	34	58	21	83	105	188	44.1	5.3	1.3	0
10.7	20:04	28.1	59	24	113	41	25	67	98	165	40.6	3.6	3.6	0
6.7	18:10	24.1	33	17	9	4	2	0	0	0	0	0	0.9	0
0	10:55	15.2	3	22	3	4	1	0	0	0	0	0	0.3	0
10.5	5:27	7.9	91	3	12	5	5	0	0	0	0	0	0.6	0
14.7	20:58	23.6	36	48	74	66	48	713	680	1393	51.2	31	2.8	0
0	10:23	13.1	7	9	1	1	1	0	0	0	0	0	0.6	0
10.2	24:33	29.5	93	129	64	55	58	0	0	0	0	0	1.6	0
7.5	15	21.3	19	8	25	8	8	7	6	13	53.8	0.5	1.7	0
4.3	8:03	11.5	104	7	16	9	12	75	80	155	48.4	4.6	1.1	0
2.2	14:47	19.7	31	64	30	12	8	0	0	0	0	0	1.3	0
10.9	10:12	14.6	134	19	28	12	21	4	6	10	40	0.2	0.8	0
10	15:53	21.3	171	19	43	16	28	28	38	66	42.4	1.5	1.3	0

Player	Team	Pos	GP	G	A	P	PIM	+/-	PP	SH	GW	OT	S
Ruzicka, Stefan	PHI	R	14	1	3	4	27	5	0	0	0	0	10
NHL Totals			55	4	13	17	47						
Ryan, Bobby	ANA	R	23	5	5	10	6	-1	3	0	0	0	37
NHL Totals			23	5	5	10	6						
Ryan, Michael	BUF	C	46	4	4	8	30	-4	0	0	0	0	60
NHL Totals			65	7	6	13	32						
Ryder, Michael	MTL	R	70	14	17	31	30	-4	1	0	2	0	134
NHL Totals			314	99	108	207	156						
Rypien, Rick	VAN	C	22	1	2	3	41	-5	0	0	0	0	8
NHL Totals			29	2	2	4	50						
Sakic, Joe	COL	C	44	13	27	40	20	-4	5	0	1	0	124
NHL Totals			1363	623	1006	1629	608						
Salei, Ruslan	COL	D	82	6	24	30	98	-4	1	0	1	0	111
NHL Totals			758	38	129	167	935						
Salo, Sami	VAN	D	63	8	17	25	38	8	6	0	1	0	122
NHL Totals			537	67	153	220	184						
Salvador, Bryce	NJD	D	64	1	10	11	54	12	0	0	1	0	29
NHL Totals			455	16	47	63	424						
Samsonov, Sergei	CAR	L	61	14	22	36	16	-1	3	0	2	1	109
NHL Totals			657	192	262	454	135						
Samuelsson, Mikael	DET	R	73	11	29	40	26	21	3	0	1	0	249
NHL Totals			385	67	101	168	194						
Sanderson, Geoff	EDM	L	41	3	10	13	16	-7	0	0	0	0	40
NHL Totals			1104	355	345	700	511						
Sarich, Cory	CGY	D	80	2	5	7	135	2	0	0	0	0	57
NHL Totals			616	12	84	96	724						
Satan, Miroslav	NYI	R	80	16	25	41	39	-11	5	0	4	0	171
NHL Totals			947	337	348	685	416						
Sauer, Kurt	COL	D	54	1	5	6	41	17	0	0	0	0	28
NHL Totals			288	4	22	26	214						
Savard, Marc	BOS	C	74	15	63	78	66	3	4	0	2	0	196
NHL Totals			659	170	405	575	624						
Schaefer, Peter	BOS	L	63	9	17	26	18	4	0	0	0	0	91
NHL Totals			556	98	161	259	198						
Schneider, Mathieu	ANA	D	65	12	27	39	50	22	5	0	2	1	139
NHL Totals			1197	212	490	702	1165						
Schremp, Rob	EDM	C	2	0	0	0	0	-1	0	0	0	0	3
NHL Totals			3	0	0	0	0						
Schubert, Christoph	OTT	D	82	8	16	24	64	7	1	0	0	0	137
NHL Totals			218	20	39	59	168						
Schultz, Jeff	WSH	D	72	5	13	18	28	12	0	0	0	0	36
NHL Totals			110	5	16	21	44						

S%	TOI/G	Sft/G	Hits	BkS	MsS	GvA	TkA	FOW	FOL	Tot	FO%	%Tm	S/G	PS
10	8:39	12.4	9	3	5	1	4	0	5	5	0	0.6	0.7	0
13.5	11:15	15.3	20	5	12	7	11	1	0	1	100	0	1.6	0
6.7	9:52	13.2	27	14	16	11	8	0	2	2	0	0	1.3	0
10.4	13:14	16.4	122	15	56	12	29	5	14	19	26.3	0.4	1.9	0
12.5	8:06	12.3	28	10	3	3	6	44	62	106	41.5	8.6	0.4	0
10.5	19:59	23.7	11	21	31	33	24	296	290	586	50.5	24.1	2.8	0
5.4	22:26	28	162	135	51	35	13	0	1	1	0	0	1.4	0
6.6	23:38	30.2	36	79	73	46	18	0	0	0	0	0	1.9	0
3.4	19:47	26.1	75	104	22	26	19	0	1	1	0	0	0.5	0
12.8	15:53	19.8	12	17	36	25	29	0	3	3	0	0	1.8	0
4.4	16:15	21	74	21	64	29	20	6	8	14	42.8	0.3	3.4	0
7.5	10:09	13.5	8	7	11	18	20	12	11	23	52.2	0.9	1	0
3.5	18:49	26.1	157	64	40	44	27	0	0	0	0	0	0.7	0
9.4	18:19	19.8	19	22	65	51	52	19	19	38	50	0.8	2.1	0
3.6	18:41	26.9	48	59	18	23	25	0	0	0	0	0	0.5	0
7.7	20:31	24.9	38	11	58	76	47	802	753	1555	51.6	36.1	2.6	0
9.9	14:57	19	32	16	40	13	15	3	4	7	42.8	0.2	1.4	0
8.6	22:17	23.6	78	56	81	34	35	0	0	0	0	0	2.1	0
0	6:57	9.5	0	0	1	1	0	0	1	1	0	0.7	1.5	0
5.8	13:34	17.6	187	36	45	37	23	1	3	4	25	0	1.7	0
13.9	18:05	23.8	61	90	24	50	23	1	0	1	100	0	0.5	0

Player	Team	Pos	GP	G	A	P	PIM	+/-	PP	SH	GW	OT	S
Schultz, Nick	MIN	D	81	2	13	15	42	9	0	0	0	0	52
NHL Totals			448	19	58	77	180						
Scuderi, Rob	PIT	D	71	0	5	5	26	3	0	0	0	0	28
NHL Totals			219	2	21	23	94						
Seabrook, Brent	CHI	D	82	9	23	32	90	13	4	0	2	0	152
NHL Totals			232	18	70	88	254						
Sedin, Daniel	VAN	L	82	29	45	74	50	6	12	0	7	2	247
NHL Totals			560	148	232	380	228						
Sedin, Henrik	VAN	C	82	15	61	76	56	6	4	1	2	1	141
NHL Totals			564	87	291	378	322						
Seidenberg, Dennis	CAR	D	47	0	15	15	18	6	0	0	0	0	80
NHL Totals			225	9	45	54	76						
Sekera, Andrej	BUF	D	37	2	6	8	16	5	0	0	1	1	28
NHL Totals			39	2	6	8	18						
Selanne, Teemu	ANA	R	26	12	11	23	8	5	7	0	2	0	87
NHL Totals			1067	552	606	1158	469						
Semenov, Alexei	SJS	D	22	1	3	4	36	-8	1	0	0	0	23
NHL Totals			164	6	19	25	192						
Semin, Alexander	WSH	L	63	26	16	42	54	-18	10	0	2	0	185
NHL Totals			192	74	63	137	180						
Sestito, Tommy	CBJ	L	1	0	0	0	17	0	0	0	0	0	0
NHL Totals			1	0	0	0	17						
Setoguchi, Devin	SJS	R	44	11	6	17	8	6	3	0	2	0	105
NHL Totals			44	11	6	17	8						
Shanahan, Brendan	NYR	R	73	23	23	46	35	-2	11	0	3	2	265
NHL Totals			1490	650	690	1340	2460						
Shannon, Ryan	VAN	R	27	5	8	13	24	-1	4	0	0	0	34
NHL Totals			80	7	17	24	34						
Sharp, Patrick	CHI	R	80	36	26	62	55	23	9	7	7	1	209
NHL Totals			276	75	60	135	232						
Shelley, Jody	SJS	L	62	1	6	7	135	-4	0	0	0	0	41
NHL Totals			411	12	24	36	1116						
Sheppard, James	MIN	C	78	4	15	19	29	0	0	0	1	0	57
NHL Totals			78	4	15	19	29						
Sillinger, Mike	NYI	C	52	14	12	26	28	-10	3	2	2	1	94
NHL Totals			1042	238	308	546	644						
Sim, Jon	NYI	L	2	0	1	1	2	-1	0	0	0	0	8
NHL Totals			309	52	46	98	206						
Simon, Chris	MIN	L	38	1	2	3	59	-2	0	0	0	0	27
NHL Totals			782	144	161	305	1824						
Sjostrom, Fredrik	NYR	L	69	12	9	21	22	-2	2	2	2	0	110
NHL Totals			279	34	41	75	134						

S%	TOI/G	Sft/G	Hits	BkS	MsS	GvA	TkA	FOW	FOL	Tot	FO%	%Tm	S/G	PS
3.8	20:10	28.8	101	147	40	37	20	0	0	0	0	0	0.6	0
0	18:44	24.3	32	110	17	25	21	0	0	0	0	0	0.4	0
5.9	21:29	25.5	167	106	36	41	21	0	1	1	0	0	1.9	0
11.7	19:03	23.5	11	14	87	38	24	17	21	38	44.7	0.8	3	0
10.6	19:30	24.2	19	15	52	56	31	643	726	1369	47	30	1.7	0
0	18:50	24.4	110	81	30	12	7	1	0	1	100	0	1.7	0
7.1	19:37	23.8	19	50	17	15	14	0	0	0	0	0	0.8	0
13.8	18:07	21.3	6	2	27	30	7	34	33	67	50.7	4.6	3.3	0
4.3	15:14	22	24	17	13	17	0	0	0	0	0	0	1	0
14.1	16:54	17.4	20	14	89	81	40	4	7	11	36.4	0.3	2.9	0
0	4:36	9	1	0	0	0	1	0	0	0	0	0	0	0
10.5	14:14	18.2	64	17	35	20	17	11	6	17	64.7	0.7	2.4	0
8.7	18:30	23.7	47	47	75	33	32	6	2	8	75	0.2	3.6	0
14.7	12:53	17.6	10	8	18	3	13	32	50	82	39	5.4	1.3	0
17.2	18:46	24.8	50	27	64	22	44	305	289	594	51.3	13.6	2.6	0
2.4	5:51	8.4	93	5	9	6	2	0	2	2	0	0	0.7	0
7	10:36	16.9	40	22	27	20	28	272	383	655	41.5	14.9	0.7	0
14.9	18:36	23.7	28	25	37	32	30	578	449	1027	56.3	34.6	1.8	0
0	14:18	17	4	0	0	0	1	0	0	0	0	0	4	0
3.7	7:10	10.4	17	8	6	9	5	2	0	2	100	0	0.7	0
10.9	12:07	17.3	103	21	36	12	19	6	30	36	16.7	0.9	1.6	0

Player	Team	Pos	GP	G	A	P	PIM	+/-	PP	SH	GW	OT	S
Skille, Jack	CHI	R	16	3	2	5	0	1	0	0	0	0	23
NHL Totals			16	3	2	5	0						
Skoula, Martin	MIN	D	80	3	8	11	26	-16	0	0	1	1	63
NHL Totals			643	37	132	169	308						
Skrastins, Karlis	FLA	D	60	2	3	5	32	-11	0	0	1	0	45
NHL Totals			599	23	74	97	283						
Slater, Jim	ATL	C	69	8	5	13	41	-10	0	2	0	0	95
NHL Totals			214	23	29	52	149						
Smaby, Matt	TBL	D	14	0	0	0	12	-6	0	0	0	0	7
NHL Totals			14	0	0	0	12						
Smid, Ladislav	EDM	D	65	0	4	4	58	-15	0	0	0	0	45
NHL Totals			142	3	11	14	95						
Smith, Jason	PHI	D	77	1	9	10	86	-4	0	0	0	0	58
NHL Totals			945	40	128	168	1052						
Smith, Mark	CGY	C	54	1	3	4	59	-6	0	0	0	0	27
NHL Totals			377	23	47	70	457						
Smith, Nathan	PIT	C	13	0	0	0	2	0	0	0	0	0	3
NHL Totals			17	0	0	0	2						
Smith, Wyatt	COL	C	25	0	3	3	8	-4	0	0	0	0	25
NHL Totals			211	10	2	12	65						
Smithson, Jerred	NSH	C	81	7	9	16	50	-9	0	2	2	0	61
NHL Totals			241	17	28	45	171						
Smolinski, Bryan	MTL	C	64	8	17	25	20	-6	1	0	2	0	89
NHL Totals			1056	274	377	651	606						
Smyth, Ryan	COL	L	55	14	23	37	50	-4	2	0	3	1	168
NHL Totals			843	284	317	601	671						
Sobotka, Vladimir	BOS	C	48	1	6	7	24	1	0	0	1	0	40
NHL Totals			48	1	6	7	24						
Sopel, Brent	CHI	D	58	1	19	20	28	9	0	0	0	0	56
NHL Totals			492	40	161	201	251						
Souray, Sheldon	EDM	D	26	3	7	10	36	-7	2	0	1	0	71
NHL Totals			532	69	127	196	857						
Spacek, Jaroslav	BUF	D	60	9	23	32	42	7	7	0	1	0	95
NHL Totals			621	65	193	258	477						
Spezza, Jason	OTT	C	76	34	58	92	66	26	11	0	6	0	210
NHL Totals			322	116	229	345	223						
Spiller, Matthew	NYI	D	9	0	1	1	7	-2	0	0	0	0	6
NHL Totals			68	0	2	2	74						
St. Louis, Martin	TBL	R	82	25	58	83	26	-23	10	2	5	0	241
NHL Totals			608	208	297	505	212						
St. Pierre, Martin	CHI	C	5	0	0	0	0	-3	0	0	0	0	2
NHL Totals			21	1	3	4	8						

S%	TOI/G	Sft/G	Hits	BkS	MsS	GvA	TkA	FOW	FOL	Tot	FO%	%Tm	S/G	PS
13	11:58	16.6	15	4	10	3	3	2	2	4	50	0.4	1.4	0
4.8	20:28	27.9	71	101	24	49	15	0	0	0	0	0	0.8	0
4.4	18:36	26	42	105	30	16	17	0	0	0	0	0	0.8	0
8.4	10:23	14.2	84	29	21	9	26	191	176	367	52	9.1	1.4	0
0	12:08	16.3	31	12	5	2	2	0	0	0	0	0	0.5	0
0	17:51	21.8	92	95	16	35	18	0	0	0	0	0	0.7	0
1.7	17:56	25	142	204	29	33	11	1	0	1	100	0	0.8	0
3.7	5:56	9.7	44	6	14	10	11	31	26	57	54.4	1.7	0.5	0
0	7:40	10.5	14	4	3	1	0	40	35	75	53.3	9.8	0.2	0
0	11:38	16.7	10	10	9	4	11	55	53	108	50.9	7.6	1	0
11.5	12:04	18.3	128	44	18	18	36	298	274	572	52.1	12.1	0.8	0
9	13:07	17.8	45	36	40	19	30	382	356	738	51.8	19.9	1.4	0
8.3	19:36	23.7	31	8	47	38	27	13	20	33	39.4	1	3.1	0
2.5	8:50	12.6	64	12	17	4	12	120	127	247	48.6	8.9	0.8	0
1.8	20:18	23.4	35	122	21	31	13	0	0	0	0	0	1	0
4.2	24:20	25.8	29	24	42	31	18	0	0	0	0	0	2.7	0
9.5	22:58	26	78	75	41	43	12	0	0	0	0	0	1.6	0
16.2	20:40	22.3	18	18	85	96	44	729	716	1445	50.4	33	2.8	0
0	19:47	21.4	11	17	2	7	1	0	0	0	0	0	0.7	0
10.4	24:17	25.2	34	45	97	63	65	3	9	12	25	0.2	2.9	0
0	15:16	20	3	1	0	3	2	33	26	59	55.9	20.4	0.4	0

Player	Team	Pos	GP	G	A	P	PIM	+/-	PP	SH	GW	OT	S
Staal, Eric	CAR	C	82	38	44	82	50	-2	14	0	7	0	310
NHL Totals			327	124	159	283	239						
Staal, Jordan	PIT	C	82	12	16	28	55	-5	3	0	4	0	183
NHL Totals			163	41	29	70	79						
Staal, Marc	NYR	D	80	2	8	10	42	2	0	0	0	0	78
NHL Totals			80	2	8	10	42						
Stafford, Drew	BUF	R	64	16	22	38	51	3	1	0	5	0	103
NHL Totals			105	29	36	65	84						
Stafford, Garrett	DET	D	2	0	0	0	0	0	0	0	0	0	1
NHL Totals			2	0	0	0	0						
Staios, Steve	EDM	D	82	7	9	16	121	-14	1	0	0	0	73
NHL Totals			759	50	128	178	1078						
Stajan, Matt	TOR	C	82	16	17	33	47	-11	2	1	3	0	127
NHL Totals			314	56	71	127	163						
Stastny, Paul	COL	C	66	24	47	71	24	22	3	0	4	1	138
NHL Totals			148	52	97	149	66						
Stastny, Yan	STL	C	12	1	1	2	9	0	0	0	0	0	10
NHL Totals			53	2	6	8	38						
Steckel, David	WSH	C	67	5	7	12	34	1	0	0	1	0	66
NHL Totals			79	5	7	12	36						
Steen, Alexander	TOR	L	76	15	27	42	32	0	2	1	2	0	169
NHL Totals			233	48	74	122	100						
Stempniak, Lee	STL	R	80	13	25	38	40	0	3	0	2	0	162
NHL Totals			219	54	63	117	95						
Sterling, Brett	ATL	L	13	1	2	3	14	-2	0	0	0	0	14
NHL Totals			13	1	2	3	14						
Stewart, Anthony	FLA	C	26	0	1	1	0	-1	0	0	0	0	21
NHL Totals			46	2	3	5	4						
Stewart, Gregory	MTL	L	1	0	0	0	5	0	0	0	0	0	2
NHL Totals			1	0	0	0	5						
Stewart, Karl	TBL	L	9	0	0	0	2	-2	0	0	0	0	2
NHL Totals			69	2	4	6	68						
Stillman, Cory	OTT	L	79	24	41	65	24	-15	11	0	6	1	166
NHL Totals			839	234	368	602	406						
Stoll, Jarret	EDM	C	81	14	22	36	74	-23	8	3	1	0	187
NHL Totals			286	59	106	165	238						
Stone, Ryan	PIT	C	6	0	1	1	5	-1	0	0	0	0	3
NHL Totals			6	0	1	1	5						
Stortini, Zachery	EDM	R	66	3	9	12	201	3	0	0	0	0	38
NHL Totals			95	4	9	13	306						
Straka, Martin	NYR	C	65	14	27	41	22	5	3	1	2	0	116
NHL Totals			954	257	460	717	360						

S%	TOI/G	Sft/G	Hits	BkS	MsS	GvA	TkA	FOW	FOL	Tot	FO%	%Tm	S/G	PS
12.3	21:38	26	99	33	108	46	56	767	941	1708	44.9	34	3.8	2
6.6	18:16	24.5	86	57	66	37	40	507	695	1202	42.2	25.6	2.2	0
2.6	18:48	24.5	124	62	53	37	33	0	0	0	0	0	1	0
15.5	13:31	16.9	62	20	32	26	15	8	13	21	38.1	0.5	1.6	0
0	6:45	11	1	0	1	1	0	0	0	0	0	0	0.5	0
9.6	22:01	24.7	81	187	44	84	33	1	0	1	100	0	0.9	0
12.6	18:54	24.7	89	47	43	41	52	615	678	1293	47.6	27.7	1.5	0
17.4	21:04	26.1	16	31	49	33	54	561	540	1101	51	30.5	2.1	0
10	10:59	16.4	16	6	9	0	0	27	34	61	44.3	9.6	0.8	0
7.6	13:33	20.4	91	42	31	21	31	507	393	900	56.3	23.3	1	0
8.9	18:05	24.1	62	36	80	46	27	59	120	179	33	4.1	2.2	0
8	15:53	21.2	103	13	66	24	37	4	7	11	36.4	0.2	2	0
7.1	12:23	15.6	6	1	9	2	4	2	1	3	66.7	0.3	1.1	0
0	6:08	8.7	14	5	4	2	4	0	0	0	0	0	0.8	0
0	11:26	13	2	0	1	1	1	0	0	0	0	0	2	0
0	4:06	6.1	6	1	2	2	1	0	0	0	0	0	0.2	0
14.5	18:58	22.9	69	22	69	35	32	7	10	17	41.2	0.3	2.1	0
7.5	17:56	23.9	122	61	68	35	39	677	552	1229	55.1	27	2.3	0
0	6:25	10.5	7	3	2	0	1	3	2	5	60	1.3	0.5	0
7.9	8:10	11.7	99	17	11	12	5	3	4	7	42.8	0.1	0.6	0
12.1	18:37	23.4	24	32	46	32	31	7	12	19	36.8	0.5	1.8	0

Player	Team	Pos	GP	G	A	P	PIM	+/-	PP	SH	GW	OT	S
Stralman, Anton	TOR	D	50	3	6	9	18	-10	0	0	0	0	40
NHL Totals			50	3	6	9	18						
Streit, Mark	MTL	D	81	13	49	62	28	-6	7	0	3	0	165
NHL Totals			205	25	84	109	70						
Strudwick, Jason	NYR	D	52	1	1	2	40	0	0	0	1	1	21
NHL Totals			488	11	27	38	678						
Stuart, Brad	DET	D	72	6	17	23	69	-10	2	0	1	0	132
NHL Totals			579	59	170	229	372						
Stuart, Colin	ATL	L	18	3	2	5	6	2	0	1	1	0	19
NHL Totals			18	3	2	5	6						
Stuart, Mark	BOS	D	82	4	4	8	81	2	0	0	1	0	60
NHL Totals			114	5	6	11	105						
Stumpel, Jozef	FLA	L	52	7	13	20	10	-11	3	0	1	0	64
NHL Totals			957	196	481	677	245						
Sturm, Marco	BOS	L	80	27	29	56	40	11	10	1	5	1	229
NHL Totals			760	205	211	416	360						
Sundin, Mats	TOR	C	74	32	46	78	76	17	10	1	4	0	259
NHL Totals			1305	555	766	1321	1065						
Suter, Ryan	NSH	D	76	7	24	31	71	3	1	0	1	0	138
NHL Totals			229	16	55	71	191						
Sutherby, Brian	ANA	C	50	1	1	2	64	-4	0	0	0	0	49
NHL Totals			304	26	36	62	338						
Sutton, Andy	NYI	D	58	1	7	8	86	-6	0	0	1	0	57
NHL Totals			490	28	85	113	871						
Svatos, Marek	COL	R	490	28	85	113	871	13	3	0	6	1	140
NHL Totals			193	75	44	119	138						
Sydor, Darryl	PIT	D	74	1	12	13	26	1	1	0	0	0	59
NHL Totals			1171	95	389	484	722						
Sykora, Petr	PIT	R	81	28	35	63	41	1	15	0	4	0	201
NHL Totals			845	275	353	628	371						
Taffe, Jeff	PIT	L	45	5	7	12	8	2	1	0	1	0	56
NHL Totals			145	20	20	40	34						
Talbot, Maxime	PIT	C	63	12	14	26	53	8	0	2	1	0	80
NHL Totals			186	30	28	58	165						
Tallackson, Barry	NJD	R	3	0	0	0	0	0	0	0	0	0	0
NHL Totals			16	1	1	2	2						
Tallinder, Henrik	BUF	D	71	1	17	18	48	5	0	0	0	0	70
NHL Totals			320	15	61	76	210						
Tambellini, Jeff	NYI	L	31	1	3	4	8	-9	0	0	0	0	43
NHL Totals			79	4	13	17	24						
Tanabe, David	CAR	D	18	1	2	3	8	2	0	0	0	0	12
NHL Totals			449	30	84	114	245						

S%	TOI/G	Sft/G	Hits	BkS	MsS	GvA	TkA	FOW	FOL	Tot	FO%	%Tm	S/G	PS
7.5	12:48	17	32	23	16	26	12	0	0	0	0	0	0.8	0
7.9	17:31	20	59	62	59	42	40	0	1	1	0	0	2	0
4.8	12:56	19	65	42	8	21	16	0	0	0	0	0	0.4	0
4.5	21:09	26.7	118	95	46	48	16	0	4	4	0	0.1	1.8	0
15.8	12:19	16.7	25	9	5	7	14	4	3	7	57.1	0.6	1.1	0
6.7	15:22	19.9	101	74	21	26	6	0	0	0	0	0	0.7	0
10.9	17:22	21.8	39	22	29	22	18	329	314	643	51.2	20.9	1.2	1
11.8	17:59	24.2	50	25	64	22	25	10	24	34	29.4	0.7	2.9	0
12.4	20:04	26.8	33	34	98	54	21	945	768	1713	55.2	40.8	3.5	0
5.1	20:34	24.5	57	75	49	38	33	0	0	0	0	0	1.8	0
2	8:35	13.3	67	17	15	8	8	128	150	278	46	9.9	1	0
1.8	18:09	22.1	86	99	30	17	30	0	0	0	0	0	1	0
18.6	13:39	18.8	36	7	44	18	21	1	2	3	33.3	0	2.3	0
1.7	17:33	23	36	102	37	21	7	0	0	0	0	0	0.8	0
13.9	16:50	21.1	26	19	97	25	22	9	6	15	60	0.3	2.5	0
8.9	9:35	13.7	52	10	23	7	9	74	78	152	48.7	5.9	1.2	0
15	15:27	21.1	66	37	16	18	18	231	282	513	45	14.2	1.3	0
0	7:03	11	2	0	0	0	0	0	0	0	0	0	0	0
1.4	21:02	24.4	34	118	32	52	16	0	0	0	0	0	1	0
2.3	10:25	13.2	19	11	7	7	8	0	0	0	0	0	1.4	0
8.3	11:58	16.1	8	13	4	7	2	0	0	0	0	0	0.7	0

Player	Team	Pos	GP	G	A	P	PIM	+/-	PP	SH	GW	OT	S
Tanguay, Alex	CGY	L	78	18	40	58	48	11	3	2	3	0	121
NHL Totals			609	177	362	539	311						
Tarnasky, Nick	TBL	C	80	6	4	10	78	-15	1	0	1	0	91
NHL Totals			169	11	9	20	162						
Tarnstrom, Dick	CBJ	D	48	3	11	14	52	-11	1	0	0	0	44
NHL Totals			306	35	105	140	254						
Thomas, William	PHX	R	7	0	0	0	0	-2	0	0	0	0	9
NHL Totals			40	9	8	17	10						
Thorburn, Chris	ATL	R	73	5	13	18	92	-4	0	0	1	0	72
NHL Totals			114	8	16	24	168						
Thoresen, Patrick	PHI	L	38	2	6	8	14	-10	0	0	0	0	39
NHL Totals			106	6	18	24	66						
Thornton, Joe	SJS	C	82	29	67	96	59	18	11	0	5	2	178
NHL Totals			754	240	516	756	775						
Thornton, Scott	LAK	L	47	5	3	8	39	1	0	0	1	0	35
NHL Totals			941	144	141	285	1459						
Thornton, Shawn	BOS	L	58	4	3	7	74	-1	0	0	1	0	65
NHL Totals			137	8	11	19	232						
Timonen, Kimmo	PHI	D	80	8	36	44	50	0	3	1	1	0	125
NHL Totals			653	87	258	345	398						
Tjarnqvist, Mathias	PHX	L	78	4	7	11	34	-1	0	0	0	0	90
NHL Totals			173	13	19	32	60						
Tkachuk, Keith	STL	C	79	27	31	58	69	-2	12	1	1	0	177
NHL Totals			1055	500	484	984	2102						
Tlusty, Jiri	TOR	C	58	10	6	16	14	-12	2	0	2	0	69
NHL Totals			58	10	6	16	14						
Toews, Jonathan	CHI	C	64	24	30	54	44	11	7	0	4	1	144
NHL Totals			64	24	30	54	44						
Tollefsen, Ole-Kristian	CBJ	D	51	2	2	4	111	-3	0	1	0	0	21
NHL Totals			126	4	5	9	236						
Tolpeko, Denis	PHI	R	26	1	5	6	24	-4	0	0	0	0	24
NHL Totals			26	1	5	6	24						
Tootoo, Jordin	NSH	R	63	11	7	18	100	-8	0	0	1	0	98
NHL Totals			232	22	23	45	408						
Torres, Raffi	EDM	L	32	5	6	11	36	-4	1	0	2	0	87
NHL Totals			307	67	59	126	255						
Tucker, Darcy	TOR	R	74	18	16	34	100	-8	7	0	3	1	152
NHL Totals			813	197	239	436	1296						
Tukonen, Lauri	LAK	R	1	0	0	0	0	0	0	0	0	0	1
NHL Totals			5	0	0	0	0						
Turris, Kyle	PHX	C	3	0	1	1	2	-5	0	0	0	0	11
NHL Totals			3	0	1	1	2						

S%	TOI/G	Sft/G	Hits	BkS	MsS	GvA	TkA	FOW	FOL	Tot	FO%	%Tm	S/G	PS
14.9	18:45	25.1	42	24	44	57	36	7	13	20	35	0.4	1.6	0
6.6	8:14	10.8	119	45	16	1	21	4	5	9	44.4	0.2	1.1	0
6.8	19:22	22.3	22	71	30	24	7	0	0	0	0	0	0.9	0
0	13:08	18.9	10	2	6	0	1	0	0	0	0	0	1.3	0
6.9	8:56	12.4	89	19	21	10	18	12	8	20	60	0.4	1	0
5.1	11:45	16.2	42	5	15	21	13	41	59	100	41	4.6	1	0
16.3	21:23	24.6	60	31	53	103	55	785	700	1485	52.9	34.8	2.2	0
14.3	8:47	13.2	49	14	19	24	7	18	22	40	45	1.5	0.7	0
6.2	7:23	10.4	67	10	23	6	8	2	5	7	28.6	0.2	1.1	0
6.4	23:34	29.5	64	129	54	56	26	0	0	0	0	0	1.6	0
4.4	13:38	19.6	86	78	40	17	18	15	31	46	32.6	1	1.2	0
15.3	16:51	23	92	17	72	33	32	552	566	1118	49.4	25.1	2.2	0
14.5	10:55	14.4	39	16	31	8	17	1	1	2	50	0	1.2	0
16.7	18:40	24.6	27	13	31	8	29	509	447	956	53.2	27.3	2.2	0
9.5	12:18	18.1	91	20	12	9	2	0	0	0	0	0	0.4	0
4.2	8:16	12	15	1	15	11	6	0	0	0	0	0	0.9	0
11.2	9:53	14.1	64	5	45	16	16	2	2	4	50	0.1	1.6	0
5.7	17	22.4	55	10	34	26	9	13	7	20	65	1	2.7	0
11.8	16:26	20.5	126	52	70	33	19	13	12	25	52	0.5	2.1	0
0	9:48	16	1	0	0	3	0	0	0	0	0	0	1	0
0	19:45	22.3	0	3	2	2	2	17	25	42	40.5	27.1	3.7	0

Player	Team	Pos	GP	G	A	P	PIM	+/-	PP	SH	GW	OT	S
Tyutin, Fedor	NYR	D	82	5	15	20	43	5	1	0	0	0	131
NHL Totals			250	15	51	66	159						
Umberger, R.J.	PHI	C	74	13	37	50	19	0	4	0	3	0	173
NHL Totals			228	49	67	116	78						
Upshall, Scottie	PHI	R	61	14	16	30	74	2	3	0	1	0	128
NHL Totals			156	31	41	72	134						
Valabik, Boris	ATL	D	7	0	0	0	42	-2	0	0	0	0	5
NHL Totals			7	0	0	0	42						
Van Ryn, Mike	FLA	D	20	0	2	2	14	-2	0	0	0	0	16
NHL Totals			326	27	91	118	246						
Vandermeer, James	CGY	D	75	3	14	17	110	6	2	0	0	0	72
NHL Totals			267	17	51	68	389						
Vandermeer, Pete	PHX	L	2	0	0	0	0	0	0	0	0	0	0
NHL Totals			2	0	0	0	0						
Vanek, Thomas	BUF	L	82	36	28	64	64	-5	19	0	9	2	240
NHL Totals			245	104	92	196	176						
Vasicek, Josef	NYI	C	81	16	19	35	53	1	0	2	2	0	126
NHL Totals			460	77	106	183	311						
Veilleux, Stephane	MIN	L	77	11	7	18	61	-13	0	0	0	0	136
NHL Totals			280	30	37	67	214						
Vermette, Antoine	OTT	L	81	24	29	53	51	3	4	3	3	0	175
NHL Totals			297	71	68	139	163						
Versteeg, Kris	CHI	R	13	2	2	4	6	-1	0	0	0	0	21
NHL Totals			13	2	2	4	6						
Vishnevski, Vitaly	NJD	D	69	2	5	7	50	-12	0	0	0	0	48
NHL Totals			552	16	52	68	494						
Visnovsky, Lubomir	LAK	D	82	8	33	41	34	-18	3	0	1	0	153
NHL Totals			499	70	209	279	214						
Vlasic, Marc-Edouard	SJS	D	82	2	12	14	24	-12	1	0	0	0	72
NHL Totals			163	5	35	40	42						
Volchenkov, Anton	OTT	D	67	1	14	15	55	14	0	0	1	0	71
NHL Totals			296	10	60	70	223						
Voros, Aaron	MIN	L	55	7	7	14	141	-7	0	0	1	0	52
NHL Totals			55	7	7	14	141						
Vrbata, Radim	PHX	R	76	27	29	56	14	6	7	3	5	1	246
NHL Totals			422	102	124	226	118						
Vyborny, David	CBJ	R	66	7	19	26	34	-8	2	0	0	0	106
NHL Totals			543	113	204	317	228						
Wagner, Steve	STL	D	24	2	6	8	8	-4	1	0	0	0	25
NHL Totals			24	2	6	8	8						
Walker, Matt	STL	D	43	1	1	2	61	-3	0	0	0	0	47
NHL Totals			175	1	10	11	275						

S%	TOI/G	Sft/G	Hits	BkS	MsS	GvA	TkA	FOW	FOL	Tot	FO%	%Tm	S/G	PS
3.8	20:26	27.2	218	112	52	41	25	0	0	0	0	0	1.6	0
7.5	17:52	23.4	64	59	46	32	40	45	72	117	38.5	2.6	2.3	0
10.9	13:20	18.4	86	14	47	25	19	2	5	7	28.6	0.1	2.1	0
0	16:41	21.9	10	11	4	6	1	0	0	0	0	0	0.7	0
0	17:48	23.4	21	19	8	5	4	0	0	0	0	0	0.8	0
4.2	19:38	25.2	124	67	26	37	20	0	0	0	0	0	1	0
0	7:33	10.5	2	1	0	0	0	0	0	0	0	0	0	0
15	16:51	19.6	45	24	87	60	33	6	7	13	46.2	0.2	2.9	0
12.7	15:51	19.5	75	31	59	29	58	615	490	1105	55.6	24.2	1.6	0
8.1	14:31	23.1	113	25	46	24	19	17	28	45	37.8	1	1.8	0
13.7	17:34	23	49	25	61	49	29	690	527	1217	56.7	26.1	2.2	0
9.5	15:52	19.8	15	6	5	1	4	2	1	3	66.7	0.4	1.6	0
4.2	15:32	18.8	140	82	22	15	7	0	0	0	0	0	0.7	0
5.2	22:59	26.6	60	118	78	91	40	1	7	8	12.5	0.1	1.9	0
2.8	21:36	28.1	24	85	54	37	12	0	0	0	0	0	0.9	0
1.4	20:30	24.9	153	209	39	32	23	0	0	0	0	0	1.1	0
13.5	9:11	15.3	96	5	19	10	8	3	12	15	20	0.4	0.9	0
11	18:12	23.7	13	19	64	19	24	7	12	19	36.8	0.4	3.2	1
6.6	15:29	21.3	36	23	21	12	25	21	36	57	36.8	1.5	1.6	0
8	18:28	23.6	36	24	15	10	5	0	0	0	0	0	1	0
2.1	15:53	21.4	45	41	8	10	10	0	0	0	0	0	1.1	0

Player	Team	Pos	GP	G	A	P	PIM	+/-	PP	SH	GW	OT	S
Walker, Scott	CAR	R	58	14	18	32	115	-3	4	2	4	2	122
NHL Totals			746	141	233	374	1091						
Wallin, Niclas	CAR	D	66	2	6	8	54	-18	0	0	0	0	60
NHL Totals			406	16	38	54	323						
Walter, Ben	NYI	C	8	1	0	1	0	-1	1	0	0	0	6
NHL Totals			18	1	0	1	4						
Walz, Wes	MIN	C	11	1	3	4	6	-5	0	0	0	0	9
NHL Totals			607	109	151	260	343						
Wanvig, Kyle	TBL	R	7	1	0	1	7	-1	0	0	1	0	10
NHL Totals			75	6	9	15	94						
Ward, Aaron	BOS	D	65	5	8	13	54	9	0	0	3	2	68
NHL Totals			697	40	88	128	630						
Ward, Jason	TBL	R	79	8	6	14	42	-18	1	1	0	0	85
NHL Totals			335	36	45	81	169						
Warrener, Rhett	CGY	D	31	1	3	4	21	-2	0	0	0	0	15
NHL Totals			714	24	82	106	899						
Weaver, Mike	VAN	D	55	0	1	1	33	1	0	0	0	0	33
NHL Totals			204	3	22	25	93						
Weber, Mike	BUF	D	16	0	3	3	14	12	0	0	0	0	12
NHL Totals			16	0	3	3	14						
Weber, Shea	NSH	D	54	6	14	20	49	-6	5	0	2	1	152
NHL Totals			161	25	45	70	151						
Weight, Doug	ANA	C	67	10	15	25	32	4	2	0	1	0	96
NHL Totals			1131	265	704	969	897						
Weiss, Stephen	FLA	C	74	13	29	42	40	14	4	0	4	0	132
NHL Totals			323	61	102	163	117						
Welch, Noah	FLA	D	4	0	0	0	7	1	0	0	0	0	0
NHL Totals			33	3	4	7	33						
Weller, Craig	PHX	R	59	3	8	11	80	-7	0	0	1	0	72
NHL Totals			59	3	8	11	80						
Wellwood, Kyle	TOR	C	59	8	13	21	0	-12	5	0	1	0	57
NHL Totals			189	31	77	108	14						
Wesley, Glen	CAR	D	78	1	7	8	52	-3	0	0	1	0	63
NHL Totals			1457	128	409	537	1045						
Westcott, Duvie	CBJ	D	23	1	3	4	30	-10	1	0	0	0	27
NHL Totals			201	11	45	56	299						
White, Colin	NJD	D	57	2	8	10	26	-5	0	0	1	0	27
NHL Totals			522	17	72	89	708						
White, Ian	TOR	D	81	5	16	21	44	-9	0	0	2	0	116
NHL Totals			169	9	44	53	94						
White, Todd	ATL	C	74	14	23	37	36	-12	6	1	4	2	111
NHL Totals			488	111	169	280	178						

S%	TOI/G	Sft/G	Hits	BkS	MsS	GvA	TkA	FOW	FOL	Tot	FO%	%Tm	S/G	PS
11.5	16:37	21.2	98	33	56	16	31	21	27	48	43.8	1.3	2.1	0
3.3	18:07	26.4	134	91	29	26	17	0	1	1	0	0	0.9	0
16.7	6:05	8.8	2	2	2	2	1	10	23	33	30.3	7.8	0.8	0
11.1	13:48	22.6	1	8	4	5	8	62	73	135	45.9	21.8	0.8	0
10	10:09	13.4	12	3	2	1	1	1	0	1	100	0.2	1.4	0
7.4	20:44	24.5	143	119	37	18	5	0	0	0	0	0	1	0
9.4	12:32	16.3	48	50	30	19	48	18	27	45	40	1	1.1	0
6.7	13:25	19.3	32	18	6	16	7	0	1	1	0	0	0.5	0
0	14:01	19.8	45	38	13	26	15	0	1	1	0	0	0.6	0
0	16:40	21	45	12	4	9	0	0	0	0	0	0	0.8	0
3.9	19:29	23.3	115	44	56	17	17	0	0	0	0	0	2.8	0
10.4	14:36	18.9	48	21	39	27	12	290	324	614	47.2	16.5	1.4	0
9.8	17:35	23.7	26	26	47	29	30	613	585	1198	51.2	27.1	1.8	0
0	8:04	11.8	6	2	2	4	1	0	0	0	0	0	0	0
4.2	10:22	14.5	123	10	23	11	10	0	2	2	0	0	1.2	0
14	12:38	15.5	5	18	30	20	15	178	147	325	54.8	9.8	1	0
1.6	16:05	24.5	85	110	29	17	15	0	0	0	0	0	0.8	0
3.7	16:25	20.5	18	14	11	7	3	0	0	0	0	0	1.2	0
7.4	19:40	24	106	73	20	24	20	0	0	0	0	0	0.5	0
4.3	18:48	23.7	96	79	55	60	26	0	0	0	0	0	1.4	0
12.6	18:25	22.8	37	37	25	27	78	543	623	1166	46.6	27.1	1.5	0

Player	Team	Pos	GP	G	A	P	PIM	+/-	PP	SH	GW	OT	S
Whitney, Ray	CAR	L	66	25	36	61	30	-6	6	0	4	0	204
NHL Totals			910	279	455	734	337						
Whitney, Ryan	PIT	D	76	12	28	40	45	-2	7	1	1	0	119
NHL Totals			225	32	105	137	207						
Wideman, Dennis	BOS	D	81	13	23	36	70	11	9	0	1	0	171
NHL Totals			223	27	58	85	224						
Williams, Jason	CHI	C	43	13	23	36	22	-2	6	0	4	1	101
NHL Totals			296	66	92	158	115						
Williams, Jeremy	TOR	R	18	2	0	2	4	-3	0	0	0	0	16
NHL Totals			20	4	0	4	4						
Williams, Justin	CAR	R	37	9	21	30	43	2	2	0	0	0	106
NHL Totals			459	121	185	306	316						
Willsie, Brian	LAK	R	53	4	8	12	30	-8	0	0	0	0	62
NHL Totals			334	51	53	104	203						
Wilson, Clay	CBJ	D	7	1	1	2	2	3	0	0	0	0	12
NHL Totals			7	1	1	2	2						
Winchester, Brad	DAL	L	7	1	1	2	2	-9	0	0	0	0	36
NHL Totals			119	5	8	13	153						
Winchester, Jesse	OTT	C	1	0	0	0	2	0	0	0	0	0	1
NHL Totals			1	0	0	0	2						
Winnik, Daniel	PHX	L	79	11	15	26	25	-3	0	0	1	0	122
NHL Totals			79	11	15	26	25						
Wirtanen, Petteri	ANA	C	3	1	0	1	2	1	0	0	1	0	1
NHL Totals			3	1	0	1	2						
Wisniewski, James	CHI	D	68	7	19	26	103	12	1	1	0	0	82
NHL Totals			137	11	32	43	178						
Witt, Brendan	NYI	D	59	2	5	7	51	-8	0	0	0	0	58
NHL Totals			783	23	84	107	1285						
Wolski, Wojtek	COL	L	77	18	30	48	14	10	4	0	6	1	158
NHL Totals			162	42	62	104	32						
Woywitka, Jeff	STL	D	27	2	6	8	12	2	0	0	0	0	25
NHL Totals			87	3	14	17	49						
Wozniewski, Andy	TOR	D	48	2	7	9	54	5	0	0	0	0	34
NHL Totals			76	2	10	12	81						
Yandle, Keith	PHX	D	43	5	7	12	14	-12	4	0	0	0	72
NHL Totals			50	5	9	14	22						
Yelle, Stephane	CGY	C	74	3	9	12	20	-4	0	1	0	0	62
NHL Totals			844	85	154	239	426						
York, Michael	PHX	L	63	6	8	14	4	-8	4	0	1	0	85
NHL Totals			578	127	195	322	135						
Young, Bryan	EDM	D	2	0	0	0	0	-1	0	0	0	0	0
NHL Totals			17	0	0	0	10						

S%	TOI/G	Sft/G	Hits	BkS	MsS	GvA	TkA	FOW	FOL	Tot	FO%	%Tm	S/G	PS
12.3	18:56	23.7	13	23	84	29	41	3	2	5	60	0.1	3.1	0
10.1	22:26	25.3	30	117	38	53	11	0	0	0	0	0	1.6	0
7.6	25:09	26.8	62	110	100	63	22	0	0	0	0	0	2.1	0
12.9	16:34	20.3	27	8	22	25	6	9	6	15	60	0.6	2.3	0
12.5	7:20	9.5	11	6	6	7	3	0	4	4	0	0.3	0.9	0
8.5	19:17	24.7	43	23	36	25	27	5	8	13	38.5	0.5	2.9	0
6.5	10:37	14.9	42	13	24	10	12	14	10	24	58.3	0.8	1.2	0
8.3	16:55	21.3	2	2	4	2	0	0	0	0	0	0	1.7	0
2.8	7:34	10.1	57	4	9	6	7	0	2	2	0	0	0.9	0
0	14	19	1	0	0	0	0	0	0	0	0	0	1	0
9	14:06	20.3	75	46	30	17	30	65	89	154	42.2	3.3	1.5	0
100	4:11	7.3	0	0	0	2	0	5	6	11	45.4	6.4	0.3	0
8.5	17	21.7	113	67	34	22	11	0	0	0	0	0	1.2	0
3.4	21:46	23.7	135	133	20	28	15	0	0	0	0	0	1	0
11.4	15:55	20.3	54	21	44	37	40	24	24	48	50	1.1	2.1	0
8	16:04	21.7	15	25	10	15	4	0	0	0	0	0	0.9	0
5.9	14:10	19.8	43	56	18	33	7	0	0	0	0	0	0.7	0
6.9	14:04	20.3	13	33	19	16	14	0	0	0	0	0	1.7	0
4.8	11:56	18.2	93	30	21	13	27	190	191	381	49.9	8.9	0.8	0
7.1	11:59	16.4	24	17	21	8	14	104	101	205	50.7	5.6	1.3	0
0	2:08	3	1	0	0	0	0	0	0	0	0	0	0	0

Player	Team	Pos	GP	G	A	P	PIM	+/-	PP	SH	GW	OT	S
Zajac, Travis	NJD	C	82	14	20	34	31	-11	5	0	1	0	155
NHL Totals			162	31	45	76	47						
Zanon, Greg	NSH	D	78	0	5	5	24	-5	0	0	0	0	38
NHL Totals			148	3	12	15	62						
Zednik, Richard	FLA	R	54	15	11	26	43	-5	6	0	5	0	140
NHL Totals			675	183	163	346	517						
Zeiler, John	LAK	R	36	0	1	1	23	-6	0	0	0	0	18
NHL Totals			59	1	3	4	45						
Zetterberg, Henrik	DET	C	75	43	49	92	34	30	16	1	7	0	358
NHL Totals			355	152	180	332	122						
Zherdev, Nikolai	CBJ	R	82	26	35	61	34	-9	7	0	3	0	254
NHL Totals			283	76	105	181	164						
Zhitnik, Alexei	ATL	D	65	3	5	8	58	-8	0	0	1	1	79
NHL Totals			1085	96	375	471	1268						
Zidlicky, Marek	NSH	D	79	5	38	43	63	-5	4	0	0	0	122
NHL Totals			307	35	140	175	299						
Zigomanis, Michael	PHX	C	33	2	1	3	6	-7	0	0	0	0	35
NHL Totals			167	19	14	33	58						
Zubov, Ilja	OTT	C	1	0	0	0	0	0	0	0	0	0	0
NHL Totals			1	0	0	0	0						
Zubov, Sergei	DAL	D	46	4	31	35	12	6	2	0	0	0	84
NHL Totals			1058	152	615	767	337						
Zubrus, Dainius	NJD	R	82	13	25	38	38	2	4	0	2	0	128
NHL Totals			771	151	247	398	487						
Zyuzin, Andrei	CHI	D	32	2	3	5	38	-11	1	0	0	0	34
NHL Totals			496	38	82	120	446						

S%	TOI/G	Sft/G	Hits	BkS	MsS	GvA	TkA	FOW	FOL	Tot	FO%	%Tm	S/G	PS
9	16:44	20.9	57	15	59	21	44	528	504	1032	51.2	24	1.9	0
0	18:27	22.2	160	176	23	25	36	0	0	0	0	0	0.5	0
10.7	17:35	21.6	51	26	53	15	22	0	2	2	0	0	2.6	0
0	8:28	12.8	102	14	8	7	7	12	19	31	38.7	1.5	0.5	0
12	22:04	26.6	31	16	111	59	53	666	544	1210	55	28.8	4.8	0
10.2	19:22	23.7	37	18	87	60	48	12	17	29	41.4	0.6	3.1	0
3.8	19:01	22.7	67	54	45	36	24	0	0	0	0	0	1.2	0
4.1	20:49	23.3	83	84	36	36	39	0	0	0	0	0	1.5	0
5.7	12:24	18.1	26	12	15	4	12	196	132	328	59.8	18	1.1	0
0	14:38	18	3	0	0	0	1	2	3	5	40	8.9	0	0
4.8	25:41	24.6	14	41	41	45	30	0	0	0	0	0	1.8	0
10.2	15:41	20.6	77	17	53	21	35	80	64	144	55.6	3.3	1.6	0
5.9	14:58	19.2	29	35	12	10	6	0	0	0	0	0	1.1	0

Regular Season

Goalie	Team	GP	W	L	OL	SA	GA	GAA	SV
Aebischer, David	PHX	1	0	1	0	33	3	3.00	30
NHL Totals			106					2.52	
Anderson, Craig	FLA	17	8	6	1	535	35	2.25	500
NHL Totals			21					2.93	
Aubin, J-Sebastien	ANA	19	5	6	1	385	44	3.19	341
NHL Totals			80					2.93	
Auld, Alex	BOS	32	12	13	5	827	77	2.68	750
NHL Totals			58					2.85	
Backstrom, Niklas	MIN	58	33	13	8	1629	131	2.31	1498
NHL Totals			56					2.17	
Beckford-Tseu, Chris	STL	1	0	0	0	9	1	2.22	8
NHL Totals			0					2.22	
Bernier, Jonathan	LAK	4	1	3	0	118	16	4.03	102
NHL Totals			1					4.03	
Biron, Martin	PHI	62	30	20	9	1865	153	2.59	1712
NHL Totals			170					2.56	
Boucher, Brian	SJS	5	3	1	1	103	7	1.76	96
NHL Totals			80					2.77	
Brodeur, Martin	NJD	77	44	27	6	2089	168	2.17	1921
NHL Totals			538					2.20	
Bryzgalov, Ilja	PHX	64	28	25	6	1829	147	2.44	1682
NHL Totals			52					2.46	
Budaj, Peter	COL	35	16	10	4	849	82	2.57	767
NHL Totals			61					2.70	
Clemmensen, Scott	TOR	3	1	1	0	62	10	3.90	52
NHL Totals			8					2.95	
Cloutier, Dan	LAK	9	2	4	1	247	28	3.44	219
NHL Totals			139					2.78	
Conklin, Ty	PIT	33	18	8	5	1013	78	2.51	935
NHL Totals			48					2.60	
Crawford, Corey	CHI	5	1	2	0	112	8	2.14	104
NHL Totals			1					2.51	
Denis, Marc	TBL	10	1	5	0	199	28	4.05	171
NHL Totals			112					3.02	
Dipietro, Rick	NYI	63	26	28	7	1779	174	2.82	1605
NHL Totals			116					2.78	
Dubielewicz, Wade	NYI	20	9	9	1	627	51	2.70	576
NHL Totals			16					2.55	

Sv%	SO	G	A	PIM	TOI		W	L	SA	GA	Sv %
						Shootout					
0.909	0	0	0	0	59:55						
0.912	13										
0.935	2	0	1	2	934:56						
0.904	4										
0.886	0	0	0	0	827:42		1	1	4	2	0.500
0.900	7										
0.907	3	0	0	0	1,722:17		2	3	15	5	0.667
0.903	5										
0.920	4	0	0	2	3,408:38		1	6	21	12	0.429
0.923	9										
0.889	0	0	0	0	26:37						
0.889	0										
0.864	0	0	0	0	238:23						
0.864	0										
0.918	5	0	1	8	3,539:04		2	6	20	13	0.350
0.911	23										
0.932	1	0	0	0	238:06						
0.898	14										
0.920	4	0	4	6	4,635:03		8	4	43	11	0.744
0.913	96										
0.920	3	0	0	2	3,613:59		5	5	29	9	0.690
0.915	5										
0.903	0	0	1	2	1,911:31		1	2	9	4	0.556
0.903	5										
0.839	0	0	0	0	154:20		1	0	3	1	0.667
0.888	2										
0.887	0	0	0	2	489:10		1	0	4	1	0.750
0.898	15										
0.923	2	0	1	4	1,865:33		2	3	15	7	0.533
0.909	4										
0.929	1	0	0	0	224:09						
0.915	1										
0.859	0	0	0	2	414:56		1	0	3	0	1.000
0.902	16										
0.902	3	0	6	18	3,707:05		3	2	21	6	0.714
0.905	14										
0.919	0	0	0	0	1,132:23		2	1	13	4	0.692
0.920	0										

Goalie	Team	GP	W	L	OL	SA	GA	GAA	SV
Elliott, Brian	OTT	1	1	0	0	29	1	1.00	28
NHL Totals			1					1.01	
Ellis, Dan	NSH	44	23	10	3	1147	87	2.34	1060
NHL Totals			24					2.36	
Emery, Ray	OTT	31	12	13	4	800	88	3.13	712
NHL Totals			71					2.71	
Ersberg, Erik	LAK	14	6	5	3	452	33	2.48	419
NHL Totals			6					2.48	
Fernandez, Manny	BOS	4	2	2	0	95	16	3.93	79
NHL Totals			127					2.49	
Fleury, Marc-Andre	PIT	35	19	10	2	909	72	2.33	837
NHL Totals			76					2.95	
Garon, Mathieu	EDM	47	26	18	1	1359	118	2.66	1241
NHL Totals			86					2.81	
Gerber, Martin	OTT	57	30	18	4	1619	145	2.72	1474
NHL Totals			100					2.60	
Giguere, Jean-Sebastien	ANA	58	35	17	6	1508	117	2.12	1391
NHL Totals			191					2.43	
Grahame, John	CAR	17	5	7	1	424	53	3.75	371
NHL Totals			97					2.79	
Greiss, Thomas	SJS	3	0	1	1	50	7	3.26	43
NHL Totals			0					3.26	
Halak, Jaroslav	MTL	6	2	1	1	151	10	2.11	141
NHL Totals			12					2.71	
Harding, Josh	MIN	29	11	15	2	838	77	2.94	761
NHL Totals			16					2.61	
Hasek, Dominik	DET	41	27	10	3	855	84	2.14	771
NHL Totals			389					2.20	
Hedberg, Johan	ATL	36	14	15	3	1026	111	3.46	915
NHL Totals			89					2.92	
Hiller, Jonas	ANA	23	10	7	1	578	42	2.06	536
NHL Totals			10					2.06	
Holmqvist, Johan	DAL	47	21	16	6	1164	129	3.04	1035
NHL Totals			48					2.99	
Howard, James	DET	4	0	2	0	95	7	2.13	88
NHL Totals			1					2.56	
Huet, Cristobal	WSH	52	32	14	6	1479	118	2.32	1361
NHL Totals			83					2.43	

Sv%	SO	G	A	PIM	TOI	W	L	SA	GA	Sv %
0.966	0	0	0	0	59:42					
0.966	0									
0.924	6	0	0	0	2,228:33	2	1	9	4	0.556
0.923	6									
0.890	0	0	0	6	1,689:20	1	3	15	7	0.533
0.907	8									
0.927	2	0	0	0	798:59	1	1	9	2	0.778
0.927	2									
0.832	1	0	0	0	244:07	1	0	3	0	1.000
0.912	14									
0.921	4	0	1	0	1,857:26	1	0	3	0	1.000
0.905	11									
0.913	4	0	0	8	2,657:59	10	0	32	2	0.938
0.906	14									
0.910	2	0	2	6	3,197:07	2	2	16	5	0.688
0.911	9									
0.922	4	0	0	4	3,310:19	6	5	30	10	0.667
0.915	29									
0.875	0	0	1	4	847:31	1	0	3	2	0.333
0.898	12									
0.860	0	0	0	0	128:49					
0.860	0									
0.934	1	0	0	0	284:40	0	1	3	1	0.667
0.913	3									
0.908	1	0	1	0	1,570:34	2	2	14	6	0.571
0.916	3									
0.902	5	0	1	12	2,350:04	3	2	12	3	0.750
0.922	81									
0.892	1	0	1	16	1,927:14	5	3	31	7	0.774
0.899	11									
0.927	0	0	1	0	1,223:05	2	1	12	5	0.583
0.927	0									
0.889	2	0	1	0	2,549:13	1	0	4	1	0.750
0.890	3									
0.926	0	0	0	0	197:04					
0.915	0									
0.920	4	0	2	0	3,048:53	4	3	18	5	0.722
0.918	17									

Goalie	Team	GP	W	L	OL	SA	GA	GAA	SV
Regular Season									
Johnson, Brent	WSH	19	7	8	2	500	46	2.67	454
NHL Totals			99					2.62	
Joseph, Curtis	CGY	9	3	2	0	181	17	2.55	164
NHL Totals			449					2.78	
Keetley, Matt	CGY	1	0	0	0	2	0	0.00	2
NHL Totals			0					0.00	
Khabibulin, Nikolai	CHI	50	23	20	6	1389	127	2.63	1262
NHL Totals			274					2.69	
Kiprusoff, Miikka	CGY	76	39	26	10	2096	197	2.69	1899
NHL Totals			159					2.37	
Kolzig, Olaf	WSH	54	25	21	6	1423	153	2.91	1270
NHL Totals			301					2.70	
LaBarbera, Jason	LAK	45	17	23	2	1341	121	3.00	1220
NHL Totals			29					3.04	
Lacosta, Daniel	CBJ	1	0	0	0	5	0	0.00	5
NHL Totals			0					0.00	
Lalime, Patrick	CHI	32	16	12	2	835	86	2.82	749
NHL Totals			191					2.53	
Leclaire, Pascal	CBJ	54	24	17	6	1379	112	2.25	1267
NHL Totals			41					2.71	
Legace, Manny	STL	66	27	25	8	1648	147	2.41	1501
NHL Totals			164					2.31	
Lehtonen, Kari	ATL	48	17	22	5	1560	131	2.90	1429
NHL Totals			75					2.82	
Leighton, Michael	CAR	3	1	1	0	68	7	2.66	61
NHL Totals			11					3.01	
Lundqvist, Henrik	NYR	72	37	24	10	1823	160	2.23	1663
NHL Totals			104					2.27	
Luongo, Roberto	VAN	73	35	29	9	2029	168	2.38	1861
NHL Totals			197					2.60	
MacDonald, Joey	NYI	2	0	1	1	73	6	3.00	67
NHL Totals			3					3.11	
MacIntyre, Drew	VAN	2	0	1	0	22	3	2.95	19
NHL Totals			0					2.95	
Mason, Chris	NSH	51	18	22	6	1278	130	2.90	1148
NHL Totals			58					2.61	
McElhinney, Curtis	CGY	5	0	2	0	51	5	2.00	46
NHL Totals			0					2.00	

Sv%	SO	G	A	PIM	TOI	W	L	SA	GA	Sv %
								Shootout		
0.908	0	0	0	0	1,032:01					
0.902	13									
0.906	0	0	0	2	399:40					
0.907	51									
1.000	0	0	0	0	9:22					
1.000	0									
0.909	2	0	2	4	2,891:56	2	4	19	7	0.632
0.908	38									
0.906	2	0	2	8	4,398:19	3	3	17	6	0.647
0.915	26									
0.892	1	0	2	8	3,153:38	2	4	34	11	0.676
0.906	35									
0.910	1	0	0	2	2,420:42	2	1	10	5	0.500
0.903	2									
1.000	0	0	0	0	13:09					
1.000	0									
0.897	1	0	0	8	1,828:06	3	0	9	2	0.778
0.905	35									
0.919	9	0	2	2	2,986:27	3	4	23	10	0.565
0.911	10									
0.911	5	0	2	4	3,665:41	2	3	17	4	0.765
0.914	23									
0.916	4	0	2	4	2,706:46	4	3	18	5	0.722
0.913	11									
0.897	0	0	0	0	158:09					
0.900	3									
0.912	10	0	0	2	4,304:48	6	7	42	13	0.690
0.917	17									
0.917	6	0	3	4	4,232:32	6	8	54	15	0.722
0.919	38									
0.918	0	0	0	0	120:25					
0.898	0									
0.864	0	0	0	0	61:06					
0.864	0									
0.898	4	0	1	0	2,691:58	1	4	13	5	0.615
0.913	12									
0.902	0	0	0	0	149:55					
0.902	0									

Regular Season

Goalie	Team	GP	W	L	OL	SA	GA	GAA	SV
Miller, Ryan	BUF	76	36	27	10	2104	197	2.64	1907
NHL Totals			112					2.69	
Nabokov, Evgeni	SJS	77	46	21	8	1802	163	2.14	1639
NHL Totals			208					2.37	
Niittymaki, Antero	PHI	28	12	9	2	739	69	2.91	670
NHL Totals			47					3.08	
Norrena, Fredrik	CBJ	37	10	19	6	856	89	2.72	767
NHL Totals			34					2.76	
Osgood, Chris	DET	43	27	9	4	976	84	2.09	892
NHL Totals			363					2.43	
Patzold, Dimitri	SJS	3	0	0	0	20	4	5.45	16
NHL Totals			0					5.51	
Pavelec, Ondrej	ATL	7	3	3	0	190	18	3.11	172
NHL Totals			3					3.11	
Price, Carey	MTL	41	24	12	3	1282	103	2.56	1179
NHL Totals			24					2.56	
Quick, Jonathan	LAK	3	1	2	0	62	9	3.83	53
NHL Totals			1					3.84	
Ramo, Karri	TBL	22	7	11	3	632	64	3.03	568
NHL Totals			7					3.05	
Rask, Tuukka	BOS	4	2	1	1	88	10	3.26	78
NHL Totals			2					3.25	
Raycroft, Andrew	TOR	19	2	9	5	509	63	3.92	446
NHL Totals			82					2.87	
Rinne, Pekka	NSH	1	0	0	0	8	0	0.00	8
NHL Totals			1					2.59	
Roloson, Dwayne	EDM	43	15	17	5	1204	119	3.05	1085
NHL Totals			139					2.60	
Sabourin, Dany	PIT	24	10	9	1	596	57	2.75	539
NHL Totals			12					2.89	
Sanford, Curtis	VAN	16	4	3	1	313	32	2.83	281
NHL Totals			30					2.80	
Schwarz, Marek	STL	2	0	1	0	17	6	7.20	11
NHL Totals			0					4.92	
Smith, Mike	TBL	34	15	19	0	848	84	2.59	764
NHL Totals			27					2.45	
Stephan, Tobias	DAL	1	0	0	1	40	2	1.97	38
NHL Totals			0					1.98	

Sv%	SO	G	A	PIM	TOI		W	L	SA	GA	Sv %
						Shootout					
0.906	3	0	1	6	4,474:18		4	7	33	14	0.576
0.908	7										
0.910	6	0	2	12	4,560:56		6	6	40	18	0.550
0.911	40										
0.907	1	0	0	0	1,424:01		1	0	3	0	1.000
0.898	3										
0.896	2	0	1	0	1,959:32		0	4	10	4	0.600
0.901	5										
0.914	4	0	3	0	2,408:53		2	3	16	8	0.500
0.907	47										
0.800	0	0	0	0	43:35						
0.800	0										
0.905	0	0	0	2	347:16						
0.905	0										
0.920	3	0	2	0	2,413:22		3	2	22	4	0.818
0.920	3										
0.855	0	0	0	0	140:31						
0.855	0										
0.899	0	0	1	4	1,268:43		0	1	2	2	0.000
0.896	0										
0.886	0	0	0	0	184:24						
0.886	0										
0.876	1	0	0	0	964:42		0	1	6	2	0.667
0.900	6										
1.000	0	0	0	0	29:24						
0.917	0										
0.901	0	0	1	2	2,340:12		5	4	37	10	0.730
0.909	22										
0.904	2	0	0	2	1,241:31		4	1	26	6	0.769
0.898	2										
0.898	0	0	1	2	679:02		0	1	4	2	0.500
0.900	4										
0.647	0	0	0	0	49:38						
0.786	0										
0.901	3	0	1	12	1,945:41		2	0	6	0	1.000
0.905	6										
0.950	0	0	0	0	60:38						
0.950	0										

Regular Season

Goalie	Team	GP	W	L	OL	SA	GA	GAA	SV
Taylor, Daniel	LAK	1	0	0	0	10	2	6.00	8
NHL Totals			0					6.00	
Tellqvist, Mikael	PHX	22	9	8	2	607	56	2.75	551
NHL Totals			36					3.07	
Theodore, Jose	COL	53	28	21	3	1367	123	2.44	1244
NHL Totals			183					2.65	
Thibault, Jocelyn	BUF	12	3	4	2	214	28	3.31	186
NHL Totals			238					2.75	
Thomas, Tim	BOS	57	28	19	6	1731	136	2.44	1595
NHL Totals			73					2.80	
Toivonen, Hannu	STL	23	6	10	5	566	69	3.44	497
NHL Totals			18					3.37	
Toskala, Vesa	TOR	66	33	25	6	1824	175	2.74	1649
NHL Totals			98					2.49	
Turco, Marty	DAL	62	32	21	6	1543	140	2.31	1403
NHL Totals			207					2.15	
Valiquette, Stephen	NYR	13	5	3	3	296	25	2.19	271
NHL Totals			9					2.40	
Vokoun, Tomas	FLA	69	30	29	8	2213	180	2.68	2033
NHL Totals			191					2.57	
Ward, Cam	CAR	69	37	25	5	1870	180	2.75	1690
NHL Totals			81					2.97	
Weekes, Kevin	NJD	9	2	2	1	160	17	2.97	143
NHL Totals			98					2.90	
Weiman, Tyler	COL	1	0	0	0	10	0	0.00	10
NHL Totals			0					0.00	

| | | | | | | Shootout | | | | |
Sv%	SO	G	A	PIM	TOI	W	L	SA	GA	Sv%
0.800	0	0	0	0	20					
0.800	0									
0.908	2	0	1	2	1,224:04	0	2	16	4	0.750
0.895	6									
0.910	3	0	2	2	3,028:05	6	1	28	6	0.786
0.909	26									
0.869	2	0	0	0	507:03	0	2	10	3	0.700
0.904	39									
0.921	3	0	0	2	3,341:59	3	4	18	6	0.667
0.913	7									
0.878	0	0	0	2	1,202:29	1	2	9	2	0.778
0.890	1									
0.904	3	0	5	4	3,837:29	2	3	15	6	0.600
0.910	11									
0.909	3	0	3	16	3,628:31	3	3	23	9	0.609
0.913	33									
0.916	2	0	0	2	685:35	2	2	11	3	0.727
0.916	2									
0.919	4	0	6	4	4,030:42	5	6	41	11	0.732
0.914	25									
0.904	4	0	1	4	3,930:08	1	3	11	6	0.454
0.897	6									
0.894	0	0	0	2	343:25					
0.902	19									
1.000	0	0	0	0	15:46					
1.000	0									

2008 Draft

ROUND 1

Num.	Drafted By	Player	Pos	Drafted From
1	Tampa Bay	Steven Stamkos	C	Sarnia Sting
2	Los Angeles	Drew Doughty	D	Guelph Storm
3	Atlanta	Zach Bogosian	D	Peterborough Petes
4	St. Louis	Alex Pietrangelo	D	Niagara IceDogs
5	Toronto	Luke Schenn	D	Kelowna Rockets
6	Columbus	Nikita Filatov	L	CSKA Jr. (Russia)
7	Nashville	Colin Wilson	C	Boston University
8	Phoenix	Mikkel Boedker	L	Kitchener Rangers
9	NY Islanders	Joshua Bailey	C	Windsor Spitfires
10	Vancouver	Cody Hodgson	C	Brampton Battalion
11	Chicago	Kyle Beach	C	Everett Silvertips
12	Buffalo	Tyler Myers	D	Kelowna Rockets
13	Los Angeles	Colten Teubert	D	Regina Pats
14	Carolina	Zach Boychuk	C	Lethbridge Hurricanes
15	Ottawa	Erik Karlsson	D	Frolunda Jrs (Sweden)
16	Boston	Joe Colborne	C	Camrose Kodiaks
17	Anaheim	Jake Gardiner	D	Minnetonka H.S. (Minn.)
18	Nashville	Chet Pickard	G	Tri-City Americans
19	Philadelphia	Luca Sbisa	D	Lethbridge Hurricanes
20	NY Rangers	Michael Del Zotto	D	Oshawa Generals
21	Washington	Anton Gustafsson	C	Frolunda Jrs (Sweden)
22	Edmonton	Jordan Eberle	C	Regina Pats
23	Minnesota	Tyler Cuma	D	Ottawa 67's
24	New Jersey	Mattias Tedenby	L	HV71 Jonkoping
25	Calgary	Greg Nemisz	C	Windsor Spitfires
26	Buffalo	Tyler Ennis	C	Medicine Hat Tigers
27	Washington	John Carlson	D	Indiana Ice
28	Phoenix	Viktor Tikhonov	W	Cherepovets Severstal
29	Atlanta	Daultan Leveille	C	St. Catharines Falcons
30	Detroit	Thomas McCollum	G	Guelph Storm

ROUND 2

Num.	Drafted By	Player	Pos	Drafted From
31	Florida	Jacob Markstrom	G	Brynas Jrs.
32	Los Angeles	Vyacheslav Vojnov	D	Chelyabinsk Traktor
33	St. Louis	Philip McRae	C	London Knights

ROUND 2, cont.

Num.	Drafted By	Player	Pos	Drafted From
34	St. Louis	Jake Allen	G	St. John's Fog Devils
35	Anaheim	Nicolas Deschamps	C	Chicoutimi Sagueneens
36	NY Islanders	Corey Trivino	C	Stouffville Spirit
37	Columbus	Cody Goloubef	D	U. of Wisconsin
38	Nashville	Roman Josi	D	Bern
39	Anaheim	Eric O'Dell	C	Sudbury Wolves
40	NY Islanders	Aaron Ness	D	Roseau H.S. (Minn.)
41	Vancouver	Yann Sauve	D	Saint John Sea Dogs
42	Ottawa	Patrick Wiercioch	D	Omaha Lancers
43	Anaheim	Justin Schultz	D	Westside Warriors
44	Buffalo	Luke Adam	C	St. John's Fog Devils
45	Carolina	Zac Dalpe	C	Penticton Vees
46	Florida	Colby Robak	D	Brandon Wheat Kings
47	Boston	Maxime Sauve	C	Val-d'Or Foreurs
48	Calgary	Mitch Wahl	C	Spokane Chiefs
49	Phoenix	Jared Staal	R	Sudbury Wolves
50	Colorado	Cameron Gaunce	D	Mississauga St. Michael's Majors
51	NY Rangers	Derek Stepan	C	Shattuck St. Mary's
52	New Jersey	Brandon Burlon	D	St. Michael's Buzzers
53	NY Islanders	Travis Hamonic	D	Moose Jaw Warriors
54	New Jersey	Patrice Cormier	C	Rimouski Oceanic
55	Minnesota	Marco Scandella	D	Val-d'Or Foreurs
56	Montreal	Danny Kristo	R	US National Under 18 Team
57	Washington	Eric Mestery	D	Tri-City Americans
58	Washington	Dmitri Kugryshev	R	CSKA Jr. (Russia)
59	Dallas	Tyler Beskorowany	G	Owen Sound Attack
60	Toronto	Jimmy Hayes	R	Lincoln Stars
61	Colorado	Peter Delmas	G	Lewiston MAINEiacs

ROUND 3

Num.	Drafted By	Player	Pos	Drafted From
62	San Jose	Justin Daniels	C	Kent H.S. (Conn.)
63	Los Angeles	Robert Czarnik	C	US National Under 18 Team
64	Atlanta	Danick Paquette	R	Lewiston MAINEiacs
65	St. Louis	Jori Lehtera	C	Tappara Tampere
66	NY Islanders	David Toews	C	Shattuck St. Mary's
67	Philadelphia	Marc-Andre Bourdon	D	Rouyn-Noranda Huskies
68	Chicago	Shawn Lalonde	D	Belleville Bulls

ROUND 3, cont.

Num.	Drafted By	Player	Pos	Drafted From
69	Phoenix	Michael Stone	D	Calgary Hitmen
70	St. Louis	James Livingston	R	Sault Ste. Marie Greyhounds
71	Anaheim	Josh Brittain	L	Kingston Frontenacs
72	NY Islanders	Jyri Niemi	D	Saskatoon Blades
73	NY Islanders	Kirill Petrov	R	Kazan Ak-Bars
74	Los Angeles	Andrew Campbell	D	Sault Ste. Marie Greyhounds
75	NY Rangers	Evgeny Grachev	C	Yaroslavl Jrs. (Russia)
76	Phoenix	Mathieu Brodeur	D	Cape Breton Screaming Eagles
77	Boston	Michael Hutchinson	G	Barrie Colts
78	Calgary	Lance Bouma	C	Vancouver Giants
79	Ottawa	Zack Smith	C	Swift Current Broncos
80	Florida	Adam Comrie	D	Saginaw Spirit
81	Buffalo	Corey Fienhage	D	Eastview H.S. (Minn.)
82	New Jersey	Adam Henrique	C	Windsor Spitfires
83	Anaheim	Marco Cousineau	G	Baie-Comeau Drakkar
84	Philadelphia	Jacob DeSerres	G	Seattle Thunderbirds
85	Anaheim	Brandon McMillan	C	Kelowna Rockets
86	Montreal	Steve Quailer	R	Sioux City Musketeers
87	St. Louis	Ian Schultz	R	Calgary Hitmen
88	Los Angeles	Geordie Wudrick	L	Swift Current Broncos
89	Dallas	Scott Winkler	C	Russell Stover
90	NY Rangers	Tomas Kundratek	D	Trinec Ocelari HC
91	Detroit	Max Nicastro	D	Chicago Steel

ROUND 4

Num.	Drafted By	Player	Pos	Drafted From
92	San Jose	Samuel Groulx	D	Quebec Remparts
93	Washington	Braden Holtby	G	Saskatoon Blades
94	Atlanta	Vinny Saponari	R	US National Under 18 Team
95	St. Louis	David Warsofsky	D	US National Under 18 Team
96	NY Islanders	Matt Donovan	D	Cedar Rapids RoughRiders
97	Boston	Jamie Arniel	C	Sarnia Sting
98	Toronto	Mikhail Stefanovich	C	Quebec Remparts
99	Phoenix	Colin Long	C	Kelowna Rockets
100	Florida	A.J. Jenks	L	Plymouth Whalers
101	Buffalo	Justin Jokinen	R	Cloquet H.S. (Minn.)
102	NY Islanders	David Ullstrom	W	HV 71 Jrs. (Sweden)
103	Edmonton	Johan Motin	D	Bofors IK

ROUND 4, cont.

Num.	Drafted By	Player	Pos	Drafted From
104	Buffalo	Jordon Southorn	D	Prince Edward Island Rocket
105	Carolina	Michal Jordan	D	Plymouth Whalers
106	San Jose	Harri Sateri	G	Tappara Jrs. (Finland)
107	Columbus	Steven Delisle	D	Gatineau Olympiques
108	Calgary	Nick Larson	L	Waterloo Black Hawks
109	Ottawa	Andre Petersson	W	HV 71 Jrs. (Sweden)
110	Colorado	Kelsey Tessier	C	Quebec Remparts
111	NY Rangers	Dale Weise	R	Swift Current Broncos
112	New Jersey	Matt Delahey	D	Regina Pats
113	Anaheim	Ryan Hegarty	D	US National Under 18 Team
114	Calgary	T.J. Brodie	D	Saginaw Spirit
115	Minnesota	Sean Lorenz	D	US National Under 18 Team
116	Montreal	Jason Missiaen	G	Peterborough Petes
117	Tampa Bay	James Wright	C	Vancouver Giants
118	Columbus	Drew Olson	D	Brainerd H.S. (Minn.)
119	Ottawa	Derek Grant	C	Langley Chiefs
120	Pittsburgh	Nathan Moon	C	Kingston Frontenacs
121	Detroit	Gustav Nyquist	C	Malmo Jrs

ROUND 5

Num.	Drafted By	Player	Pos	Drafted From
122	Tampa Bay	Dustin Tokarski	G	Spokane Chiefs
123	Los Angeles	Andrei Loktionov	C	Yaroslavl Jrs. (Russia)
124	Atlanta	Nicklas Lasu	L	Frolunda Jrs (Sweden)
125	St. Louis	Kristoffer Berglund	D	Bjorkloven IF
126	NY Islanders	Kevin Poulin	G	Victoriaville Tigres
127	Columbus	Matt Calvert	L	Brandon Wheat Kings
128	Toronto	Greg Pateryn	D	Ohio Junior Blue Jackets
129	Toronto	Joel Champagne	C	Chicoutimi Sagueneens
130	Toronto	Jerome Flaake	L	Cologne Sharks
131	Vancouver	Prabh Rai	C	Seattle Thunderbirds
132	Chicago	Teigan Zahn	D	Saskatoon Blades
133	Edmonton	Philippe Cornet	L	Rimouski Oceanic
134	Buffalo	Jacob Lagace	L	Chicoutimi Sagueneens
135	Columbus	Tomas Kubalik	R	Plzen HC
136	Nashville	Taylor Stefishen	L	Langley Chiefs
137	Columbus	Brent Regner	D	Vancouver Giants
138	Montreal	Maxim Trunev	F	Cherepovets Jr. (Russia)

ROUND 5, cont.

Num.	Drafted By	Player	Pos	Drafted From
139	Ottawa	Mark Borowiecki	D	Smiths Falls Bears
140	Colorado	Mark Olver	C	Northern Michigan University
141	NY Rangers	Chris Doyle	C	Prince Edward Island Rocket
142	New Jersey	Kory Nagy	C	Oshawa Generals
143	Anaheim	Stefan Warg	D	Vasteras Jrs. (Sweden)
144	Washington	Joel Broda	C	Moose Jaw Warriors
145	Minnesota	Eero Elo	L	Lukko Jrs. (Finland)
146	San Jose	Julien Demers	D	Ottawa 67's
147	Tampa Bay	Kyle De Coste	R	Brampton Battalion
148	NY Islanders	Matt Martin	L	Sarnia Sting
149	Dallas	Philip Larsen	D	Vastra Frolunda HC Goteborg
150	Pittsburgh	Alexander Pechurski	G	Magnitogorsk Jr. (Russia)
151	Detroit	Julien Cayer	C	Northwood Prep (N.Y.)

ROUND 6

Num.	Drafted By	Player	Pos	Drafted From
152	Tampa Bay	Mark Barberio	D	Moncton Wildcats
153	Los Angeles	Justin Azevedo	C	Kitchener Rangers
154	Atlanta	Chris Carrozzi	G	Mississauga St. Michael's Majors
155	St. Louis	Anthony Nigro	C	Guelph Storm
156	NY Islanders	Jared Spurgeon	D	Spokane Chiefs
157	Columbus	Cameron Atkinson	R	Avon Old Farms H.S. (Conn.)
158	Toronto	Grant Rollheiser	G	Trail Smoke Eaters
159	Phoenix	Brett Hextall	C	Penticton Vees
160	Tampa Bay	Luke Witkowski	D	Ohio Junior Blue Jackets
161	Vancouver	Mats Froshaug	C	Linkoping Jr.
162	Chicago	Jonathan Carlsson	D	Brynas IF Gavle
163	Edmonton	Teemu Hartikainen	C	Kalpa Jrs. (Finland)
164	Buffalo	Nick Crawford	D	Saginaw Spirit
165	Carolina	Mike Murphy	G	Belleville Bulls
166	Nashville	Jeff Foss	D	R.P.I.
167	Colorado	Joel Chouinard	D	Victoriaville Tigres
168	Calgary	Ryley Grantham	C	Moose Jaw Warriors
169	Chicago	Ben Smith	R	Boston College
170	Colorado	Jonas Holos	D	Sarpsborg
171	NY Rangers	Mitch Gaulton	D	Erie Otters
172	New Jersey	David Wohlberg	C	US National Under 18 Team
173	Boston	Nicolas Tremblay	C	Smiths Falls Bears
174	Washington	Greg Burke	L	New Hampshire Jr. Monarchs

ROUND 6, cont.

Num.	Drafted By	Player	Pos	Drafted From
175	NY Islanders	Justin DiBenedetto	C	Sarnia Sting
176	Dallas	Matt Tassone	C	Swift Current Broncos
177	San Jose	Tommy Wingels	C	Miami University (Ohio)
178	Philadelphia	Zac Rinaldo	C	Mississauga St. Michael's Majors
179	Chicago	Braden Birch	D	Oakville Blades
180	Pittsburgh	Patrick Killeen	G	Brampton Battalion
181	Detroit	Stephen Johnston	L	Belleville Bulls

ROUND 7

Num.	Drafted By	Player	Pos	Drafted From
182	Tampa Bay	Matias Sointu	R	Ilves Jrs (Finland)
183	Los Angeles	Garrett Roe	L	St. Cloud State
184	Atlanta	Zach Redmond	D	Ferris State University
185	St. Louis	Paul Karpowich	G	Wellington Dukes
186	San Jose	Jason Demers	D	Victoriaville Tigres
187	Columbus	Sean Collins	C	Waywayseecappo Wolverines
188	Toronto	Andrew MacWilliam	D	Camrose Kodiaks
189	Phoenix	Tim Billingsley	D	Mississauga St. Michael's Majors
190	Florida	Matt Bartkowski	D	Lincoln Stars
191	Vancouver	Morgan Clark	G	Red Deer Rebels
192	Chicago	Joe Gleason	D	Edina H.S. (Minn.)
193	Edmonton	Jordan Bendfeld	D	Medicine Hat Tigers
194	San Jose	Drew Daniels	R	Kent H.S. (Conn.)
195	Carolina	Samuel Morneau	L	Baie-Comeau Drakkar
196	Philadelphia	Joacim Eriksson	G	Brynas Jrs.
197	Boston	Mark Goggin	C	Choate Academy (Conn.)
198	Calgary	Alexander Deilert	D	Djurgarden Jrs. (Sweden)
199	Ottawa	Emil Sandin	L	Brynas IF Gavle
200	Colorado	Nathan Condon	C	Wausau H.S. (Wisc.)
201	Nashville	Jani Lajunen	C	Blues Jrs (Finland)
202	New Jersey	Harry Young	D	Windsor Spitfires
203	Tampa Bay	David Carle	D	Shattuck St. Mary's
204	Washington	Stefan Della Rovere	L	Barrie Colts
205	New Jersey	Jean-Sebastien Berube	L	Rouyn-Noranda Huskies
206	Montreal	Patrick Johnson	C	U. of Wisconsin
207	Nashville	Anders Lindback	G	Almtuna
208	Anaheim	Nick Pryor	D	US National Under 18 Team
209	Dallas	Mike Bergin	D	Smiths Falls Bears
210	Pittsburgh	Nicholas D'Agostino	D	St. Michael's Buzzers
211	Detroit	Jesper Samuelsson	C	Timra Jrs. (Sweden)

Off-Season Transactions 2008

SATURDAY, JULY 12

Team	Player	Pos	Type	Details	From
San Jose	Marcel Goc	C	Re-signed	One-year contract	

FRIDAY, JULY 11

Team	Player	Pos	Type	Details	From
Minnesota	Corey Locke	C	Traded	for Belle	Montreal
Ottawa	Brendan Bell	D	Signed as free agent	One-year contract	
Pittsburgh	Connor James	LW	Signed as free agent		
Tampa Bay	Chris Gratton	C	Re-signed	One-year contract	
Anaheim	Brennan Evans	D	Signed as free agent	Two-year contract	
Anaheim	Steve Montador	D	Signed as free agent	One-year contract	
Washington	Boyd Gordon	C	Signed	One-year contract	
Vancouver	Rob Davison	D	Signed as free agent		
Montreal	Shawn Belle	D	Traded	for Locke	Minnesota

THURSDAY, JULY 10

Team	Player	Pos	Type	Details	From
NY Rangers	Martin Straka	LW	Signed with European team	HC Plzen-Czech League	
Edmonton	Jason Strudwick	D	Signed as free agent	One-year contract	
Tampa Bay	Zenon Konopka	C	Signed as free agent	Two-year contract	
Washington	Eric Fehr	RW	Re-signed	One-year contract	
Vancouver	Pavol Demitra	LW	Signed as free agent		
St. Louis	Mike Weaver	D	Signed as free agent		
Columbus	Nikita Filatov	LW	Signed	Three-year contract	

WEDNESDAY, JULY 9

Team	Player	Pos	Type	Details	From
Atlanta	Eric Boulton	LW	Re-signed	Multi-year contract	
Atlanta	Mike Hoffman	RW	Signed as free agent		
Atlanta	Grant Stevenson	C	Signed as free agent		
Atlanta	Junior Lessard	RW	Signed as free agent		
San Jose	Christian Ehrhoff	D	Re-signed	Three-year contract	
Ottawa	Ray Emery	G	Signed with European team	Atlant Mystichy-Russian League	
Nashville	Josh Gratton	LW	Signed as free agent	One-year contract	
Florida	Anthony Stewart	C	Re-signed		
Edmonton	Jean-Francois Jacques	LW	Re-signed	Two-year contract	
Edmonton	Marc Pouliot	C	Re-signed	Two-year contract	
Tampa Bay	Andrew Hutchinson	D	Signed as free agent	Two-year contract	
NY Islanders	Brendan Witt	D	Contract extended	Two-year contract extension	
Carolina	Chad LaRose	LW	Re-signed	One-year, $875K contract	

WEDNESDAY, JULY 9, cont.

Team	Player	Pos	Type	Details	From
Washington	Brooks Laich	C	Re-signed	Three-year contract	
Washington	Sergei Fedorov	C	Signed as free agent	One-year contract	
Montreal	Josh Gorges	D	Re-signed	Three-year contract	
Columbus	Michael Peca	C	Signed as free agent	One-year contract	

TUESDAY, JULY 8

Team	Player	Pos	Type	Details	From
Ottawa	Jason Smith	D	Signed as free agent	Two-year contract	
NY Rangers	Paul Mara	D	Signed as free agent	One-year contract	
Pittsburgh	T.J. Kemp	D	Signed as free agent	One-year contract	
Pittsburgh	Adam Henrich	LW	Signed as free agent	One-year contract	
Tampa Bay	Evgeny Artyukhin	RW	Re-signed	Multi-year contract	
Tampa Bay	Brandon Bochenski	RW	Signed as free agent	Two-year contract	
Tampa Bay	Mark Recchi	RW	Signed as free agent	One-year contract	
NY Islanders	Joe Callahan	D	Signed as free agent	One-year contract	
Anaheim	Brendan Morrison	C	Signed as free agent	One-year contract	
Vancouver	Steve Bernier	RW	Signed	One-year, $2.5 million contract	
Montreal	Jaroslav Halak	G	Re-signed	Two-year contract	
St. Louis	Steve Bernier	RW	Signed to an offer sheet	One-year, $2.5 million offer sheet	
Columbus	Clay Wilson	D	Re-signed	One-year contract	
Columbus	Andrei Plekhanov	D	Signed	Two-year contract	
Columbus	John Vigilante	LW	Signed as free agent	One-year contract	

MONDAY, JULY 7

Team	Player	Pos	Type	Details	From
Minnesota	Tomas Mojzis	D	Signed as free agent	Multi-year contract	
Minnesota	Jesse Schultz	RW	Signed as free agent	One-year contract	
Ottawa	Greg Mauldin	C	Signed as free agent	One-year contract	
Pittsburgh	Matt Cooke	LW	Signed as free agent	Two-year contract	
Pittsburgh	Janne Pesonen	LW	Signed as free agent	One-year contract	
Pittsburgh	Ben Lovejoy	D	Signed as free agent	One-year contract	
Toronto	Matt Stajan	C	Re-signed	Two-year contract	
Carolina	Dennis Seidenberg	D	Signed	One-year, $1.2 million contract	
Philadelphia	Arron Asham	RW	Signed as free agent	Multi-year contract	
Calgary	Todd Bertuzzi	LW	Signed as free agent	One-year contract	
Anaheim	David LeNeveu	G	Signed as free agent	One-year contract	
Montreal	Ryan Flinn	LW	Signed as free agent	One-year contract	
Columbus	R.J. Umberger	C	Signed	Four-year contract	
Chicago	Matt Walker	D	Signed as free agent	One-year contract	

SUNDAY, JULY 6

Team	Player	Pos	Type	Details	From
Minnesota	Barry Brust	G	Signed	Multi-year contract	
Minnesota	Owen Nolan	RW	Signed as free agent	Multi-year contract	

FRIDAY, JULY 4

Team	Player	Pos	Type	Details	From
San Jose	Dan Boyle	D	Traded	w/ Lukowich for Carle, Wishart & picks	Tampa Bay
San Jose	Brad Lukowich	D	Traded	w/ Boyle for Carle, Wishart & picks	Tampa Bay
Buffalo	Craig Rivet	D	Traded	with 2010 pick for two 2nd-rnd picks	San Jose
NY Rangers	Jaromir Jagr	RW	Signed with European team	Avangard Omsk-Russian League	
Toronto	Mikhail Grabovski	C	Signed	One-year contract	
Tampa Bay	Matt Carle	D	Traded	w/ Wishart, picks for Boyle & Lukowich	San Jose
Tampa Bay	Ty Wishart	D	Traded	w/Carle & picks for Boyle, Lukowich	San Jose
Calgary	Rene Bourque	LW	Signed		
Vancouver	Mark Cullen	C	Signed as free agent		
Vancouver	Steve Bernier	RW	Traded	for 2009 3rd-rnd pick & 2010 2nd-rnd pick	Buffalo

THURSDAY, JULY 3

Team	Player	Pos	Type	Details	From
Minnesota	Antti Miettinen	RW	Signed as free agent	Multi-year contract	
Dallas	Francis Wathier	LW	Re-signed	Two-year contract	
Dallas	Landon Wilson	RW	Signed as free agent	One-year contract	
Dallas	Garrett Stafford	D	Signed as free agent	Two-year contract	
Dallas	Maxime Fortunus	D	Signed as free agent	Two-year contract	
San Jose	Rob Blake	D	Signed as free agent	One-year contract	
NY Rangers	Markus Naslund	LW	Signed as free agent		
NY Rangers	Dmitri Kalinin	D	Signed as free agent		
Pittsburgh	Marc-Andre Fleury	G	Re-signed	Seven-year contract	
Pittsburgh	Ruslan Fedotenko	LW	Signed as free agent	One-year contract	
Pittsburgh	Miroslav Satan	RW	Signed as free agent	One-year contract	
Florida	Chris Beckford-Tseu	G	Signed as free agent	Two-year contract	
Florida	Steven MacIntyre	D	Signed as free agent	Two-year contract	
Florida	Rory Fitzpatrick	D	Signed as free agent	Two-year contract	
Florida	James DeLory	D	Signed as free agent	Three-year contract	
Edmonton	Taylor Chorney	D	Signed	Three-year contract	
Toronto	John Mitchell	C	Signed	Two-year contract	
Toronto	Greg Scott	LW	Signed as free agent	Three-year contract	

Team	Player	Pos	Type	Details	From
Toronto	Dominic Moore	C	Signed as free agent	One-year contract	
Toronto	Mikhail Grabovski	C	Traded	for Pateryn & 2010 2nd-rnd pick	Montreal
Tampa Bay	Scott Jackson	D	Signed as free agent	Three-year contract	
Tampa Bay	Wyatt Smith	C	Signed as free agent	One-year contract	
NY Islanders	Chris Lee	D	Signed as free agent		
NY Islanders	Peter Mannino	G	Signed as free agent	One-year contract	
NY Islanders	Mike Iggulden	C	Signed as free agent	One-year contract	
NY Islanders	Yann Danis	G	Signed as free agent	One-year contract	
NY Islanders	Mitch Fritz	LW	Signed as free agent	One-year contract	
NY Islanders	Brett Skinner	D	Signed as free agent	One-year contract	
NY Islanders	Kurtis McLean	C	Signed as free agent	One-year contract	
Carolina	Dwight Helminen	C	Signed as free agent	One-year, $475K contract	
Phoenix	Matt Jones	D	Re-signed	Two-year contract	
Phoenix	Brian McGrattan	RW	Signed	One-year contract	
Phoenix	David Hale	D	Signed as free agent	Two-year contract	
Phoenix	Derek Nesbitt	RW	Signed as free agent		
Phoenix	Francis Lessard	RW	Signed as free agent		
Washington	Keith Aucoin	RW	Signed as free agent	Two-year contract	
Montreal	Greg Pateryn	D	Traded	for Grabovski	Toronto
Montreal	Marc Denis	G	Signed as free agent	One-year contract	
Montreal	Cedrick Desjardins	G	Signed as free agent	Two-year contract	
Montreal	Georges Laraque	RW	Signed as free agent	Three-year contract	
Montreal	Alex Henry	D	Signed as free agent	One-year contract	
St. Louis	Yan Stastny	C	Signed as free agent	Two-year contract	
Colorado	Chris Durno	LW	Signed as free agent		
Colorado	Daniel Tjarnqvist	D	Signed as free agent	One-year contract	

WEDNESDAY, JULY 2

Team	Player	Pos	Type	Details	From
Minnesota	Kurtis Foster	D	Re-signed	One-year contract	
Atlanta	Ron Hainsey	D	Signed as free agent	Five-year contract	
Dallas	B.J. Crombeen	RW	Re-signed	One-year, $550K contract	
Dallas	Sean Avery	LW	Signed as free agent	Four-year, $15.5 million contract	
Ottawa	Jarkko Ruutu	LW	Signed as free agent	Three-year contract	
Ottawa	Shean Donovan	RW	Signed as free agent	Two-year contract	
Detroit	Marian Hossa	RW	Signed as free agent	One-year contract	
NY Rangers	Dan Fritsche	C	Traded	Four-player trade	Columbus
NY Rangers	Nikolai Zherdev	RW	Traded	Four-player trade	Columbus

Team	Player	Pos	Type	Details	From
Pittsburgh	Evgeni Malkin	C	Contract extended	Five-year contract extension	
Pittsburgh	Brooks Orpik	D	Signed as free agent	Six-year contract	
Tampa Bay	Ryan Craig	C	Re-signed	Two-year contract	
Tampa Bay	Janne Niskala	D	Signed	One-year contract	
NY Islanders	Doug Weight	C	Signed as free agent	One-year contract	
Carolina	Joni Pitkanen	D	Signed	Three-year, $12 million contract	
Carolina	Josef Melichar	D	Signed as free agent	One-year, $1 million contract	
Philadelphia	Riley Cote	LW	Re-signed	Three-year contract	
Calgary	Curtis Glencross	LW	Signed as free agent	Three-year contract	
Calgary	Pete Vandermeer	LW	Signed as free agent		
Calgary	Jim Vandermeer	D	Signed as free agent	Three-year contract	
Anaheim	Stu Bickel	D	Signed as free agent	Three-year contract	
Phoenix	David Spina	LW	Re-signed		
Phoenix	Al Montoya	G	Re-signed		
Phoenix	Drew Fata	D	Signed as free agent		
Washington	Tyler Sloan	D	Signed		
Washington	Graham Mink	LW	Signed as free agent		
Vancouver	Nolan Baumgartner	D	Signed as free agent		
Vancouver	Alexandre Bolduc	C	Signed as free agent		
Vancouver	Curtis Sanford	G	Signed as free agent		
Vancouver	Ryan Johnson	C	Signed as free agent	Two-year contract	
Boston	Petteri Nokelainen	C	Re-signed	Multi-year contract	
Columbus	Kristian Huselius	LW	Signed as free agent	Four-year contract	
Columbus	Christian Backman	D	Traded	Four-player trade	NY Rangers
Columbus	Fedor Tyutin	D	Traded	Four-player trade	NY Rangers
Colorado	Wojtek Wolski	LW	Re-signed	Two-year contract	

TUESDAY, JULY 1 (first day of free agency)
407 PLAYERS FILE FOR FREE AGENCY

Team	Player	Pos	Type	Details	From
Anaheim	Corey Perry	RW	Re-signed	Five-year contract	
Boston	Blake Wheeler	RW	Signed as free agent	Three-year contract	
Boston	Michael Ryder	RW	Signed as free agent	Three-year contract	
Buffalo	Patrick Lalime	G	Signed as free agent	Two-year contract	
Calgary	Brandon Prust	C	Re-signed		
Calgary	David Van der Gulik	RW	Re-signed		
Calgary	Mark Giordano	D	Signed		
Calgary	Rene Bourque	LW	Traded	for conditional 2nd-rnd pick	Chicago

Team	Player	Pos	Type	Details	From
Calgary	Ryan Wilson	D	Signed as free agent		
Carolina	Anton Babchuk	D	Signed	One-year, $1 million contract	
Carolina	Joni Pitkanen	D	Traded	for Cole	Edmonton
Carolina	Ryan Bayda	LW	Signed as free agent	One-year, $475K contract	
Carolina	Tim Conboy	D	Signed as free agent	Two-year, $975K contract	
Carolina	Wade Brookbank	LW	Signed as free agent	One-year, $475K contract	
Chicago	Brian Campbell	D	Signed as free agent	Eight-year contract	
Chicago	Cristobal Huet	G	Signed as free agent	Four-year contract	
Colorado	Andrew Raycroft	G	Signed as free agent	One-year contract	
Colorado	Darcy Tucker	RW	Signed as free agent	Two-year contract	
Colorado	Per Ledin	LW	Signed as free agent	One-year contract	
Columbus	Mike Commodore	D	Signed as free agent	Five-year contract	
Columbus	Raffi Torres	LW	Traded	for Brule	Edmonton
Detroit	Brad Stuart	D	Signed as free agent	Four-year contract	
Detroit	Ty Conklin	G	Signed as free agent	One-year contract	
Edmonton	Erik Cole	RW	Traded	for Pitkanen	Carolina
Edmonton	Gilbert Brule	C	Traded	for Torres	Columbus
Florida	Cory Stillman	LW	Signed as free agent	Three-year contract	
Los Angeles	Denis Gauthier	D	Traded	w/ pick for Hersley & Lukacevic	Philadelphia
Minnesota	Andrew Brunette	LW	Signed as free agent	Multi-year contract	
Minnesota	Craig Weller	RW	Signed as free agent	Multi-year contract	
Minnesota	Marek Zidlicky	D	Traded	for Jones & 2009 2nd-rnd pick	Nashville
Montreal	Andrei Kostitsyn	LW	Re-signed	Three-year, $9.75 million contract	
Nashville	Drew MacIntyre	G	Signed as free agent	One-year contract	
Nashville	Ryan Jones	LW	Traded	w/ 2009 2nd-rnd pick for Zidlicky	Minnesota
New Jersey	Barry Tallackson	RW	Re-signed		
New Jersey	Bobby Holik	C	Signed as free agent		
New Jersey	Brian Rolston	LW	Signed as free agent	Four-year, $20 million contract	
New Jersey	Bryce Salvador	D	Re-signed	Four-year contract	
New Jersey	David Clarkson	RW	Re-signed	Two-year contract	
New Jersey	Jay Pandolfo	LW	Re-signed	Three-year contract	
New Jersey	Matt Halischuk	RW	Signed		
New Jersey	Vladimir Zharkov	RW	Signed		

Team	Player	Pos	Type	Details	From
NY Islanders	Mark Streit	D	Signed as free agent	Five-year contract	
NY Rangers	Aaron Voros	LW	Signed as free agent		
NY Rangers	Andreas Jamtin	LW	Signed as free agent		
NY Rangers	Matt Zaba	G	Contract extended		Edmonton
NY Rangers	Michal Rozsival	D	Signed as free agent	Four-year contract	
NY Rangers	Patrick Rissmiller	LW	Signed as free agent		
NY Rangers	Stephen Valiquette	G	Re-signed		
NY Rangers	Wade Redden	D	Signed as free agent	Six-year contract	
Ottawa	Alex Auld	G	Signed as free agent	Two-year, $2 million contract	
Philadelphia	Glen Metropolit	C	Signed as free agent	Two-year contract	
Philadelphia	Nate Raduns	RW	Signed as free agent	One-year contract	
Philadelphia	Ned Lukacevic	LW	Traded	w/ Hersley for Gauthier & pick	Los Angeles
Philadelphia	Ossi Vaananen	D	Signed as free agent	One-year contract	
Philadelphia	Patrik Hersley	D	Traded	w/ Lukacevic for Gauthier & pick	Los Angeles
Philadelphia	Randy Jones	D	Re-signed	Two-year contract	
Philadelphia	Sean Curry	D	Signed as free agent	Two-year contract	
Phoenix	Kurt Sauer	D	Signed as free agent	Four-year contract	
Phoenix	Mikkel Boedker	LW	Signed	Three-year contract	
Phoenix	Todd Fedoruk	LW	Signed as free agent	Three-year contract	
Phoenix	Viktor Tikhonov	RW	Signed	Three-year contract	
Pittsburgh	Eric Godard	RW	Signed as free agent	Three-year contract	
Pittsburgh	Mark Eaton	D	Signed as free agent	Two-year contract	
Pittsburgh	Pascal Dupuis	LW	Re-signed	Three-year contract	
St. Louis	David Backes	RW	Re-signed	Three-year, $7.5 million contract	
Tampa Bay	Adam Hall	RW	Signed as free agent	Three-year contract	
Tampa Bay	David Koci	LW	Signed as free agent	One-year contract	
Tampa Bay	Olaf Kolzig	G	Signed as free agent	One-year contract	
Tampa Bay	Radim Vrbata	RW	Signed as free agent	Three-year, $9 million contract	
Toronto	Curtis Joseph	G	Signed as free agent	One-year contract	
Toronto	Jeff Finger	D	Signed as free agent	Four-year contract	
Toronto	Niklas Hagman	LW	Signed as free agent	Four-year contract	
Vancouver	Darcy Hordichuk	LW	Signed as free agent	Two-year contract	
Vancouver	David Backes	RW	Signed to an offer sheet	Three-year, $7.5 million offer sheet	
Vancouver	Kyle Wellwood	C	Signed	One-year contract	
Washington	Jose Theodore	G	Signed as free agent	Two-year contract	
Washington	Mike Green	D	Signed	Four-year contract	

MONDAY, JUNE 30

Team	Player	Pos	Type	Details	From
Atlanta	Alexei Zhitnik	D	Became UFA	Contract bought out by team	
San Jose	Jody Shelley	LW	Re-signed	Two-year contract	
Buffalo	Paul Gaustad	C	Re-signed	Four-year contract	
Detroit	Andreas Lilja	D	Signed	Two-year contract	
Florida	Rostislav Olesz	LW	Signed	Six-year contract	
Edmonton	Lubomir Visnovsky	D	Traded	for Stoll & Greene	Los Angeles
Tampa Bay	Gary Roberts	LW	Signed	One-year contract	
Tampa Bay	Ryan Malone	LW	Signed	Seven-year contract	
Tampa Bay	Vaclav Prospal	LW	Signed	Multi-year contract	
Tampa Bay	Janne Niskala	D	Traded	for 2009 6th-rnd pick	Philadelphia
Los Angeles	Matt Greene	D	Traded	w/ Stoll for Visnovsky	Edmonton
Los Angeles	Jarret Stoll	C	Traded	w/ Greene for Visnovsky	Edmonton
Philadelphia	Tim Ramholt	D	Traded	for Greentree	Calgary
Calgary	Kyle Greentree	LW	Traded	for Ramholt	Philadelphia
Columbus	Duvie Westcott	D	Became UFA	Contract bought out by team	
Colorado	Adam Foote	D	Re-signed	Two-year contract	
Colorado	John Michael Liles	D	Re-signed	Four-year contract	

SUNDAY, JUNE 29

Team	Player	Pos	Type	Details	From
Tampa Bay	Brian Rolston	LW	Traded	for conditional draft pick	Minnesota
Philadelphia	Steve Eminger	D	Signed	One-year contract	

All-time and Active Leaders

GAMES PLAYED

Career		
1	Gordie Howe	1767
2	Mark Messier	1756
3	Ron Francis	1731
4	Dave Andreychuk	1639
5	Scott Stevens	1635
6	Chris Chelios	1616
7	Larry Murphy	1615
8	Raymond Bourque	1612
9	Alex Delvecchio	1549
10	John Bucyk	1540

Active		
1	Chris Chelios	1616
2	Brendan Shanahan	1490
3	Glen Wesley	1457
4	Luke Richardson	1415
5	Mark Recchi	1410
6	Trevor Linden	1382
7	Joe Sakic	1363
8	Rod Brind'Amour	1324
9	Jeremy Roenick	1321
10	Mike Modano	1320

GOALS

Career		
1	Wayne Gretzky	894
2	Gordie Howe	801
3	Brett Hull	741
4	Marcel Dionne	731
5	Phil Esposito	717
6	Mike Gartner	708
7	Mark Messier	694
8	Steve Yzerman	692
9	Mario Lemieux	690
10	Luc Robitaille	668

Active		
1	Brendan Shanahan	650
2	Jaromir Jagr	646
3	Joe Sakic	623
4	Mats Sundin	555
5	Teemu Selanne	552
6	Mike Modano	528
7	Mark Recchi	522
8	Jeremy Roenick	509
9	Keith Tkachuk	500
10	Sergei Fedorov	472

ASSISTS

Career		
1	Wayne Gretzky	1963
2	Ron Francis	1249
3	Mark Messier	1193
4	Raymond Bourque	1169
5	Paul Coffey	1135
6	Adam Oates	1079
7	Steve Yzerman	1063
8	Gordie Howe	1049
9	Marcel Dionne	1040
10	Mario Lemieux	1033

Active		
1	Joe Sakic	1006
2	Jaromir Jagr	953
3	Mark Recchi	859
4	Mats Sundin	766
5	Chris Chelios	763
6	Mike Modano	755
7	Nicklas Lidstrom	726
8	Doug Weight	704
9	Jeremy Roenick	694
10	Brendan Shanahan	690

POINTS

	Career	
1	Wayne Gretzky	2857
2	Mark Messier	1887
3	Gordie Howe	1850
4	Ron Francis	1798
5	Marcel Dionne	1771
6	Steve Yzerman	1755
7	Mario Lemieux	1723
8	Joe Sakic	1629
9	Jaromir Jagr	1599
10	Phil Esposito	1590

	Active	
1	Joe Sakic	1629
2	Jaromir Jagr	1599
3	Mark Recchi	1381
4	Brendan Shanahan	1340
5	Mats Sundin	1321
6	Mike Modano	1283
7	Jeremy Roenick	1203
8	Teemu Selanne	1158
9	Sergei Fedorov	1146
10	Rod Brind'Amour	1114

POWER-PLAY GOALS

	Career	
1	Dave Andreychuk	274
2	Brett Hull	265
3	Phil Esposito	249
4	Luc Robitaille	247
5	Mario Lemieux	236
6	Brendan Shanahan	235
7	Marcel Dionne	234
8	Dino Ciccarelli	232
9	Mike Gartner	217
10	Joe Neiuwendyk	215

	Active	
1	Brendan Shanahan	235
2	Joe Sakic	205
3	Keith Tkachuk	193
4	Teemu Selanne	190
5	Jeremy Roenick	183
6	Jaromir Jagr	181
7	Mark Recchi	180
8	Mats Sundin	155
9	Mike Modano	149
10	Sergei Fedorov	142

SHORT-HANDED GOALS

	Career	
1	Wayne Gretzky	73
2	Mark Messier	63
3	Steve Yzerman	50
4	Mario Lemieux	49
5	Butch Goring	40
6	Dave Poulin	39
7	Jari Kurri	37
8	Sergei Fedorov	36
9	Theoren Fleury	35
10	Dirk Graham	35

	Active	
1	Sergei Fedorov	36
2	Brian Rolston	33
3	Joe Sakic	32
4	Mats Sundin	31
5	Mike Modano	29
6	Jeremy Roenick	28
7	Rod Brind'Amour	27
8	Michael Peca	25
	Martin St. Louis	25
10	Mike Sillinger	24

SHOTS ON GOAL

Career

1	Raymond Bourque	6206
2	Marcel Dionne	5366
3	Al MacInnis	5157
4	Mike Gartner	5090
5	Wayne Gretzky	5089
6	Brendan Shanahan	5009
7	Brett Hull	4876
8	Steve Yzerman	4602
9	Jaromir Jagr	4596
10	Phil Esposito	4595

Active

1	Brendan Shanahan	5009
2	Jaromir Jagr	4596
3	Joe Sakic	4575
4	Mats Sundin	3931
5	Mike Modano	3882
6	Sergei Fedorov	3867
7	Chris Chelios	3607
8	Teemu Selanne	3551
9	Rob Blake	3516
10	Mark Recchi	3407

SHOOTING %

Career

1	Craig Simpson	23.66
2	Charlie Simmer	22.34
3	Paul MacLean	21.41
4	Mike Bossy	21.18
5	Yvon Lambert	19.85
6	Rick Middleton	19.69
7	Blaine Stoughton	19.52
8	Alex Tanguay	19.43
9	Darryl Sutter	19.42
10	Rob Brown	19.41

Active

1	Alex Tanguay	19.43
2	Gary Roberts	18.53
3	Andrew Brunette	17.73
4	Mark Parrish	17.46
5	Tomas Holmstrom	16.49
6	Brenden Morrow	16.36
7	Dany Heatley	16.12
8	Jeremy Roenick	15.75
9	Daniel Briere	15.65
10	Teemu Selanne	15.54

PENALTY MINUTES

Career

1	Tiger Williams	3966
2	Dale Hunter	3565
3	Tie Domi	3515
4	Marty McSorley	3381
5	Bob Probert	3300
6	Rob Ray	3207
7	Craig Berube	3149
8	Tim Hunter	3146
9	Chris Nilan	3043
10	Rick Tocchet	2972

Active

1	Chris Chelios	2873
2	Gary Roberts	2533
3	Brendan Shanahan	2460
4	Donald Brashear	2440
5	Keith Tkachuk	2102
6	Brad May	2093
7	Luke Richardson	2053
8	Chris Simon	1824
9	Owen Nolan	1727
10	Ian Laperriere	1631

PLUS / MINUS

Career		
1	Larry Robinson	730
2	Bobby Orr	597
3	Raymond Bourque	528
4	Wayne Gretzky	518
5	Bobby Clarke	506
6	Serge Savard	460
	Denis Potvin	460
8	Guy Lafleur	453
9	Bryan Trottier	452
10	Brad McCrimmon	444

Active		
1	Nicklas Lidstrom	378
2	Chris Chelios	351
3	Jaromir Jagr	275
4	Sergei Fedorov	257
5	Peter Forsberg	242
6	Gary Roberts	240
7	Scott Niedermayer	184
8	Jere Lehtinen	183
9	Keith Carney	164
10	Patrick Elias	162

WINS (GOALIE)

Career		
1	Patrick Roy	551
2	Martin Brodeur	538
3	Ed Belfour	484
4	Curtis Joseph	449
5	Terry Sawchuk	447
6	Jacques Plante	437
7	Tony Esposito	423
8	Glenn Hall	407
9	Grant Fuhr	403
10	Dominik Hasek	389

Active		
1	Martin Brodeur	538
2	Curtis Joseph	449
3	Dominik Hasek	389
4	Chris Osgood	363
5	Olaf Kolzig	301
6	Nikolai Khabibulin	274
7	Jocelyn Thibault	238
8	Evgeni Nabokov	208
9	Marty Turco	207
10	Roberto Luongo	197

SHUTOUTS

Career		
1	Terry Sawchuk	103
2	Martin Brodeur	96
3	George Hainsworth	94
4	Glenn Hall	84
5	Jacques Plante	82
6	Alec Connell	81
	Dominek Hasek	81
	Tiny Thompson	81
9	Ed Belfour	76
	Tony Esposito	76

Active		
1	Martin Brodeur	96
2	Dominek Hasek	81
3	Curtis Joseph	51
4	Chris Osgood	47
5	Evgeni Nabokov	40
6	Jocelyn Thibault	39
7	Roberto Luongo	38
	Nikolai Khabibulin	38
9	Olaf Kolzig	35
	Patrick Lalime	35

GAA

1	Alec Connell	1.912
2	George Hainsworth	1.933
3	Charlie Gardiner	2.024
4	Lorne Chabot	2.039
5	Tiny Thompson	2.077
6	Marty Turco	2.148
7	Dave Kerr	2.149
8	Martin Brodeur	2.201
9	Dominek Hasek	2.202
10	Ken Dryden	2.235

Active

1	Marty Turco	2.148
2	Martin Brodeur	2.201
3	Dominek Hasek	2.202
4	Manny Legace	2.311
5	Miikka Kiprusoff	2.371
6	Evgeni Nabokov	2.374
7	J.S. Giguere	2.427
8	Chris Osgood	2.429
9	Manny Fernandez	2.494
10	Patrick Lalime	2.535

SAVE %

Career

1	Dominik Hasek	0.922
2	Roberto Luongo	0.919
3	J.S. Giguere	0.915
4	Miikka Kirpusoff	0.915
5	Manny Legace	0.914
6	Tomas Vokoun	0.914
7	Martin Brodeur	0.914
8	Marty Turco	0.913
9	Manny Fernandez	0.912
10	Evgeni Nabokov	0.911

Active

1	Dominik Hasek	0.922
2	Roberto Luongo	0.919
3	J.S. Giguere	0.915
4	Miikka Kirpusoff	0.915
5	Manny Legace	0.914
6	Tomas Vokoun	0.914
7	Martin Brodeur	0.914
8	Marty Turco	0.913
9	Manny Fernandez	0.912
10	Evgeni Nabokov	0.911

Darcy Norman

Born and raised in small-town northern Ontario, and with no shortage of ice in the winter, Darcy has lived and breathed hockey from the tender age of five. Playing from Tykes to the Junior level, the University of Alberta Economics major retains his passion for the game by turning it into a study that reflects his educational pursuits involving numbers and data analysis. Darcy has a strong belief that reading numbers is the only truly objective method of analysis, be it on the stock market or the sports page.

OverTime Books

If you enjoyed *Hockey Stats & Facts 2008–09*, be sure to check out these other great titles from OverTime Books:

THE HOCKEY QUIZ BOOK: The Best Humorous, Challenging & Weird Questions & Answers
by J. Alexander Poulton

Have you ever wondered which goaltender holds the record for lowest goals-against average? What about who signed the longest contract in professional hockey history or which player is known as "the Hammer"? Find out the answers to those questions and many more in this hockey aficionado must-have!

Softcover • 5.25" X 8.25" • 256 pages • ISBN13 978-1-897277-31-7 • $18.95

HOCKEY QUOTES
Compiled by J. Alexander Poulton

Hockey players, coaches and managers have uttered some of the greatest, funniest and most memorable phrases in sport history. This book is a selection of those exceptional words spoken when hockey heroes swap game-day for wordplay.

Softcover • 5.25" X 8.25" • 168 pages • ISBN10 1-897277-02-4
• ISBN13 978-1897277-02-7• $9.95

CANADIAN HOCKEY TRIVIA: The Facts, Stars & Strange Tales of Canadian Hockey
by J. Alexander Poulton

Hockey is so much a part of Canadian life that the theme song to *Hockey Night in Canada* had called our unofficial national anthem. Read the fascinating facts from Canada's favorite game such as the almost-forgotten Winnipeg Falcons, who were the first Canadian team to win Olympic gold in 1920 and Dennis O'Brien, who holds the record for most NHL teams played for in a single season.

Softcover • 5.25" X 8.25" • 168 pages • ISBN13 978-1-897277-01-0 • $9.95

GREATEST STANLEY CUP VICTORIES: The Battles and the Rivalries
by J. Alexander Poulton

A look back at some of the NHL's most memorable battles for hockey supremacy.

Softcover • 5.25" X 8.25" • 168 pages • ISBN13 978-1897277-06-5 • $9.95

WEIRD FACTS ABOUT CANADIAN HOCKEY: Strange, Wacky & Hilarious Stories
by Peter Boer

Hockey, our national sport, is played everywhere from urban cul-de-sacs to NHL arenas. Gamers are rife with tales of the odd, the strange, the funny and, occasionally, the disturbing side of hockey history.

Softcover • 5.25" X 8.25" • 160 pages • ISBN13 978-0-9737681-2-1 • $9.95

Lone Pine Publishing is the exclusive distributor for OverTime Books.
If you cannot find these titles at your local bookstore, contact us:

Canada: 1-800-661-9017   USA: 1-800-518-3541